HINDUISM

Scriptures
&
Practices

HINDUISM

SCRIPTURES
&
PRACTICES

Prabha Duneja

GEETA SOCIETY
2822, Camino Segura, Pleasanton, CA 94566, U.S.A
Tel.: 925-484-5411; Fax.: 925-417-5946
email: duneja@aol.com, website: www.holygeeta.com

AUTHOR

Prabha Duneja
2822, Camino Segura,
Pleasanton, CA 94566, U.S.A
Tel.: 925-484-5411; Fax.: 925-417-5946
email: duneja@aol.com
website: holygeeta.com

EDITORIAL

Norris W. Palmer, PhD
Professor, Theology & Religious Studies
Saint Mary's College of California

Vandana Makker
Literature & Language Teacher

PUBLISHER

ARC Publishers
acutrack.com

ISBN: 978-0-9858596-0-2
LIBRARY OF CONGRESS CONTROL NUMBER: 2012943855

CONTENTS

Acknowledgements

The variety of topics on Hinduism presented in this book have been written over the past several years in close association with great Vedic scholars, the exponents of yoga and meditation, the learned Hindu priests, and numerous saints and sages who have crossed my path on this spiritual journey and shared their words of wisdom and rich experiences of yogic communion. My gratitude goes to all of them for their valuable teachings and guidance.

Special thanks are due, however, to my husband Amritji and our son Anshuman for their continuous encouragement and sincere support in the completion of this noble work. I feel immensely indebted to my respected grandparents Sri & Smt. Ganga Ramji, my parents Dr. & Mrs. Manohar Lalji, and my uncle Professor Nand Lalji who initiated me in the study of Vedic literature and Bhagawad Geeta at the early age of eight. I convey my sincere gratitude to Dr. Norris W. Palmer, the professor of Religious Studies at Saint Mary's College of California, who carefully edited the book and has been kind enough to give a Foreword to the volume. I am also thankful to Vandana Makker, a literature and language teacher, for her in depth proofreading and useful encouraging comments on the early drafts. I wish to express my heartfelt appreciation to dear Divya Lambah for her loving assistance in typing my handwritten drafts into a computer processed manuscript.

Last but not least, I want to thank Matt Shields, Brian Schmille, Scott Donovan, Raj Barman, Jason Lau, Jan Thomas, Sri J.L. Gupta 'Chaitanya', and my longtime friend Manorama Iyer, for their valuable help in processing the preliminary work.

– Prabha Duneja

Preface

Over the last 15 years, I have had the opportunity to speak on Hinduism at interfaith conferences, the Parliament of World's Religions, the Commonwealth Club San Francisco, and at numerous schools, colleges, churches, and temples both in the United States and abroad. Everywhere, I noticed a sincere interest of the audiences in the study of ancient Hindu scriptures and religious practices; and quite often I received requests for the recommendation of a book that would explain the essential features of the Hindu religion in a short and simple format. Observing the immense popularity of Hinduism in the West and a sincere request for another book, I decided to compile the several topics of my lectures on the fundamentals of the Hindu religion, which I have been sharing with students at the universities and with other admirers of Hindu philosophies, customs, and ceremonies.

In this book I have sincerely endeavored to give an introduction to the study of the Hindu religion both in its theoretical as well as practical aspects. Beginning from an introduction to the Holy Vedas, Upanishads, and Manusmriti, through the great epics—the Ramayana and the Mahabharata, with a brief summary of the Bhagawad Geeta, the Hindu gods and goddesses, festivals and the customs of our rich cultural heritage, I have tried to cover a wide spectrum of subjects to the interest of the younger generation, from a new and contemporary way of life. The short and succinct summary of the Vedic rites and rituals, *Patanjali Ashtanga Yoga* and meditation makes the book more faithful to its subject.

The Vedic religious practices have been created and supported by some spiritual concepts and loyalty to the perseverance of these traditions has been emphasized over centuries. The entire social structure in Hindu society is centered in religious beliefs, followed by Hindu families through the ages. The contents of all the essays are intended to add depth to the clear understanding of time-honored spiritual traditions that form the significant features of Hindu culture. Each topic offers valuable insights into the systematic exploration of the subject. I hope the explanation of the vital aspects of Hindu religion covered in the following pages will provide an enlightened perspective, in this age of increased curiosity and the desire to create a global family.

In the course of my writing this concise commentary on the Hindu scriptures, occasionally, I was struck by a sense of awe and wonder as I glanced through the passages of the Holy Vedas, Upanishads, and other scriptures. It has been one of the most wondrous experiences of my life. I was really overwhelmed by the intellectual abilities, the heightened intuition, and the mesmerizing yogic powers of the divine sages, who compiled their valuable theses on scientific research and spiritual experiences. In connection with each of the topics addressed in this book, I have genuinely attempted to provide sufficient information from the texts concerned, in order to satisfy the immediate need of the beginners, who are interested in the multi-faceted aspects of Hinduism.

Although, most of these lectures have been revised

for publication, still the informal style has been retained to some extent, which I thought had some significant value in itself. Also the readers may come across some repetition because of the essential character of the subject matter and my continuous effort to find the bridges that would connect the preceding chapter with the next; but I am sure that the inspired spontaneity in explanation will keep the interest alive for optimum benefits. It is hoped that the message of the melodious hymns of the Vedas, the profound treatises on Upanishads, and the timeless wisdom of the Bhagawad Geeta presented here will evoke in many the earnest desire to pursue the detailed study of these great scriptures and enrich their lives.

While sharing my understanding of Hinduism, I have often felt the living presence of those great Rishis who encapsulated the Divine wisdom in their yogic unity with the soul, and also shared their knowledge with their most inquisitive disciples at the *Gurukuls* (schools) of ancient India. The description of the notable celebrities in the two great epics the Ramayana and the Mahabharata aroused my genuine devotion to Lord Rama and Lord Krishna. Even while writing on Hindu gods and goddesses I often felt in personal communion with the deities and sharing the subjective experience of spiritual ecstasy. The explanation of Hindu *Samskaras* and the popular religious practices has also come quite spontaneously because of my direct involvement in the performance of Hindu rites and rituals over the past several years in the USA and abroad. In these essays I have tried to give only a few glimpses of the great philosophical treatises and the highly cherished spiritual practices of Hindu religion, which are truly beyond accurate counting and descriptions.

I hope this book will offer a valuable overview of the connecting points into the study of Hinduism through the ages. I have made sincere efforts to present before the modern world, the timeless wisdom of Hindu scriptures treasured over centuries and to answer the questions I have often encountered from my audiences at schools, colleges, and conferences. I sincerely believe that this elegant edition will open another door to enter into the spirit of Hindu philosophies and help in the mobilization of our inherent spiritual intimacy centered in the Supreme-soul. There are hundreds of books on Hinduism written by the learned exponents of Hindu heritage. All these commentaries by learned Indians as well as erudite Western scholars are worthy of genuine respect and appreciation.

This book is only a humble addition to the work which has been accomplished by the previous expounders of Hinduism. I feel immensely blessed that the essential philosophies and the performance of the spiritual practices of Hindu rites and rituals, which I have enjoyed sharing with others over the last several years, is finally going to be presented as a commentary to the admirers of Hindu traditions.

May the teachings of the Holy scriptures and Yogic unity with the Supreme-soul bless everyone with the power of enlightened love, devotion, spiritual intimacy, and true knowledge—restoring peace, happiness, and harmony on Earth.

– Prabha Duneja

Foreword

The reader of *Hinduism—Scriptures & Practices* is in for a real joy. For many decades Prabha Duneja has been foremost among that rare sort of deeply devoted religious practitioners who also direct an equal share of their attention to interpreting their tradition to those outside the fold. For a dozen-plus years my own students at Saint Mary's College of California have been privileged to learn about Hinduism from Prabha, either directly from her when she has visited my classroom or when we have met her at a temple, or by means of her written work, most notably until now her volume *The Legacy of Yoga in Bhagawad Geeta*, which provides not only a fresh translation of the Geeta but also a deeply thoughtful commentary on it.

In all of her work, Duneja writes with the assurance of one who has not only spent decades translating sacred Hindu texts from Sanskrit into English or an equal number of years interpreting Hindu rituals and practice for those uniformed about them, but as one who understands the practice and study of Hinduism by having spent a lifetime immersed in it. In this volume, Duneja makes a unique contribution by presenting Hinduism not merely as either an ancient set of ethical codes of conduct or as a timeless philosophical outlook but, rather, as a vibrant, living tradition in which life's greatest questions and most profound meanings may be worked out.

While cognizant of the many other scholarly works already on the shelf, Duneja's voice stands out among them. This is not a volume for those interested in picking apart Hindu Scripture in its finest grammatical details. Those sorts of books already exist. Neither is this an arms-length, academic interrogation of traditions that analyzes the very life out of them. Rather, *Hinduism—Scriptures & Practices* makes it greatest contribution by extolling the virtues of those scriptures and explaining their application to daily life. This volume presents an informed and intelligent interpretation of the spiritual realities resident within Hindu Scripture and practices, allowing readers to experience firsthand how a Hindu woman understands them. In an age when tradition is often dismissed as simply "myth" or "legend," Duneja reminds us of the greater truths and essential life lessons at the very core of this tradition.

Duneja is to be rightly praised for her careful explication of Hindu beliefs and practices, which those of us raised beyond their scope often find bewildering. Whether explaining the nature of the Divine, the 16 *Samskaras*, or discussing any number of festivals, Duneja always has her sights trained on her audience and thoughtfully delivers uniformly insightful explanations. This is a volume written for those in need of careful reflection and explanation from the inside, one that doesn't devolve into the tedious and unimportant distinctions that are often drawn in the scholar's study, and obscure the larger truths of Hinduism.

It is a great pleasure to recommend this work. Persons seeking a Hindu interpretation of Hinduism will be immeasurably enriched by reading it, and all persons will be challenged to live more thoughtful lives by thoughtfully examining its pages.

Norris W. Palmer, Ph.D.
Professor, Theology & Religious Studies
Saint Mary's College of California

Reviews

Hinduism—Scriptures and Practices by Prabha Duneja is ambitious in that it introduces the four Vedas, the Upanishads, the epics and the law codes of Manu—as succinctly as possible. The author also discusses the concept of God in Hinduism and she highlights some important deities with their specific worship and iconography. To wrap the book in an encyclopedic fabric, the author devotes a separate chapter on yoga and mantra, two major aspects of Hinduism. Finally, the author introduces various festivals in the life of a Hindu and ends the book with the status of women in Hindu society from the Vedic period to modern times. This encyclopedic work is a must read for anyone who wants a quick answer to the history, philosophy, rituals and cultural meanings of symbols that are necessary to understand Hinduism at a deeper level. Mrs. Duneja has embarked on a crusade to introduce Hinduism to a seeker in a simple language, an almost impossible task when it comes to making sense of the complexity that Hinduism is. I salute her for her noble efforts.

Deepak Shimkhada, Ph.D.
Professor of Religious Studies
Claremont Graduate University
Claremont, CA

Prabha Duneja presented a class on the scriptures and practices of Hinduism as part of a comparative interfaith education series at Spiritual Life Center in Sacramento, California. Her presentation received the highest reviews from the 90 students for her informal yet vibrant teaching style, and her ability to clearly communicate the heart and soul of Hinduism to a class of mostly western minds. Duneja embodies her subject and makes the timeless wisdom of the Hindu scriptures come alive and relevant. She left us wanting more and now we have it in her latest book. *Hinduism—Scriptures and Practices* beautifully bridges the gap between the East and West, and the ancient and contemporary. I enthusiastically recommend this text for those seeking a clearer understanding of the oldest practiced religion in the world.

Rev. Michael Moran
Senior Founding Minister
Spiritual Life Center,
Sacramento, CA.

The book *Hinduism—Scriptures and Practices* by Shrimati Prabha Duneja is a wonderful introduction to the world of Hinduism and its philosophy. Known originally as *"Sanatana Dharma,"* roughly translated as "The Eternal Religion," Hinduism is like a fathomless ocean, full of priceless pearls of wisdom, fed from all sides by the rivers and rivulets of the inspiring words and revelations of the great seers and masters. Smt. Prabha's poetic and elaborate translations of quotes from the scriptures helps one's soul resonate with their deeper meaning, the conviction she portrays sweeps you into higher realms, and her direct language gives one has the feeling of being addressed personally as in an intimate conversation. Highly recommended for getting a glimpse of the roots of Hinduism.

Sri Gajananam Director
Vishnu-devananda Yoga Vedanta Center
Berkeley, CA

Prabha Duneja has created a gracious, accessible and sublime journey into the breadth and depth of Hinduism. While her book is a treasure trove of information and insight for anyone seeking to know more about the scriptures and practices of this great religion, I believe it is most distinguished as a work of love by a skilled writer. Through her engaging presentation of Hinduism, she offers her readers a rare opportunity to journey more deeply on their own path of spiritual development. This is a book I will return to many times.

The Rev. Canon Charles P. Gibbs
Executive Director
United Religions Initiative

Prabha Duneja's *Hinduism—Scriptures and Practices* is a text should be in the library of anyone who wants to know more about the Hindu religion and culture. With its primordial nature, varied texts, and countless gods and goddesses the Hindu religion often seems too vast and complex to fully comprehend, even to many of its practitioners, but this book provides thorough explanations in a format that is simple to navigate. Part reference manual and part philosophical treatise, the book explains the Hindu scriptures, festivals, and cultural and societal norms in language that is clear and easy to understand for people of all ages and backgrounds. Whether read by students, philosophers, scholars, or simply those seeking answers to their questions about Hinduism, this book serves as a go-to guide that will become indispensable.

Vandana Makker
Literature & Language Teacher

A devotee, scholar, priest and teacher who lives Hinduism through and through, Prabha Duneja is an apt guide to this profound stream of teaching and practice. She has "nut shelled" the major scriptures from Rig Veda to Bhagawad Geeta, including the Upanishads, Manusmirti, Ramayana, and Mahabharata – an extraordinary feat! Sprinkled throughout are tiny tastes of Hindu scriptures. Mrs. Duneja seamlessly weaves story and meaning to make this ancient wisdom accessible. Her evocative translations bring the Sanskrit to life and reveal its spiritual meanings. For anyone seeking a deeper grounding in Hinduism, this book will open the door to a house of treasure.

Rev. Jan Thomas, MSW
Interfaith Minister & Spiritual Director

Hinduism—Scriptures and Practices, Prabha Duneja's newest book, provides a comprehensive and very readable guide to Hinduism. With great skill and sensitivity, Prabha Duneja weaves together a concise, yet thorough, description of all of the major Hindu scriptures with a comprehensive guide to Hindu deities, rituals, and practices. This is an excellent resource guide for scholars, students, and those seeking a deeper understanding of the many facets of Indian religion and culture.

In addition, Prabha's writing is clear and direct and she makes a difficult subject very accessible to the average reader. At the same time, her in-depth knowledge of Sanskrit makes this a valuable key for scholars in the field in Eastern religions. No other book combines the extensive depth of scholarship that Prabha Duneja demonstrates so easily with the spirit of *bhakti*, or devotion. This book reveals the true heart and soul of Hinduism, not just from an academic level, but also from the insight of one who is an accomplished spiritual teacher and master of the practice of yoga. I think it is this quality that makes this book so appealing and accessible. She makes a very serious study a delight to read in a volume relevant to the modern world.

Nowhere has so much relevant and interesting scholarship on Hinduism been compiled so concisely and beautifully in one volume. Prabha combines information on all stages of Hinduism, from the earliest Vedas, through the major epics and stories of the Ramayana and Mahabharata, including guidance on the practice of meditation, *pranayama*, and ritual. There is no other book like this, which integrates so expertly Hindu wisdom and practice. It deserves a place in all libraries.

Sujan Burgeson, Ph.D.
Professor of Religious Studies
Yuba College, CA

Prabha Duneja is well-known in the San Francisco Bay Area for her insightful talks on Hinduism. She has a unique talent for conveying Indian thought and practical spiritual life to Western audiences. Her new book *Hinduism—Scriptures and Practices* is an excellent addition to her growing contribution to Hindu literature. May the Supreme Spirit shower His blessings on her efforts. I hope modern readers and seekers will appreciate it.

Swami Prabuddhananda
Vedanta Society of Northern California
San Francisco, CA

It has been a joy and privilege to know and serve with Prabha Duneja in our Tri-Valley Interfaith ministries and in the Tri-Valley Coalition for Peace. I have been deeply enriched by our conversations, by her generous sharing of her writings and meditation recordings, as well as her presentations in a variety of settings.

Reading Prabha's newest book on Hinduism has been a wonderful gift, offering knowledge and bringing a deeper appreciation for the depth and richness of the Hindu religion. Spending time with this book has provided a spiritual "retreat" as these rich spiritual truths offered nourishment for my own spiritual journey. I have been reminded of the universal truths that reside in all faiths and the call of the Divine to work for peace, harmony, and well-being for all of Creation.

Prabha's book will serve as an excellent textbook for college students and a rich resource for adult education classes in the community. Prabha has an ability to make the complexity and richness of the Hindu philosophy, sacred writings, faith stories, theology, and festivals accessible to a wide audience. Whether one is just beginning the journey of exploring the vastness of the Hindu faith or is seeking a deeper understanding and knowledge, this book will be an important companion and guide.

This book is a vital and well-written resource containing a wealth of information. But it is much more. What shines through each page is the author's deep and abiding knowledge, understanding and practice of her faith. She writes as one with not only a profound grasp of her topic, but as one who lives and breathes and practices her faith in who she is and all she does. Her embodiment of peace, harmony, and enlightenment is evident and inspiring. She is indeed one who *"experiences the presence of the indwelling-soul at the shrine of heart and exhilarates in joy. . ."*

Rev. Dr. Martha Williams
United Christian Church
Livermore, CA

Once again Prabha Duneja has given us a comprehensive insight into the beliefs, scriptures, and practices of Hinduism and to their evolution over many millennia, from before the existence of most current religions. She describes the God of Hinduism in the unmanifest form as the one pervasive unifying power and soul of the universe, and tells of the deities depicted in Hindu temples as the manifestations of the one God, which adherents have added over time to help them visualize and personify the one God.

As I read her description of the Bhagawad Geeta and the teachings of the Divine man, Sri Krishna, I am reminded of the gospels and the teachings of Jesus. She summarizes the whole of the Ramayana, an epic tale of heroes of extreme virtue, power, and magic. The magnificent Mahabharata epic, which has no parallel in Western literature, is only sampled in this book. I have seen scenes from both of these grand moral allegories on the walls of Angkor Wat in Cambodia.

Professor Duneja discusses yoga, meditation, detachment,

liberation, karma, and self-perfection in transcendence over many life cycles. She describes the scriptures, which contain the beliefs, ethics, practices, prayers, and hymns of Hinduism. She describes the deities and festivals.

She begins with a long introduction, which places all of these elements of Hinduism in context, and ends with an insightful discussion of the role of Hindu women through the course of their history, a tale of submergence and reemergence in current times.

This treatise might be the text for initiation into Hinduism, or a thoroughly enjoyable introduction for those of us seeking a cultural familiarity with this religion. It certainly prepares you and whets your appetite to read closer to the original epics, philosophy, and religious writings.

Thomas J Gilmartin, Ph.D.
Ex. Senior Scientist
University of California
Lawrence Livermore National Lab

In this book, Prabha Duneja brings it all together, giving a complete tour of the brimful and profound world of Hinduism with the tone of a loving and patient teacher. She is uniquely suited for this task. But Duneja is not just a scholar; she is also a living, breathing spiritual practitioner. Her chapters are infused with the real joy of religious commitment.

Brian Stein-Webber
Executive Director, Interfaith Council
Contra Costa County, CA

In this engaging and extensive study of Hinduism,

Prabha Duneja offers the reader a literary feast of insight and information. Written with scholarly detail and passion for the subject, *Hinduism—Scriptures and Practices*, collects the many and varied features of this faith tradition into a study which is both thorough and moving. As a novice in my understanding of the richness and variety of Hindu practices, scriptures and figures I was, nevertheless, captivated and engaged in the explications Ms. Duneja offers the reader. For those deeply experienced with the Hindu faith – as practitioners on the inside or scholars and students from the outside – one cannot fail to appreciate the encyclopedic quality of this work. All of that information is undergirded by the obvious delight of the author in plumbing the depths of the tradition and by using extensive quotes in Sanskrit, which are translated for an English-reading audience. From a brilliant scholar and teacher, whose deep passion for her faith resonates from every page, this is a work that beginners and the initiated will find an essential resource for study and reference.

Rev. Chuck Johnstone
Asbury United Methodist Church
Livermore, CA

Prabha Duneja's book is a remarkable treasure, unlocking the timeless wisdom of ancient Hindu scriptures in easy-to-understand language. She has made a vast body of Hindu literature available to the modern English reader. I am in awe of her grasp of the material and the simplicity with which she has expressed it. As a learned Hindu priest, she explains how modern practitioners can celebrate the *Samskaras*, the 16 lifelong rites of passage, which infuse deep spiritual meaning into our lives. As a teacher and a non-Hindu, I can use the fascinating chapters on the Ramayana (the life story of Sri Rama) and the Bhagawad Geeta as teaching tools for character education for my students. Every Hindu family must have this book to help anchor their lives in these deep spiritual practices. Mrs. Duneja's sincere love for all people, Hindu and non-Hindu, shines out from every page.

Kristina M. Seher
Head of School
The Principled Academy
San Leandro, CA

Whenever I teach world religion I always invite Prabha Duneja to give a guest lecture. Her vast knowledge, deep inner peace, and enthusiasm for the Hindu way radiate when she speaks. This book embodies those same qualities. All who want a detailed introduction to Hinduism from someone who loves and follows that spiritual path will profit from this work.

Dr. Scott Sinclair
Assistant Prof. of Religion
Dominican University of CA

Prabha Duneja has written a guide to Hinduism that fully encompasses this beautiful tradition from her viewpoint inside a life built on devotional practice. It is an accessible explication of the scriptures, the methods of worship, and the cultural historical through line to Hindu practices today. Prabha's love shines through as she brings her readers on a pilgrim's journey into the powerful learning that comes with encounters with

Divinity. Duneja is a straightforward storyteller whose wisdom shines through her simple, joyful exaltation in the humor and depth of the teachings.

Rosana Schutte
Unity of Berkeley
Berkeley, CA

This engaging introduction to Hinduism radiates affection and reverence for the texts and practices that have guided its author's spiritual life and her love of God. With an expert's knowledge, Prabha Duneja reviews the greatest Hindu scriptures, introduces us to the gods and goddesses as if they were family, teaches us about the One great spiritual reality (*Parabrahman*) from which everything derives, and explicates the major Hindu spiritual practices of yoga, meditation, mantra-chanting and devotional worship, all the while conveying Hinduism's unique ways of accomplishing the work that is common to all authentic spiritual traditions – transforming self-centered life toward life centered in the Real.

Professor Phillip Novak
Dept. Of Philosophy and Religion
Dominican University of California

Prabha Duneja is to be commended for her tireless efforts to shine the glorious light of Vedic teachings into today's world, especially through her books, classes, and lectures for interfaith groups. In her latest work, *Hinduism—Scriptures and Practices*, she has provided an introduction to Hinduism that is warmly welcoming to those who are newly exploring this religions' principles and practices. Drawing from her teaching experience, she has anticipated and responded to many questions readers may have about Hinduism. This book also gives us a divine glimpse into the highest Vedic ideals, so needed in our world today.

Rev. Ellen Grace O' Brian
Founder and Spiritual Director
Center for Spiritual Enlightenment

"Since ancient times India has been famous for its wisdom and its thought. The ancient Persians, Greek, and Romans were eager to learn from its sages and philosophers. When, in the eighteenth century, the first translations of some Upanishads and the Bhagawad Geeta became available to the West, European philosophers rhapsodized about the profundity and beauty of these writings. Here they encountered a fusion of philosophy and religion, a deep wisdom and a concern with the ultimate, that had no parallel in either contemporary Western philosophy or Western religion. Indian philosophy is highly sophisticated and very technical and surpasses in both in volume and subtlety."

-Prof. Klaus K. Klostermaier

Introduction

Hindu religion, or *Sanatan Vedic Dharma*, is the ancient code of conduct supported by the voice of the inner-Self. *Sanatan Vedic Dharma* is as old as human civilization itself. It has evolved over thousands of years. Since Vedic knowledge developed originally in the Indus Valley, it is also known as Hindu Religion. The oldest and the most prominent scriptures of Hindu *Dharma* are the four Vedas, the Upanishads, Manusmriti, the Ramayana, the Mahabharata, and the Bhagawad Geeta. The essential message of these Holy books is to live in peace and harmony with ourselves, with other people, and with nature. The hymns of the Vedas describe the glories of the Supreme power and the perennial inter-dependence, which exists between God, nature, and the other created beings. In the Vedas there are beautiful illustrations of the origin of the world and detailed descriptions of the bounties and blessings of nature.

The four Vedas, the Rigveda, the Yajurveda, the Samaveda, and the Atharvaveda, have been revealed to the four privileged sages—Agni, Vayu, Aditya, and Angira—at the beginning of creation. The Rigveda was revealed to the great sage Agni, the Yajurveda to sage Vayu, the melodies of the Samaveda were revealed to the great Rishi Aditya, and the great sage Angira was blessed with the hymns of the Atharvaveda. In the Vedic hymns we find a remarkable fusion of spirituality, philosophy, science, and religion. The power and glory of God have been represented by the traditional Vedic personification of gods and goddesses. Each of these four Vedas has one *Upaveda* (sub-Veda),that is, for the Rigveda—Ayurveda (the science of life),the Yajurveda—Dhanurveda (the military science), the Samaveda—Gandharvaveda (the science of sound), and the Atharvaveda—Arthaveda (multiple branches of knowledge). The entire message of the Vedas revolves around the theme of living a healthy, happy, prosperous, creative, and productive life while keeping in mind the global welfare. The last prayer of the Rigveda is, "*Aum Sam gachchhaddhvam, sam vadaddhvan sam vo manamsi janatam. Deva bhagam yatha purve sam janana upasate*" (Rig.10.191),which means, "May we all prosper with mutual understanding, mutual intimacy, respect, love and care while staying in touch with the voice of God, as advised by our predecessors."

Manusmriti, also known as *The Ordinances of Manu,* holds a revered place amongst the other sacred scriptures of Hindu religion. *Smriti* as the word explains itself, is the knowledge reproduced in different versions based on the sacred knowledge of ancient literature. Manusmriti was compiled during the early centuries of the Vedic Era as a codification of the guiding rules for the proper management of society in almost all walks of human life, according to time and place. It is a compendium of ancient wisdom, systematically epitomizing the rules of practice in religion, political, social, and cultural life of people. It outlines the laws for the organization of a peaceful society; the administration of a country; source of revenue; methods of conducting trade, business, provisions for good education and medical care and also the punishment of criminals and offenders. The institutes of sacred law proclaimed by Manu in Vedic times, however modified and changed to some extent throughout the history, still serves as a decisive authority in various fields of life in Hindu society. The ethical code of Manu was written for the proper development of society, where everybody would live with mutual respect, in peace and harmony with each other, and promote economic progress, better standards of life and freedom. This great work of the learned sage Manu opens the door to the understanding of the entire subsequent social structure of Hindu society in the Vedic Era.

Although there are a variety of topics in the book in reference to an ideal cultural setup in society, the most popular ones refer to *Varna-Ashrama-Dharma*—which means the respective duties and rights of an individual at the different stages of life; the Caste System, the four *Ashramas* (stages) of life, and the ritualistic performance of 16 *Samskaras*, or the purificatory sacraments.

The word *Samskara* is a combination of two words— *Sams* and *Kara*—*Sams* means "all auspicious" or "which purifies" and *Kara* means "performance"; so *Samskara* means "the performance of certain rituals in order to give sanctity and purification to human thoughts and aspirations." The closest english word that explains the literal meaning of *Samskara* is the ritualistic sanctification or sacrament. Although fully blessed with subjective awareness of the indwelling supreme-soul, inner knowledge, and wisdom, human beings still need guidance at every step. These sacred rituals are performed at various stages of one's entire life, beginning from the time of conception in the mother's womb until the last moment of death for the peaceful transition of the human soul to another world. In Manusmriti, there is a detailed description of the 16 *Samskaras* from Chapter Two onwards, in reference to *Varna-Ashrama-Dharma*.

Beside the purificatory ceremonies performed at various stages of life, the Vedas recommend the performance of some daily rituals in order to improve the quality of life, such as daily *yajna*, yoga and meditation. *Yajna*, a well-known religious term of the Vedic tradition literally means "the act which helps the individual to live in harmony with everybody and everything." The spirit of *yajna* conveys the ideal of interdependence, continuity and the survival of the creation. The performance of *yajna* makes the inner world blend peacefully into the physical world.

The importance of yoga and meditation has been highly emphasized in Vedic tradition. The most popular word of Vedic literature 'yoga' has been derived from Sanskrit root word '*yuj*', which literally means "the alignment of mind, body and spirit in order to experience a union and communion with the indwelling-soul." It is the communion of human soul with Divine. In ancient days, the *yoganushasama* (yoga discipline) was taken as a necessity in order to live a healthy and wholesome life. People started their day with the early morning worship of the Sun. There are many hymns in the Vedas that describe the festival of sunrise when the golden light is scattered through the rift of the clouds. There are 12 yogic postures for *Surya Namaskara* (salutation to Sun), each flowing into another very gracefully and graciously energizing each cell in the body.

After these exercises the body feels thoroughly refreshed and peaceful. The yogic practice of early morning rejuvenates each cell in our body, helps in proper absorption of calcium, eliminates many toxins, and also helps in meditation. The experience of unity in yoga remains with the person for the rest of the day and the heavenly glow is carried on in the activities of daily life. The peace and purity of the meditative hours lingers in the memory long after the moment itself is gone. The other ideal time for yogic exercises and meditation is the mysterious hour of sunset. The beautiful twilight, the quietness across the horizon is very helpful in meditation and the mind becomes receptive to the call of the Divine. The union of day and night described as *Sandhya* in the Vedas helps the mind and body to glide into relaxed moments and experience the union with the indwelling-soul. The momentary hush and pause in nature promotes inner peace, helps to disengage the mind from all the activities of daytime, and experience the yogic alignment, which brings deep relaxation.

In reference to the caste system or *Varna-Dharma* in Hinduism, it is believed that people initiated by their inborn nature choose the kind of work that suits their likings and aspirations—this has brought into existence the four-fold work order in society. In olden days when people started living in small groups and started to form communities, they gradually realized that they had naturally divided themselves into four major sections. The division took place quite naturally, according to the social needs, for the benefit of society.

The system of division has helped the community in maintaining mutual respect, inter-dependence, cooperation, and perfect fellowship. The four categories have been named Brahmin, Kshatriya, Vaishya, and Shudra. This division, which was originally based on the inherent potential of the individuals, has been defined as the caste system. The word 'caste' is self-explanatory—it means the role a person has assigned himself to play in his lifetime for the time being. This specific role played by the person, born of his instinctive nature, becomes his assigned duty or *Dharma*. For example, serenity, self-control, asceticism, purity, forgiveness, simplicity, righteousness, honesty, knowledge of the scriptures, and strong faith in God are the characteristics of a Brahmin born of his innate nature. A Brahmin is the one who lives in the consciousness of the supreme *Parabrahman* and manifests the purity of the Self through his thoughts, words, and deeds. His manners express proper alignment with the inner-divinity. His lifestyle is expected to be simple and the epitome of renunciation, self-dedication, and service to the entire mankind. He is expected to teach the Holy scriptures, perform the religious rituals and guide other people into a pure lifestyle.

In ancient times the learned Brahmins, the Rishis, and the sages used to be on the advisory boards of the Kings. Since the political and the economic life of the people is expected to derive its guidance from God, the Kings always consulted these learned scholars for proper guidance in administration. These men of wisdom have been known as royal priests and royal sages who always looked into the true interests of society.

As a Brahmin is considered to be an embodiment of godliness, the other class which is next in scale is the Kshatriya; the embodiment of heroism, splendor, steadfastness, dexterousness, generosity, and lordliness. The Sanskrit aphorism *'Kshatat traayate iti Kshatriyah,'* meaning the one who protects others from *Kshati* (injury) is a Kshatriya. The duty of a Kshatriya is to enforce the laws of *Dharma* for the well-being of society. He should make sure that righteousness is being upheld in reverence and people are doing their duties, while keeping in mind the welfare of others. Whenever there is decline of ethical values, the Kshatriya class is expected to be alert and help the community in the restoration of law and order. The protection of a country, society, and community is the first and foremost duty of a Kshatriya. To exhibit valor, heroism, patriotism, skill, promptitude, generosity, compassion, self-sacrifice, and self-confidence in the battle-field are the other hallmarks of a genuine Kshatriya. The King as a Kshatriya ruler becomes the embodiment of God and his life becomes dedicated to the service of his citizens.

The next class in hierarchy of *Varna-Dharma* is that of Vaishyas—the businessmen or merchants. Agriculture, cattle-rearing and commercial operations are the duties performed by the Vaishyas born of their innate nature. The Vaishyas are endowed with special business talents and help the administrators in the economic growth of the country. The fourth category is that of Shudras, the routine workers, the proletariat and laborers who are good at carrying out instructions and contribute only a small fraction of their inherent potential.

This hierarchical distribution of people in conformity with their personal choice or *Swabhava* (inborn nature) becomes conducive to the peace and progress of society. Each and every station of duty is very significant and holds its proper importance for the development of society. In general, we notice that people in society are not equal in their intellectual abilities, capabilities and capacities, but each and every person is a substantial contributor of his unique abilities in his own special way. This classification in society proceeds from personal *swabhava* (inborn nature). The four-fold division in society is psychological and universal. It is created by the people, of the people, and for the people.

In reference to the status of women in Hindu society, the ancient Hindu scriptures declare graciously, "*Yatra naryastu pujyante, ramante tatra devatah, yatraitaastu na pujyante sarvastatra aphalah kriyah*" (Manusmriti.3.56), meaning, "To the family where women are given due respect and protection, the celestials (gods) shower their blessings perennially—but where they are not respected, all other efforts to seek happiness become ineffectual and the downfall of that family is inevitable." There is another famous saying in the sacred books of Hindu *Dharma* "Next to God we are indebted to woman, first for the life itself and then for making it worthwhile." A woman is indeed the nucleus around which everything in family and society revolves.

Since Vedic times (which is anywhere beyond 5000 B.C.E.) Hindu women have enjoyed a very honorable status in society. A famous Hindu prayer, *"Tvameva mata ca pita tvameva"* which means, O' Lord, you are my mother and father—indicates clearly the honor and respect of women in the ritualistic Vedic worship. According to the Taittiriya Upanishad the first lesson a child learns from the teacher is, *"Matridevo bhava"* (1.11.2) meaning, "Let your mother be the embodiment of God to you." A mother's influence is the most powerful factor in molding the character of an individual. In a Hindu family, mother is the epitome of purity, chastity, and unselfish love for her children.

In the Epic period, good education was regarded as an important accomplishment to be well placed in life. At homes as well as at the *Gurukuls* (schools) of ancient India, both boys and girls were educated together. Fine arts, music, dancing, needlework, cooking, and painting were especially included in the academic curriculum for girls. There is also a description in some scriptures about women being great archers, skillful chariot riders in the army, and great teachers par-excellence. The most enlightening dialogue between the great sage Yajnavalkya and the lady philosopher Gargi in Brihadaranyaka Upanishad has always drawn the attention of scholars and men of letters around the world. The

Atharvaveda also refers to highly educated women as head of the educational institutes, and government offices.

The young girls were also given the *Upanayana* (sacred thread) and encouraged to study the Vedas and be an active participant in the performance of rituals at home and also in society. The Yajurveda (8.1) documents clearly, "A young daughter who has observed *Brahmacharya Ashrama* should be married to a man who is educated and learned like her." In general, the young girls got married in their late teens or sometimes even later than that and they also had a decisive voice in the selection of their husbands. The Rigveda mentions that parents invited suitors to their homes and the daughter had the freedom of choosing her husband. This tradition was called *Swyamvara*, meaning, "self-choice of husband by the woman."

In the Vedic Era women neither covered their heads nor veiled their faces; they enjoyed sufficient freedom at home and also in their involvement of public affairs. But the repeated attacks on India by Arab invaders and other foreigners over the past centuries disturbed the entire setup in Hindu families. During such hostile aggressions, and also when invaders became the rulers, the chastity and dignity of women were often threatened. In many cases Hindu women sacrificed their life instead of yielding to the humiliations and insults enforced by the assailants. Gradually, Hindu society became very concerned and quite protective about the honor of women. Their freedom was curtailed and in order to protect their personal respect and chastity they started veiling their faces in public. The formal education of women also became a serious issue of genuine concern for parents.

In the early 19th century when India was being ruled by the British Empire, some great Hindu leaders raised a strong voice against the prevailing evils such as the *Sati* (self-immolation) custom, the child marriage, the seclusion of women, and many other issues related to the suppression and education of women in Hindu society. They started several reform movements in cooperation with the government.

At the dawn of 1901 when Mahatma Gandhi started the movement of India's freedom from British Empire, he wrote extensively in newspapers and also spoke fervently in a decisive voice about the importance of social freedom and education of women in Hindu society. A wave of awakening went across the country and thousands of women came out of seclusion and entered the public domain with men. After the independence of India in 1947, equal rights for men and women have been incorporated in the constitution.

Although, it is quite true that in Hindu society there is still a small fraction of social structure where women are not treated equally due to the lingering deep-rooted influence of previous generations, when the foreigners were ruling India. In modern India generally women do not cover their heads or veil their faces except in some remote villages. After independence, the democratic secular government of India has been constantly struggling to safeguard the women's interest and bring back the ancient glory of the Vedic Era when women were privileged with equal rights in almost every single field of life. At present, a Hindu woman enjoys sufficient freedom at home and in society, while living by the time-honored cherished ideals of Hinduism.

About the concept of God in Hinduism, the hymns of Vedas and the verses of Bhagawad Geeta describe gloriously that the essence of all life is God. The Isha Upanishad opens with the declaration, *"Ishavasyam idam sarvam yatkin cha jagatyam jagat,"* (Isha.1.1) meaning, "The entire universe is permeated by the Supreme Lord, God is the source of all the sentient and insentient and everything belongs to the Almighty." The Supreme power exists diffusing its abundance in everything, which is within the boundaries of perception and even beyond that. The cosmic-soul is the omnipotent substratum from where the plurality of the world is projected.

Everything in the macrocosm as well as in the microcosm is energized by the cosmic energy, Supreme *Parabrahman*— the pure consciousness. The Hindu trinity—Brahma, Vishnu, and Maheshwara (Shiva) are the three expressive aspects of the Supreme *Parabrahman*. Lord Brahma as distinct from *Parabrahman* is the creator, Lord Vishnu the sustainer, and Maheshwara (Shiva) the annihilator as well as the regenerator. If we look closely at Hindu trinity, we see three identical faces of Divine, power projections of pure consciousness. All the deities may appear to be independent; in fact they are the different facets of the pure consciousness. The Vedic sages have declared jubilantly, *"Ekam sad vipra bahudha vadanti"* (Rig.1.164.46), meaning, "One alone exists; sages and mystics call it by various names." Hindu gods and goddesses are the personification of the ultimate infinite Supreme Reality, answering and satisfying the devotees who seek help with prayers and meditation.

For example, the worship of Lord Vishnu initiates people to live a life with the spirit of *yajna*, which conveys the ideal of mutual inter-dependence, continuity, and the survival of creation. Helping each other selflessly and living in peace and harmony with ourselves, with other people and nature. The Divine consort of Lord Vishnu is Sri Lakshmi who guides people for making money by appropriate means and also making the appropriate use of money while keeping in mind the global welfare.

The worship and meditation on Shiva is also one of the most cherished rituals in Hinduism. There are innumerable temples and shrines with the images of Shiva in the form of '*Yogi Raja*' absorbed in peaceful deep meditation as well as the symbolic *Lingam* form which is generally made of black or white stone rounded both at the top and bottom to indicate that it does not stand or arise from anywhere in space or time. It has neither beginning nor end. The three horizontal lines on the *Shivalingam* indicate the three qualities of the polarized creative force of nature—the three *Gunas: Sattvic, Rajasic* and *Tamasic*. The worship of Shiva is performed with the most sacred ritual of *abhishekam* in which water is offered on the top-most part of *Shivalingam* in an unbroken stream with uninterrupted chanting of sacred hymns with one pointed concentration. The divine sages have described it as— "*Sajatiya vritti pravah*" meaning, "continuous, single-minded contemplation on God." In the process of *abhishekam* the devotee prays for unity with the source of life in an unbroken stream of devoted thoughts. The Divine consort of Lord Shiva is goddess Parvati, who is worshiped for alignment with *Para Shakti* (the divine potency), which is holding everything together and is reflected through everything.

In the worship of Sri Ganesha, which forms an important part of almost all the Hindu rituals, the devotee seeks blessings for inner-enlightenment, clarity of vision, purity of mind and intellect. *Gana* means the chief elements that constitute the body of the universe and *Esha* means the master who controls the combined movement of every atom and every molecule, which keep the wheel of creation in motion. The symbolism in prayers indicates the efforts of the individual-soul seeking liberation from seven deadly sins such as, lust, anger, greed, envy, sloth, egoism, gluttony, and alignment of the conditioned-self with pure-self.

In the religious tradition of Hindu *Dharma*, there are some goddesses who are worshipped independently as well as with their Divine spouse. Mother Saraswati, the Divine consort of Brahma, is worshipped as the embodiment of knowledge, wisdom, purity and serenity. The Goddess is addressed as *Gynana Sakti,* meaning, "the expressive aspect of divine potency that enriches our life with the knowledge of material world as well as the higher mysteries of soul." Mother Durga, the personification of the totality of the powers of Brahma, Vishnu, and Shiva, is worshipped for annihilation of negative tendencies. The consort of Kala, the all devouring time, is the Divine Mother Kali, who is worshipped for victory over time and blessings for living in the tissue of the present moment.

In most of the temples, besides the important shrines of Lord Shiva, Lord Vishnu, Sri Hanuman, Lord Rama, Lord Krishna, and other gods and goddesses; there is generally a shrine of nine cosmic bodies known as *Navagraha Mandala*, for special worship, where the devotee seeks alignment with nature for peace and prosperity. All the worships in a Hindu family are performed while giving due importance to the five basic elements—fire, air, ether, earth, and water, presiding *Nakshatra* (constellation) the birth sign, the position of Sun, Moon, and other planets.

For a Hindu, God is a living reality and there is a constant effort to stay aligned with the pure luminous soul, become alert about the activities of mind and body, make the right choices and feel relaxed. According to Hindu sages it is very important to remember that human life is a great gift of God. Human beings are blessed with subjective awareness of the soul. It is only in human life that we get an opportunity for self-analysis, self-realization, God-realization, and *moksha* (liberation). That is why for a Hindu every little bit of activity is centered in God. People have shrines at homes, at work places, schools, and hospitals. There are rituals to bless a new car, new house, business, etc. People greet each other with '*Namaste*' meaning, "The one in me salutes and bows to the one in you." It is honoring divinity in others which promotes cosmic intimacy and brings people closer to each other in a relaxed spiritual bond.

Hinduism believes that the Supreme-soul also manifests as

God-incarnate. Although the God-incarnate appears to be an ordinary human being, he remains rooted in the transcendental-Self. His body is a cosmic body and his mind is the cosmic mind. The Supreme-soul incarnates to enlighten people to recognize their own divinity through their own efforts. The God-incarnate comes down to the level of humans, in order to educate them into the graciousness of human life. He strengthens their faith in God and also their respect for the laws of *Dharma*. He shows his personal compassion for people and inspires them into godliness and helps people to realize the values of *Dharma* (righteousness).

Although there is a description of ten God incarnations in the Hindu Puranas, only two are generally worshiped by people: Lord Rama and Lord Krishna. The Ramayana, which describes the life story of Lord Rama, ranks among the greatest religious classics of the world. Apart from its poetic excellence and literary grandeur, it is also considered to be a Holy scripture by Hindu families. The other highly respected unique scripture is the Bhagawad Geeta, the holy dialogue between Lord Krishna and Arjuna. The message of the Bhagawad Geeta has been held in deep reverence by the sages, philosophers and learned scholars all over the world. It is one of the most well known revered texts among the other scriptures of the world. Along with the most prominent Hindu scriptures as mentioned earlier, the ancient sages also wrote the Puranas. In the Puranas the philosophical truths of the Vedas and Upanishads are presented through stories, anecdotes, and parables. There are 18 Maha-Puranas, but the most popular ones are Bhagavata Purana, Vayu Purana,

Vishnu Purana, Skanda Purana, Garuda Purana, Padma Purana, Markandeya Purana, and Shiv Purana.

In reference to the religious symbols in Hinduism there are some which present the totality of the Supreme-soul and also the path leading to alignment with the indwelling-self, gods, goddesses and cosmic bodies. The Holy syllable *Aum* is the most well known symbol of Hinduism, which has been highly glorified in the Vedas. The sound of *Aum* is the whisper from the unified field of pure consciousness to itself. This sound from *Brahma nada* wraps the entire creation. Everything in the macrocosm as well as in the microcosm is the sequential unfolding of this mysterious sound, which is whispering and manifesting through every molecule and every atom.

According to Mandukya Upanishad (1.3-4-5), *Aum* symbolizes the triads in time and space and also the four states of consciousness. 'A' stands for the waking state (conscious level), 'U' describes the dream state, and 'M' stands for the *Sushupti*—dreamless, deep sleep. When written in Sanskrit, there is a curved line on the top, which indicates the fourth state of consciousness, which is beyond dreamless, deep sleep. It is called *Turiya* in meditation, when the individual-soul goes through the gap into unity with the universal-soul. This half syllable leads the meditator into deep silence and inner peace. The dot on the curved line represents the Supreme Divinity in us. Meditating on the dot is going into the silence of the Self. These three syllables also describe the three stages of evolution in the universe. A stands for *adimata* (beginning),

U stands for *utkarsha* (sustenance) and M stands for *mitti* (annihilation). It also describes *Akara*, *Ukara* and *Makara*-combined together *Omkara*. *Akara* stands for *Ishwara*, *Ukara* for *Mula-Prakriti* and *Makara* for *Maya Shakti*. This means that everything we see in the universe is going through an evolution. It comes into existence, it is sustained for a while and then it is gone. Everything is enclosed within the grasp of swift moving time. The mystic syllable also stands for Brahma, Vishnu and Shiva—the cosmic cycle of creation, sustenance and destruction. The primordial sound of *Aum* is called the *Brahmnada*, which holds within itself the totality of everything in the universe.

Other popular symbols used in meditation and ritualistic worship are the '*Swastika*', '*Dharma Chakra*', '*Sri Chakra*', '*Nataraja*', and '*Saligrama.*' '*Swastika*' comes from the root word *Swasti*, which means auspiciousness. It represents the omniscience of the pervasive intelligence that prevails at the substratum of the entire creation. The symbol of '*Swastika*' represents the symbol of *Aum* written in *Brahmi-lipi*, one of the very old scripts of ancient India.

'*Dharma Chakra*' represents the wholeness of the Divine. It is symbolic of the eternal cosmic law that everything we see is going through an evolution. A wheel also represents the universal field of energy and information always in motion.

Similarly the symbol of '*Nataraja*' the dramatic dancing posture of Shiva with a ring of flames all around the figure indicates the pulsating rhythm of cosmic energy, which has no beginning and no end. Another popular symbol, '*Sri Chakra*', is a geometrical diagram with a star at center, which leads the aspirant to the shrine of heart, under the wish granting tree—*kalpataru*, where the individual goes into unity with the Divine Mother.

'*Saligrama*' is a black rounded stone with a natural hole showing visible spirals inside which indicates that the true nature of the soul is veiled in many layers of conditioned consciousness and is indeed very difficult to comprehend. '*Saligrama*' is supposed to be endowed with mysterious powers which guide the individual for unity in transcendence and desire for selfless service to humanity.

In the Hindu religion there are colorful festivals celebrated throughout the year associated with India's rich cultural and religious heritage. Although each festival is associated with several legends and marks the commencement of a new season and fresh crop; the purpose of celebrating these festivals is self-purification, inner-enlightenment, and living in peace and harmony with others. It is an effort to be respectful to the bounties of nature, celebrate the changes in nature in order to get full support of nature. Performance of the ceremonies attached to these festivals dates back to the ancient civilization of the Indus Valley. These traditions along with the wisdom of elders in the family, learned sages and spiritual teachers have been passed from one generation to another so that prosperity in society may evolve both intellectually and spiritually making life peaceful, enjoyable, and prosperous.

In January, people celebrate Lohri, Pongal, and Makara Sankranti, when the Sun shines closer to 90° on the Tropic of

Capricorn. This marks the beginning of an enlightened and prosperous time for mankind. In the beginning of February and March the festivals of Shivaratri, Vasant Panchami, and Holi are celebrated in welcome of the spring season. Towards the end of March and beginning of April starts the New Shaka Samvat celebrated as New Year's Day of the Hindu lunar calendar, which also marks the beginning of nine days worship of Navaratra. Generally people fast for eight days, eating only one meal a day, and on the ninth day celebrate the birth of Lord Rama—the God-incarnate. Vaishakhi is also celebrated in April in welcome of a new crop and the arrival of summer. In the month of July, August, or September comes the celebration of Rakshabandhan, also known as Rakhi, and Janmashtami when the birth of Lord Krishna, the God-incarnate, is celebrated with deep respect, great enthusiasm, love, and devotion. In October and November again comes the nine days Navaratra-worship of Durga, Lakshmi, and Saraswati, which culminates in the celebration of Vijayadashmi—the victory of goodness over evil. Next comes the festival of Diwali or Deepavali celebrated exactly 20 days after Vijayadashmi, on the last day of the descending phase of Moon in *Ashwin*. This festival is associated with several legends and marks the advent of new crops and the winter season. Deepavali is a three-day festival, which starts with *Dhantehras* on the 13th day of the lunar calendar, and the celebration culminates in the worship of the goddess Lakshmi on the night of Deepavali.

For perfect health, peace, and harmony, the importance of vegetarian food has been highly emphasized in Hinduism.

Human teeth are meant for eating vegetarian food; and also the human intestine, which is long and narrow, is not designed to digest any type of meat. The physical body is called the "*Annamaya Kosa*" which has a direct relation with *Manomaya Kosa* (Mind), *Pranamaya Kosa* (Breath), *Vijnanmaya Kosa* (Meditative unity), and *Anandamaya Kosa* (Bliss). These various fields are inter-connected and work in unison with each other. To experience unity with the Self, the journey starts from physical body, which is *Annamaya Kosa*. The food is called '*Anna*' in Sanskrit. *Anna* is related to *Prana*—the life breath. *Prana*—is very closely connected with *Mana*, the mind.

The divine sage of the Chandogya Upanishad writes clearly, "*Annam asitam tredha vidhiyate, tasya yah sthvasitho dhatus tat purisam bhavati, yo madhyamas tan mamsam, yo nisthas tan manah,*" (5.1) meaning, "The food we eat is digested in a three-fold process. The coarsest portion becomes the feces; the middle becomes flesh and the subtlest becomes the thoughts." So it is very important to eat the specific quality of food which promotes the purity of thoughts and good health. Besides, it is not just the ingredients of food which matters, but also the way it is cooked and consumed makes a big difference. For example, when a certain recipe is given to five cooks, the results are always different because each one of them adds his own thoughts and feelings into the cooking. Good and positive thoughts in cooking do produce pleasant and enjoyable taste and also affect the temperament and health of the person who eats it. A prayer of gratitude before eating the meal has been highly emphasized in Vedic tradition. The prayer is asking for grace and blessing which brings a relaxed flow of awareness in the mind and helps the body in the proper digestion of the food. It is really important to eat the meal in a prayful mood and remain silent and relaxed while eating or have good, pleasant conversation with others at the dining table.

Freedom of faith and religious tolerance have been highly appreciated in Hinduism. The legacy of Vedic teachings has always advocated that every individual must seek his own personal confirmation from his own inherent resources. The aspirant should be properly guided and not forced into co-operation. He should be entreated and persuaded but not compelled. Free spontaneity in acceptance should be valued and respected. Every person is free to choose his own form of worship; for all paths ultimately lead to the realization of the Supreme-soul through a variety of personal spiritual experiences. In Hinduism, all paths towards the realization of God are endured and honored. The entire approach is universal and tolerant.

In reference to the concept of life after death, the Hindu religion believes in reincarnation. Death is not an end in itself, it only marks the time for change and a new beginning. The embodied-soul goes from one body to another; forced by the thoughts and memories which have been accumulated during the lifetime. The individual-soul retains its individuality from one stage to another and also from one life to another. All sorts of changes take place only at the physical level and the unchangeable, immutable soul remains untouched. The destruction of the gross body can never cause any destruction in the continuity of the indestructible soul.

The soul at one time becomes someone's father, at another time, the son, the elder brother and yet at another time the younger brother. One soul enclosed within the mind has gone through many births before, and keeps entering into new wombs. The journey of the soul is ever-renewing on the path of eternity.

Hindu sages believed in cremation of the deceased because with the burning of dead body the five basic elements—fire, earth, ether, air, and water, which constitute the bodies of all beings—merge into the five essential components, and the soul is free to enter another body based on the individual karma. The earliest description of *Antyeshti Samskara* (funeral rites) has been mentioned in Rigveda (10.16.3-5,7,13) and Atharvaveda (12.2.40-42).

From this overview of Hinduism we may gather that Hindu religion is not based merely on philosophical speculations, but is grounded in direct perception of the indwelling-soul from moment to moment. The teachings of the Holy Vedas, Upanishads, and Bhagawad Geeta assert the inherently pure divine nature of man and also suggest the appropriate means for its subjective experience. Hinduism is a way of life that helps the individual to stay aligned with the Supreme-soul and receive guidance into the activities of daily life, in order to live in peace and harmony with others and with nature. The entire social structure in Hindu society is centered in time honored religious beliefs and practices that have provided the spiritual basis for self-realization and God-realization through the ages. According to the great Hindu sages every person is a potential candidate for Divine status and ultimately must experience the presence of God within. Let the grace of indwelling Lord be perceived and expressed in all that we think, speak, and perform.

Aum-Tat-Sat
Sri Krishna Arpanamastu.
Shubham Bhuyat.

January 14, 2012   **– Prabha Duneja**

"Whenever I have read any part of the Vedas, I have felt that some unearthly and unknown light illuminated me. In the great teaching of the Vedas, there is no touch of sectarianism. It is of all ages, climes and nationalities and is the royal road for the attainment of the Great Knowledge."

-Henry David Thoreau

"The religion based on the Vedas, the *Sanatana Dharma* or *Vedic Dharma*, is the oldest of living religions and stands unrivalled in the depth and splendor of its philosophy…The more it is studied and practiced, the more does it illuminate the intellect and satisfy the heart."

-Annie Besant

"The Vedas are the most rewarding and the most elevating book which can be possible in the world."

-Arthur Schopenhauer

1

The Holy Vedas

The Word "Veda" means "sacred knowledge", which was revealed to the four great Rishis—Agni, Vayu, Aditya, and Angira—at the beginning of creation. The Vedas are called *Shruti*, meaning "the words and sounds heard by the sages in yogic unity with Supreme *Parabrahman*."

The Vedas are considered to be the divine revelation, which has been handed down to humanity as a necessary guidance in order to live in peace and harmony on earth. The ancient sages were blessed with stupendous memory; they preserved this sacred knowledge in their memory with proper accentuation and passed it on to the successive generations through oral teachings with utmost care and accuracy. Later, when the Sanskrit script was developed, the learned sages compiled the Vedic wisdom into four Holy scriptures; the Rigveda, the Yajurveda, the Samaveda, and the Atharvaveda. Vedic literature is the proud possession of mankind since the beginning of human history. The important feature of Vedic knowledge is its all pervasiveness, encompassing almost every aspect of life. In this reference Professor F. Max Muller writes, "The Vedic literature opens to us a chapter in what has been called the education of the human race, to which we can find no parallel anywhere else." He further says, "The Vedas has a twofold interest; it belongs to the history of the world and to the history of India—as long as man continues to take an interest in the history of his race, and as long as we collect in libraries and museums the relics of former ages, the first place in that long row of books which contains the records of the Aryan branch of mankind, will belong forever to Rigveda."

The hymns of the Vedas describe the glories of the Supreme Lord and the perennial interdependence, which exists between God, nature, and the other created beings. There are beautiful illustrations of the origin of the universe and detailed descriptions of the bounties and blessings of nature and how we can make the best use of the natural reservoirs while keeping in mind the global welfare. In Vedic hymns we find a remarkable fusion of spirituality, philosophy, science, and religion. As a matter of fact, almost all the different branches of knowledge and systems of Indian philosophy owe their allegiance to the Vedas. Appreciating the profundity of the holy divine revelation, Henry David Thoreau has said, "Whenever I have read any part of the Vedas, I have felt that some unearthly and unknown light illuminated me. In the great teaching of the Vedas there is no touch of sectarianism. It is of all ages, climes and nationalities and is the royal road for the attainment of the Great Knowledge. When I am at it, I feel that I am under the spangled heavens of a summer night. "

The great educator Thoreau not only read the Vedas but also recommended the study of the sacred wisdom in his lectures on philosophy. The Vedas are the living inspirations for leading a dynamic life. Professor Heeren, while writing on the sublimity of the Vedic knowledge, says, "Vedas are without doubt the oldest work composed in Sanskrit. The Vedas stand alone in their solitary splendor—standing as a beacon of divine light for an onward march of humanity." The great Russian saint and educator Leo Tolstoy also held the Vedas and Upanishads in deep reverence and spread their teachings in Russia. The Hymns of the Vedas are the inspired utterances of the great sages perceived through their heightened consciousness.

The Vedas are a unique treasure of a sacred knowledge, inspiring philosophy, cherished religious treatises, laws of nature, cosmology, meteorology, laws of science, sociology, astrology, psychology, pharmacology, mathematics, physics, chemistry, astronomy, administration, theology, and the deepest mysteries of yoga and meditation.

In reference to the magnitude of Vedic wisdom Mrs. Wheeler Wilcox, a great American scholar, says, "India - The land of Vedas, the remarkable works contain not only religious ideas for a perfect life, but also facts which science has proved true. Electricity, radium, electronics, airship, all were known to the seers who founded the Vedas."

The Vedic sages have tried to cover almost all phases of human activity, its purposefulness and attainments. The Vedas are the repository of all knowledge and wisdom. These superb poetic compositions encompass the knowledge of the whole universe, which cover the subject matter that relates to animate and inanimate. *"Yada bhutam bhavyam bhavishyashch saraam vedaat prasidyati"* is the famous saying about the Vedas—meaning, "Vedic knowledge envelopes in it the entire wisdom of the past, present, and future." It is valid for all times in every field of life, for everyone in the universe. The revered knowledge of the Vedas holds the most honorable place among the ancient teachings of the world and is definitely relevant to the philosophical and scientific development of modern generation.

The hymns of the Vedas have been categorized in three sections. The first part is known as *Samhitas*, which constitutes the mantra portion. The second part is known as *Brahmanas*, which deals with rites, ceremonies, and rituals. The third part constitutes the *Aranyakas* which describes the knowledge of the Supreme-Self. Each of the four Vedas has one *Upaveda* (sub-Veda) i.e. for the Rigveda—Ayurveda (the science of life), the Yajurveda—Dhanurveda (the military science), the Samaveda—Gandharvaveda (the science of sound), and the Atharvaveda—Arthaveda (multiple branches of knowledge).

The Rigveda

The Rigveda, which comprises 10,589 hymns, is divided into ten volumes. This unique scripture is full of prayers and poems explaining the glories of the Supreme Lord. There are many hymns that describe the festival of Sunrise when the golden light is scattered through the rift of clouds and fills the sky with the glories of crimson dawn, such as, *"Eaishayukt pravata! Suryashyodynadhi shant sthabhi subhgosha eym vi yatybhi manushan"* (Rig.1.48.7) meaning, "The rising sun from beyond the horizon fills the auspicious dawn with a hundred auras of divine light and moves on her way to bless everyone in all the directions." Also in another hymn the divine poet says, "*Ketum krivann ketve pesho mriya apeshsye. Samushderbhrijayatha,*" (Rig.1.6.3) meaning, "The blessed whispers of crimson dawn with smiles and sweet melodies awakens life across the planet with hope and new promises. Wake up O' man and offer your obeisance to the Supreme Lord who shines through everything."

"The Rigveda is truly the aspiring song of humanity", says Dr. L.M. Singhvi, "profoundly humane and compassionate, untrammelled and emancipated in its universality, deeply spiritual in its mystical depths, sincere and upright in its ethical rectitude, evocative and affirmative in the ardent enjoyment of life and its gifts, spontaneous in its sense of human togetherness, and cosmic in its reach and its world view, the Vedic literature is undoubtedly mankind's most precious treasure."

There are highly inspiring hymns in the Rigveda in which the divine poet expresses the joy of living in a peaceful integrated society—'*Vasudhaiva Kutumbakam*', meaning, "Let people on earth live like citizens of one great empire under the pure guidance of Supreme Divinity, the source of all life, that connects the entire creation." There are so many hymns where unity, integrity, and universal fraternity have been highly emphasized.

The Vedic philosophy of cosmic fellowship, moving together hand in hand to develop common ideals and purposes is beautifully expressed in these hymns, e.g., "*Aum*

Sam Gachchhadhvam Sam Vadadhvam Samvo Manamsi Jaanatam. Deva Bhaagam Yatha Purve Samjanana Upasate," (Rig.10.191) meaning, "May we assemble and communicate with each other from the purity of our heart for the common welfare of Society. May our thoughts be integrated in pursuit of higher ideals. May we become duty oriented like our wise ancestors and enjoy our assigned share of fortune". *"Aum Samano Mantrah Samitih Samani Samanam Manah Saha Chittamesham. Samanam Mantram Abhi Mantraye Vah Samanena Vo Havisha Jishome,"* (Rig.10.192) meaning, "May our prayers be universal for love and peace around the globe. May our thoughts and intentions move in accord, and may we work in unison for the common ideals and goals. May our devotional worship be alike, and may our offerings be one and the same". *"Aum Samani Vah Akutih Samana Hridayani Vah. Samanam Astu Vo Mano Yatha Vah Susahasati,"* (Rig.10.194) meaning, "May our aspirations be in perfect harmony with each other. May our thinking be peaceful and synchronous and may we all prosper while keeping in mind the universal welfare and fraternity".

These ethereal invocations from the Rigveda have always inspired everyone to hold reverence for the potential divinity that dwells wrapped up in other human beings and work together with spiritual intimacy, and relaxed understanding.

In reference to these invocative hymns of noble affirmation, Dr. L.M. Singhvi says, "These enduring verities of the Vedas are not a relic of the past, nor are they the exclusive preserve or the sole Inheritance of Indians or Indo-Aryans. They belong to the common heritage of humanity and are relevant in our world and in our age. We owe it to ourselves and to the people and the nations of the world to share this precious heritage and to disseminate its message and meaning." He further says, "The message of the Vedas remains a living legacy for every age and for all time. The indestructible spoken word of the Vedic sages stands untouched by time or the elements and has continued to travel through countless centuries like a great wave through the living substance of mind."

Vedic hymns illustrate the close relationship of man with nature, and the realization of God through an intimate revered bond with Mother Nature. The power and glory of God have been represented by the traditional Vedic personification of gods and goddesses. The Sanskrit words for god and goddess are *Deva* and *Devi*. The word *"Deva"* comes from the root word *"Div"* and means, "that radiates" or "embodies the potential dynamism, the splendor or glory and charisma of the Supreme Lord and showers blessings." There are hymns addressed to Agni (fire), Indra (king of gods), Varuna (water), Soma (Moon), Virat Purusha (cosmic man), Vayu (wind), Dhyaus (sky), Rudra (life force), Prithvi (earth), Apah (water), and Bruhaspati (celestial teacher).

The word 'Agni' is derived from the root word *'Ancu'* and *'Aga'*, the fire god. Worship of Agni has been highly glorified in the Vedas. The first hymn of the Rigveda starts with the adoration of Agni as an embodiment of Supreme *Parabrahman*. *"Aum Agnimede Purohitam Yagasya Devaritvajam Hotaram Ratnadhatamam"*, meaning, "I salute to Agni, the fire god, the most bounteous, the giver of wealth on the planet." There are hundreds of hymns dedicated in appreciation of Agni who manifests as fire on earth, as lightning in the *Indraloka* (sky), as the Sun in heaven, and as a mediator carrying the offerings of men to gods. All the traditional Vedic rituals are performed around the ceremonial fire, the personification of the Supreme Lord himself.

Varuna, the Lord of water, has always held a very revered place among the Vedic gods and goddesses. There are many hymns dedicated to the worship of Varuna that encompasses the entire universe. In some of the hymns Varuna is addressed as 'Mitra Varuna'. The word 'Vayu' is derived from the root word '*va*' meaning, motion. Vayu, the wind god, is also addressed as Anila. The 11 Rudras are the 11 *pranas* or vital airs—*prana, apana, vyana, samana, udana, naga, kurma, karkilla, devadutta, dhananjaya*, and the 11th is *atman* the consciousness. There are so many hymns dedicated to Bruhaspati, the greatest spiritual teacher par-excellence. Indra is usually addressed as Devaraja Indra—The Lord of gods and goddesses. The word 'Indra' comes from the root word '*idi*,' the god of rain. In the Rigveda there are hundreds of hymns that describe the glory of Indra. The 12 Adityas are the special aspects of sunlight over the 12 months of the year. In hymns addressed to Adityas, the aspirant seeks blessings for making appropriate use of time throughout the year. Moon, the most important star in Vedic astrology, is addressed as Chandera; the source of *Ojas*, the elixir of life. There are many hymns that describe the glory of moonlight as it pours the nectarean *Soma* in the silence of night and nourishes the food, herbs, and healing plants on earth.

The Rigveda is full of the most melodious hymns addressed to goddess Saraswati the embodiment of divine speech, knowledge, wisdom, purity, and serenity. Such as, *"Pavaka nah Saraswati vajehir vajinivati yajman vashtudhynavasuh"* (Rig.1.3.10), meaning, "May the Divine Mother of speech, the goddess Saraswati who enriches our lives with pure knowledge, bless us with the clarity of vision and be the source of inspiration and accomplishment in all our activities organized for the welfare of mankind." Also, *"Chodayitri Sunritanam Chetanti Sumatinam"* (Rig.1.3.11), meaning, "O' Divine Mother of speech Saraswati, those who are aligned with the source (Truth) are constantly inspired and guided by you. Please help us in the performance of benevolent activities that are in peace and harmony with others." *"Maho arnah Saraswati pra chatiyati ketuna Dhiyo Vishva vi Rajati"* (Rig.1.3.12), meaning, "The Divine Mother of speech sets in motion all the faculties of mind and spirit, and enlightens the intellect of devotees who are inclined to experience inner unity and spiritual maturity."

This is only a short introduction to the gods and goddesses described in the Rigveda. As stated earlier, these *Devas* and *Devis* are the personification of Supreme *Parabrahman*. All the deities may appear to be independent; in fact they are the different facets of the pure consciousness. Omniscience of the Supreme-soul is the only truth that prevails at the heart of the entire creation. There is a hymn in the Rigveda where the divine sage explains this concept quite clearly. *"Indra Mitram Varuamagnimahuratho Divya Sa Superno Gurutman. Ekam Sad Vipra Bahudha Vadantyagnim Yama Matarishvanmahu"* (Rig.1.164.46), meaning, "The Supreme-soul is called Indra (the Lord resplendent), Mitra (the most reliable friend), Varuna (the virtuous), Agni (the divine light), Yama (the ordainer), Gurutman (the celestial singer), and Matarishvan (the life force). 'One' alone exists, the learned sages call it by various names." Another hymn, "*Aum Shano Mitra Sham Varunah Shano bhavatvaryama Shano Indro Bruhaspati Shano Vishnu Rukramah*" (Rig.1.90.9) meaning, "May the Sun god giver of life on planet be gracious to us, Varuna the most virtuous, be kind to us, Aryana the god of justice be gracious to us, Devraj Indra the giver of rain showers, be gracious to us, Bruhaspati the great spiritual teacher be gracious to us, Lord Vishnu the great pervasive intelligence be gracious to us."

Ayurveda, the science of life, is the *Upaveda* (sub-Veda) of the Rigveda. Ayurveda describes anatomy, pharmacology, physiology, medicinal herbs, astrology, and bacteriology. There is also a long description of surgical instruments and procedures applied in all types of surgeries. Ayurveda gives an elaborate description of the three *Gunas* and also the three *doshas* (*Kapha*, *Vata*, and *Pitta*) inherently present in the physical and psychological makeup of every individual. These *Doshas* are the subtle influential tendencies, present in all human beings, though in different degrees. The three *doshas* form a twisted rope of self-programmed behavior that manifests through various kinds of ailments in the human body. Ayurveda gives guidelines to the understanding of doshas that leads to good health, peace and happiness. It is the holistic approach to restore and maintain the perpetual alignment of mind body and spirit.

The medical science as practiced in ancient India mentions some important branches of general medicine such as, *vishgadvirodhicprashanm* (toxicology), *kaumar-*

bhrityakam (pediatrics), *shalyapehtkam* (surgery), *bhutvidya* (psychotherapy), *rasayanam* (rejuvenation), *vajikarnam* (virilification) and also the ailments of eyes, ears, nose, throat, and the lungs. Ayurveda is full of hymns that indicate special guidance to the doctor. The great sage asserts that a physician, besides being well-versed in the field of medicine, should also live a pure, austere, and balanced life, dedicated to the service of mankind. His attitude should be always relaxed, compassionate, and supportive. The study of medical literature, ethical behavior, responsible performance of duties, and interest in helping others are the characteristics of a competent *vaidya* (doctor).

There is a long description of *Oshadhi* (medicinal) hymns in the Rigveda such as *Asravati, Somavati, Urjayanti, Prisniparni, Pippali*, etc. Besides the use of these healing herbs, there are also hymns that illustrate the importance of pure water itself, a cure in several ailments; such as, "*Apsu antaramritam apsu bheshajam apam uta prasastye, deva bhavata vajinah*" (Rig.1.23.19) meaning, "The pure water is indeed the elixir of life; It has the power of eliminating toxicity from body. There is healing balm and medicinal herbs in water. Know their proper use and become enlightened and wise." Similarly another hymn, "*Apsu me somo abravid antar bhesheja, Agnim ca Vishvasambhavam apas ca Vishvabheshajih*" meaning, "The men of wisdom have acclaimed that water contains all the disease dispelling herbs, used for physical and emotional ailments, and also the fire, the benefactor of the universe."

There are hundreds of hymns about Ayurveda (the science of life) scattered all over the four Vedas, especially in the Atharvaveda. These hymns provide an easy guide to the use of herbal compounds and basic steps for perfect health. The divine sage has declared jubilantly that every person on earth should aspire to live a good healthy life for at least 100 years. *"Aum Tachchakshur devahitam purastach chhukram uchcharat. Pashyema sharadah shatam jivema sharadah shatam shrinuyama sharadah shatam prabravama sharadah shatam adinah syama sharadah shatam bhuyashcha sharadah shatat"* (Rig. 7.66.16) (Yajur.36.25), meaning, "O' Self-effulgent Supreme Lord, the giver of life on planet, with thy grace may I live a healthy, happy and peaceful life. May my eyes be blessed with good vision for 100 years, may I be blessed with healthy hearing and melodious speech for 100 years. May I be blessed with noble thoughts and live an independent and prosperous life dedicated to the service of mankind."

The Yajurveda

The Yajurveda gives an elaborate description of *yajnas* performed during the lifetime. The total number of mantras in the Yajurveda is 2,086. The vedic sages have explained the glory of living a prosperous life with a spirit of *yajna*.

The word *yajna* (sacrifice) indicates the mutual dependence, which exists between the created beings and the cosmic powers. It is a network of services performed selflessly by human beings, gods, and mother nature. The cosmic powers have appeared with creation in order to maintain and to sustain life on earth.

For example, the Sun fills the earth with energy and

light, the air carries vapors, and then the rainwater helps the food to grow. Food helps the sustenance of life on earth. The entire work-order in nature is closely related to the activities of human beings. As the cosmic forces are working in co-operation with each other to sustain life on earth, similarly human beings are expected to be respectful to the bounties of nature and work selflessly in co-operation with each other to support life on earth. It is the combined effort of everyone that keeps the wheel of creation in motion. It is indeed a participatory world where everything and everybody contributes in some way or the other.

The melodious hymns of the Yajurveda provide a large description of '*yajna*' meant to bring equilibrium, peace, happiness, freedom, and prosperity in society. For example, in performance of daily *Agnihotra*, the herbs, medicinal roots, and leaves mixed with clarified butter are offered in the holy fire, with chanting of special hymns in order to create harmony at the physical, psychological, and spiritual levels of awareness. While hands pour the *ghee* (clarified butter) and mixture of herbs, the chanting of hymns guide the mind into yogic unity with the source and saturates the air with positive energy. The herbs used for offerings are fumigating substances and highly beneficial for cleansing of the environment. The divine sage explains the concepts of *yajna* quite melodiously, "*Sambarhirankam havisa ghritena samadityairvasubhib sammarudhib. Samnindro visvadeve-bhiranktam divyam nebhogacchatu yat svaha*" (Yajur.2.22), meaning—"May the *Ahuti* (oblation) of *ghrita* (*ghee*) mixed with other substances rise unto the space: and after being absorbed with heavenly rays, water and air, energize the cosmic bodies and bless people on earth with enlivening showers of rain; golden rays of Sun, clean air and nourishing *Soma* for good health, wealth and prosperity."

There are many hymns in the Yajurveda where the divine sage has used the term *yajna* with its expanded meaning and contents. It is the spirit of *yajna* that leads the individual to yogic unity with the soul. *Yajna*, is not just limited to the activity of igniting fire at the sacred shrine, and giving some oblations in names of gods. The ideology of *yajna* steps beyond that, it is the alignment of the individual-soul with the totality of the universe. The great seer expounds upon the meaning and suggests that one's entire life should be lived in the spirit of *yajna*, like selfless offering to the service of the Divine. The hidden significance of *yajna* has been explained from various points of view, such as: "*Ayuryajnena kalpatam, prano yajnena kalpatam, chakshur yajnena kalpatam, shrotam yajnena kalpatam, prishtam yajnena kalpatam, yajno yajnena kalpatam,prajapateh praja abhuma svardeva aganma mritabhuma*" (Yajur.9.21), meaning—"May my entire life move in spirit of *yajna* (sacrifice) dedicated to the service of God. May my life breath be tuned to the spirit of *yajna*. May my vision be aligned to the source and observe everything with the spirit of *yajna*. May my hearing be tuned to the selfless service to humanity. May my healthy backbone always stay aligned with the Supreme-soul and ready for the silent call of Divine for service to mankind. May all our noble deeds and cherished services be performed in the spirit of holy *yajna*. O' Lord of the universe I offer myself from the totality of my being at your service and with thy grace may I experience Bliss." The sacred hymn continues, "*Vagyayajñena kalpatam, manoyajñena kalpatam, atma yajnena kalpatam, brahm yajnena kalpatam, jyotir yajnena kalpatam, svarg yejnena kalpatam*" (Yajur.18.29), meaning—"May my speech be blessed by the Divine Mother Saraswati and prosper in the spirit of *yajna*, May my mind be perennially absorbed in the ecstasy of divine love and remain dedicated to self-less service of God, May my individual-soul prosper in the spirit of *yajna*. May the all-pervasive intelligence move in the spirit of *yajna*, may everyone remain guided by the divine light into self-less service of Divine, and may the eternal happiness be secured through the spirit of *yajna*." "*Prano yajñena kalpatam, apano yajñena kalpatam, viano yajñena kalpatam, udano yajñena kalpatam, samano yajñena kalpatam*" (Yajur.22.33), meaning—"May my life-breath, as it moves in and out of the body be totally tuned to the source and also to self-less service of humanity. May the downward breath, diffusive breath, upward breath from the bottom of spine and digestive breath in stomach, move incoherence with the spirit of *yajna*."

In these hymns the great Rishi gives many examples, saying that some people offer material goods in *yajna* while others offer their egocentric individual-self as an offering to the Supreme Lord. Some people offer their sense of hearing and other senses in the austerity of self-control; others offer the objects of senses into the fire of self-discipline. Some others offer the actions of senses and the activity of *prana*, into the yogic fire of self-control lit by the flame of wisdom. The aspirant offers every little function of his *prana* into the contemplation of God. The activity of breathing is *Prana*, the downward movement of breath and out of body is *Apana*. The contraction and expansion of breath in the heart is called *Vyana*; the movement of breath in assimilation of food in the stomach is called *Samana*. When the life force is pulled upward from the base of the spine, it is called *Udana*. In the yogic meditation when the life breath is offered into the life breath—*pranayama*, the rhythm of *prana* becomes harmonized. It stabilizes the activities of the mind and the individual goes in unity with the soul and completes the *yajna* of life. He is blessed with the rich experience of his own immortality.

There is also another famous mantra in which the great seer speaks about liberation from the fear of death and the joy of living in eternity. *"Aum Tryambakam yajamahe sugandhim pustivardhanam urvarukmiva bandhanat mrityormuksiya ma'mritat"* (Yajur.3.60)—meaning, "May our awakened intuition guide us in living a life selflessly dedicated to the service of Supreme Divinity; which eventually liberates everyone from the anxiety of death making us eligible to experience immortality."

The great *Mahamrityunjaya* mantra is addressed to the indwelling Supreme Lord for a long healthy, wholesome life and liberation from the fear of death. The constant devoted repetition of this mantra connects the individual to the source of life and he is blessed with the experiential knowledge of his own immortality; which brings liberation from the fear of death and also the rich experience of being ageless, timeless, and immortal.

The *Upaveda* (sub-Veda) of the Yajurveda is Dhanurveda, which gives an elaborate description of military science, a treatise written on administration, weapons, arms, and ammunitions. There are hymns that illustrate the concept of *Rashtra* (kingdom) and also the head of the kingdom as *Indra, Rajan* (King), or *Samrat* (Emperor). The king has been regarded as the embodiment of God, because he takes care of people in all respects. He protects, fosters, and also guides his subject into righteousness. The king is expected to lead an austere, religious, spiritual, and disciplined life, without being attached to the royal pleasures. It is very important for the king to live a simple and virtuous life dedicated to the service of mankind. If the king upholds *Dharma* and lives by the gospel of selfless service, people are automatically inspired to follow the lead. The characteristics of an honorable king are to exhibit valor, heroism, steadfastness, skill, promptitude, generosity, compassion, and Lordliness.

The great sage gives an inspiring description of a prosperous, integrated community in these hymns, "*Aum a Brahman brahmano brahmavarchasi jayatam. A rashtre rajanyah shura ishavyoativyadhi maharatho jayata dogdhri dhenurvodhandvaanasuh saptih purandhir yosha jaishnu ratheshtha sabheyo yuvasya yaja-manasya viro jayatam nikame nikame nah parjanyo varshatu phalavatyo na oshadhayah   pachyantam   yoga-kshemo   nah   kalpatam"* (Yajur.22.22), meaning—"O' Supreme Lord, may our *Rashtra* (kingdom) be blessed with learned scholars of highest caliber, brave warriors and great statesmen imbued with high moral values and dedicated to the service of country; heroic skilled archers with piercing shafts, cows giving abundant milk, stout oxen and swift horses, virtuous women of great accomplishments, ever victorious valorous men and civilized youths always marching forward with renewed enthusiasm. May our fields be blessed with timely rain showers, and trees bearing fruits in season and may each one of us has the insight and ability for proper acquisition and preservation of riches."

In reference to the military science in the Yajurveda, the great Vedic scholar Indra Dev Khosla writes, "There is an elaborate description of army divided into various categories, land force, air force, and all the soldiers equipped with many kinds of weapons and skilled in the strategy of warfare. There is a hymn that explains this concept clearly: *"Namah Senabhyah Senanibhyasca Vo namo rathibhyo, arthebhyashca Vo namo. Namah Kshatribhya, Sangrihitribhyashca Vo namo namo mahadbhya, arbhakebhyasca Vo Namah"* (Yajur.16.26), meaning, "Our Salutation to the great warriors, to respectable commanders, the warriors fighting from chariots and the drivers of the chariots. Salutation to all those who fight the enemy either on land or in the air." In relation to the defense of a country the Vedic sage says, *"Shashtrene rakshite Rashtre shastrachinta pravartate"* meaning, "When the country is well protected through arms, only then, there can be peace, prosperity, and all kinds of development." There are so many hymns about the defense planning and at the same time seeking peaceful negotiations with others. The head of the state is expected to have an attitude of tolerance, respect, and hospitality towards all varieties and diversities in different communities and countries.

There is a beautiful prayer in the Yajurveda for universal peace and harmony. *"Aum dyauh shantirantariksam shantih prithivi shantirapah shantirosadhayah shantih vanaspatayah shantirvisve devah shantirbrahma shantih sarvam. Shanti. Shantireva shantih sa ma shantiredhi. Aum shanti, shanti, shanti"* (Yajur.36.17), meaning—"O' all pervading Lord; may there be peace in all the three regions of the universe. May the water reservoirs be peaceful, may the medicinal plants be peaceful. May the forests be peaceful, may all the bounties of nature be peaceful. May the cosmic powers be peaceful. May our knowledge become a source of peace to us and others. May everybody be blessed with peace and harmony. May there be peace and peace only."

The Samaveda

The Samaveda has been upheld to be the most honorable text on the philosophy of devotional music. It refers to ecstatic melodies, music, art, drama, and the science of sound. The *Upaveda* (sub-Veda) of the Samaveda is Gandharvaveda. In the Samaveda there are 1875 mantras imbued with sweet melodies of devotional love for God and the beauties of nature. The word 'Sama' has been derived from 'Sama-shantvene' meaning, "That renders inner peace and tranquility." The hymns of this Veda are an expression of the exhilarating spiritual experience of the divine sage.

The glory of the celestial chants of the Samaveda has been explained in the *Brahmanas* and in other spiritual literature of the Vedic religion. The Shatapatha describes, *"Sarvesa va esha vedanam raso yatsam"* meaning, "Samaveda is the quintessence of all the Vedas." The Gopatha describes *"Samaveda eva yasha"* meaning, "Samaveda is glorious, splendid and illustrious." The hymns of the Samaveda are used in devotional music and also for proper knowledge of *Swara* (sound). In the very first hymn the divine sage says, *"Agna a yahi vitaye grinano havyadataye ni hota satsi barhisi"* (Sama 1.1), meaning, "O' Adorable Lord we seek your guidance, please come and bless the dedicated devotees with inner enlightenment and true knowledge. Take your seat at the inner-most shrine of our hearts and eliminate the darkness that pervades around us."

In the Samaveda there is a long description of primordial sound meditation and the enjoyment of mystical divine nectar *Soma*, which drips from *Binduvisarga* (source of the elixir) and creates the feeling of blissful intoxication. The taste of this blissful elixir cannot be described in words and also cannot be compared with any other taste in the world. It supersedes all other tastes of the material world. It renders peace and contentment. The nectar originates in the *Sahasrara*, cascades through *Binduvisarga*, and drips from *Lalana chakra* at the point located in the upper palate, right in the back of throat along the route of *Sushumna*. In this reference Swami Satya Prakash Saraswati says, "In the Samaveda the Supreme reality is invoked with highest reverence and affection by the devotee, utterly sincere in his invocations, and the result is the gradual outflow of a devotional elixir, highly exhilarating, pleasing and enlightening. The Supreme reality is the source of this elixir *Soma* and the infinitesimal self is the recipient. The fluid of ecstasy, at the start, tickles in drops and in last stages, it flows in streams and channels." He further says, "The superb flowing *Soma*—a fluid of conceptual experience, a personification of what is known as *Satya* (Truth), *Jyoti* (Light), and immortality." *Soma*, the divine nectar, is a supreme purifier because it is fulfillment in itself and also a means for increased spiritual progress at the same time. In description of *Soma* (the elixir of life), the divine sage says, "*Imamindra sutam piba Jyesthamamartye madam sukrasya tvabhysksarandhara ritasya sadane*" (Sama.344,949), meaning, "Enjoy this immortalizing elixir, flowing from the source in spiritual exhilaration. Experience the inner light, truth, purity, and meditative unity with resplendent Supreme-self." There is another mantra that also indicates the experience of spiritual exhilaration, "*Anas te gantu matsaro vrisha mado varenyah sahavam indra sanasih pratanasad amartyah,*" meaning—"O' Lord may our offering in spiritual ecstasy be acceptable to you; for it gives inner peace, good health, wealth, and prosperity. It is enjoyable and very precious to us. It eliminates the negative tendencies and is immortal."

There are many hymns in the Samaveda where the individual-soul seeks blessings for living perpetually in a state of everlasting spiritual ecstasy. The divine sage upholds the path of '*Upasana*' (sincere devotion) to be the noblest and most rewarding in life. The mantras are imbued with deep philosophical messages and composed in phenomenal musical notes. The liturgy is very sophisticated and exhilarating. The great sage sings the blessings of nature with grace and style.*"Pri prasishyadet kavih sindhorurmavadhi sritah: karum Bibhrat Puruspraham"* (Sama.486), meaning—"Let us tune to the exhilarating music of the divine poet. He plays upon the golden harp in the brisk morning air, giving a wake-up call, its rhythm and melody goes across the horizon into the endless canopy of sky, the ocean waves dance with the echo from heaven, the earth is filled with whispers of blessings, and life is renewed everywhere."

The mother earth, the ocean, the sky, and cosmic bodies all are held together by the eternal symphony vibrating across the universe. There is another hymn in which the great Rishi draws our attention towards the ever renewing sweet melodies played with the change of seasons throughout the year, *"Vasant ennue rantaya grisham ennue rantaya varshannue sharado, hemanta, shishirennue rantaya,"* (Sama.616) meaning, "Enjoy the celestial fragrance in spring, silently overflowing across the green meadows and flowering groves. The summer with its own beauty of sighs and murmurs, calls upon the blessed showers from heaven with thunder and dazzling flashes, to nurture the life on earth. The serene whisper of leaves in autumn, and cool breeze in winter with new hopes and promises, all are the expressions of divine magnificence in space and time." The hymns of the Samaveda express the subtle joy of living a life that is in perfect harmony with the rhythm of the universe, where the unconscious relationship with the Supreme-soul becomes more conscious, real, and alive. The conceptual reality becomes experiential and subjective.

The Atharvaveda

The Atharvaveda is a unique scripture, which comprises the total of 5,977 mantras. The *Upaveda* (sub-Veda) of the Atharvaveda is Arthaveda; which describes various branches of education, i.e. the metallurgical, mechanical and technical engineering, aircrafts, finances, economics, telegraph, sociology, and statistics. A part of the Atharvaveda deals with diversified sciences such as healing herbs and treatments for various types of ailments, physics, chemistry, pharmacology, psychology, arithmetic, astronomy, and astrology. The hymns of this Veda encompass almost every aspect of human life such as matrimony and friendship, prayers for progeny, happy married life, solidarity of family, cattle rearing, and the spiritual bond that exists between human beings and Mother Earth. There are many hymns, addressed to Mother Earth in which the divine sage calls upon the celestial energy that aids the earth's evolution and helps balance the impact of human life. The famous *Prithvi Sukta* of the Atharvaveda, which is redolent with unique melodious hymns, have been chanted with deep respect and reverence by the learned priests over generations and still catches our attention with renewed resonance. The divine poet says, "O' Earth let thy hills, snowy mountains, and valuable forest be pleasant, enjoyable and useful. Upon the brown and black multi-colored earth, which is guarded by Indra, may I stand unharassed, unhurt and unwounded." "I call upon thee O' Mother Earth who has nurtured us since the beginning of creation. Thou are bounteous, beautiful, pure, and patient, maintained by the ordinance of *yajna*. May thou help us to have quick growth and enjoy our share of food" (Atharva.12.1.11-13).

In reference to the science of life, the ancient seers have given us the gift of the Atharvaveda, the monumental treatise on the theory and practice of traditional medicine in ancient India. There is a long description of ailments and the recommended remedies for each one of them. The great sage mentions about different types of fevers and their distinct symptoms and cures from hymns 1.22.1 to 1.22.4 and from 5.22.1 to 5.22.14, such as, *"Tritiyakam vitritiyam sadandimut shardam, takmanam shitam, ruran graishman nashaya varshikam"* (Atharva.5.22.13) meaning, "Fever that comes every third day—intermittent fever or comes every fourth day or which comes daily. Then there are seasonal fevers, fever that comes in autumn, fever in summer due to excessive heat, or in rainy season accompanied by extreme shivering, fever due to dryness in winter and also fever due to chest congestion, accompanied by severe bronchitis and pneumonia." It also explains about the body types of people who suffer from different kinds of fever, and the prescribed remedies for each one of them. There are special herbs described in 5.22.2 to 5.22.4, that help to improve the immunity and also resistance to fever. The Atharvaveda mentions about piles and its treatment in the hymn 11.25.3, for sciatica in 2.9.1, for skin diseases in 6.17.1, for tuberculosis in 7.76.5, and for hair diseases from 6.136.1 to 6.136.3. There is a long description on bacteriology that gives names of germs such as *Keshi, Sunama, Chaturaksha,* and so on. The divine sage also writes about surgery and the herb *Viryavati* in 6.139.5 that joins the incision and promotes healing.

There are hymns in the Atharvaveda 11.4.16 that give the general classification of healing pursued in Vedic times. For example, healing with special mantras, with natural remedies direct from herbs and nectarean *Soma*, with yoga and meditation, and also with the specific compounds prepared by the learned physicians. Besides the medicinal herbs there are also references of water therapy in the Atharvaveda. In the hymn 1.5.2 the great Rishi says, "*Shivtam rasa*" – meaning, "Water is the enjoyable sacred drink" and "*Apsu Vishvani Bheshjani*", "Water is very beneficial, it contains all sorts of remedial properties." The hymns 1.4.3 and 1.6.4 illustrate different kinds of sources of water and how each one contains specific properties and how it relates to good health and healing in body. The divine sages declare, "Water with all its nutritious values and healing powers to be the sovereign remedy for mankind."

There is a description of Sun healing in the Atharvaveda. The great seer indicates clearly in the hymns 2.32.1 that, "Sunlight kills all worms," and also in hymn 9.8.22 that, "Sunlight eliminates toxicity from body and cures limb-pains." The chemistry of metals and gem therapy has also been discussed in detail. There are many hymns in reference to gold, silver, copper, and iron being used in medicines and also as general tonic.

In reference to Astronomy and Astrology in the Atharvaveda the divine sage gives the fundamentals of science that deal with heavenly bodies and the relationship that exists between the human mind, body, and the stars and planets. Each heavenly body radiates a specific type of celestial energy, which is closely connected with the physical as well as the psychological makeup of human beings and definitely forms a significant part of Vedic astrology. In the Atharvaveda the hymn 8.9.6 gives a description of the 'winter solstice', when the northern course of the Sun starts and the duration of the daylight is lengthened for six months; and also the 'summer solstice', when the southern course of the Sun starts and the daylight is shortened over the period of six months. The divine sage also mentions about the 12 birth signs of astrology in the hymn 10.8.4. Each birth sign is called a '*Rashi*' and occupies 30° of a 360° circle moving from birth sign Aries to Pisces. Among these 12 birth signs are equally placed the 27 constellations into fractions of 13° and 20 minutes. These constellations are called *Nakshatras* in Sanskrit, and each one of them is possessed with a specific type of energy. Some of these hold divine energy and others demonic. The names are *Ashvini, Bharani, Kritika, Rohini, Mrigshirash, Ardra, Punarvasu, Pushya, Ashlesha, Magha, Purvaphalguni, Uttaraphalguni, Hasta, Chitra, Swati, Vishakha, Anuradha, Jyeshtha, Mool, Purvashadha, Uttarashadha, Shravan, Dhanishtha, Shattara, Purvabhadrapada, Uttarabhadrapada,* and *Revati.* The position of the presiding *Nakshatra* (constellation) at the time of birth plays a significant role in the natal chart, and usually parents name their baby by the specific alphabets connected with the energy of that constellation. In general, the important projects of life are also commenced under the influence of an auspicious *Nakshatra* for success and peaceful completion.

The astrological significance of these constellations is determined in relation to the movements of the Moon. Since the Moon is the most important star in Vedic astrology; the birth sign and constellation in effect at any specific time are the ones that the Moon has conjoined. Sun signs are important to some extent but the natal chart is always prepared with the position of the Moon in relation to the ruling constellation at the time of birth. The divine sage has given a detailed explanation of these *Nakshatras* (constellations) in hymns 19.7.2 to 19.7.5 and also from 19.8.1 and 19.18.2. In reference to the six seasons and 12 months of the year, those have been named on the basis of presiding *Nakshatra*, there is also a description of *Adhikamasa* (13th month) which occurs every third year (Atharva.13.3.8).

The hymns on the development of Arithmetic, Geometry, and Algebra are scattered all over the Atharvaveda and also in the Rigveda and the Yajurveda. There are hymns where the divine sage mentions about '*Yog*' (addition), '*Viyog*' (subtraction), '*Gunan*' (multiplication), '*Bhag*' (division), '*Varg*' (square), '*Vargamool*' (squareroot), '*Dhanmool*' (cube root). The consecutivity of numbers goes to 100 and then up to millions, billions, and trillions. The Vedic numerical system as described in the Vedas presents a simple but a powerful system of writing and memorizing. The hymns like "*ekacsh me, dashsh me,*" from (Atharva.5.15.1-11) and from

(Yajur.18.24.25) explain a unique style of memorizing. There are hymns in which the simplifying, multiplying, and adding of fractions have been illustrated in a very interesting method. It is singing and playing with numbers in poetry. It is really difficult to comprehend the heightened abilities of those great seers who wrote these mathematical treatises for mankind.

This short introduction to the four Vedas is summarized with the blessings of the great Gayatri mantra, which is written in the first three Vedas: Rig, Yajur, and Sama. In the Vedas, Gayatri has been given the name '*Vedmata*' meaning, "the mother of knowledge and wisdom." The glory of Gayatri has been described throughout the Vedic literature. It is believed that the essence of all the Vedic mantras is combined into the 24 syllables of Gayatri. There is a famous aphorism, "*Gayante Trayanti iti sa Gayatri*" meaning, "The mantra that liberates the individual-soul from the false self-imposed conditions is indeed Gayatri."The ancient sages have declared that anybody who worships the rising Sun with the recitation of Gayatri receives special blessings for good health, wealth and prosperity in life. The worshippers of the Sun usually live a very long healthy life.

There are thousands of translations of Gayatri mantra, by great Vedic scholars and learned sages. The great Rishi who compiled Devi Bhagavatam describes the glory of Gayatri in these words: "*Sarva ved sar bhuta Gayatriastu Samarchana, Brahmadyopi sandyayam tha dhyayanthi japanti cha,*" meaning, "The worship with Gayatri mantra constitutes the entire essence of all the Vedas. Even Brahma himself meditates on Gayatri." Swami Dayanand Saraswati, a great commentator on the Vedas, has given the meaning of Gayatri in these words: "O' Divine power, you are the creator and sustainer of the universe, May we meditate on thy glorious splendor, and offer all our activities to your humble service. Bless us with spiritual and intellectual strength. Please illuminate our mind with thy grace and inspire our spiritual perception. May thy kindness direct our thoughts towards the righteous path."

The great Gayatri mantra is easy to recite, it can be used in prayers by everybody in the world. It is a compact prayer, and in most cases does prepare the individual for all kinds of advanced spiritual progress in life. According to ancient Vedic tradition, Gayatri mantra should be taught as the first lesson to each child of the family. It should be introduced as the first prayer to the youngster. The importance of learning Gayatri mantra has been highly emphasized at the time of *Upanayana Samskara* (the sacred thread ceremony).

The great Gayatri mantra, *"Aum bhurbhuvah svah, tatsaviturvarenyam bhargo devasya dheemahi, dhiyo yo nah prachodayat,"* (Rig. 3.62.10) (Yajur.36.3) meaning:

Aum — The Holy syllable that represents God

Bhur—Physical-self

Bhuvah—Psychological-self

Svah—Spiritual-Self

Tat—That

Savitur—The Creator of the Universe

Varenyam—The Supreme being to worship

Bhargo—The embodiment of light

Devasya—The bestower of Bliss

Dheemahi—May we meditate on Thee

Dhiyoyo nah—Who purifies our intellect

Prachodayat—May guide us in the right direction

The recitation of the three words, "*Bhur, Bhuvah, and Svah*", connects the individual to the three levels of consciousness, i.e. physical, psychological, and spiritual. *Bhur* symbolizes the physical body composed of five elements: fire, air, ether, earth and water. The word *Bhuvah* signifies the thought process as a controller of the astral body or inner nature. *Svah* refers to the indwelling light of the soul. Gayatri *Japam* brings harmony at all three levels of consciousness. It keeps electrifying thoughts with spiritual power. It purifies thoughts, speech, and action. In the Gayatri mantra the aspirant calls upon the Divine mother, Savitur—for inner enlightenment, clarity of vision, purity of mind and intellect, precision of thoughts, inner integrity, and right guidance in the activities of daily life.

"In the whole world there is no study so beneficial and so elevating as that of the Upanishads. It has been the solace of my life, it will be the solace of my death."

-Arthur Schopenhauer

"On the tree of wisdom there is no fairer flower than the Upanishads, and no finer fruit than the *Vedanta* philosophy."

-Paul Deussen

"The Upanishads have shown an unparalleled variety of appeal during the long centuries and have been admired by different people, for different reasons, at different periods."

-Dr. S. Radhakrishnan

"Upanishads are the source of the *Vedanta* philosophy, a system in which human speculation seems to me to have reached its very acme."

-Prof. F. Max Muller

2

The Upanishads

The perennial philosophy of the Upanishads has been a unique source of spiritual guidance and enlightenment to mankind for centuries. These great spiritual treatises imbued with various branches of knowledge and rich mystical experiences of the learned sages are also known as *Vedanta*. As stated earlier, the hymns of Vedas have been categorized into three sections: the first part, which is called *Samhitas*, that constitutes the mantra portion; the second is *Brahmanas* that describes the rites and rituals; and the third is *Aranyakas*, which illustrates the mysteries of the soul. The Upanishads, which are the most interesting part of *Aranyakas*, is the concluding portion of the Vedas. The words *"Vedasya antah"* literally means, "The Vedic knowledge culminating in the joy of rich personal experience."

The *Samhitas* and *Brahmanas* which represent the 'Karma-Khanda' (the performance of rituals), purifies and prepares the individual step by step for the study of deep philosophies which constitute the *"Gyana-Khanda"* (knowledge of the Self) of the Holy Upanishads. The entire purpose of performing Vedic rituals is self-purification. Reciting of hymns in daily prayers, *yajna* and other austerities connect the day-to-day life of the individual with the presence of the Supreme-soul and create awareness at the physical as well as at the psychological levels of consciousness. Performance of rituals is a meaningful approach that provides insight into the understanding of our body, mind, the codes of moral ethics, and social obligations that serve as a prerequisite for inner enlightenment and direct perception of Truth. The hymns of Vedas unfold the knowledge of the soul along with the knowledge of the manifested divinity. It is the intimacy with the indwelling-soul, which marks the fundamental basis for the acquaintance with everything that exists within and without. When a true aspirant moves from *Samhitas* to *Brahmanas* and later into the hymns of *Aranyaka*, he comes to the realization that mere performance of rituals is not enough for the first hand experience of inner divinity and he is spontaneously led into the study of the soul.

The Upanishads are the repository of divine knowledge, which has been imparted to the inquisitive disciples in the form of questions and answers. The word "Upanishad" literally means, "To sit nearby devotedly." The entire teaching of the Upanishads is set between the teacher and the disciple. These great men of wisdom, the ancient seers while living at the *Gurukul* (school) located in far-off forests, revealed the deepest mysteries of the soul to their students, who approached them with guileless hearts, humility, and serious inquiry. These divine sages of unique caliber and personal yogic experience were also invited by kings in royal assemblies and spiritual retreats where they discussed and shared the most sacred truths of life with their inspired pupils.

There was a perfect freedom of thoughts and expressions. The variety of interpretations in Upanishads indicates clearly, the free spontaneity in thoughts and acceptance. The Vedic seers emphasized that each individual must seek his personal confirmation from his own inherent resources. The aspirant should be guided properly, not forced into co-operation; he should be entreated and persuaded but not compelled. It is really interesting to notice how the same subject has been discussed in each Upanishad with renewed enthusiasm and increased logical clarity. The Holy Upanishads are not the philosophical explanations of a single Rishi or a prophet, these are the teachings compiled from many discourses and dialogues between the divine seers and their students. The ancient seers not only shared the metaphysical speculations, but also the sacred wisdom combined with their own experiential knowledge of the soul. Although the names of the renowned sages like Yajnavalkya, Aruni, Pippalada, Sandilya, Svetaketu, and Balaki are mentioned during the dialogues, but like all the early Vedic literature, the names of the authors of Upanishads are not mentioned anywhere.

The teachings of Upanishads are indeed a compendium of timeless wisdom, which presents a complete vision of both the theoretical knowledge of the Supreme-soul—*Brahmavidya* and also the techniques to experience the transcendental Reality, which is the substratum of the universe. The philosophical concepts contained in the Upanishads are universal and addressed to the entire mankind. Each chapter is replete with inspiring anecdotes and the subjective experiences of the inspired seers, which makes the study of esoteric subjects quite fascinating and enjoyable at every step. These revered treatises that represent the *Vedanta* in its original form, have been held in deep reverence over generations. In the words of Dr. S. Radhakrishnan "The Upanishads are respected not because they are a part of *Shruti* or revealed literature and so hold a reserved position, but because they have inspired generations of Indians with vision and strength, by their inexhaustible significance and spiritual power. Indian thought has constantly turned to these scriptures for fresh illumination and spiritual recovery or recommencement, and not in vain. The fire still burns bright on their altars. Their light is for the seeing eye and their message is for the seekers after Truth." He further says, "The Upanishads have shown an unparalleled variety of appeal during the long centuries and have been admired by different people, for different reasons, at different periods. They are said to provide us with a complete chart of the unseen Reality, to give us the most immediate, intimate and convincing light on the secret of human existence."

The Upanishads, the ancient writings, have been acknowledged to be the source of profound philosophies by great scholars all around the world. There are so many well-known commentaries by revered, learned Indians as well as western erudite scholars. The work of Adi Shankaracharya, the divine saint who introduced the Upanishads as *Vedanta* philosophy, created a powerful impact on the literary world. The traditional commentaries on the principal Upanishads by Adi Shankaracharya are indeed the most valuable contribution and have always served as the most intelligible guide for many commentators. The other revered translators and commentators of the past have been Raja Rammohan Roy (1816-19), S.Sitaram Shastri and Ganganath Jha (1898-1901), S.C.Vasu (1902), Rajender Lal Mitra, and the well known works of Swami Prabhavananda and Swami Nikhilananda. The Upanishads have been also translated into Persian by Prince Mohammed Dara Shikoh (1656-57) and then into Latin by Anguetil Duperron (1801-1802). Among the western scholars who were fascinated by the study of Upanishads and also translated with brief commentaries are Prof. F. Max Muller (1879-84), Paul Deussen (1897 and 1906), G.R.S. Mead (1896), E.B. Cowell (1861), Sir William Jones (1799), W.D. Whitney (1890), Gough (1882), A.B. Keith (1925), R.D. Ranade (1926), R.E. Hume (1931), and many others. All of the translations and commentaries by Indian as well as by western scholars are worthy of genuine respect and appreciation.

Schopenhauer, an outstanding thinker and philosopher, who was deeply impressed by the study of the Upanishads says, "In the whole world there is no study so beneficial and so elevating as that of the Upanishads. It has been the solace of my life, it will be the solace of my death. Upanishads are a product of the highest wisdom—It is destined sooner or later to become the faith of the people." He always emphasized that his own philosophy was powerfully impregnated by the fundamentals of the doctrines of the Upanishads.

Paul Deussen, a renowned German philologist, says, "The Upanishads are the deep still mountain tarn fed from the pure waters of the everlasting snows, lit by clear sunshine, or by night mirroring the high serenity of the Stars on the tree of Indian wisdom, there is no fairer flower than the Upanishads, no finer fruit than the *Vedanta* philosophy." He further says, "The philosophical conceptions unequalled in India or perhaps anywhere else in the world, are to tackle every fundamental problem of philosophy." The Upanishads are indeed the scriptures of true knowledge, in which are enshrined the unique revelatory *Mahavakyas*—the great key spiritual statements, such as, *"Aham brahmasmi"*—I am *Brahman*—I am the totality. *"Tat tvam asi"*—Thou art That, *Brahman.*"Ayam Atma Brahma"*—This *Atman* (Self) is *Brahman. "Prajnanam Brahma"*—*Brahman* is pure-consciousness (Bliss). These unique spiritual statements declare the Truth not as an abstract intellectual speculation but the Truth as experienced in spontaneous self-discovery. These *Mahavakyas* express the wonder and beauty of the exalted experience of yogic unity with the Supreme-soul in transcendence—the state of infinite Bliss. These key sentences assert the inherent divinity of every individual-soul and also the concept of God. In the words of Sri Aurobindo, "The Upanishads abound with passages which are at once poetry and spiritual philosophy of an absolute clarity and beauty, but no translation empty of the suggestions and the grave and subtle and luminous sense echoes of the original words and rhythms can give any idea of their power and perfection." He further says, "There is in some of the prose

Upanishads another element of vivid narrative and tradition which restores for us though only in brief glimpses the picture of that extraordinary stir and movement of spiritual enquiry and passion for the highest knowledge which made the Upanishads possible. The scenes of the old world live before us in a few pages, the sages sitting in their groves ready to test and teach the comer, princes and learned Brahmins and great landed nobles going about in search of knowledge."

The Upanishads are the teachings of those great seers who perennially lived in the awareness of the Supreme-soul and experienced spiritual intimacy from moment to moment—*Sakshatkrit Dharmana* as described in our ancient scriptures. The unique dialogues in the Upanishads are the purest expression of true knowledge. According to Rabindranath Tagore, "The symbolical expressions of the Upanishads are like an eternal source of light which still illumines and vitalizes the religious mind of India. They are the revelation of infinite Reality—*Ananda-rupam Amritam*, in deathless form of joy."

The Upanishads contain a variety of inspiring passages directly spoken by the Vedic sages to their earnest students who approached them with genuine thirst for knowledge. The dynamic style of Upanishadic teaching indicates step by step guidance with active involvement of the students in understanding the systematized statements into the mysteries of the universe and the Supreme-soul. Prof. F. Max Muller, the most well known scholar and educator of Germany who edited the voluminous series *the Sacred Books of the East* and also translated some of the principal Upanishads says, "Upanishads are the source of the *Vedanta* philosophy, a system in which human speculation seems to me to have reached its very acme." His translations, accompanied by detailed explanations, are respectfully used by students seeking information on the religions of the world. Upanishads are the interesting dialogues where the mysteries of the Supreme *Parabrahman* (Pure consciousness) have been discussed with broader goals that eventually lead the aspirant to inner fulfillment and enlightenment. Vedic literature mentions around 108 Upanishads, but Adi Shankaracharya has written commentaries on 11, which are considered to be the principal Upanishads. These 11 are Isha, Kena, Katha, Prashna, Mundaka, Mandukya, Taittiriya, Aitareya, Chandogya, Brihidaranyaka, and Shvetashvatara.

Isha Upanishad

The Isha or Ishavasya Upanishad, which is a part of the Yajurveda, opens with the declaration that omniscience of the Supreme Lord is the only truth, which lies at the heart of the entire creation. The Supreme power exists, diffusing its abundance in everything, which is within the boundaries of perception and beyond that. The cosmic-soul is the omnipotent substratum from where the plurality of the world is projected. The Lord of the universe individualizes itself as individual manifestation wherever the mediums are made available. In the words of Swami Chidbavananda, "Lord is expressing Himself; whatever catches our imagination, draws our attention, sends us into raptures and infuses bliss into us, that is none, but the glory of the Lord." It is really amazing how the Supreme Lord Himself becomes everything, which is manifested.

The Absolute *Brahman* pervades the entire creation. God is the source of everything, the animate and inanimate. It is *Shakti* (the divine potency)—which is expressing itself everywhere. *"Ishavasyam idam Sarvam yatkin cha jag-atyam jagat, Tena tyaktena bhunjitha ma gridhah Kasyas viddhanam,"* (Isha.1.1) meaning, "The entire universe is permeated by the Supreme Lord, God is the source of all the sentient and insentient and everything belongs to the Almighty. Enjoy things of this world while abandoning attachment to them and try not to be greedy and possessive. Do not covet the wealth of others." In this first hymn of the Isha Upanishad the divine sage glorifies the omniscience of the Supreme Lord and shares the profound message of enjoying everything in the world with an attitude of detachment. The great Rishi enlightens us about the individual responsibility of every person, and the importance of living in peace and harmony with others in society and nature. Everything in the world is meant to be shared with others; one should never covet the wealth of other people. The individual should enjoy the comforts of life, as a blessing from God with the spirit of sharing and renunciation. The words *"Tena tyaktena bhunjithah"* have been beautifully explained by Dr. S. Radhakrishnan: "Enjoy all things by renouncing the idea of a personal proprietary relationship to them. When the individual is subject to ignorance, he is not conscious of the unity and identity behind the multiplicity and so cannot enter into harmony and oneness with the universe and thus fails to enjoy the world, when however he realizes his true existence which is centered in the Divine, he becomes free from selfish desires and enjoys the world, being in a state of non-attachment." In this mantra the wise sage suggests sincerely that everybody must realize the call of mutual give and take, which has been passed on to the entire creation since antiquity. The spirit of relinquishment creates equilibrium, peace, happiness, freedom, and prosperity in society. It promotes the attitude of service and sacrifice.

In the next mantra, which is a continuation of the same message, the learned Rishi explains the secret of detachment in life and how an individual can actually experience freedom from the bondage of karma and aspire to live a blessed life for 100 years. The great Rishi says, "*Kurnnaveh karmanijijivishechchtam samah evam tvayi nanyathetosti na karm lipyate nare* (Isha.1.2)—meaning, "In this world, while performing the assigned work (karma) selflessly, one should desire to live the full span of 100 years. This is how a man can stay liberated from the bondage of karma."

In the first hymn of this Upanishad the divine seer enlightens us about the omniscience of the Supreme Lord and in these hymns, he declares the rewards of accepting the presence of the Divine in everything and learning to live in the awareness of the indwelling-soul. It is the acceptance of the presence of Supreme Lord in our day-to-day activities which initiates the individual to develop an intimate relationship with God and then he naturally offers all the work as a service to the Divine. Living a life in transcendental consciousness rewards the individual with sanctity and austerity and also an attitude of detached service. It is the understanding of the truth that every activity proceeds from the indwelling light, and every bit of work is performed by the indwelling-self; such actions become selfless and benefit the individual as well as the society in which he lives. The person lives his life in an alignment with God and performs all the work in complete co-partnership with God. The perpetual alignment with the soul liberates the individual from egoistic individuality, jealousy, greed, sense of possession, and the desire for the fruits and rewards of his actions. The enlightened attitude keeps him detached and free, even though he is constantly engaged in actions. As the consciousness of the presence of Divine blossoms, the entire life style becomes calm peaceful and blessed. The inner unity, peace, and security help the individual to rise above the futility of worldly fame and also the desire of accumulation and recognition. The great sage asserts that while accepting the omniscience of the Supreme Lord, a person should live a life which is completely attuned to the consciousness of the Self and dedicated to the selfless service of the Divine for a full life-span of 100 years here, and freedom hereafter.

In the third hymn the wise sage mentions that the deluded people who are not consciously aligned with the indwelling-soul and are not receptive to the voice of the

Supreme-Self involve themselves in harmful dealings and create problems for others. They are always motivated by selfish desires and act with totally impure resolves. These deluded arrogant people are hurled into the wombs of demons only. They are born again and again to the lower grades of life, which corresponds to their conditioned aptitude. The human birth, instead of being an opportunity for spiritual growth and liberation, proves to be a total waste for them and that constitutes the most tragic fall and failure of human life.

The next few hymns describe the immanence, as well as the transcendental remoteness, of the Supreme-soul. The presence of the indwelling-soul can be experienced by everyone through the functions of the sensory organs and it still transcends everything. The person who has trained himself to live his life in the consciousness of the indweller, for him God surely resides in the temple of the heart, while for others, He is far away. Contemplation at the shrine of heart creates spiritual intimacy with the soul, which is the key that opens the doorway to an intimate relationship with others. The individual beholds the self abiding in all beings and all beings in the Self. He sees equality everywhere. To enter into cosmic unity is the culmination of all yogic austerities. The moment a person recollects his Divine inheritance, he is bound to act from the depth of his spiritual nature, which is pure, clean, and unconditional. Divine nature holds no duality, a God-realized person beholds nothing else but a reflection of the Supreme-Self alone, in everybody and everything. *"Ishavasyam idam Sarvam*—The entire universe is pervaded by God alone."

Kena Upanishad

The Kena Upanishad comprises a part of *Talavakara Brahmana* of Samaveda. The teaching of this Upanishad has four sections, the first two are in verse and the remaining two in prose. The metrical portion explains the magnificence of the Supreme *Parabrahman* and the prose part dwells upon the glories of Supreme-soul as *Ishwara*. The Kena Upanishad opens with a question from a disciple who approached the teacher with deep humility and asked, "Holy Sir, at whose command does the mind pursue the desired objects, and the vital force move? Who makes the tongue speak? Who is the effulgent being that directs the movements of eyes and activities of sound in the ears?" The divine sage begins his answer in the second hymn (1.2) saying, "The Supreme spirit is the ear of the ear, the mind of the mind, speech of the speech, breath of the breath and also the eye of the eye. Having known the essentiality of that luminous-self, the man of wisdom discards the masks of false identifications and becomes immortal upon his departure from this world." He further explains, "That the absolute Truth is indeed beyond the reach of sensory perception. It is formless, nameless inexplicable, indefinable, unthinkable, far above the known and also unknown."

In the next few hymns the Rishi tells his disciple about the magnificence of that Supreme power, which permeates the entire creation. He wants his student to be awakened from the systematic self-deceptive logical explanation and engage in the subtlest adventure of experiencing the one beyond the boundaries of existent and non-existent. The pure luminous spirit manifests through everything, which can be seen with the eyes, touched, tasted and experienced through other senses. *Brahman* is the energizer as well as the experiencer of all the sensory objects and yet remains unattached and aloof as a silent witness. The super power can be experienced through the functions of the sensory organs and still transcends everything. The Supreme-self is eternal, pure, lucid, awakened, and devoid of all modifications. The person who perceives this truth with the eye of wisdom and heightened intuition, surely attains liberation in due course of time.

In reference to the magnanimity of *Parabrahman*, the Rishi tells a story about the war between the gods and demons, as described in ancient scriptures, and asserts the truth that pure consciousness is the power behind all the apparent powers, life behind all apparent life forms, and the grace behind everything that appears to be graceful.

Omniscience of the Supreme Lord is the only truth that lies at the heart of everything in the universe. The great sage winds up the profound metaphysical discussion with word, *Tadvanam*—"Dearest of all". He enlightens his students about the ecstasy of divine love and the joy of inner Bliss which is within the access of every human being. The wise sage enunciates the doctrine of self-realization and God-realization through faith, devotional love, austerities, self-discipline, and the performance of duty without attachment. He assures that if a person seeks for God, from the depth of his heart and with firm resolve, he is definitely blessed with the grace of the Lord and the absolute Truth is revealed to him in due course of time. It is ardent devotion, which leads the aspirant to the consummation of ultimate union with the Supreme Lord.

Katha Upanishad

The Katha Upanishad which comprises a part of the Yajurveda is the most widely known, of all the Upanishads. There are many commentaries written on this Upanishad by Indian as well as European and American scholars. Many well-known western educators have described it as, "one of the perfect specimens of the mystic philosophy and poetry of the ancient Hindus." The reason why the Katha Upanishad has been held in deep interest and is a widely translated scriptural text is because of its theme, "The journey of soul". It is an interesting dialogue between Nachiketa and Yama (the god of death). Nachiketa inquires about the mystery of death. "*Yeyam Prete vichikitsa manushye stity eke nayam astiti chaike etat vidyam anusistas tvayaham varanam esha varastriteeyah*" (Katha.1.1.20), meaning, "There has been a doubt in regards to the death of a man, some say that he exists and others say he does not. Enlighten me about the truth and let this be my third boon."

As we see, people usually feel surprised over the phenomenon of life, as from where it comes and where it goes. Death has been one of the most baffling problems of man. Among all the other fears, the most common and the dreaded one is the fear of death. It is not only unpredictable, it is overpowering too, because at the sudden call of death one feels utterly helpless. There is no escape from death and that is why Nachiketa requests Yama to unfold his secret.

The dialogue becomes really interesting in the upcoming hymns as Yama answers the profound metaphysical questions of Nachiketa in these words: *"Na jayate mriyate va vipascin nayam kutashcin na babhuva kashcit ajo nityahshashvato' yam purano na hanyante hanyamane sharire"* (Katha.1.2.18). Yama enlightens Nachiketa about the immortality of the soul and the perishable and ever changing nature of the physical body. The soul is immortal, imperishable, immutable, non-changing, and inexplicable. The absolute Truth about the soul is veiled in many layers of conditioned consciousness and it is very difficult to comprehend. In general, it is very hard to find someone who has the perceptual and experiential knowledge of the soul or the one who has understood its essential nature, by reading and by hearing from others. It is only when an individual transcends the boundaries of mind and intellect, he perceives the essentiality of the soul, and is also blessed with the rich experience of his own immortality that underlies the visible mortality of body. He looks upon the transmigration of soul as merely changing garments.

At one point in hymn 1.2.20 the god of death enlightens Nachiketa about the spiritual experience of proximity with the soul at the shrine of heart, which ushers the individual into yogic unity and the rich experience of understanding the nature of the soul. The realization of the Supreme Lord at the innermost region of the heart is easy and the most rewarding experience of life.

The mysterious power of the Holy syllable *Aum* has been also mentioned in hymns 1.2.15 and 1.2.16. Meditation with the mystic syllable *Aum* has been highly exalted in the Vedas and in the other Holy scriptures. It is the most beneficial austerity, which reveals almost all the mysteries of the macrocosm as well as the microcosm. It is an introduction to the various branches of knowledge such as the physical-self, the psychological-self, and the spiritual-self. The holy syllable *Aum* represents the transcendental Supreme *Parabrahman*; that is why all the hymns in Vedas start with *Aum*. Every type of penance, *yajna*, yoga and worship becomes ennobled and sanctified by uttering the sacred word *Aum* at the commencement. The simple practice of repeating the holy syllable *Aum*, and always remaining aware of its sound is in itself an austerity that purifies the thinking faculty and initiates the mind to be receptive to the voice of God, which gradually leads to the subjective experience of the soul.

In reference to the progressive realization of the Supreme-soul, the god of death, Yama, gives a hierarchy of the various levels of consciousness; declaring that beyond the senses are the objects of senses and beyond that is the mind; subtler than the mind is the intellect and subtler than intellect is the embodied-soul and beyond that is the unmanifest Supreme-soul. In the hymns 1.3.12 and 13, it is clearly indicated that the regular practice of yogic unity in meditation helps the person to bring his scattered thoughts together into a reflective state of mind in order to comprehend the presence of soul within. It integrates mind, body, and spirit and sets up a spiritual force, which ushers the aspirant into conscious alignment with the source—the Supreme *Parabrahman*. A yogi who is steadfast in his vows and constantly connected with the indwelling-soul, he is blessed with the experiential knowledge of his own immortality, which brings liberation from the fear of death and also the rich experience of being ageless, timeless, and immortal.

The teachings of the first chapter are concluded with an inspiring message in the hymn 1.3.14, "Arise, awake, and achieve which is yours, with the help of those who have experienced the truth; the wise proclaim that the path of God-realization is sharp like the edge of a razor and hard to step on." The wise sage exhorts mankind to wake up from the circular patterns of conditioned thinking and comprehend the truth behind the perceptual boundaries of senses. He declares that human beings are not just the passive victims of some unknown destiny, every person has the ability and wisdom to improve the quality of life, be liberated from the fear of death, and enter into the totality of the infinite Bliss at the time of departure from the world.

Katha Upanishad Chapter Two is a continuation of the teachings from the previous hymns, that instinctively our senses are accustomed to be *bahirmukhi,* that is, in the habit of chasing sense objects in the material world. In general people remain involved in the transitory pleasures of the mundane world and miss the joy of spiritual intimacy with the soul. Out of many millions, scarcely a few strive for inner-Bliss and out of those true aspirants, the man of wisdom directs his attention towards the inner treasure and perceives the presence of inner Divinity at the shrine of his heart. This experience of unity with the transcendental-self comes as a unique blessing. The person is enlightened about the essential truth that "I am separate from the mind and body, I am the knower of the body." Self-realization is to be able to realize the Self, as the witness of all activities at the various states of consciousness. It is the experiential knowledge of the soul which liberates the person from the bondage of karma and the fear of death.

In the upcoming hymns of this chapter in the third *Valli* there is a beautiful description of the tree of life, presented with the unique allegory of an *Ashwattha* tree. *Ashwattha* means, "that which will not remain the same till tomorrow." It is perpetually changing, constantly growing, and expanding in all directions. It has been declared as *Sanatana* (eternal) by the knower of Truth. *Ashwattha* also stands for the tree of the banyan family, which is constantly expanding by throwing the branches down into the ground, to become roots again. The tree of *Samsara*, which is the world of actions and experiences with its roots above, in the Supreme consciousness, is indeed the individual body as well as the cosmic body. Roots upward means the life starts from the roots that are settled in the *Brahmarandhra* (the crown of the head) in the form of thoughts, latencies, and *Samskaras*. Life is an expression of information fed by the software of memories in the *Brahmarandhra*. The seat of *Brahman* is in the *Brahmarandhra* from where the entire body is nourished and sustained. The pure consciousness is the creator, sustainer and annihilator. All the beings emerge from Supreme *Parabrahman*—sustained by *Parabrahman* and into Supreme consciousness they enter and merge again. Yama the god of death says, "This is that *Tattva*, O' Nachiketa about which you have inquired."

In the next few hymns Nachiketa is enlightened about the great secret that liberates the individual-soul from the bondage of karma and ushers towards immortality. Yama makes it very clear that the bondage of a man is rooted in his infatuation for worldly desires. Overwhelmed by various desires and yearnings every individual feels trapped and helpless. Pursuit of false values imprisons the embodied-soul. Yama tells Nachiketa that anybody who has the strength to withdraw his mind from the cravings of the worldly desires, he becomes satisfied in the tranquility of the transcendental-Self, and attains liberation in due course of time. The Yogi who lives in unity with the indwelling-soul, he naturally leaves his body meditating on the Supreme-soul. At the time of death, he directs his breath upward towards the top of the head (crown *chakra*). Of all the 101 arteries of the heart, there is one which goes upward towards the crown of the head—the tenth gate of the body—*Brahmarandhra*. Departing from this gate from the top of the head he becomes immortal.

Prashna Upanishad

Prashna Upanishad belongs to Atharvaveda, where the great Rishi Pippalada and his disciples, Sukesha, Satyakama,

Gargya, Kaushalya, Bhargava, and Kabandhi are engaged in truly scientific inquiry into the mysteries of the soul, along with the mysteries of the phenomenal world. The first question from Kabandhi the son of Katya pertains to the source of creatures on earth. Kabandhi approached the great Rishi with deep humility and asked, "Venerable Sir, whence, verily, are all these creatures born?" (1.3). The divine sage starts his answer from the next hymn 1.4 and explains that at the beginning of creation, Prajapati (the Lord of creation) came into existence as *Prana* (life force) and *Rayi* (matter). *Prana* "the primal energy" is the Sun and *Rayi* "the matter" is the Moon. *Rayi* is thus the material world that includes gross and subtle, visible or invisible. In this illustration the teacher makes it very clear to his student that matter derives its existence from the primal energy exactly as the Moon receives its light from the Sun. It is the potency of the Supreme spirit —*Prana*, which vitalizes the matter and makes it grow and manifest itself as the most spectacular creation. It is the primal energy which is holding everything together and is reflected through everything. Matter is indeed the cosmic mother of the entire spectacular universe and *Ishwara* (God) is the cosmic father. The multitude of beings comes into existence from the union of matter and the Supreme-soul. One Supreme power, the primal energy, becomes manifest through innumerable forms and shapes within various grades of potentialities bound by their own latencies.

The second question in relation to the sustenance of the creation comes from Bhargava Vaidarbhi, who approached the great seer and asked, "O' Venerable Sir, how many gods hold together this body? Which of them are most vibrant, and who among them is the greatest?" The divine sage starts his answers with a brief introduction of the gods and goddesses— the cosmic powers that help the sustenance of everything in macrocosm as well as microcosm. These natural forces such as fire, air, ether, earth, water, the five senses of perception and five of action, and the five types of *Prana*s (the life force) are addressed as gods and goddesses because they are constantly working to support life.

The Sanskrit word for gods and goddesses is *Deva* and *Devi*—The word *Deva* comes from the root word *'Div'* means to shine or who radiates the potential dynamism of the Supreme spirit and help unconditionally. Besides the five chief elements fire, air, ether, earth, and water that constitute the body of the universe, there are gods and goddesses in the human body, which help the different organs to work in perfect co-operation with one another. For example the presiding *Deva* of eyes are the Sun and Moon, of the speech is Agni (fire), and of the hearing is Aakash (ether). The *Deva* of the organs of defecation is Yama; of the reproductive organs Prajapati and the controller of hands and arms is Indra. The presiding *Deva* of forehead is Shankara and of digestion is Vaishvanara. As a matter of fact our hands and five fingers are also the five *Devas*, which act as the switchboard for the entire body. The thumb is Agni (fire), the index finger is Vayu (air), the middle finger is Aakash (ether), the ring finger is Prithvi (earth), and the little finger is Varuna (water).

Elaborating upon the concept of gods and goddesses in our body the great Rishi relates an imaginary episode to his students which answers the next part of the question, "Who illuminates them? And which is the greatest?" The sage Pippalada reveals the secret about the superiority of *Prana*. He explains in detail that *Prana* is indeed the life force or the life energy that sustains the entire creation. Among the gods in body, *Prana* is the chief that illuminates, energizes, regulates, directs the sensory organs, and controls all the functions of the body. It sustains and maintains the body. All these *Devas* in the body work under the direct control and power of the *Prana* (life-force). None of these have any independent existence of their own. There is one vital force that presides over the inner cosmos and guides the entire functioning of the body. All the voluntary and involuntary activities of the body are only various manifestations of the life force—*Prana*. The moment when the divine light, *Prana* leaves the human body it is declared dead and ready to be cremated or buried. The consciousness in body is addressed as *Prana*, Rudra or Shiva. When Shiva leaves the body, it is declared as "*Shava*"—dead. *Shava* is a Sanskrit word that stands for "dead body". *Prana*, the life force, is indeed the essence of the entire manifestation, whether it concerns the individual body or the cosmic body.

The third question about the nature of *Prana* came from Kaushalya, the son of Ashvala. He approached the Maharishi with a guileless heart and asked, "Holy Sir, of what is *Prana* born; how does it enter the body? And how does it distribute itself and establish itself and also how does it go out of the body? How does it hold together the external (physical body) and internal (mind and soul)?" The sage Pippalada explains the answer to the third question through an example and tells his students that *Prana* is born of the soul. Like a man and his shadow, the soul and *Prana* are inseparable; and it enters the body bound by the desires of mind from past lives. The individual *Prana* is a wave which emerges from the wholeness of the soul without disturbing its peace and serenity. *Prana* is essentially one with *Atman* (the soul), but also distinct because of its separate self-assumed identity which is wrapped around the *Sankalpa*–the thoughts. The individualized *Prana* enclosed within the mind has gone through many births before, and keeps entering into new wombs.

Now coming to the second part of the questions, how does *Prana* sustain and maintain the functions of body? The great Rishi describes the five-fold nature of *Prana*, which is merely a functional division. The one primary *Prana* divides into five types, i.e. *Prana, Apana, Samana, Vyana,* and *Udana* in accordance to its location and movement in body. *Prana* (inhalation) is the life-breath as it moves inward and provides basic energy to the body. *Apana* (exhalation) means the air that moves outward. *Apana* controls the elimination of carbon dioxide through breath, also the elimination of stool and urine. The expelling of semen, menstrual fluid and the fetus are also the functions of '*Apana*'. At the subtle levels of consciousness *Apana* helps in releasing the stored emotions. *Samana* is active in the middle region of the body i.e. the navel, where energy is centered and digestion takes place. It works in the gastrointestinal tract and helps in digestion at all levels. *Vyana* is the vital energy primarily in the region of heart and lungs but it governs circulation on all levels.

The divine sage further explains that the soul dwells in the lotus of the heart. There are 101 arteries, from each of these proceed another 100, those are still smaller, and from each of those again 72 thousand branching arteries, in which *Vyana* (diffused breath) moves. In explanation of *Udana* the teacher gives answer to the next part of the question—how *Prana* departs from the body. *Udana* (upward moving breath), primarily moves along the route of *Sushumna Nadi*, from the bottom of the spine to the crown of the head and provides nourishment to the whole body. The Rishi Pippalada tells that at the time of death, it is surely the *Udanaprana* (the life-force) that settles in the ruling thought of the individual and while leaving the body, leads the embodied-soul to be reborn according to its good, bad, and mixed deeds respectively. The Rishi concludes his answer with the words, that anyone who understands the origin of *Prana*, how it enters the body, how it abides there in its five-fold division and its relation to the indwelling-soul, he attains immortality.

The fourth question was brought forward by Gargya Sauryayani in relation to the nature of the Supreme-self and the various layers of human consciousness. He approached the great Rishi Pippalada and asked, "O' Venerable Sir, when a man's body goes to sleep, who sleeps and who remains awake? Who beholds the wonder of dreams, who experiences pleasure, and, in the case of sound sleep, in whom are all these established?" The divine sage explains that when the mind withdraws itself from the senses of perception and action and gradually settles into *Manomaya Kosha* (the subtle body), the gross body feels relaxed and the person goes to sleep; in sleep when the mind is centered in the subtle body, which is the reservoir of thoughts, memory, latencies and *Samskaras*, the mind becomes very active and beholds its own immensity. In dreams the mind revives its past impressions, what has been seen is seen again; and whatever has been heard is heard again; whatever has been experienced in different places or far away regions returns to the consciousness in strange details. The sage goes to the extent of telling his students that the sum total of all those incidents seen and unseen, heard and unheard, enjoyed or not enjoyed, both the real and unreal are experienced by the individual while dreaming in sleep. In this reference Adi Shankaracharya has written that the unseen, unheard, and unenjoyed that a man experiences in the dream are in context with the things that were seen, heard, and enjoyed in past lives.

In the next few hymns, the Rishi describes the dreamless sleep and the nature of the Supreme-soul. He tells Gargya that when the mind is calm and peaceful and gradually starts identifying with the radiance of the indwelling spirit, the mind glides into dreamless, deep sleep. The quiet and restful mind resorts to the silence of the Self and the gross body feels relaxed and rejuvenated. Dreamless sleep is the alignment of the five cosmic elements, the ten organs of perception and action, mind, intellect, ego, and the Supreme spirit. In the next hymn (4.9) the Rishi moves a step further and enlightens his students about the mysteries of the onlooker, the seer, the observer, the spectator, and the Lord of the entire creation. He says that even in deep sleep, when the physical body and the subtle body both are at rest, there is someone who is witnessing the state of complete rest and joy of perfect unity with the Higher-self. Who is that observer? This is indeed the silent onlooker who resides in the hearts of all—The Supreme spirit. The Lord dwells in the body and beholds everything as a silent witness. The great sage emphasizes the fact that anybody who perceives this truth with the eye of wisdom and sufficient discrimination, surely attains liberation in due course of time.

The fifth question in Prashna Upanishad comes from Satyakama, the son of Shibi. Approaching the great sage Pippalada with profound reverence he asked, "Venerable Sir, if a man meditates upon the *Omkara*—The holy syllable *Aum*, throughout his life, what shall be his reward after death?" The divine sage starts his answer in the next hymn (5.2) and then elaborates upon the glory of *Omkara*. He explains that *Omkara—Aum* is *Brahman*—both the immanent and transcendent, the pure luminous Higher-self and the conditioned-self, the personal and impersonal; with meditation on the sound of the holy syllable *Aum*, the man of wisdom may attain either the one or the other. The teacher distinguishes the different grades of confluences, A for *Akara*, U for *Ukara* and M for *Makara*; the three put together are *Aum— Omkara*. *Aum* symbolizes the triad in time and space and also the three stages, A-*Akara* is the waking state, U-*Ukara* is *Svapna* (dreams) and M-*Makara* is *Sushupti* (deep sleep). When written in Sanskrit—there is a curved line on the top *Ardhamatra* which indicates the fourth state of consciousness which is beyond dreamless, deep sleep; when the individual-soul peacefully glides through the gap into the unity with the Supreme-soul. This is the state of aesthetic consciousness called *Turiya*—the unified field which is beyond the three levels of consciousness.

In meditation on the sound of *Aum*, each syllable resonates with a specific sound, touching the specific level of consciousness. Each level of consciousness has its own style and capacity of comprehending inherent wisdom and knowledge of the Self; and as the aspirant moves from the fields of conditioned consciousness into the mysteries of Super-consciousness; each step provides a basis for spontaneous awakening at the next. It is indeed a great mystery! That is why the wise sage educates his disciple quite cautiously and informs that although the rewards of meditation with the sound of *Aum* are assured, but in direct proportion to the intelligent comprehension of its meaning. He makes it clear that knowledge is indeed better than practice carried on without proper insight. In order to achieve the complete benefit of meditation with the sound of *Aum*, one must allow the meaning to penetrate the subtle understanding.

In reference to the grades of benefits, the divine sage tells Satyakama that when the individual meditates on the holy syllable *Aum* even with little knowledge of its meaning but with special emphasis on the first syllable 'A', he becomes enlightened, and after his death, he is reborn in the family of the learned, where he resumes his practice for further progress towards the attainment of the final goal. He further adds, that, "The person who meditates upon the sound of *Aum* with deeper understanding of its meaning and increased emphasis on A and U (first and second letters) he definitely ascends closer to the joy of inner Bliss. He lives in ecstasy of Divine love and carries that Bliss wherever he goes. After death he returns again to earth, possessed with godly qualities and blessed with all the favorable conditions for the completion of his goal. He is intuitively persuaded towards the path of God-realization and *Moksha* (liberation)." In the next hymn the Rishi proceeds further and asserts that anybody who meditates on *Omkara—Aum*, with the totality of his being, consciously following the sound A, U, and M each marching into the other interconnectedly and harmoniously, he definitely attains unity with the Supreme *Parabrahman* and enters into infinite Bliss at the time of departure from the world.

The sixth question about the identity of *Sodasha Kala Purusha*—the person with 16 parts—came from Sukesha, the son of Bharadvaja. He requested guidance of the great Rishi saying, "O' great teacher tell me where is that person of 16 forms?" The Rishi Pippalada starts his answer from the next hymn (6.2) and explains the secrets of *Para* and *Apara Prakriti*. He tells Sukesha, "Right here within the body itself dwells the soul in whom all these parts arise. He elaborates the answer with a detailed description of the

16 parts of the subtle body and gross body as indicated in *Samkhya* Philosophy with some modifications, i.e. *Prana*, *Shraddha* (faith), *Panchbhuta* (light, air, ether, earth, water), *Indriyam* (the senses of action and perception), *Mana* (mind), and *Annam* (food), *Viryam* (vital vigor), austerity, mantras, the hymns and formulae, Karma (the actions), *Lokah*—the worlds whose acquisition is conditioned by the deed and *Nama* (name), as the individual distinctness." He further adds, that these 16 parts originate from the Supreme *Purusha*, and, at the dawn of self-realization, they all merge together into the Supreme spirit with their names and forms. He tells Sukesha, "As the flowing rivers whose destination is the sea, having reached there, disappear into the ocean, losing their names and forms, similarly in the blessed moments of inner-awakening the names and forms merge into the wholeness of the Supreme-soul." The great Rishi concluded, saying, "I have explained to you everything about the Supreme spirit which is within the comprehension of human intellect." The disciple thanked the great Rishi Pippalada and bowed with profound respect.

Mundaka Upanishad

The Mundaka Upanishad belongs to Atharvaveda. It has three chapters, each of which has two sections. This Upanishad derives its name from the root word *"Munda"* which means "to shave off"—which is quite apt, in reference to the teachings of this Upanishad. The theme of Mundaka Upanishad is the distinct understanding of the knowledge of the soul that leads the aspirant into detachment from the pleasures of the material world, and perpetual alliance with the Supreme *Parabrahman*. It is snapping off the desires for worldly enjoyments and living with single minded devotion for God. It is shaving off the false identifications at the dawn of inner awakening.

The Mundaka Upanishad begins with a question from Shaunaka, the owner of a very big monastery, who duly approached the great sage Angira and asked, "O' Venerable Sir, what is that by knowing which all else becomes known?" The divine sage started his answer by saying, "There are two kinds of knowledge as declared by the knower of *Brahman*. The *Para* means 'the transcendental' and the *Apara* means 'related to the mundane world.'" He further added that the knowledge of the Rigveda, the Yajurveda, the Samaveda, the Atharvaveda, Phonetics, Rituals, Grammar, Etymology, Philology, Metrics, and Astrology is considered '*Apara*'; while the transcendental knowledge that ushers to the realization of the immortal supreme spirit is called '*Para*'. He intimates his disciple with various aspects of manifest Divinity saying, "As the web comes out of the spider and is withdrawn, as plants grow from the soil and hair from the body of man, so springs the universe from the eternal *Brahman*." The Supreme spirit, the essence of all life is indeed the creator, the sustainer, and the annihilator of the entire creation.

The divine sage enlightens about the unfailing rewards of performing the Vedic rituals and also alerts that the performance of these rituals without proper insight can surely distract the mind from the goal of self-realization and liberation. He further adds that the people who practice spirituality merely for the attainment of earthly pleasures and lordship, they keep revolving into the rounds of birth, death, and rebirth until they realize the bondage for themselves and make efforts for their liberation. The great Rishi indicates the necessity of guidance from a Guru (preceptor) who is well versed in the study of ancient scriptures and established in *Brahman*. The Guru should be approached with reverence, humility, and with an attitude of service. In his description of the glories of *Parabrahman* the divine sage tells that the cosmic-soul is the omnipotent substratum, from where plurality of the world is projected. The Absolute *Brahman* pervades the entire creation. Heaven is His head, the Sun and Moon His eyes, the four quarters His ears, the revealed scriptures His voice, the air is His breath, the universe is His heart. From His feet came the earth. He is the innermost self of all, from Him arises the Sun-illumined sky, the ocean and the mountain, the herbs and life sustaining elements. From Him are born the gods of manifold descent, the celestials, men, beasts, birds, the life sustaining breath, rice and barley, austerity, faith, truth, continence, and the law. The Supreme power individualizes itself as individual manifestations in millions of forms and shapes. He further adds that Self-luminous *Brahman*, the light of lights, although present everywhere can be perceived as seated within the lotus of the heart in everyone. The realization of the Supreme Lord at the shrine of heart is easy and most rewarding experience of life. It is easy because the individual is not seeking something distant, not something foreign and alien; it is very much known, familiar and one's own indwelling-self. Spiritual experience of proximity with the Divine at the heart center prepares the individual for the devotional love of God. When an ardent devotee concentrates at the heart center with the celestial sound of Holy syllable *Aum*, he goes into yogic unity with the indwelling-soul and feels immersed in the affinity of divine love.

After presenting a detailed description of the omni-science of the Supreme-soul, the great sage Angira enlightens his disciple about the essentiality of individualized-self. He tells him that the embodied-self is an eternal fragment of the cosmic-self. It is only due to ignorance that the embodied-soul forms a separate identity, feels alienated, and goes through the suffering of birth, death, and rebirth again.

In reference to the perspicuous understanding of the individual-self and the transcendental-self, he gives the analogy of two birds sitting on the branches of the same tree of life. One bird is always busy enjoying the fruits of the tree while the other is only watching. The one who is involved in the enjoyment of fruits seems to be sometimes happy and some other times very unhappy; he is confused and suffers. But the one who is simply watching and remains a silent witness is always peaceful and free. The bird who is busy enjoying the fruits of the tree symbolizes the individual-soul—the '*nara*' who remains involved in the enjoyment of worldly pleasures and eventually becomes confused about the realities of life; but the one who is simply watching is the

Supreme-soul—*Narayana* Himself. The latter remains a silent witness and free. Realization of the Supreme spirit beyond the horizon of self-imposed limitations is realized when the individual-soul re-establishes his conscious relationship with the indweller and identifies himself with the divinity within.

In the process of Self-revelation, the embodied-soul acts as a seer and transcending both good and evil becomes free from impurities of mind and attains unity with *Parabrahman.* sage Angira winds up the topic with a profound statement: *"Brahmavid Brahmaiva bhavati"* (3.2.9), meaning, "He who knows *Brahman* becomes *Brahman.*" In the state of inner awakening when the knower perceives that he is not other than the known; he steps out of his self-imposed false identity and enters the realm of immortal existence. He is librated from the knots of duality and becomes immortal.

Mandukya Upanishad

The Mandukya Upanishad is a part of Atharvaveda. Although it is the shortest Upanishad, containing only 12 hymns, its message is very profound. This is considered to be one of the most important Upanishads and has been always held in deep reverence by the great sages and scholars. The *Karika* of Adi Shankaracharya's Guru, Sri Gaudapada, on Mandukya Upanishad has always served as the most valuable guide for many commentators in India as well as in foreign countries. *Karika* is the first systematic exposition of *Advaita Vedanta.* Mandukya Upanishad opens with the declaration *"Aum ity etad aksharam idam sarvam, tasyopavyakhyanam, bhutam bhavad bhavishyad iti sarvam aumkara eva, yach chanyat trikalatitam tad apy aumkara eva,"* meaning, "The holy syllable *Aum* is indeed the imperishable *Brahman* and the entire universe is the exposition of His glory. *Aum* is all that existed in past, whatever is now, whatever will be in future; and also whatsoever transcends past, present, and future is *Aum*. The holy syllable *Aum* is the essence of everything around and everything is the manifestation of *Aum*"

The great sage Manduka proceeds further and explains that this mysterious symbol of *Brahman* is both the manifest and unmanifest Divinity, and also makes it clear that "All this is verily *Brahman*."*Aum* represents the totality of everything in microcosm as well as in macrocosm, which is experienced in the four states of consciousness; namely: the waking state, the dream state, the dreamless, deep sleep state, and the fourth called *Turiya*, when the individual-self goes in unity with the cosmic-Self, the Supreme *Parabrahman*.

The great rishi indicates that in the wakeful state of consciousness, the soul is addressed as *Vaishvanara*, in which the embodied-self with seven limbs and 19 mouths experiences the mundane world. The seven limbs i.e. the fire, air, ether, earth, water, Sun, and Moon that are mentioned in the hymn, are the basic elements that constitute the individual body as well as the cosmic body. The 19 mouths refer to the five senses of perception (hearing, touch, sight, taste, and smell), the five organs of action (speech, hands feet, reproduction, and excretion), the five vital breaths (*Prana, Apana, Vyana, Udana, Samana*), the mind, intellect, ego, and the conditioned consciousness. These 19 mouths are the windows of the body, which convey the messages from the material world to the indwelling-soul. The mind interprets the data, stores it, and also feeds it back to the physical body with new and old information. It is through these 19 mouths that the individual-soul connects to everything in the world and receives experiences of pleasure and pain. The seven limbs and 19 mouths are very active in the wakeful state of consciousness and perpetually involved in experiencing and enjoying the material world.

In the next hymn 1.4 the great sage enlightens about the second state of consciousness, which refers to the dream-state, the '*Taijas*' when the indwelling-self illumined by the inner light fashions its own world based on the pre-dispositions left by the waking experiences. It is addressed as '*Taijas*' because in the dream state, the subtle body—the *Antahkaran* (the totality of the latencies), is active and presides over the inner horizon, where thoughts move mysteriously into things and form. Here also the duality prevails, the dream and the one who is conscious of the dream. The hymn 1.5 describes the third state of consciousness: the dreamless, deep sleep— '*Sushupti*', when both the waking and dreaming completely disappear. In the dreamless, deep sleep the embodied-soul transcends the thinking faculty and glides into the realm of inner silence which is beyond the perception of both external and internal objects. The fourth state of consciousness (awareness) is characterized by deep silence and inner peace. It is pure unitary consciousness in which awareness of the world and its multiplicity is completely obliterated, the individual-self resumes unity with *Prajna* (pure-wisdom) and becomes one with *Brahman*. This is the unified field of consciousness: utterly quiet, peaceful, blissful, 'One' without a second.

The divine sage concludes his message saying that it is definitely through the understanding of the holy syllable *Aum* that the mysteries of Supreme *Parabrahman* are gathered to a specific point and revealed in due course of time.

Taittiriya Upanishad

The Taittiriya Upanishad derives its name from the great spiritual teacher Taittiri; it belongs to Yajurveda. The entire Upanishad is divided into three sections called *Vallis*. The first one is the *Shikhsa Valli*, which describes the unique system of structured education at *Gurukuls* (schools) in ancient India. *Shikhsa Valli* also deals with first of the six *Vedangas* – the science of phonetics and pronunciation. The second is the *Brahmananda Valli* and the third is *Bhrigu Valli* both dealing with spiritual education, the knowledge of Supreme *Parabrahman*.

Shikhsa Valli presents a comprehensive sweep of *Gurukul* education. The education system was quite structured. *Shikhsa Valli* opens with an invocation to God to eliminate all the obstacles in the way of attaining education. The teacher seeks blessings, both for himself and his students, saying, "Let there be the radiance of spiritual knowledge for both of us, let there be the glory of wisdom for both of us." In section two the teacher expounds upon the importance of correct pronunciation and the science of articulation. He describes in detail the six limbs of speech i.e. '*Varna-Swara*' (the letters or sounds)–the vowels and the consonants and accent pitch, '*Matra*' (measure) is the accurate distribution of voice, '*Bala*' (correct emphasis) to convey the appropriate meaning. '*Sama*' is the proportionate pronunciation in regular pitch. It is modulating one's voice in order to convey effectively, '*Santanah*' (adjunct or combination). The idea is that all the above six limbs should be taken into consideration in pronouncing any letter or word. It has been highly emphasized for proper understanding of Vedic hymns and also for excellence in communication. The Vedic sages believed that a truly educated man is the one who can communicate effectively with others. After teaching the important aspects of grammar the teacher moves on to the significance of contemplation on the sound of the holy syllable *Aum.* He declares, "*Aum iti Brahma, Aum itidam sarvam*"—meaning "*Aum* is *Brahman, Aum* is all this." He who meditates on *Aum* is blessed with yogic unity and attains *Parabrahman.* In education at *Gurukuls*, yoga and meditation were introduced at a very young age for the development of a sound mind and body, which definitely helped in pursuit of higher education, in diverse branches of knowledge.

The 11th section of *Shiksha Valli* begins with the convocation address given by the teacher to the students at the time of graduation. Ordinarily, the education at *Gurukul* (school) was spread over a period of 12 years. The students studied many subjects, both sciences and humanities, and stayed at the Ashram as part of Guru's family. So in the valedictory address, one perceives the sincere concern of the teacher for the students entering into the fast moving stream of busy life. He tells his students to maintain the flow of continuity as cleanly and smoothly as possible. The speech at the convocation ceremony begins with the following words: "Speak the truth, be virtuous and perform your duties well, while keeping in mind the laws of *Dharma*. Let there be no neglect of your daily reading. Don't break the lineage of progeny (enter the married life). Swerve not from truth and never deviate from the path of virtue. Never neglect your own well-being and also never neglect your means of prosperity. Let there be no neglect of further learning and teaching and also performing Divine duties and the offerings to your ancestors. Let your mother be the god to you; let your father be the god to you; let your teacher be the god to you; let your guest also be the god to you. Practice only those actions which are faultless, not others. Whatever good practices are there among us, those are to be adopted by you not others. Always show reverence to the learned teachers. Whatever you give to others, give with love and reverence. Gifts should be given with joy, humility modesty and compassion. If at any time there is any doubt in regard of your duty or conduct, follow the practice of great souls, who are guileless, of good judgment and devoted to truth. This is the command of the scriptures, this is the teaching. This is the secret doctrine of the Vedas. These are the traditional instructions; the same way you should act; the same way you may follow."

The first section of *Brahamananda Valli* in Taittiriya Upanishad begins with an invocation in which the divine sage says, *"Aum Sahanavavatu Sahanoubhunaktu Sahaviryam Karavavahai Tejasvina Vadhitamastu Mavidhvishavahai,"* meaning, "May we both (teacher and student) be protected by the Supreme Lord, may we both be nourished and become receptive to inner guidance, may our mutual combined effort of receiving knowledge be strengthened, may our awakened intuition and knowledge be luminous and splendorous, reflecting the light of our alignment with the soul. May we both feel comfortable and respectful to each other, totally free from enmity and animosity, may peace prevail all around us." After the invocation the Rishi declares, *"Brahma-vid apnoiti param"*—the knower of *Brahman* attains the Supreme. He further adds, *"Satyam, jnanam, anantam Brahman,"* meaning, "Truth, knowledge, and infinite is *Brahman*." He who understands this, and perceives the presence of *Brahman* dwelling within the lotus of heart, becomes aligned and enjoys the ecstasy of Divine Bliss from moment to moment. In the upcoming hymns the Rishi admirably describes the journey of Self from the gross to the subtle and further into the subtlest realms of pure consciousness where the embodied-self goes into unity with the pure luminous-self and becomes perpetually aligned to the source. This is the journey through the *pancha koshas* (five sheaths), such as *Annamaya kosha, Pranamaya kosha, Manomaya kosha, Vijnanmaya kosha* and *Anandmaya kosha*. These various fields are inter-connected and work in co-operation with each other.

In order to experience unity with the Supreme-self, the journey starts from the physical body called *Annamaya kosha*, meaning—the field that is sustained by food. It has the predominance of food, which sustains the physical body. The type of food which is consumed by the individual does influence the physical body, as well as the subtle body, which is the storehouse of thoughts. *Anna* (food) is related to *Prana*—the life breath. *Prana* depends on food consumed by the body. *Prana* (life-breath) energizes the body and is also very closely connected with '*Mana*'–the mind, which is a vessel of thoughts. In the spiritual journey from the physical body to the innermost shrine of the soul, *Prana* plays a significant role; because there is a subtle and powerful relationship between body, breath, and mind. When the breathing is calm and peaceful, the mind becomes relaxed and the aspirant spontaneously enters into *Manomaya kosha* (the field of thoughts) and later into the quietness of the Self. It is the concentration with the breath control which leads the aspirant from *Annamaya kosha* (physical body) to *Pranamaya kosha* (the energy field) and further into *Manomaya kosha* (thinking faculty) and *Vijnanmaya kosha* (the experiential knowledge of the Self) and later into *Anandamaya kosha* (Bliss) the subjective experience of unity in transcendence. The ecstatic experience of conceptual unity is a blessing, which liberates the individual from all kinds of fears. The Rishi asserts, "That whatever joy, which is acceptable in this world or in others, however alluring, is definitely insignificant in comparison to *Brahma Ananda* (Bliss)." An exalted person who has experienced the inner joy of the soul is not afflicted by any anxiety. He regards honor and dishonor, pleasures and pain as only passing phases of life, and is liberated from all kinds of fears.

Bhrigu Valli, the third chapter of Taittiriya Upanishad, is another interesting dialogue between Bhrigu and his father, the great Rishi Varuna. Bhrigu respectfully approached his father and said; "O' venerable Sir please teach me about *Brahman*." The father replied, "O' dear son, that from which everything in creation emanates, by which everything is sustained and into which everything enters eventually is *Brahman*. Everything in the world is experienced, grasped, and perceived through *Brahman*, which is the *Sanatan* (eternal) principle of all existence." The Rishi further explained that *Brahman* is the substratum of the universe and can be perceived only with '*Brahman Vijnana Sadhana*' which means penance and disciplinary observances. He told Bhrigu to enter into *tapas* (austerities) and discover the essential nature of *Brahman* in quiet moments of unity with the self. During the process of tough penances the son (student) moves from one perceptual experience to another; by negation and quiet reflection, he determines for himself that Supreme *Brahman* is the power behind matter, life, mind, and intelligence, that controls each one of them. The nature of *Brahman* is indeed inexplicable. The final vision satisfies all the enquiries.

After the subjective experience of ultimate reality, everything becomes self-evident, nothing else remains to be known any more. '*Anando Brahmeti vyajanati*'— meaning, 'Bliss is *Brahman*.' The entire creation comes out of Bliss, it is sustained by Bliss and it returns into Bliss. The mystical chant towards the end of the *Bhrigu Valli* indicates the ecstatic experience of conceptual unity with Supreme *Parabrahman*. The exalted one transcends the limitation of mind and body; and exhilarates in realization of oneness with the entire creation. This *Sama* chanting expresses the lyrical and rapturous embrace of the universe. Bhrigu, the son of Rishi Varuna, perceives unity both with manifest as well as unmanifest Divinity.

Aitareya Upanishad

The Aitareya Upanishad belongs to Rigveda. It derives its name from the teacher Mahidasa Aitareya, the son of Itara. In this Upanishad the divine sage unveils the mysteries about the origin of the universe. It is rather a short Upanishad comprising only three chapters, imbued with profound wisdom. Rishi Aitareya explains that, "Before creation, all that existed was the *Atman*, the *Atman* alone, nothing else whatsoever winked. That *Atman* thought 'Let me create the worlds.'" Thus *Atman* created *Ambhas* (the region above the sky) and upheld by it; *Marichi* (sky), *Mara* (the earth)—the world of mortals, and *Apah* the region of waters beneath the earth; then their presiding deities or guardians. Later with Divine 'will' appeared the *Purusha* (individual-soul), and the divinities (fire, air, ether, earth, and water) entered the body of *Purusha*. Fire becoming speech entered the mouth, air becoming breath entered the nostrils, Sun becoming sight entered the eyes. Ether (space) becoming hearing entered the ears, earth the skin, and water becoming semen entered the generative organ, Moon becoming the mind entered the heart and so on. Finally the *Atman* (consciousness) as life-force entered into that body through the suture of the skull. The opening at the centre of head is known as '*Vidrti*' or

'*Brahmarandhra*' the door of Bliss—The seat of Supreme *Parabrahman* (Pure consciousness). It is also called *Sahasrara*—the thousand-petalled lotus. Having entered into the body, the *Atman* started identifying with mind and function of body; and became individualized as *Jivatma*. Individual-soul or *Jivatma* is essentially one with *Atman* but also distinct, because of the separate assumed identity with body. It is the identification of *Atman* with mind and body that gives momentum to the wheel of creation. Pure luminous *Atman* and *Jivatma* both exist in a mystical union. Realization of Supreme-soul beyond the individualized identity with body is perceived when *Jivatma* (embodied-self) transcends the three stages (waking, dream, and dreamless sleep) and experiences the presence of the indwelling-soul at the shrine of heart and exhilarates in joy saying "I know *Brahman*." The Rishi explains, that the one who has perceived the luminosity of the soul at the shrine of heart has been addressed as "*Idandra*" means 'I have seen'. *Idandra*—most commonly known as 'Indra' literally means the 'One' who has witnessed the presence of the Supreme-soul in the body.

The Aitareya Upanishad does not give the whole story of evolution in all its detail; it takes up the description of only *Nadaja* and *Binduja*. The creation that comes into existence out of 'Divine will' is *Nadaja*—in other words 'the expression of a mere thought'. The revered sages, the four Kumaras and Manus are the *Nadajas*. The others, born from the male and female union are called *Binduja*. After giving some glimpses of the cycle of birth-death and rebirth, the divine sage draws our attention towards the topic of rediscovery of the Supreme-soul within. *Atman* is the omnipotent substratum from where the plurality of the world is projected. The absolute *Brahman* pervades the entire creation and manifests through everything, which is seen by the eyes, touched, tasted, and experienced through the senses. God is the seed and the ultimate source of origin for beings and non-beings. The omnipresence of the Lord can be experienced and perceived everywhere and in everything. The attributes of the Supreme Lord are surely infinite and very difficult to comprehend. The person who perceives this truth, he surely attains peace and liberation in due course of time.

Chandogya Upanishad

Chandogya Upanishad belongs to the Samaveda. "*Chando Sama gayanti iti chandogah*" meaning, "Chandogya is the singer of *saman*." The Chandogya Upanishad forms the last eight chapters of the Chandogya *Brahmana* of the Samaveda. It is the second longest, voluminous of the principal Upanishads, next only to Brihadaranyaka, and has been held in profound reverence by Adi Shankaracharya and other scholars of the world. *Acharya*'s commentary is exhaustive and meticulous. It unites the diverse currents of metaphysical and mystical thoughts into a single stream of philosophy, which is quite intelligible and within the comprehension of every student of *Vedanta*. Chandogya Upanishad introduces to the students of religion and philosophy, the great seekers of truth such as Narada, Satyakama, and Svetaketu as well as the great men of wisdom like Uddalaka Aruni, Sanatkumara, and

Prajapati. The central teachings in reference to *Brahmavidya* has been presented in powerful spiritual dictums –the *Mahavakyas* such as '*Tat tvam asi*'—"Thou art That", and "*sarvam khalu idam Brahman,*—means, all this is verily *Brahman.*" Apart from religious and philosophical teachings Chandogya has other unique features, such as, its melodious text in Sanskrit, the discipline of metrical chanting, meditation on the sound of *Aum*, and the logical development of central theme in the salient sections. This Upanishad consists of eight chapters, the first five explain in detail the glory of *Upasana*, the meditation with the holy syllable *Aum* and the *Panchagni Vidya* (the knowledge of five-fold fire): the other three chapters known as *Gyankhanda* deal with the knowledge of Supreme *Parabrahman*. In Chandogya the Supreme Reality is designated as *Satya* (Truth). The luminous power of truthfulness is highly emphasized. The word *Satyam* is declared to be the designation of *Brahman*. In *Gyankhanda*, which comprises the remaining three chapters, the doctrine of enlightenment through the experiential knowledge of the Self, is highlighted. The dialogues between Rishi Uddalaka Aruni and his son Svetaketu, between Narada and Sanatkumara and also between Prajapati, Indra, and Virochana are really interesting, in which the scriptural knowledge culminates in the subjective experience of Supreme *Parabrahman*.

Chandogya Upanishad opens with the declaration '*Aum ity etad aksharam, udgitham upasita*', meaning, "One should adore, and meditate on the holy syllable *Aum* (the imperishable one) as the *Udgitha*." Singing aloud and contemplating on the sound of *Aum* as *Udgitha* exhilarates the mind and helps in going into the ecstasy of divine love. The mystic syllable *Aum* has the power to awaken within the mind the corresponding God-consciousness. In general, the Vedic scholars know the techniques of perceiving a very clear resonance of the sound of *Aum* in their mind. They start every hymn in worship with the holy syllable *Aum*, which initiates the sincere devotion and essential unity with the all-pervasive Supreme Lord. The significance of beginning the hymn with the celestial syllable represents the Lord himself to be the essence of everything. The simple practice of repeating the holy syllable *Aum* and remaining aware of the sound is in itself an austerity, which purifies the thinking faculty and makes the mind receptive to the voice of God. *Aum* meditation marks the fundamental basis for the acquaintance with everything that exists within and without. As a matter of fact, the entire creation is held together by the sound energy of *Aum* as *Udgitha*.

In the description of the all comprehensive power of *Brahmanada Aum* the divine sage explains in the hymn (1.4.5)—that anyone who contemplates on '*Aum*' with the purity of heart and undivided devotion he enters into the essentiality of '*Swara*' (primordial sound), and tastes the celestial nectar, becomes fearless and immortal in due course of time. He also affirms (1.5.1) that *Udgitha* is *Pranava* and *Pranava* is *Udgitha*. The word "*Pranava*" means, "That, by which the Supreme power is sincerely and effectively praised."*Pranava* also means, "Which runs through *Prana* (life-force), pervades at the heart of creation and is ever renewing."

With the fourth section of the fourth chapter begins the story of Satyakama Jabala, which clearly indicates that speaking truth is indeed the most honorable virtue. It keeps the person aligned with indwelling Divinity and gives inner strength, inner security, and self-respect. Speaking truth promotes the harmony of thoughts, words, and deeds, and makes the individual fearless and confident. Once upon a time Satyakama Jabala, an earnest student, approached the great Rishi Gautama and requested in utter humility to be accepted as a student. When the sage inquired about his parentage and *gotra*, Satyakama confessed with honesty and told his teacher that his mother was a servant in her young age and worked in many places. So, he was not aware of his parentage. sage Gautama was so impressed by the simplicity and truthfulness of Satyakama that he accepted him as his disciple. Speaking truth and taking pride in it, definitely reflects divine nature, which is pure and luminous. This incident also gives an insight into the liberal social structure of ancient India. It shows that for admission in *Gurukul* (school), there was no stigma of birth or caste attached to a person. The great Rishis were truly honest in their outlook and completely free from the false standards and social norms. It is mentioned that Satyakama Jabala became a great teacher himself and had many disciples.

The fifth section of the fifth chapter gives a detailed

explanation of *Panchagni Vidya*, which means, "The knowledge of five-fold sacrificial fires, arranged in the order of their subtleness." It indicates the mutual dependence which exists between the created beings and the cosmic powers. Everything in the universe which includes humans, beasts, plants, trees, water reservoirs, rocks, and the cosmic bodies, these are all knitted together through the spirit of self-sacrifice, so, that a new creation may emerge at every stage. The divine sage also explains in brief the journey of the soul—birth, death, and rebirth.

In the description of *'Panchagni'*, the Rishi tells that *'Shraddha'* or *'Bhava'* with meditative unity is poured as an oblation in *Dyuloka* (the heavenly region beyond Sun); and as a consequence of that the lunar world comes into existence. Then moonlight wrapped with *'Bhava'* (thought) itself becomes an oblation and *'Parjanya'* comes into existence. *'Parjanya'* (rain) is the second fire. When the rain pours on earth which is the third fire, the consequence is food. When the food is offered to man, who is considered to be the fourth fire, the seed of life comes into existence. The fifth fire is the woman who accepts the seed and for which the reward is the most familiar emergence of life witnessed at childbirth.

The sixth Chapter of Chandogya Upanishad opens with a very enlightening and interesting dialogue between the most revered sage Uddalaka and his 24 years old son Svetaketu. When Svetaketu Aruneya was 12 years old, his father Rishi Uddalaka asked him to go to *Gurukul* for initiation into the study of Vedas and other holy scriptures. Svetaketu honored his father's advice. He went to *Gurukul*, and after completing his education, he returned home greatly conceited, arrogant, thinking himself well read and quite opinionated. His father welcomed him warmly but also noticed the young man's conceit. The wise sage approached his son politely and inquired, if he knew that by knowing which the unhearable becomes heard, the unperceivable becomes perceived, and unknowable becomes known. Svetaketu, in his great amazement, looked at his father and said, "O' Venerable Sir, how can there be such instruction? What is the knowledge by which everything else is known?" The great sage asserted, in fact, there is the knowledge, which makes everything else known in the universe. He gave his answer with simple examples saying, "My child just as through one lump of clay, all that is made of clay is known, just as through one nugget of gold alone all that is made of gold becomes known, just as through one nail-clipper everything made of iron is known; all modifications are just names, only verbalizations based upon words—exactly so, is that knowledge of the 'Self' which makes everything else known. Just as by analyzing the components of only one drop of water, the quality of the entire water reservoir becomes known, similarly by the subjective experience of indwelling-soul, everything else in the universe becomes known."

The dialogue becomes interesting when the divine sage unfolds the mysteries of Supreme spirit, 'One' only, without a second that has entered into the entire creation. The whole universe has come into existence from 'One *Bhava*' or 'One thought' that forms the seed of primal will: "*Bahu syam prajayeti*"—which means, "May I be many." Just one thought becomes the creative force, when energized by the Supreme spirit. The thought "Let me be many" started at the beginning of the creation and is still powerful. Everything in nature is spreading out, forming various roots, seeds, and eggs. Every seed brings forth millions of similarities. Every seed has the inherent desire to become a tree, then again the tree has the inherent desire—'Let me be many' so the cycle goes on. It applies to all beings and everything in the macrocosm as well as in the microcosm. In the human body the cells are constantly splitting and giving birth to new cells. The old cells are dying and being replaced by the new ones. So, it is indeed the inherent desire "Let me be many," which is primordial, yet, still fresh all around in creation. Everything in the universe is the sequential revelation of this mysterious power, which is manifesting through every little molecule and every atom. The entire universe is the orchestration of that 'One' only without a second. That is the subtle essence of all—that is the Truth '*Sat*' that is the *Atman*. "Thou art That 'O' Svetaketu." The subtlety of the Supreme-soul is totally incomprehensible by human mind and intellect.

In this reference the Rishi tells Svetaketu to bring a fruit of the *Nyagrodha* tree, and instructs him to break it. When he breaks it open, the Rishi inquires, "What do you see there?"

Svetaketu answers, "Some seeds extremely small Venerable Sir." The Rishi further instructs, "Now break the seed and tell me what is inside the seed." Svetaketu looks at the broken seed and says, "There is nothing inside the seed. Nothing at all, Venerable Sir." Then the Rishi enunciates that although there is nothing visible inside the seed, still the seed does have all the information to become a tree. The invisible inside the seed which has no name and form is the pure being—the essence of life. That is the Truth '*Sat*' that is the *Atman*. "Thou art That O' Svetaketu." The great sage Uddalaka enlightens his son step by step about the magnificence of the Supreme spirit that prevails at the substratum of the universe. He affirms that the man of wisdom, who is perennially established in the knowledge of the Self, does recognize it instantly. He remains firmly grounded in the consciousness of the soul, and perceives the presence of *Brahman* in everything in the world.

Chapter seven of Chandogya Upanishad, which is a continuation of the theme discussed earlier opens with the most exalting dialogue between Narada and Sanatkumara, in which the divine sage unveils the truth, that in order to comprehend the mysteries of the infinite, the person does not need much pre-requisite in scriptural knowledge and philosophy. The true knowledge of the Self is inherently present in everybody; it becomes revealed when the individual resorts to the tranquility of the Self and remains aware of the inner unity from moment to moment.

The path of sincere devotion has been upheld to be the

noblest and highly rewarding in spiritual journey. The divine teacher Sanatkumara guides his disciple Narada step by step from gross to the subtle and then into the subtlest experiences of the Self. He gives a hierarchy of the various levels of consciousness. First of all, he advises Narada to meditate on 'Name' as *Brahman*—the ultimate reality. He further adds, that subtler than 'Name' is the speech and subtler than speech is the mind, subtler than mind is the *sankalpa*—'will', and indeed subtler than 'will' is the intellect. Contemplation assuredly is subtler than intellect and beyond that, is the insight, the subtlest understanding and so on. It is the progressive expansion of consciousness; that gradually leads Narada into the realization of Absolute Truth. He is introduced to the characteristics of the finite as well as the luminosity of the infinite. Sanatkumara concludes that when the heart is purified, there is constant remembrance of the God which leads to inner unity. Gradually the knots of bondage are released and the aspirant is blessed with the vision of the Supreme divinity that ushers to the shore of freedom.

In chapter eight section seven of Chandogya, is another interesting dialogue between Prajapati, Indra, and Virochana. The first mantra of this chapter declares, "That soul is free from impurities, from old age and death, from sorrow, hunger, and thirst, whose desire is the truth, whose resolve is the truth, is to be sought after, is to be inquired, is to be realized. He who knows about the soul obtains all the worlds and all the desires" (8.7.1). Having heard about the magnificence of the soul, both gods and the demons decided to seek the profound secret of the soul. Thereupon, Indra on behalf of gods and Virochana on behalf of demons, without communicating with each other approached the renowned teacher Prajapati with deep humility. Both were instructed to live there for 32 years and lead the disciplined life of a student of sacred knowledge. After the period of living as *brahmchari* and going through other austerities, they requested Prajapati for instructions into the knowledge of the *Atman* (soul). Prajapati told them that the one seen in the eye is the immortal-Self, that is *Brahman*. He further added, that the one that is seen reflected in water and mirror, is also the Self.

Later they were asked to put on their rich garments and look into the water. Indra and Virochana gazed on their reflections in the water and returning to Prajapati they said, "Sir we have seen the Self, exactly like ourselves." To that Prajapati added, "The Self, seen in these, that is immortal, the fearless, that is *Brahman*." Both Indra and Virochana were quite convinced that the reflection was the soul, they did not ask any question and went away satisfied. Unfortunately, they mistook the physical-self (the body) for the Higher-Self that is seen and not the seer. The Self who sees through the eyes and other senses is the seer; Prajapati meant that to be the *Atman*—fearless and immortal. He wanted them to look into the Truth behind the veil (the body)and not accept everything based upon the inherited habits of perceptual thinking about the world.

On his way back to gods in heaven, Indra analyzed the statement. He reasoned that the body goes through modifications and dies. Therefore it could not be the imperishable, immutable, and immortal soul. He decided to go back to Prajapati for further instruction. Prajapati asked him to live with him for another 32 years in austerity. After that he told Indra, "He who moves about happy in dreams, that is the self." But even this did not satisfy Indra because the dreaming-self is also subject to pleasure and pains, loss and gain, etc. So he requested the teacher for the clarification. Prajapati suggested him to spend another 32 years, observing strict discipline; and then he explained to Indra that when a man goes in dreamless, deep sleep and is at perfect rest, calm and peaceful that is the Self—The *Brahman*, the fearless and immortal. Indra pondered over the words, immortal and immutable, and he analyzed that in dreamless, deep sleep, in fact, the person is not conscious of any existence at all, this state is next to total annihilation. So once again he returned to Prajapati expressing his doubts about the nature of the Self. The teacher asked Indra to live with him for another five years. Thus, it is only after Indra lived the disciplined life of a student of true knowledge, Prajapati considered him receptive to understand the highest truth and secret of *Brahmavidya*.

Prajapati opened the conversation saying, "O' Maghavan (Indra), this body is mortal, always gripped by death, but within the physical body dwells the immortal Self. The body goes through changes between birth and death but Supreme-soul remains unchanging and immutable. It is due to the false identification of the embodied-self with mind and body that the individual becomes disconnected from the eternal truth. He becomes weak, fearful and disintegrated." Prajapati affirmed that, "Rising above the body consciousness, knowing the soul to be distinct from the senses and the mind, perceiving the self within the Self—one rejoices and is free." With the realization of this distinction between the body and the soul, the individual becomes acquainted with his true nature which is calm, peaceful and luminous. Anyone who experiences himself as *Atman* (soul), he never loses his contact with the source of Bliss even in the middle of everything in the world; for him the presence of soul becomes the only reality to be meditated upon. The gods, or *Sura*, who are always in tune with the luminosity of the Self, perpetually aligned with the source, they obtain all the worlds and all desires. They always live in Bliss and share the Bliss with everyone. In the world of mortals, anyone who remains grounded in the purity of the Self and perceives the distinction between the body and Self, he is blessed with everything in the world.

The other profound message conveyed in this dialogue is that the sacred knowledge of the Self can't be attained at one leap. It is acquired through a methodical endeavor, purity of mind and dedicated disciplined austerities. It is the progressive spiritualization of the embodied-self that opens the doorway into realms of transcendental-Self, and unity with the soul.

Brihadaranyaka Upanishad

Brihadaranyaka Upanishad, which is generally recognized to be the quintessence of Vedic philosophy, forms an important part of the *Shatapatha Brahmana*. It is a vast collection of spiritual treatises such as the creation of the world, the place of human beings in it, and the deep mysteries of Supreme-soul. The well-known teachings of the great sage Yajnavalkya, which includes the most enlightening debate between the great seer and the other scholars; the philosophical discussions with King Janaka, and the famous dialogue with his wife Maitreyi, have created an increased interest in the study of this Upanishad. There are many translations of this highly revered Upanishad, written by a number of scholars within a century, both in the East and in the West. The ancient commentary on Brihadaranyaka Upanishad has been written by Sri Adi Shankaracharya, which has always served as the most valuable guide for many commentators.

Brihadaranyaka Upanishad consists of three *khandas* (sections), i.e. *Madhu-khanda*, *Muni-khanda*, and *Khila-khanda*. The *Madhu-khanda* dwells upon the teachings of the basic identity of the embodied–self and the cosmic-self, the Yajnavalkya or the *Muni-khanda* provides the glimpses of analytical understanding of mysteries of Supreme *Para-brahman* and the *Khila-khanda* deals with specific modes of worship and meditation. Each khanda is imbued with philosophical teachings par-excellence.

Madhu-khanda conveys the main teachings of the *Advaita* doctrine and also presents the glimpses of the co-relation that exists between the individuals and their cosmic counterparts. The first two *Brahmanas* (parts) of *Madhu-khanda* deal with the performance of Vedic rituals meant for inner purification, and to harmonize the diverse constituents of the physical, psychological, and spiritual Self. The divine sage also explains the interdependence in nature and how the entire work-order is mutually connected. In the fifth, the sage illustrates that earth, water, fire, air, Sun, space, Moon, lightning, and thunder are like honey for all creatures and all beings are honey for them. The great pervasive intelligence that holds everything together is the pure luminous Self—the *Brahman*. The sage further clarifies the truth and tells that the Moon is honey to all beings; all beings are honey to the Moon. It is the same immortal being in the Moon and also in the creatures, who is identified with mind and body, who is the Supreme-soul as well as the individual-soul—the essence of all—'The *Brahman*'.

The Self, verily, is the Lord of all beings. As all the spokes are held together in the hub and felly of a wheel, even so all beings, all creatures, all gods, all worlds, all lives are held together in the Self. Contemplating on that luminous consciousness which is at the root of the entire manifestation is being acquainted with everything else within and without.

The fourth *Brahmana* (part) of the fourth chapter introduces the great Vedic scholar Yajnavalkya in a very interesting dialogue with his wife Maitreyi, where the great sage enlightens his wife about the subtle truth of our relationship with everybody and everything in the universe. He tells her that it is not for the sake of the husband that the husband is dear, but for the sake of the Self. It is not for the sake of wife that the wife is dear, but for the sake of the Self. It is not for the sake of sons that sons are dear, but for the sake of the Self, and so on. It is the bonding with the indwelling *Atman* (soul) which gives meaning to our relationship with others. sage Yajnavalkya wants Maitreyi to understand how the world of diversity with beings and non-beings, animate and inanimate is centered and settled in "one" unity of the Supreme-soul. The subtlety of the *Atman* (soul) is totally incomprehensible by human mind and intellect. Although the Supreme power appears to be divided among creatures, still it is undivided. The appropriate analogy which can be given in this context is that of the hologram; in which any piece separated from the hologram carries with it the totality of the object. In the language of the modern era the supreme-soul can be described as a holographic entity. The cosmic-soul is the omnipotent substratum from where plurality of the world is projected.

The sage emphasizes, the duly regulated scheme of *Shravana* (hearing), *Manan* (reflecting), and *Nididhyasna* (meditating) for self-realization. He makes it very clear that in order to comprehend the essentiality of the Supreme-Self, the aspirant has to go through these three steps. The first one *Shravana* means listening with profound respect to the guidance of the teacher, then *Manan*, which means reflection and introspection, and later *Nididhyasna* means the subjective experience in meditation. He further adds that the knowledge of the Self is the gateway to immortality.

The Upadesha in *Madhu-khanda* is appropriately and gloriously followed by the expository discourse in *Muni-khanda*. It starts with the first *Brahmana* (part) of the third chapter. Here the great spiritual teacher Yajnavalkya appears as a stalwart dialectician in King Janaka's assembly of learned philosophers and speaks intelligently and constructively towards his way to victory in elucidating the philosophical truth. It seems once the wise King Janaka on a certain occasion performed a *yajna* (sacrifice) at which many gifts were given to the priests and the learned sages. Many Vedic scholars of Kurus and Panchala had assembled there. King Janaka had a desire to know who was the most learned among the Brahmins gathered there. As a reward he had decided to offer one thousand cows, each adorned with ten gold coins tied between their horns. The king declared in the assembly, "O' Venerable Brahmins, let the greatest Vedic scholar, the wisest among you, take these cows home." No one came forward, then Yajnavalkya stood up and asked his disciple Samasrava to take home all the cows. The pupil followed the instructions instantly, but that created a commotion in the assembly. The rest of the Brahmins felt insulted and raised their voices saying, "How dare he call himself to be the wisest?" At last

Ashvala, the royal priest of King Janaka, came forward saying, "Yajnavalkya, are you quite sure you are the most learned and wisest amongst us?" The great sage Yajnavalkya who had a sense of humor replied with humility saying, "I salute to the greatest Vedic scholar, I only wish to have the cows." Thereupon Ashvala the royal priest resolved to ask him some questions. He asked questions in reference to sacrifice, the modes of worship, also about gods and the special hymns to be chanted for alignment of the physical, psychological, and spiritual realms. After Ashvala, sage Artabhaga appeared on the scene, and later they were followed by great intellectuals in the assembly.

The most enlightening dialogue in the assembly was between Yajnavalkya and the lady philosopher, Gargi, who stood as the most outstanding personality among the philosophical interlocutors, and asked some intriguing questions, in reference to *Brahmatattva*. The great sage Yajnavalkya's answers to the highly philosophical questions of Gargi constitute one of the most memorable passages of the entire debate at the palace of King Janaka. The speakers at King Janaka's court were distinguished scholars, who disclosed their contradictions and then synthetically resolved each one of them with mutual respect. Yajnavalkya had to face an intense volley of intellectual questions, but he was able to hold the discussion very intelligently, gave a profound answer to each question, and emerged being the wisest in the assembly of the great Vedic scholars.

The third *Brahmana* (part) of the fourth chapter in *Muni-khanda* also presents an inspiring dialogue between the King Janaka and the sage Yajnavalkya. Once, when the sage Yajnavalkya was present at the palace of the King Janaka, the king asked him a question with deep humility, "O' venerable sage, what is the light by which a man lives?" The sage answered, "The light of the Sun." The king asked again, "When there is no Sunlight, what is the light by which a man lives?" The sage answered, "It is the light of the Moon." The king asked further, "When there is no Moonlight, then what is the light by which a man lives?" The wise sage answered, "O' King; it is the fire by which a man lights the lamp and performs the activities." The king queried further, "After the Sun and Moon have both set, and the fire is extinguished, what serves as a light for man?" The sage replied, "O' King! The sound serves as his light and guides him to find his way and to perform his activities." The King inquired further; 'O' sage it is true indeed, but for a man who is deaf and cannot hear any sound, so what serves as his light?" To that the sage answered, "O' King the 'Self' indeed serves as his light. It is through the light of the Self, he moves around and performs all the activities of life. It is the light of the Self, that illumines the inner world as well as the outer. It is the light of the Self, which energizes every little molecule in the universe and every little cell in our body. This light is the inner intelligence, the Supreme-soul residing in our body and everywhere around." The Supreme-Self is ever luminous, omniscient, uniform, changeless, and immutable. It is the identification of the soul with the body, and attachment to the modes of nature, which becomes the cause of bondage, and the repeated rounds of birth in good and evil wombs. The slavery of the individual-self goes on until the embodied-self realizes his true identity with the Supreme-Self. The sage Yajnavalkya draws King Janaka's attention to the truth which enlightens the King about the subtle nature of the soul and discovery of Supreme-Self within the Self.

The *Khila-Khanda* of Brihadaranyaka Upanishad illustrates certain modes of meditation. Here the great Rishi asserts the inherently divine nature of man and elucidates in detail the means and methods to manifest this divinity. The subtle teachings of this Upanishad are encapsulated in the soul-elevating hymn *abhyaroha-mantra, "Aum Asato ma sad gamaya, tamso ma jyotir gamaya, mrityorma amritam gamaya"* (Brih.1.3.28) meaning—"O' God, lead me from untruth to truth, from darkness to light and from death to immortality." This is the prayer of *Jivatma* (embodied-soul) seeking freedom from the masks of dualities and ultimate alignment with the Supreme-soul. It is the progressive realization of the Self that leads the individual from less awareness to increased awareness, from darkness to light, from ignorance to inner enlightenment, from masks of duality into unity with the pure luminous-Self and at last from bondage to freedom. It is a prayer for *Atmabodha* which means, "The experiential knowledge of pure-consciousness and the blessed experience of immortality."

The most revered teachings of Brihadaranyaka also include the profound key statement called *Mahavakya—Aham brahmasmi*—I am *Brahman*—I am the totality—the pure consciousness that prevails at the substratum of the universe. This *Mahavakya* is generally given by a spiritual teacher to his disciple in initiation. The *Mahavakya*, '*Aham brahmasmi*' can set up quite powerful vibration in the body and verbally assert union with the pure consciousness. In prayerful recitation of '*Aham brahasmi*' the sound flows very easily with the breath, assimilates quickly with the thought pattern and gradually leads the aspirant to cosmic unity. It is the experience of being restored to the wholeness of *Parabrahman* and freedom from the intrigues of duality—'Free at last'. It is the highest peak of human aspiration—I am the totality. It is the state of infinite Bliss, *Mukti, Moksha*, or *Nirvana*.

The essential message of Brihadaranyaka Upanishad is summed up in the most exalted hymn—"*Aum purnamadah purnamidam purnat purnam udacyate, purnasya, purnamadaya, purnamevavashyatate,*" (Brih.5.1.1), meaning, "That is the whole, this is the whole, the whole comes out of the whole; even when the whole comes out of the whole, what is left behind is also whole." Everything in the macrocosm as well as the microcosm declares the wholeness of the Supreme-soul—the all-pervasive consciousness. A seed becomes a tree and generates thousands of seeds, each seed from the tree is complete in itself and has the potential to become a tree again;

similarly in our body, when one cell splits into two, nothing is lost; each cell is complete in itself. That is infinite, this is infinite. The infinite emanates from the infinite, even when the infinite proceeds from the infinite, there still remains the infinite.

Shvetashvatara Upanishad

Shvetashvatara Upanishad belongs to Yajurveda. It derives its name from the sage who shared its teachings with his disciples. It is a short Upanishad consisting of only 113 hymns, divided into six chapters. It is not one of the most ancient Upanishads, yet because of the profundity of its teachings, many of its hymns have been quoted by the great commentators in support of their doctrines. This Upanishad introduces the elements associated with theism, such as identifying the Supreme *Brahman* with Rudra or Lord Shiva. Devotion to personal God becomes more prominent and explicit in Shvetashvatara Upanishad. The Absolute with Name is the distinguished feature of this Upanishad. The divine sage has tried to reconcile *Jnana, Bhakti* and other paths of spiritual life. He has synthesized different philosophical and religious ideals that were prevalent at the time of its composition.

The Upanishad begins with an informal discussion among the students of the Vedas, desirous to know the eternal verities of life. It opens with the basic questions such as, "What is the cause of this universe—is it *Brahman*? Whence are we born? Why do we live? Where is our final rest? Under whose command are we bound by the law of happiness and misery? Time, inherent nature, *Niyati* (the law of karma), chance, matter (the five elements), the primal energy, womb, *Purusha* or *Jivatma*—none of these nor a combination of these, can be the final cause of the universe, for they also are effects and exist to serve the soul. Even the individual-self cannot be the cause being subject to the law of pleasure and pain, it is not free."

After quiet reflection and meditation, these *brahmavadinis* (students) perceived within themselves the luminous power of the Divine, that remains hidden behind the veil of *Gunas*—*Sattva*, *Rajas*, and *Tamas*. The indwelling-soul, that is experienced in deep meditation is essentially one with Supreme-soul; but also distinct because of its separate self-assumed identity with the modes of nature (three *Gunas*). The *Gunas* are the primary constituents of nature and are surely the cause of bondage for the embodied-soul. These qualities—the '*Sattva*, *Rajas*, and *Tamas*', bind the pure imperishable soul into the strings of conditioned behavior and into the repeated rounds of birth, death, and rebirth. These modes of nature definitely create confusion for the individual-soul and the latter forgets its true identity. As a matter of fact, the entire creation is a drama, orchestrated by these three qualities inherent in Mother Nature.

In the next few hymns from the fourth onward, the world is metaphorsized with a wheel, *Brahmachakra,* in which the embodied-soul flutters about identifying with the three *Gunas*, and moves into the repeated rounds of birth, death, and rebirth. The infinite spirit feels finite and bound in all respects. It revolves upon the wheel, in bondage to the laws of karma. *Brahmachakra* indicates the subservience of all beings to the command of the triad of nature. The realization of the Supreme-soul beyond the slavery of *Gunas* is realized, when *Jivatma* (individual-soul) starts identifying with the pure luminous indwelling-soul. In the process of self-revelation the *Jivatma* is reminded of his Divinity and primordial relationship with the Supreme-soul. The person is awakened to the Truth that the pure luminous soul is indeed the essence of everything in the universe. The mantra (1.15) of this Upanishad explains this concept gloriously: "Just as the oil in the sesame seeds, butter hidden in the curd, water in the sediments of the spring, fire in the wood, so is the Supreme Divinity veiled within one's own Self and can be perceived by true austerity and knowledge of the soul."

In the second chapter of this Upanishad, the importance of prayer and meditation has been highly glorified, as the most valuable means for inner awakening and the subjective experience of ultimate reality. It is through regular practice of meditation that the individual is introduced to the masks of triad in nature as well as to the luminosity of the indwelling pure-self. In the hymns 2.8 onwards, the procedure of going into meditation and the experience of inward vision have been explained step by step. First of all, it is important to find a quiet place for meditation. A secluded place, like a forest, mountain peak, or a cave is ideal, because it helps the inner thoughts and feelings to blend with the serenity and purity of nature. The importance of a quiet and clean place has been highly recommended because during the meditation period, when the nerves are being trained to go into peace, even the slightest disturbance can create imbalance and deviate the attention from the goal in contemplation. The recommended posture for meditation requires the proper alignment of lower back, neck, shoulder, and head. This is the vertical alignment which helps the mind to withdraw attention from the body and enter into the silence of the soul where the yogi conceives the vision, in forms, which resemble fog, smoke, sun, wind, fireflies, lightning, crystal, and moon. These are the signs that indicate the gradual success in practice of *Dhyanayoga* (meditation). As the aspirant moves into the realms of pure-consciousness, the mind feels relaxed; and exhilarates in yogic unity with Supreme *Parabrahman*. When the yogi perceives the *Brahmatattva* through the light of *Atmatattva* (soul), he is liberated from all impurities and all fetters.

In chapter three of Shvetashvatara Upanishad the highest reality is identified with Rudra (Shiva), "who rules all these worlds with his ruling powers. He creates the entire universe, sustains it, and withdraws it, into himself eventually." Rudra is the bestower of exalted joy, peace, happiness, and master of everything and everyone involved in the play of life. In the hymns starting from 3.2 the divine sage declares with the most melodious words, *"Eko hi Rudro na dwityaesthu,"*meaning, "Truly Rudra is 'One' without a second." The great Rishi sings the adoration of Lord Rudra in profound reverence and heartfelt devotional love. It is a very spontaneous gesture of the one who has experienced the spiritual intimacy with the indwelling-soul, in deep exuberance. It is the exalted state of being overjoyed at the immanence of the Lord. The seer calls upon Rudra, the primal, ancient *Purusha* and the ultimate support of the universe, who is the knower and also the ultimate object of all knowledge. The Rishi pays respectful salutation to the Lord Shiva from the depth of his heart.

These hymns are highly melodious, poetic and also deeply philosophical. The Supreme Divinity is addressed as Rudra, Shiva, Shankara, and Maheshwara. The intimacy that is expressed in these hymns reflects the primordial relationship of *Jivatma* (individual-soul) and *Paramatma* (cosmic-soul). The Absolute *Brahman* pervades the entire creation. The hymn 3.14 explains that the Supreme being, who has thousands of heads, thousands of eyes and feet, and envelops the entire universe; though transcendent can be intimated as residing in the lotus of heart, at the center of the body only ten fingers above the navel. Also the mantras from 3.16 to 3.17 describe the omniscience of the Lord jubilantly, "His hands and feet are everywhere, his eyes and faces are in all directions. He exists in the world enclosing everything within. The super power can be experienced by everyone through the functions of the sensory organs and still transcends everything." The aspirant who takes refuge in the Lord with intellectual apprehension of truth, coupled with proper insight and devotion, he surely conceives the subtlety of the *Atman* (soul) and perceives the Self, by the Self, within the Self, and declares, "I know Him" (3.21).

The hymns in chapter six are also very melodious in which the great sage sings the glories of the Supreme Lord in ecstasy of divine love. It is indeed in the Shvetashvatara Upanishad, where the metaphysical speculations culminate into a subjective experience and loving adoration of God. The sage indicates that it is not merely the intellectual comprehension; it is surely the deep subjective apprehension, which makes the experience of indweller possible. Blessed are those who constantly live in the awareness of the indwelling soul with love and devotion, they are definitely liberated from the impurities of mind and attain unity with God. The aspirant who is awakened to the Blissful State of inner tranquility, he appreciates and enjoys the proximity of the Lord with genuinely aroused devotion and dedication. He worships the Lord from the very core of his being and from the totality of his heart. He feels elevated, exhilarated and exalted in every moment of life. The echo of inner unison helps him to maintain his devotional ecstasy. It keeps the covenants renewed perpetually. An aura of ineffable devotion and dedication prevails over his mind, which keeps him charged with the unique power of yogic communion. After the experience of the indwelling-soul in yogic unity the person becomes aligned with the entire universe. He is blessed to perceive the 'One' existing in many and the many existing in 'One' (6.11). The entire universe is pervaded by God alone. He serves the Lord through each and every one of his activities by constant adoration and meditation. Absolute surrender to God with innocence, honest devotion, and determination is indeed the most reliable and all-sufficing method of God-realization. Let the Supreme Lord possess the individual and become the means and goal simultaneously.

"Steadfastness, forbearance, self-restraint, non-stealing, purity of mind and body, control over the sense-organs, illumined intellect, knowledge of the Self, truthfulness, and absence of anger—these ten are the hallmarks of *Dharma*."

Manusmriti (6.92)

"Non-violence, truthfulness, non-avarice, purity of thoughts, words and deeds, and self-control are the *Dharma* of mankind, so said Manu"

Manusmriti (10.63)

3

Manusmriti

Manusmriti, also known as *The Ordinances of Manu,* holds a revered place amongst the other sacred scriptures of Hindu religion. *Smriti* as the word explains itself, is the knowledge reproduced in different versions based on the sacred knowledge of ancient literature. Manusmriti was compiled during the early centuries of Vedic Era as a codification of the guiding rules for the proper management of society in almost all walks of human life, according to time and place. It is a compendium of ancient wisdom, systematically epitomizing the rules of practice in religion, political, social, and cultural life of people. It outlines the laws for the organization of a peaceful society; the administration of a country; source of revenue; methods of conducting trade, business, provisions for good education and medical care, and also the punishment of criminals and offenders. The institutes of sacred law proclaimed by Manu in Vedic times, however modified and changed to some extent throughout the history, still serves as a decisive authority in various fields of life in Hindu society. Dr. Coke Burnell, a well known scholar and educator, who translated *The Ordinances of Manu,* says,

"However, it is not merely for the terse exposition of tenets that this work is important; it sums up an ideal or a philosophy of life which has provided substance and sustenance to its followers."

The ethical code of Manu was written for the proper development of society, where everybody would live with mutual respect, in peace and harmony with each other, and promote economic progress, better standards of life and freedom. This great work of the learned sage Manu opens the door to the understanding of the entire subsequent social structure of Hindu society in the Vedic Era. In the words of Dr. R. N. Sharma, "It is a standard and most authoritative work on Hindu law and presents the normal form of Hindu society and civilization. It is a storehouse of information on social, cultural, religious, ethical, educational, political, judicial and geographical life of the period and this is perfectly natural." He further says, "Manu's importance in Indian history lies in the fact that it was he, who gave the stamp of sanctity and permanence to the Socio-political institutions of land and left to Indian world the first code of civil and criminal laws."

For example, in reference to the rights and duties of a King, there is a verse in Manusmriti which indicates that the person who has the clear understanding of the four-fold sacred path of *Dharma* (Virtue), *Artha* (Wealth), *Kama* (Pleasure), and *Moksha* (Liberation) and upholds righteousness under all circumstances is truly a King. It is further added that even the King who deviates from the path of *Dharma* should be duly punished. It is the duty of the King to yield to the power and submit to punishment for the breaches of *Dharma*. The ethical values, as set by the laws of *Dharma* was itself deemed to be the real restoring power over King's court. In the words of Charles Drekmeier, "The Hindu king never enjoyed the immunity that accompanied the European concept of the divine right of kings. Rather than divine right, we must speak of divine obligation; the duty of the King to protect the social order."

Manu's greatness among the lawgivers of antiquity like Hammurabi's is self-evident. In short, Manusmriti has commanded great respect and authority for centuries and is still an indispensable guide to the understanding of ancient Indian social order. It provides remarkable guidance, which embraces almost all facets of human life. Ever since the first English translation of Manusmriti by Sir William Jones in 1794 became known to the educators in Europe, the book has won the interest and admiration of several well-known scholars in England, France, Germany, Russia, and other countries. Manusmriti has been translated, edited, and published by many erudite commentators in India as well as in foreign countries. Among the Sanskrit and Hindi works, the commentaries of Medhatithi, Govindaraja, Kullukabatta, Raghvananda, as well as of Sarvajnanarayana have been quite popular and consulted by many scholars and men of letters from time to time. The law codes of Manu have been translated into English by Sir William Jones in 1794 and G. C. Houghton in 1825, later Hüttner Loiserleur Deslongchamps in

German and Elmanevich in French respectively.

Although there are a variety of topics in the book in reference to an ideal cultured setup in society, but the most popular ones are referred to *Varna-Ashrama-Dharma*, which means, the respective duties and rights of an individual in the different spheres of life i.e. the four *Ashramas* (stages), the Caste System, and the Hindu *Samskaras* (sacraments).

The Four Ashramas or Stages of Life

The great Seers of the Holy Vedas have declared jubilantly that every person should aspire to live a healthy, happy, and prosperous life for 100 years while following the four-fold sacred formula *Dharma* (Virtue), *Artha* (Wealth), *Kama* (Pleasure), *Moksha* (Liberation). The first three i.e., *Dharma-Artha-Kama*, constitute the path of *Pravrithi*, which means, active involvement in the world as a responsible member of family and society. The fourth one, *Moksha* guides the individual towards the path of *Nivrithi*, which means renunciation and liberation.

Maharishi Manu has divided the ideal span of 100 years into four successive stages of life or 'Four *Ashramas*', namely *Brahmacharya, Garhasthya, Vanaprastha,* and *Sannyasa*, each of which is marked by specific responsibilities and obligations. The *Ashrama* System was believed to be in accordance with the laws of *Dharma*, and it was considered to be the sacred duty of every person to follow it respectfully. These four stages of life that formed an ideal course of intellectual, psychological, and spiritual growth helped the individual in his journey to the pursuit of truth, self-realization, and God-realization.

(1) Brahmacharya Ashrama

The first 25 years are *Brahmacharya Ashrama*—the stage that covers the period of good education in life. This is the time when the student cultivates his special abilities and prepares himself for future service to society. The youngster is expected to be devoted to the attainment of knowledge in his or her selected field of education and also observes abstinence.

(2) Garhasthya Ashrama

The second stage of life from 25 to 50 years is the stage of a householder or family man; which has been upheld to be the most honorable and respectable of the four *Ashramas* because a married couple supports the other three *Ashramas* and also the society. In reference to respect for *Garhasthya Ashrama* says Swami Nikhilananda in his lectures on Hinduism, "Husband and wife are co-partners in their spiritual growth, and the family provides a training ground for the practice of unselfishness. A healthy householder is the foundation for a good society, discharging his duties as a teacher, soldier, statesman, merchant, scientist, or manual worker. He should be ambitious to acquire wealth and enjoy comforts but not by deviating from the path of righteousness." This is the time to make the best use of the intellectual and professional abilities, to raise a good family and participate enthusiastically in the economic growth of society. At this second stage of life the fourfold purpose i.e. *Dharma-Artha-*

Kama-Moksha is actualized in all dimensions and the abstract truths and the aphorisms of the Holy scriptures become clear and distinct to understand.

(3) Vanaprastha Ashrama

The third stage of life, which is from 50 to 75 years, is *Vanaprastha Ashrama*, wherein the individual gradually prepares himself to retire from the worldly activities. He lives a simple life, and spends more time in the study of sacred scriptures, mantra meditation, performance of appropriate rituals according to the scriptural injunctions, and selfless service to society.

(4) Sannyasa Ashrama

This is the next stage of life anywhere from the age of 75 to 100 when a person is ready to withdraw himself completely from social obligations and spend maximum time in yoga, meditation, the devotional love of God, and service to humanity. He lives in utmost simplicity. Even though not living at the Ashram in a remote forest, the individual becomes very detached from family and remains perpetually absorbed in the ecstasy of divine love and surrenders his will to the will of God. Maharishi Manu had planned the *Ashrama* system in a very organized manner, that while exiting from the previous and entering into the next stage, the individual willingly and naturally discards each layer of attachment to the previous, so much so, that by the time he enters the *Sannyasa* he feels like a citizen of the world and dedicates his life to the service of mankind.

In accordance with the four stages of life thus outlined by the divine sage Manu, the life becomes enjoyable, creative, productive, calm, and peaceful at every step. "The four-fold plan of life still prevails in Hindu families," says Dr. S. Radhakrishnan, "Every state is necessary and so far as it is necessary it is good. The blossom does not deny the leaf and the leaf does not deny the stalk nor the stalk the root. The general rule is that we should pass from stage to stage gradually."

The Caste System (Varna-Dharma)

The classification into four types of work-order based upon the intrinsic qualities and inborn inclinations of human beings has been defined as the caste system or *Varna-Dharma* in Manusmriti and other ancient scriptures. In the olden days when people lived in small groups and started to form communities, they gradually realized that they had naturally divided themselves into four major categories. The division took place quite naturally according to the social needs and individual temperament of people. The system of division has helped the community in maintaining mutual respect, inter-dependence, cooperation, and perfect fellowship. The functions of the different classes were regarded as equally important to the well-being of the whole. The Vedic knowledge and serenity of the teachers, the patriotism and heroism of the soldiers, the enthusiasm and honesty of businessmen, the patience and loyalty of the servants and laborers, all contributed to the social growth of the country.

The four categories have been named Brahmin,

Kshatriya, Vaishya, and Shudra. This division, which was originally based on the inherent potential of the individuals, has been defined as caste system. The word 'caste' is self-explanatory—means the role a person has assigned himself to play in his lifetime for the time being. This specific role played by the person, born of his instinctive nature, becomes his assigned duty or *Dharma*. For example, serenity, self-control, asceticism, purity, forgiveness, simplicity, righteousness, honesty, knowledge of the scriptures, and strong faith in God are the characteristics of a Brahmin born of his innate nature. He is expected to teach the Holy scriptures, perform the religious rituals and guide other people into a pure lifestyle. A Brahmin is the one who lives in the consciousness of the supreme *Parabrahman* and manifests the purity of the Self through his thoughts, words, and deeds. His manners express proper alignment with the inner Divinity. His lifestyle is expected to be simple and the epitome of renunciation, self-dedication, self-sacrifice, and service to entire mankind. In ancient times the learned Brahmins, the Rishis, and the sages used to be on the advisory boards of Kings. Since the political and the economic life of the people is expected to derive its guidance from the Supreme-Self, the Kings always consulted these learned scholars for proper guidance in administration. These men of wisdom have been known as royal priests and royal sages who always looked into the true interests of society.

As a Brahmin is considered to be an embodiment of godliness, the other class (caste) which is next in scale is the Kshatriya; the embodiment of heroism, splendor, steadfastness, dexterousness, firmness in the battlefield, generosity, and lordliness. The Sanskrit aphorism *Kshtai trayate iti Kshatriya*—meaning, "The one who protects others from *Kshtai* (injury) is a Kshatriya." The duty of a Kshatriya is to enforce the laws of *Dharma* for the well-being of society. He should make sure that righteousness is being upheld in reverence and people are doing their duties, while keeping in mind the welfare of others. Whenever there is decline of ethical values, a Kshatriya class is expected to be alert and help the community in restoration of law and order. The protection of a country, society, and community is the first and foremost duty of a Kshatriya. To exhibit valor, heroism, patriotism, skill, promptitude, generosity, compassion, self-sacrifice, and self-confidence on the battlefield are other hallmarks of a genuine Kshatriya. The King as a Kshatriya ruler becomes the embodiment of God and his life becomes dedicated to the service of his citizens.

The next class in hierarchy of *Varna-Dharma* is that of Vaishyas—the businessmen or merchants. Agriculture, cattle-rearing and commercial operations are the duties performed by the Vaishyas born of their innate nature. The Vaishyas are endowed with special business talents and help the administrators with the economic growth of the country. The fourth category is that of Shudras the routine workers, the proletariat and laborers who are good at carrying out instructions and contribute only a small fraction of their inherent potentials.

This hierarchical distribution of people in conformity

with their personal choice or *Swabhava* means the inborn nature becomes conducive to the peace and progress of society. Each and every station of duty is very significant and holds its proper importance for the development of society. Spiritualism, introspectiveness, management, leadership, productivity, and service, these are the duties of the four character types based upon their innate natural disposition. In the words of Dr. S. Radhakrishnan, "*Varna* rule recognizes that different men contribute to the general good in different ways, by supplying directly urgent wants of which all are conscious and by being in their lives and work, witnesses to truth and beauty. Society is a functional organization and all functions, which are essential for the health of society, are to be regarded as socially equal. Individuals of varying capacities are bound together in a living organic social system. All men are not equal in their capacities but all men are equally necessary for society and their contributions from their different stations are of equal value." He further says, "While it was the intention of the scheme to develop the requisite spirit and tradition in the members of the classes by a proper employment of the forces of heredity and education, it was not viewed in a rigid way. In special cases individual and groups changed their social class. Sage Vishwamitra, Ajmidha, and Puramidha were admitted to the status of Brahmin class and even composed Vedic hymns. Yaska in his Nirukta tells us that of two brothers, Santanu and Devapi, one became a Kshatriya King and the other a Brahmin priest. Kavasa, the son of a slave girl, Ilusa, was ordained as a Brahman priest at a sacrifice. There was healthy social mobility and for long,

Varnas did not become hereditary, crystallized castes. In some of the old books it is clearly mentioned that the great Empire builders, the Nandas, the Mauryas, and Guptas were not from the Kshatriya class. Since many foreign tribes were absorbed in Hindu society they also made their adjustment according to their caliber."Manusmriti (10.65) documents this very clearly "A Shudra may switch to the cast of Brahmin and similary a Brahmin may switch to the caste of shudra."

There are many hymns in ancient Hindu scriptures that clearly indicate the truth that classification in society has originated and proceeded from the personal *Swabhava* (innate nature) of every individual. The word *Swabhava* combines two words—*Swa* means the indwelling-self and *bhava* means the thoughts. So *Swabhava* literally means "the conditioned-self." Every individual is guided by his own personal thoughts and inclinations and finds his fulfillment in the particular field of action as initiated by his inborn nature. The psychological make-up expresses itself in physical make-up and the personal choice of the individual. The division of work in society is psychological and universal. Sri Krishna tells in the Bhagawad Geeta that each and every individual is very special and it is the responsibility of a person to explore his or her unique potential and try to enhance it. The society should also provide the opportunity and means for the full expression of one's intrinsic nature 'the *Swabhava*' which eventually becomes one's own *Swadharma*. People everywhere follow the law of their own instinctive behavior and assign themselves the work accordingly. It is indeed so true that the four-fold system in society becomes created by itself—by the people, of the people, and for the people. Each and every individual is the creator of the role he has chosen for himself to play in his lifetime. A similar type of concept has been described by Gerald Heard in his book *Man the Master*. He writes, "It seems that there have always been present in human community four types or Strata consciousness. The Aryan-Sanskrit sociological thought, which first defined and named this four-fold structure of society, is as much ours as India's."

A famous verse in the great epic Mahabharata explains that all the people on Earth belonged to one class, they were all born as Brahmins and the four groups became established on account of their innate inclinations and occupation. The great scholar Rene Guenon also supports the theory of this classification in society based on the inborn nature of the individual in his famous book *Hindu Doctrines*. "The particular nature of each individual necessarily comprises from the beginning, all the tendencies and aptitudes which will be developed and manifested in the course of his existence, and which for instance, will determine his qualification for this or that social function, this being the point that more especially concerns us here." He further says, "It will be easily understood that we have here the basis of a organization that is truly hierarchical, that is to say in conformity with the nature of beings, following the interpretation we have given of the notion of *Dharma*."

The human evolution has not proceeded in one straight

line. It has gone through jerks from side to side with many ups and downs. It has always worked through the intertwined phases of physical, psychological, intellectual, spiritual, and the unknown. In the words of Sri Aurobindo, "There is always in human nature, something of all these four personalities, developed or undeveloped, wide or narrow, suppressed or rising to the surface, but in most men, one or the other tends to predominate and seems to take up sometimes the whole space of action in the nature. And in any society we should have all four types."

The divine sage Manu has made it quite clear that an empire needs some men of wisdom and scholars for proper guidance in day-to-day life and when the society is faced with conflict of duties. Every community needs research and scientific development for all kinds of progress and advancement. The muscular strength is essential for the protection of the nation and for maintaining law and order in the country. Economic growth, food, and trade are also mandatory for the harmonious development and manual labor is definitely required for the proper maintenance of society. Each and every station of duty is very significant for the balanced development of society. It is the sincere and enthusiastic attitude towards one's own self-assigned work that brings peace and satisfaction at the individual level as well as global.

Hindu Samskaras

The 16 *Samskaras* outlined in the Manusmriti, provide the basis of Hindu rites of passage. The word *Samskara* is a combination of two words—*Sams* and *Kara*—*Sams* means "all auspicious" or "which purifies" and *Kara* means "performance"; so *Samskara* means "the performance of certain rituals in order to give sanctity and purification to human thoughts and aspirations." The closest english word that explains the literal meaning of *Samskara* is the ritualistic sanctification or sacrament. Although fully blessed with subjective awareness of the indwelling Supreme-soul, inner knowledge, and wisdom: human beings still need guidance at every step. These sacred rituals are performed at various stages of the entire life, beginning from the time of conception in mother's womb until the last moment of death for the peaceful transition of the human soul to another world. The performance of these rituals helps the individual to stay aligned with the source of life and receive guidance from time to time in order to live a creative, productive, and virtuous life, which is in peace and harmony with society. The codes of virtuous living, explained during the performance of ceremonies, are etched in the deepest layers of consciousness as valuable impressions that motivate the entire range of activities during life and help the individual to stay on the right track under all circumstances.

As a matter of fact in classical Sanskrit literature, the word "*Samskara*" has been used with expanded meaning and contents. It is the performance of purificatory rituals in the interest of all-round human welfare; and also the word "*Samskara*" has been used in reference to the deep rooted thoughts, impressions, and latencies stored in the software of the soul from many previous lives that instigate new actions in the present life.

The moment when the baby is conceived in the mother's womb, it is the thoughts of the mother, the thoughts of the father, and the thoughts of the incoming soul, that enter together as one unified thought in the consciousness of the mother. This triple combination of thoughts and impressions —*Samskaras* expresses itself in the overall personality of a person. So every individual-soul enters the world with some positive aspirations but also with some negative impressions. With the performance of these *Samskaras* and by providing the aura which is conducive to moral values; the individual-soul remains aligned with the Supreme-soul and the lingering shadows of the negative thoughts and latencies start fading in the early years of life and the future growth becomes quite balanced, relaxed, and healthy. It is an effort to eliminate the hostile influences and seek blessings of the beneficial ones, so that a person may receive timely guidance and help from God for proper growth in all respect. When there is a proper development of mind, intellect and body, the person contributes substantially towards the economic growth and welfare of society.

In reference to this the great scholar F. Max Müller says, "The prescription of these ceremonies by the ancients disclose the deep rooted tendency in the heart of man, to bring the chief events of human life into contact with a higher power, and to give to our joys and sufferings a deeper significance and a religious sanctification."

The performance of *Samskaras* are quite educational for the person at the individual level as well as the family and the entire society at large. It promotes inner enlightenment, clarity of thoughts, and mutual respect. The great sage Manu realized the necessity of consciously molding and transforming the personality of an individual and made it very clear in his teachings that the human beings become blessed with divine qualities by good education, observing vows, and undergoing the ritualistic worships at the various stages of life.

In Manusmriti there is a detailed description of the 16 Samskaras from Chapter two onwards—in reference to *Varna-Ashrama-Dharma*. The sequence in which these rituals are performed over the entire course of lifetime is *Garbhadhana, Punsavana, Seemantonayana, Jaatkarma, Naamkarana, Nishkramana, Annaprashana, Chudakarama, Karnavedha, Upanayana, Vedarambha, Samavartana, Vivaha* and *Grahasthashrama, Vanaprastha, Sannyasa,* and *Antyeshti Samskara.*

(1) Garbhadhana Samskara

The auspicious ceremony in which a man seeks blessings for his wife to conceive a healthy baby is called *Garbhadhana Samskara*. The learned priest fixes the propitious day and time according to the astrological calculations and the ritual is solemnized in a set pattern. First of all both husband and wife invoke the blessings of Sun god, the giver of life on the planet. In Sun worship the water is offered facing east with special hymns; the water reflects the healing energy of the Sun and rejuvenates each and every cell in the body. Afterwards the husband recites the prayer hymns from Vedas and makes a request to the Supreme Divinity to help his wife conceive a healthy baby. At the time of *Garbhadhana Samskara*, some particular mantras are chanted in adoration of Lord Vishnu the bestower of boons and bounties in life. The worship of the nine celestial bodies also forms an important part of the rituals performed during the *Garbhadhana Samskara*. According to Vedic astrology these nine cosmic bodies, such as Sun, Moon, Mars, Mercury, Jupiter, Venus, Saturn, along with the ascending and descending nodes of Moon—known as Rahu and Ketu hold a strong relationship with human mind and body. In worship the husband seeks blessing for the conducive influence of the cosmic bodies for his wife at the time of conception. The couple also recites some prayers in the name of their ancestors to be blessed with noble children who will give continuity to the family lineage. At the completion of ceremonial worship, the elders in the family bless the couple.

(2) Punsavana Samskara

This ritual is performed in the second or third month of pregnancy when both the husband and wife express their gratitude to the Supreme Divinity and seek blessings for the healthy growth and protection of the baby in the mother's womb. They also recite some auspicious mantras in welcome of the soul coming to their family. In the performance of *Punsavana Samskara*, a few drops of the juice of a stem from a banyan tree is poured into the right nostril of the pregnant lady with special hymns for the birth of a healthy child. In the ancient Ayurvedic books the great sage Susruta has written quite clearly that the extract from the stem of banyan tree is saturated with properties of comforting the fetus and relieving all kinds of troubles during pregnancy. A special sacred thread is tied to the left wrist of the expectant mother for good health and inner peace. She is also guided to regulate her diet and eat nutritious food that includes barley, rice, yogurt, *ghee*, boiled milk mixed with saffron, almonds, and green vegetables. The couple is guided to make time for daily prayers and try to live in love, peace, and harmony with each other.

(3) Seemantonayana Samskara

Among the series of pre-natal ritualistic ceremonies, *Seemantonayana Samskara* is the most important and also popular in Hindu families. This *Samskara* is performed anywhere between the sixth and eighth months of pregnancy in the ascending phase of Moon. The day and time is fixed in conjunction with one of the auspicious *Nakshatras* (constellations) such as *Pushya, Punarvasu, Anuradha, Shravana,* or *Mrigshirash.* The ceremony starts with prayer hymns in which the couple seeks blessings of gods and goddesses, and the full support of cosmic bodies for safety during the pregnancy period and at the time of childbirth. The hymns recited during the ceremony, indicate protection as well as guidance for the expectant mother i.e. the type of nutritious food she should eat, the good friends with whom she should associate, and the kind of books she should read. The expectant mother is advised to be careful about the selection of T.V. programs and also the display of pictures around the house. In this reference the great sage Manu has written, "*Yadrisham bhajate nari sutam sute tatha vidham, Tasmat praja—Vishuddhyartha striyam rakshet prayatnatah,*" meaning, "the kind of images a woman draws in her mind during her pregnancy, create a strong influence upon the thinking facility of the unborn baby. Therefore the expectant mother should always live in a healthy environment."

According to the Vedic sages this is the time in pregnancy when the baby is quite alert in the womb and shares most of the experiences of the mother. So it is very important for her to handle everything with special caution and care because the baby absorbs the lingering shadows of all the joys and sorrows she goes through. The significance of listening to joyous spiritual music, which is conducive to the healthy growth of the fetus, has been highly emphasized for the well being of both the mother and the baby.

After invoking the blessings of Lord Vishnu, the husband of the expectant mother calls upon the presiding deity of the full Moon—Raka, to bless the unborn baby with beauty, grace, and emotional strength. Afterwards he pours a few drops of aromatic oil on his wife's head while making a nice parting of hair in the center and repeats the Vedic hymn, "*Aum Bhur Bhuah Swah*"—which means, coordination of physical, psychological, and spiritual self. A garland made from auspicious *Udumbara* leaves and flowers is also given to the pregnant lady by her husband. The gentle head massage and parting of hair by the husband is an expression of his love and support and it also symbolizes the removal of negative energies and all the undesirable shocks during pregnancy.

Special mantras are recited for coherent brain development and increased intellectual abilities of the unborn infant. Also at some point during the ceremony the husband gently touches the woman's stomach and recites this hymn from Charak Samhita, "*Aum ahirasi ayurasi sarvatah pratisthasi, dhata tva dadhatu vidhata tva dadhatu brahmavarcasa bhavediti*"— meaning, "O' dear baby, May you be endowed with the radiance of the Sun. May you be blessed with a long life and respected everywhere. May the supreme Lord always be with you and nourish you. May you reflect the divine radiance."

Towards the completion of the rituals, special offerings of *Khichri* (cooked mixture of rice, mung beans, *ghee*, and coconut) are made by the expectant mother with special hymns and the husband seeks blessings for the healthy nourishment of the mother and her baby. Afterwards he requests his wife to look at her reflection in a small bowl full of melted *ghee*, saying, "*Kim Pashyasi*—What do you see my dear?" The wife replies, "*Prajaam Pashyaami*—I see my baby." Thereafter the expectant mother receives all kinds of traditional gifts from the elders in the family and other relatives, and also everybody showers their blessings saying, "*Aum vira-sustvam bhava, Jiva-sustvam bhava, Jivapatni tvam bhava,*" meaning, "May you give birth to a brave healthy baby and always enjoy the love and respect of your husband." At the time of blessings the sweet melody of *Veena* is played with the Vedic hymns. According to Samaveda the celestial sound of *Veena* is considered to be very conducive to general health of the expectant mother and the baby and also it increases the mother's suckling ability and confers several psychological benefits for the safety and comfort at the time of childbirth.

(4) Jaatkarma Samskara

This ritual is solemnized within a day or two after the birth announcement of the baby. The father of the newborn recites the sacred hymns from Vedas and welcomes the infant into his family. He holds the baby in his lap and feeds the newborn with a few drops of a special mixture made with *ghee* and honey. He also writes *Aum* on the lips of the infant with a gold or silver spoon while chanting the holy syllable *Aum* accompanied by the celestial sound of conches. At this point the infant is blessed with sacred words. The father whispers in the baby's ear, *"Tvam vedo-asi"* meaning, "You are the knowledge of Vedas." He also recites the *Ayushya* hymns for ensuring a long life for the newborn such as, *"Aum shatam jiva sharado vardhamana, shatam hemanta, chatum vasantam,"*— meaning, "O' dear child, may God bless you with the joy of hundreds of beautiful springs, summers, autumns, and winters." Afterwards the traditional sweets are prepared and shared with friends, relatives, and co-workers. Special gifts are given to Brahmins and other needy individuals in the community. In some cases this ceremony can be combined with the naming ceremony.

(5) Naamkarana Samskara

Naamkarana literally means the naming ceremony, which is generally performed 13, 21, or 101 days, after the birth of the child. This wide option has been given to the parents due to the convenience of the family and also the health of the mother and the baby. And also these dates can be postponed a little bit due to the astrological calculations. As things stand at present in modern societies, the parents generally have to name their baby within a day or two, while the mother and the newborn are in the hospital; but it is still important to perform the ritual later at home, for spiritual sanctity.

According to Vedic astrology, there is a strong relationship between human mind and body and the stars and planets. It is believed that the cosmic combination at the time of birth plays a significant role in the overall personality of a person. So, during the performance of the naming ceremony the proper worship of the presiding constellation at the time of birth, the lunar date and the birth sign has been highly recommended. Generally, the information about the exact moment of birth (time and date) is given to the family priest immediately after birth so that he or she can prepare the horoscope or natal chart for the baby ahead of the particular time selected for the ceremony, and also inform the parents about the auspicious alphabets for the name; which connotes to the energy of the presiding constellation at the time of birth. For example if a baby is born under the influence of *Rohini Nakshatra* (constellation) the name should start with letters such as A, V, K. The Vedic sages have also emphasized that the given name to the child should be quite influential, auspicious, meaningful and easy to pronounce. It is also important to have at least two vowels in the name, which helps the child to stay perpetually aligned with the celestial sound of *Aum*.

The performance of naming ceremony starts with the chanting of prayer hymns. Afterwards the mother brings the infant dressed in new clothes and hands over the baby to the father from the right side, and returns back to her seat on the left side of her husband. The father holds the baby in his lap while keeping the head towards the north. First of all, he affectionately thanks his wife for bearing a child who is the joy and hope of the family, then after checking the flow of the baby's breath from both nostrils, they start the *yajna*. Special offerings are made to Prajapati (the creator), the presiding lunar *tithi* (date), *Nakshatra* (constellation), and their deities at the time of birth and also the Sun god, Moon, and other cosmic bodies. Thereafter the father, leaning towards the baby, chants the Vedic hymns and makes a formal announcement of the given name saying, "*Aum Ko'si Katamoasi Kasyaasi Ko Naamaasi. Yasya te naamam—tamanmahi yam twaa somey— naatitripam bhur bhuvah swah suprajaah prajaabhih syaam surviro veeraih suposhah poshaih* (Atharva.7.29). *Aum Ko'si Katamo Asi Esho asi amrito asi, Aahaspatyam maasam pravisha assau*"—(add the given name of the baby)" The meaning and the substance of these hymns: "O' dear child you are indeed a blessing to our family, you are a little spark of supreme *Parabrahman* the master of the universe. Your name connotes the feeling of joy and happiness. May you be called by this name (given name to baby) with respect and dignity by everybody, for many more generations. May you be awakened to the consciousness of Divine and enlighten the lives of other people. May God bless you with good health and other comforts of life. Endowed with intelligence, may you observe the rules of good and healthy living. You are an eligible candidate for Divine status, your essentiality is Divine—always remember that."

After this the father formally joins the hands of the baby and makes him or her salute the supreme Lord and also the chief priest and other Brahmins who came to bless. He also gives gifts and a generous amount of money to the learned Brahmins. A variety of sweets are prepared for this special ceremony and joyously shared with friends and relatives. Towards the completion of the ritualistic worship the baby receives gifts and blessings from parents, grandparents, other members of the family, and friends.

Blessings for a Baby Girl: *Eiam Kumari (name) Tvam Ayushmati, Buddhimati, Vidyavati, Dhanavati, Dharmavati Srimati Bhava...*

Meaning, O' Dear (name) May God bless you with long happy life, with increased intelligence, good education, prosperity, good marriage, and always be with you—love and peace

Blessings for a Baby Boy: *Eiam Kumara* (name)*Tvam Ayushman, Buddhiman,Vidyavan, Lakshmivan, Kantiman, Sriman Bhava...*

Meaning, O' Dear (name) may you be blessed with a long, happy, healthy, prosperous life; endowed with increased intelligence, good education, and leadership.

(6) Nishkramana Samskara

This simple ritual is performed on the day of the first outing for the baby; which is generally 40 days after the child's birth. Early morning at sunrise the baby is given a gentle massage with almond oil and bath and then dressed in a new outfit. First of all, the parents take the baby to the shrine of the family deity at home and then they go out in the front yard for *Aditya-darshana* (salutations to the Sun god). The father holds the baby straight upwards facing east and formally makes the child salute the Sun god, the giver of life on planet. The mother offers water to the rising Sun and they both recite the 'Veda mantra', "*Aum tachhakshur-devahitam purastaat-chhukra muchcharat, pashyema Sharadah Shatam, Jeevam Sharadah Shatam, Shrinuyam Sharadah Shatam, Prabravam Sharadah Shatam- Deenaah Syaama Sharadah Shatam, bhuyascha Sharadah Shataat*" (Rig.7.66.16)—meaning, "The Almighty Lord, omnipresent, omniscient, and resplendent, who pervades in the world, enveloping everything, may bless our organs of sight, hearing and speech to be healthy up to an age of 100 years, and may we enjoy full freedom throughout our lives."

Surya Namaskara is an act of introducing the baby to the importance of Sun worship, which forms an important part of daily rituals in Hindu families. Generally, after the Sun worship the parents take the child to the temple for Lord's *darshana* (vision) and blessings. They make charities in the name of the newborn and pray for good health and happiness. Afterwards at night, when the Moon shines with its calmness from the distant horizon, the baby is brought out again in the courtyard for *Chandera Darshana* (salutations to the Moon god). The divine light of the Moon is considered to be the repository of sapful *Soma* or nectarean elixir that gives nourishment to everything on earth. The parents offer water to the Moon god and seek blessings for healthy growth of their baby. Later after the special worship at home the baby receives all kinds of gifts from grandparents and relatives.

(7) Annaprashana Samskara

This is the auspicious ceremony in which the baby is fed with solid food for the first time. The ritual of *Annaprashana* is held in the sixth month, after the birth of the baby, in the ascending phase of moon. In the performance of this ritual the parents seek blessings of the Divine Mother *Annapurna* (the goddess of food), to bless their child with good food, which promotes longevity, purity, intellectual abilities, strength, good health, and cheerfulness. Food is called '*Anna*' in Sanskrit. *Anna* is related to *prana*—the life breath, which energizes the body and is also closely connected with *Mana*—the mind. The Vedic sages made it very clear that the purity of mind—the thinking faculty is deeply influenced by the purity of diet. So it is very important to eat the specific quality of food that promotes longevity and the purity of thoughts. For perfect health, sound mind and body, the importance of vegetarian food has been highly emphasized in Hinduism.

For *Annaprashana* ceremony a light, nutritious meal (porridge) which includes rice, milk, and honey is cooked for the baby. Thereafter, a special worship is conducted by the family priest in which the melodious Vedic hymns are recited for the child to be blessed with healthy food throughout his life. The food is first offered to the deity for blessings and later the baby is fed with *prasad* (blessed food) while the priest and parents recite the Vedic hymns on behalf of the baby "*Aum annapateannasya no dheyanamivasya shushminah, prapra dataram tarisaurjam no dhehi dvipade chatushpada*" (Yajur.11.83), meaning, "May the food I eat be beneficial for my body and may everyone be blessed with food."

After the ritualistic worship of feeding the baby with cereal, everybody shares the *prasad* and the special sweets prepared for the ceremony. The child is blessed with words such as '*Tvamannapatiranado Vardhamano Bhuva*' meaning, "O' dear child may you be blessed with variety of foods for yourself and to share with others." Charitable gifts that include all kinds of food items are given to the Brahmins and also distributed among the poor and homeless. Sometimes when the ceremony is performed at the temple, the parents organize an *Annadana* (free meal) feast for all the family members, friends, and other visitors at the holy sanctuary.

(8) Mundana or Chudakarma Samskara

The ceremony of head shaving is performed in the first or third year from the date of the child's birth; which marks the transition from babyhood to childhood, from less awareness to increased awareness. In reference to the importance of *Mundana* ceremony there are hymns in Ayurveda and other holy scriptures that clearly indicate, "Life is definitely prolonged by tonsure; therefore it should be performed by all means." According to the divine sage and Ayurvedic physician Sushrut, "during pregnancy when the baby is in the mother's womb and floats in the amniotic fluid, there are sticky and greasy substances in that fluid, which give protection to the skin but also stick heavily to the scalp, to protect the crown of the baby's head. This scaly layer, which is called 'cradle crust', makes the follicles very weak and can become the cause of dandruff later. Therefore, it is necessary to shave off the baby's early hair, in order to protect the scalp from skin disorders and for healthy hair growth in future. It is also believed that after the first haircut, the baby's scalp is exposed to sunlight for a while and receives nourishment of Vitamin D for the proper growth of the body.

From the viewpoint of Ayurvedic science, sometimes, when the mother goes through some illness or emotional stress during the pregnancy the baby shares the stress and it is generally absorbed in the hair; so the procedure of head shaving in early years marks a new beginning for balanced growth of the child. The Mundaka Upanishad which has been named after *Mundana* ceremony, glorifies the importance of tonsure for the progressive realization of the soul. In tonsure ceremony the haircut is given with special hymns and also in certain steps, in order to enlighten the baby about *Brahmarandhra* (the crown *chakra*) the yogic pathway, which connects the physical body to the cosmic body. It is at this point, the ancient sages used to grow a long tuft of hair as a symbol of their perpetual yogic alignment with the Supreme-soul.

An auspicious day and time is fixed for *Mundana Samskara* and the performance of the ritual starts with Vedic prayers. The parents of the baby sprinkle water towards East, West, North, and South while placing saucers filled with rice, barley, mung beans and black sesame seeds around the shrine. After reciting the prayer hymns the parents request the barber to give the first haircut to their baby. The expert barber properly moistens the hair with lukewarm water, divides it into four bunches, and starts cutting from the right, left, front, and back respectively, while the learned priest guides the barber with appropriate hymns from the holy scriptures. After the haircut, all of the hair is carefully picked up with wet dough or cow dung and saved in a small bag. Later on, the hair along with the beans from the four saucers is buried in a small pit in the vicinity of water. Thereafter, the mother gives the baby a gentle head massage and bath with yogurt and then brings back the little one to the ceremonial seat of worship for blessings. Everybody showers blessings with flowers while the priest recites the special hymns.

(Repeat the blessings from Naamkarana Samskara)

(9) Karnavedha Samskara

The ritual of piercing the ears is performed in the second or third year, after the birth of the baby. 'Sushruta Samhita' and 'Charaka Samhita', the most revered treatises on Ayurveda, have highlighted the importance of *Karnavedha* ceremony in connection to the physical as well as emotional well-being of the individual. The divine sage Sushruta writes,

"Ears of a child should be pierced for protection from evil spirits, negative energy, various ailments, along with the purpose of wearing jewelry." He further explains quite clearly, "Piercing of ear in the upper portion close to the temple area protects the body from hydrocele and hernia. Thus, it is a precaution taken in early years of life so that the chances of these health problems can be minimized."

On the auspicious day fixed for ear-piercing ceremony the child is given a special bath for the total cleanliness of the body and then dressed with clean new clothes. The parents seek blessings of gods and goddesses while holding their child in their lap facing towards the east. Thereafter, the priest recites the special hymns from Yajurveda meant for the *Karnavedha* ceremony and the expert physician starts the piercing of the right ear, followed by the left. Towards the end of the entire procedure the child receives blessings and gifts from elders in the family.

(10) Upanayana Samskara

The ceremony of investiture with sacred thread is called the *Upanayana or Yajnopaveet Samskara*, which is generally performed at the age of eight and above, when the youngster is enlightened about the importance of good education in life and his or her responsibilities as a respectable member of the family and community. According to Vedic tradition the *Upanayana Samskara* is regarded a spiritual rebirth; and the one so initiated is known as '*dwija*' which means 'twice born', because it signifies entrance into an enlightened and cultured way of life. *Upanayana* literally means, "bring close to *Shiksha* (education) and *Diksha* (initiation) or tuition and intuition." *Upanayana* also means "higher vision" or "nearsight". It is during the performance of this sacred ritual when the youngster is introduced to 'Gayatri mantra', which opens the doorway to inner enlightenment and heightened intuition. The other words generally used for this special ritual are '*Janeu*' ceremony or *Yajnopaveet Samskara*, which also stands for initiation into the understanding of mutual interdependence that provides bases for global intimacy, collective awareness, and worldwide teamwork.

In ancient times, traditionally the sacred thread ceremony was performed at the beginning of formal education at *Gurukul* (school). The scheme of education outlined by the Vedic sages helped the young boys and girls to prepare themselves for their future responsibilities at the individual level as well as global. The *Upanayana Samskara* has been compared with Bar Mitzvah and Bat Mitzvah in Jewish culture and 'Coming of Age Ceremony' in other ethnic traditions. It is also quite similar to the '*Naujat*' (new birth) ceremony of Zoroastrianism in which *Kusti* (the sacred thread) is given to the youngster.

An auspicious day and time are fixed astrologically for *Upanayana Samskara*. Generally the ceremony is scheduled during the ascending phase of moon and also when the Sun is in Northern hemisphere. The sacred ritual is performed in a series of set patterns. First, the *Acharya* (learned priest) offers a yellow scarf to the youngster saying, *"Aum yenendraay brihaspatir, Vaasah parya-dadhaat amritam"*—which means,

"As the divine Guru Bruhaspati gave Devraj Indra the pious cloth to wear and perform the *yajna* on earth so I give this to you with blessings." The youngster salutes and bows in reverence to the learned teacher, accepts the scarf, and sits on the west side of the *Yajnakunda* (ceremonial fire) facing east. The performance of ritual starts with the chanting of prayer hymns from the Vedas. After seeking the blessings of gods and goddesses, the youngster is initiated into the sacred chants of Gayatri mantra, "*Aum Bhurbhuvah Svah. Tatsaviturvarenyam, bhargo devasya Dhimahi. Dhiyo yo nah prachodayat*" (Rig.3.62.10). The learned priest repeats the sacred hymn a few times with his student and then explains that the recitation of the first three words namely '*bhur, bhuvah, swah*' connect the individual to the three levels of consciousness, i.e. physical, psychological, and spiritual. The regular chanting of Gayatri mantra keeps electrifying our thoughts with spiritual powers. It creates alignment of mind, body, and spirit. In Gayatri mantra the aspirant calls upon the Divine Mother 'Savitur' for inner enlightenment, clarity of vision, purity of mind and intellect, precision of thoughts, inner integrity and right guidance into the activities of daily life.

Learning to recite the Gayatri mantra is a very important feature of the *Yajnopaveet* ceremony. Once the student is taught the recitation of Gayatri mantra methodically, he or she is expected to recite it at least few times every day, especially at sunrise and sunset.

After initiation into the great Gayatri mantra the *Acharya* (learned priest) gives the sacred thread in the hands of the youngster and guides him to wear it while chanting the following hymn, "*Aum yajnopaveetam paramam pavitram prajaapater—yat Sahijam purastaat. Aayushya magram pratimunch Shubhram yajnopaveetam balam astu tejah. Yajnopaveeta masi yajnyasya twaa yajnopaveetena upanahyaami*"—which means, "this sacred thread is really special, and the auspicious tradition to wear, has been passed from one generation to another since time immemorial. It is a reminder of your participation in keeping the wheel of creation in motion. Accept it and wear it, with respect and dignity. You are going to be blessed with physical and emotional strength, happiness and longevity."

The youngster wears the *yajnopaveet* (sacred thread) over his left shoulder, falling underneath the right arm, up to the waistline on the right side. The sacred thread is supposed to be worn for the rest of one's life after the *Upanayana Samskara* has been performed. It is only once a year, on the specific date as per Hindu lunar calendar, when the old thread is discarded and replaced by the new one. The sacred thread is circular, consisting of three cords, tied together by a knot called *Brahmagranthi*. The three cords of *Yajnopaveet* are intended to remind the wearer of the three important duties, obligations or *Rihna* (debt) in life; such as '*Pitri Rihna*', '*Rishi Rihna*', and '*Daiva Rihna*'.

Pitri Rihna—means, gratitude towards the parents who gave this beautiful life and raised us with love and care. It is the duty of every individual to be respectful to parents, grandparents and other members of family and also after completing desired education, one should enter the married life, which gives continuity to the age old traditions of family. Human life is a great gift of God, a vehicle of self-realization. A family unit contributes substantially towards peace, happiness, and the integrity of a community and country.

Rishi Rihna—means, understanding the importance of good education in life and to remain respectful to teachers, Gurus, and the great scholars of past and present for their valuable contribution. Human potential is enormous. Every person is born with unique abilities and it is the essential duty of each individual, to enhance his or her unique talents and contribute something new and beneficial, which is conducive to the well-being of society at present and also in the future.

Daiva Rihna indicates the mutual dependence, which exists between the created beings and cosmic powers. It conveys the ideology of interdependence, continuity and the survival of creation. *Deva* literally means, "the one who gives selflessly." The cosmic powers have appeared with creation in order to maintain and sustain life on the planet. It is the duty of every individual to be respectful to the bounties of nature and make the appropriate use of these blessings. And also, each generation is indebted to the previous one, in the sustenance and maintenance of life on earth. It is indeed a participatory world and since the human beings have been blessed with increased awareness and heightened intelligence every individual bears the highest responsibility in maintaining the work order on earth.

After giving a long description of the three obligatory

duties in relation to the three strands of *Yajnopaveet*, the *Acharya* (learned priest) tells the youngster to pronounce the following vows.

1) *Pitri Rihna*—The youngster speaks, "I (name) will always respect my parents and take good care of them in sickness and old age," and further adds, "I will observe the discipline of celibacy till I marry and carry the family traditions with respect and dignity."

2) *Rishi Rihna*—"I (name) will always approach my teachers with profound reverence and humility and try to attain the highest possible knowledge in the field of education I choose; also I will make the most appropriate use of my professional abilities while keeping in mind the global welfare"

3) *Daiva Rihna*—"I (name) promise to live my life in peace and harmony with nature and with others in society. O' God give me the insight and strength to be an enthusiastic participant in the *yajna* (selfless service)—that prevails at the substratum of the universe."

This marks the dawn of a new Era in the life of a youngster, when he or she is introduced to the life of perfect and stern discipline. The codes of moral ethics and social obligations explained during the performance of ritual, serve as the prerequisites for proper physical and spiritual growth. Throughout the ceremony, the youngster is reminded to be goal oriented, focused and steadfast in vows; and if the student lives up to the guidance, he or she is bound to be a successful scholar, and fit to share the responsibilities of life.

Towards the completion of the ritual, special Gayatri *yajna* is performed, in which all the other members of family and friends also participate joyously. After *Purna ahutee* (Last oblation) the youngster stands up and circumambulates around the sacred fire three times and returns back to the seat. The performance of entire ceremony culminates in the last part of the ritual known as *Bhiksha* (alms)—wherein the youngster goes to his or her parents and grandparents and requests saying, *"Bhavati bhikshaamdehi"* which means, "Please give me alms and blessings." The alms collected by the youngster are offered at the feet of the learned priest with respect and gratitude. The parents of the youngster also give gifts and a generous amount of money to the *Acharya* and other Brahmins who came to bless their child. Afterwards the youngster comes back to his or her seat, sits near the *yajnakunda* and everybody showers blessings while the learned priest speaks the *Punyahvachana.*

Blessings for Girl: *Iyam Kumari (*add the name here*) Tvam Ayushmati, Buddhimati, Vidyavati, Dhanvati, Dharmvati Bhava…*

Meaning and substance—Dear (name) May God give you ability, insight, and strength to live your life by the laws of *Dharma* set by the holy teachers, Gurus and *Acharyas.* May God bless you with a long life, heightened awareness, improved academic performance, good health, prosperity, and always be with you—love and peace.

Blessings for Boy: *Iyam Kumara (*add the name

here*)* *Tvam Ayushman, Buddhiman,Vidyavan, Lakshmivan, Kantiman, Bhava...*

Meaning and substance—Dear (name) May God give you ability, insight, and strength to live your life by the laws of *Dharma* set by the holy teachers, Gurus, and *Acharyas*. May God bless you with a long life heightened awareness, improved academic performance, good health, prosperity, and always be with you—love and peace.

A large variety of special delicacies are prepared for the auspicious occasion and shared with the attendees.

(11) Vedarambha Samskara

The performance of this ritual marks the beginning of higher education or in modern language we can say the commencement of college education. It is called *Vedarambha* because Vedic teachings are all comprehensive; it covers the variety of subjects that relate to the animate and inanimate. The Vedas are the repository of knowledge and wisdom, which is valid for all times in almost every field of life. Vedic literature is a unique treasure of inspiring philosophy, cosmology, meteorology, laws of science, psychology, pharmacology, physics, chemistry, administration, and others.

In Vedic tradition a good academic career has been highly emphasized for both boys and girls. According to an appendix in the Manusmriti the girls held equal rights for higher education at *Gurukuls* (schools). The term university, although new in modern times, has been quite familiar through the ages in Hindu society.

Vedarambha Samskara is generally performed anywhere from the age of 16 to 18 at the commencement of higher education at college. It also marks the beginning of an important phase of life when the youngster is enlightened about further responsibilities of receiving higher education at the university. Throughout the worship the youngster recites special hymns from the Holy scriptures and seeks blessings, for heightened intuition, increased creativity, positive enthusiastic attitude towards life, purity of intellect, high academic performance and right guidance into day-to-day life. In *Vedarambha Samskara* the worship of the Divine Mother Saraswati (the goddess of education), forms an important feature of the ritual.

An auspicious day and time is fixed for the ceremony and the worship starts with the chanting of prayer hymns from the holy Vedas. The learned priest recites the mantras invoking the presence of the goddess and the youngster is advised to seek blessings of the Divine Mother, Saraswati. Towards the completion of the worship the student repeats the prayer, "*Mata Saraswati Namastubhyam varde Kamarupini Vidyarambh karishyami Sidher bhavatu mae Sada,*" which means, "O' Divine Mother Saraswati, I salute and bow to you in reverence. You are the giver of boons and bounties; today as I start my higher education please be with me, guide me, and bless me with success in the chosen field of education." The ceremony ends with the melodious chanting of Gayatri mantra and prayers for a successful academic career of the student. Thereafter, the youngster formally goes to the *Acharya* (learned priest) with his parents and they offer him gifts and a generous amount of money with deep respect and gratitude.

Next, the youngster returns to the ceremonial seat of worship for special blessings from the learned priest and other members of family and friends. Everybody showers blessings with flowers while the priest recites the hymns. (Repeat the blessings from *Upanayana Samskara*)

(12) Samavartana Samskara

This ceremony is performed at the completion of formal education at *Gurukul* or college. *Samavartana* literally means "returning home" from the university or *Gurukul*, after graduating. It is a welcome home ceremony, when the young graduate is received with love and pride by his parents, relatives, and friends. An auspicious day is fixed for the performance of the ritual and the ceremony starts with the chanting of Vedic hymns. After invoking the presence of gods and goddesses, the *Acharya* (learned teacher) congratulates and counsels the graduate saying, "I am so proud of everything you have accomplished with hard work and dedication. May your future be filled with many more wonderful opportunities for further learning, and to excel in your field of education. Always take pride in the performance of your work and make the best use of your knowledge, while keeping in mind the global welfare. Speak the truth, be virtuous and perform your duties devotedly. You must show respect to the men of wisdom and remain receptive to their teachings and guidance. Don't break the lineage of progeny—enter the married life and keep the traditions of family alive."

Afterwards, the *Acharya* who is conducting the ceremony tells the graduate to recite the special mantras from the Vedas and seek blessings for successful career, good health, and prosperity. Towards the completion of the ritual, all the attendees chant the sacred Gayatri mantra devotedly, and everybody makes special offerings. Later, the *Acharya* is honored with a beautiful garland and all kinds of other gifts by the celebrated graduate and family. The ceremony ends with blessings from parents, grandparents, relatives, and friends with the following words:

(Blessings for the graduate)

Dear (name) May God bless every moment of your life and guide you at every step. May you remain associated with learned scholars, men of wisdom those are cultured, industrious, and courageous in performing their duties and fulfilling the task of philanthropy.

(13) Vivaha Samskara
(Vedic Marriage Ceremony)

Vivaha Samskara is the most elaborate out of the 16 *Samskaras* described in Vedic tradition. Marriage is a special relationship ordained by God Himself. It is a spiritual partnership between a man and woman that helps them to live an honorable life of nobility, virtue, and *Dharma*. In an ideal marriage the general interests of both husband and wife are perfectly reconciled. They both stand by each other under all circumstances of life. Moreover, the marriage is not just a union of bride and groom, it is the beginning of a very strong bond between two families for many future generations. It marks the beginning of a life of extended responsibilities. Married life is a graceful way of living in community, which helps the individual to fulfill his or her personal legitimate desires and also the society in which he or she lives. The proper growth of every individual primarily depends upon the solidarity of a family that comes into existence only with the sacred act of marriage. A family is the most honorable institute of informal education, where the parents enlighten their children into the timeless wisdom of life.

The *Vivaha Samskara* (wedding ceremony) is the cherished ritual that marks the beginning of *Garhasthya Ashrama*; which has been upheld to be the most respectable of the '*Four Ashramas*' as described in the Hindu tradition. The Vedic sages have declared jubilantly that every person should aspire to live a good healthy life for 100 years and they suggested dividing it into '*Four Ashramas*'. First 25 years is *Brahmacharya Ashrama*—the time for good education, for both boys and girls; the next 25 to 50 years is *Garhasthya Ashrama*—the stage of a householder or a family man. The third stage from 50 to 75 years is *Vanaprastha Ashrama*, the retired life, and the fourth stage of 75 to 100 years is *Sannyasa Ashrama*—the time for dedicated study of the Holy scriptures, yoga, meditation, self-realization, and God realization.

In Manusmriti, the divine sage glorifies the life of a householder and regards it as the center and prop of the whole social structure. The '*Garhasthya Ashrama*' has been given utmost importance because it marks the transition from studentship to householder and it also forms the foundation for the remaining two stages of life. Since three quarters of human life depends upon the success of a good marriage, the institution of marriage has been upheld in high esteem since time immemorial.

An auspicious date and time is fixed astrologically for the performance of *Vivaha Samskara* (wedding ceremony) and the bride and groom embark on a new phase of life enriched by their sacred union with the blessings of God, and their parents, relatives and friends.

The traditional wedding ceremony is performed in a series of rituals wherein the bride and groom are enlightened about the essentials of married life that help them to establish the foundations of a happy, enjoyable marriage on a firm footing. The wedding rituals are performed around the *Agni-yajna* (ceremonial fire), which represents the Supreme-Lord to be the witness of the ceremony. The performance of the sacred ritual follows a set pattern:

I. Swagatam—(The welcoming)

The groom arrives at the wedding venue with his family and friends in a procession and at the entrance they are received with warm respect by the bride's family. The parents, grandparents, and close relatives of the bride and groom exchange garlands to signify the new extended relationship. The bride's mother along with other ladies, performs a short welcome ceremony for the groom and then he is led to the *mandap* (ceremonial stage) for the wedding ceremony.

II. Ganesha Puja

After the groom is seated at the ceremonial stage the priest begins the ceremony with an invocation to Lord Ganesha. The Rigveda declares *"Gananam twa Ganapatim havamahe"* which means, "I invoke the blessings of Ganapati or Ganesha, the master of *Ganas*—the chief elements that constitute the body of the universe." Also special offerings are made to Lord Varuna (The Water god) and a copper pitcher filled with water, and covered with betel leaves, coconut, and flowers is placed near the *Havankunda* (the sacred fire pot to perform the ritual).

III. Madhuparka

The bride's parents offer a mixture of yogurt and honey to the groom, which is considered to be very refreshing and auspicious. This tradition dates back to Vedic Era, when a householder offered sweet yogurt to his guests as a way of welcoming them.

IV. Jaimala—(exchanging of garlands)

The bride, escorted by her sisters and friends, enters the ceremonial *mandap* with the resonating sound of conch shells. The bride and groom greet each other and exchange the garlands, which symbolizes their voluntary acceptance. Thereafter, they move towards the site of *Havankunda* (sacred fire pot) and take their seats facing East. The bride sits on the right side of the groom.

V. Kanyadaan—(Pious act of giving away the bride

with respect and blessings)

After the bride and groom are seated, the learned priest recites the eight prayer hymns from the Holy Vedas to invoke the blessings of various deities. He sprinkles water in four directions for purification and then invites the parents of the bride to the ceremonial *mandap* (stage) for performing the pious act of *Kanyadaan*. He reads the famous hymn from Manusmriti—"*Yatra naryastu pujante, ramante tatra devata, yatretastu na pujante sarvastra aphla kriya*" (Manusmriti.3.56), meaning, "To the family where women are given due respect and protection, the celestials (gods) shower their blessings perennially—but where they are not respected, all other efforts to seek happiness become ineffectual." He further adds that according to the divine sage Manu, when a girl is born, it is the duty of parents to give her special care and good education. She should be protected and respected under all circumstances until she is given in the responsible hand of her husband. After marriage, it is the duty of the husband to be a good provider, and sincerely concerned about her comfort. She should be given due respect and also consulted for everything. And later in old age it becomes the duty of the son or son-in-law to take good care of her and always be quite respectful.

In *Kanyadaan*, the bride's parents entrust the groom with their daughter, forming a life long union. The bride's father holds his daughter's right hand and places it over the right hand of the groom with green betel leaf, coconut, and a handful of rice and says, *"Twadiyam vastu govindam tubhyameva samarpaye*—O' Dear (name of the groom) you have come to my house as an embodiment of Divine. You are Vishnu and my beautiful daughter is Lakshmi, you are the Rigveda and she is the *Richa* (mantra) of the Holy Veda, you are Samaveda and she is the melody, I offer the hand of my adorable daughter in yours, in the sacred relationship of marriage." The groom respectfully declares his acceptance, and thereafter the parents bless the bride and groom wishing them a very happy and prosperous life together.

VI. Yajna—(Lighting the sacred fire)

After the pious act of acceptance, the bride and the groom start the *yajna* together. The word *yajna* (sacrifice) indicates mutual dependence that exists within the family. The performance of special *Vivah Homa* (marriage *yajna*) for wedding ceremony educates the couple as they enter into their new phase of life.

The *yajna* begins by lighting the sacred fire in the *Havankunda*. The priest recites the Vedic hymns while the bride and groom make oblations with *ghee* (clarified butter) and *samagri* (mixture of sacred herbs). The special offerings are made to the nine cosmic bodies in order to seek peace and harmony in nature. The *Navagraha* (nine cosmic bodies) worship is performed with nine types of grains that symbolize the colors of the birthstones generally worn by people. The presiding deities of the birth signs of the bride and groom and the ruling *Nakshatra* (constellation) of the day are also invoked for peace and prosperity in their married life. The *Vivah Homa* (marriage *yajna*) also features the chanting of specific Vedic hymns in which the bride and groom seek blessings for good health, peace and harmony in family. Oblations are offered to Lord Pushan, Bhaga and Aryaman, who are the presiding deities over love, peace, prosperity, and conjugal fidelity. The number of *Homas* that are conducted during the ceremony are such as:

- *Servaprashcit Homa*—Seeking forgiveness of mistakes.

- *Atha Dukhnivark Homa*—Praying for the strength to endure the ups and downs of life.

- *Abhayataan Homa*—Prosperity in all dimensions while keeping in mind the laws of *Dharma*.

- *Rashtrabhrit Homa*—Acceptance of responsibilities towards the community and country at large.

- *Jaya Homa*—The bride and groom also seek the blessings of Lord Vishnu and the Divine Mother Lakshmi for peace and happiness in married life.

VII. Gathbandhan—(Tying the sacred knot)

At the completion of *yajna*, the mothers of the bride and groom tie the groom's *dupatta* (scarf) to the bride's scarf symbolizing the couple's everlasting union and commitment.

VIII. Shila-Arohan—(Placing the foot on a small stone)

Thereafter, they both stand up facing east, and the groom requests the bride to ascend the auspicious stone and pray for steadfastness in her vows.

IX. Mangal Phera—(Auspicious circumambulation of *Agni*)

The bride and groom walk together four times around the holy fire of *yajna*, while the learned priest recites the hymns from Vedas. At each round the bride prays to the Lord that may her transition from her father's home to her husband's home be auspicious, pleasant, enjoyable, and permanent. She prays for a long life for her husband and accepts her responsibilities in married life. At the beginning of each round the bride's brother fills her hands with puffed rice, which she offers in *yajna* assisted by the groom. Each round represents the highly cherished four-fold formula of *Dharma* (righteousness), *Artha* (prosperity), *Kama* (pleasure), and *Moksha* (liberation). The bride leads the groom in first three rounds, which constitute the path of *Pravrithi* (active life in the world). The groom leads in the fourth round, which symbolizes the path of *Nivrithi*, when they pursue their spiritual goals in peace and harmony with each other. At the completion of the fourth round the bride and groom change their seats. The bride sits on the left side of the groom and she agrees to be declared from Miss (maiden name) to Mrs. (husband's family name).

X. Paani-Grahana—(Holding of Bride's hand)

Afterwards, when they are both seated comfortably, the groom holds the bride's right hand and they both promise each other unconditional love, respect and togetherness throughout their lives. They take the vows for peace, happiness, harmony, mutual respect, and creating an ideal family life.

Bridegroom: "O' Dear, in the name of *Dharma* I hold your hand in the purity of love and accept you to be my *Dharmapatni* (wedded wife), as long as we both shall live."

Bride: "O' Dear, I do feel honored being your *Dharmapatni* (wedded wife) and you my *Dharmapati* (wedded husband) in the name of *Dharma*."

Bridegroom: "O' gracious lady, you are a blessing to me and my family. May your transition from your parents home to my home be auspicious. May God bless us with noble children who will carry the good name of both the families."

Bride: "O' dear, I promise to remain true and faithful to you and help you to carry your family traditions."

Bridegroom: "May our mutual love and faith in each other blossom perennially as we move along in maturity and old age."

Bride: "May we both enjoy the gracefulness of old age and pursue our spiritual goals together in peace, and harmony with each other."

Bridegroom: "I shall promise to remain faithful to you and lead a pure, honest, and dedicated married life."

Bride: "O' dear I shall always be faithful to you and live by the laws of *Dharma*—truth, honesty, and purity of thoughts, words and deeds."

Both husband and wife take sincere vows that they will help in fulfillment of each other's hopes and desires in worldly prosperity as well as in spiritual growth.

XI. Saptapadi—(Seven steps)

The seven steps together are solemnized by walking around the sacred fire that embodies the Supreme Lord, being the principle witness of the ceremony. In *Saptapadi* the bride and groom stand side by side at the north of the *Havankunda*. The groom holds the bride, with his right hand and they take seven steps together, seeking the grace for domestic felicities, mutual love, and cooperation in married life. The groom requests the bride at each step as they walk together—

- O' Dear (name of the bride) let us take the first step to seek the blessings of Divine Mother, "Isha", the goddess of nourishing food.

- The second step, for good health, strength, emotional stability, and positive attitude towards the activities of daily life.

- The third step, for wealth and prosperity.

- The fourth step, for all comforts of married life together.

- The fifth step, to be blessed with noble children, grandchildren, and great grandchildren

- The sixth step to be blessed with all the seasonal needs of life.

- The seventh step for sincere friendship, faith, respect, loyalty, and eternal unity in married life.

XII. Dhruva Darshan—(Looking at the Pole Star) and **Surya Chintan**—(Blessings of Sun god)

After completing the ritual of seven steps around the sacred fire, the bride and groom resume their seats again facing east. First of all they salute and bow to the Sun god and pray for a long, healthy, prosperous life together and also the joy of their healthy children and grandchildren. Then the groom requests the bride to look at the auspicious Pole star and says, "O' dear let us pray for the purity of love, devotion, and stability in married life. May God help us to be firm in our vows, be an ideal couple to guide others into the gracefulness of happy married life."

XIII. Shapath-Aashwasan—(Mutual assertion)

Next, the bride and groom place their right hands on the other's heart and speak the Vedic hymn which means, "O' dear may we both enclose each other in the purity of our hearts and honor the sacred relationship of marriage."

XIV. Sindoor Daan and Mangal Sutra

Afterwards, the groom puts *sindoor* (red vermillion powder) at the bride's hair parting and welcomes her into his life as his eternal partner. He also helps her to wear the *Mangal-Sutra* (auspicious wedding necklace) around her neck and seeks blessings of Divine Mother Parvati for their eternal unity in married life. At this point, seven married women are requested to come to the *mandap* (the stage) and bless the new bride with rose petals.

(Although not a part of traditional Hindu ceremony the bride and groom can exchange wedding rings at this time.)

XV. Aashirwad—(Blessings)

Thereafter, while the learned priest recites the auspicious blessings from the holy scriptures, the parents, grandparents, relatives, and friends bless the newlyweds with saffron colored rice.

Blessings: "*Iamu Dampati, praspara anukula bhava vivardhain. Ati Shaita prema anuraga sam sapto bhuyat. Sri Lakshmi Narayana yog eva yogo bhuyat. Sakal bhoga, bhagya, aishwarya, grhastha jeevan tushti bhuyat. Dharma, Artha, Kama, Moksha phala siddhir bhavatu—Aum shubham bhavati*", which means, "May this couple be blessed with eternal union in married life, peace, happiness, good health, wealth, prosperity, and the joy of children and grandchildren. May God help them to live by the laws of *Dharma* and enrich their lives with His grace and guidance." The *punyavachana* or the auspicious words of blessings from the attendees, marks the completion of the rituals for the wedding ceremony.

(14) Vanaprastha Samskara

The performance of this ceremony takes place when a person graciously enters into the third stage of life, *Vanaprastha Ashrama*. According to Manusmriti, at a certain age in life, when the householder feels free from the responsibilities of married life and especially when he becomes a grandfather and the skin begins to show wrinkles, he should perceive the inner call for further spiritual advancement and plan to perform this ritual. *Vanaprastha Samskara* is a transition from one stage of life into another, in which the individual gracefully and joyously accepts the arrival of old age and seeks the blessings for self-study in solitude and selfless service to mankind. This stage of life is obviously a preparation for total detachment later.

An auspicious date and time is fixed and the ceremony is performed in the presence of other family members and friends. After everybody is seated at the site of *yajna*, both the husband and wife, dressed in simple clothes, come and take their seats near the *Havankunda* and then the learned priest starts the performance of ritual. First of all he recites the prayer hymns from the Vedas to invoke the blessings of gods and goddesses and then requests the couple to make special oblations. During the ceremony the retired couple is enlightened about their transition from the path of *Pravrithi* (active family life) into *Nivrithi* (detachment and liberation) when they pursue their spiritual goals independently in perfect harmony with each other. They both take the vows to retire gradually from the family involvements and also live a very disciplined, simple, austere life of total abstinence. They are instructed to spend more time in the study of sacred scriptures, mantra meditation and selfless service to humanity. Towards the completion of ceremony the husband gives back the *Yajnopaveet* (the sacred thread) to his wife and they both promise unconditional help and respect to each other in their spiritual journey towards the liberation of the soul. After, *Purna-ahutee* (last oblation) in the sacred *yajna*, the retired couple is blessed by the priest for good health, happiness, and undivided devotion to God.

(15) Sannyasa Samskara

The initiation into an ascetic way of life is *Sannyasa Ashrama pravesh Samskara*. This ritual is performed when the individual is ready to withdraw himself completely from family obligations and spend maximum time in yogic meditation, devotional love of God, and can also enlarge his scope for global service to entire mankind. At this point in life, the person gracefully enters into *Sannyasa* for which the entire life has been a preparation; the path of *Nivrithi*— the gateway to freedom and *Moksha*. He lives in utmost simplicity. Even though not living in an Ashram (monastery), the initiated *Sannyasi* becomes quite detached from family life and remains perpetually absorbed in the ecstasy of divine love and surrenders his will to the will of God. His bonds with the family start snapping slowly and he transcends the personal attachments. He overcomes all the desires for worldly enjoyments, develops chastity of mind and body, and starts identifying himself with the luminosity of the soul. At this fourth stage of life the person is exclusively focused upon his individual spiritual growth as well as the other fellow beings. He or she becomes a global citizen and genuinely engaged in various philanthropic and humanitarian activities along with his or her own pursuit of inner enlightenment, peace, and liberation. A true renunciate is emotionally integrated, determined, quite mature and performs all of his activities skillfully, faithfully, diligently with an attitude of service. His ideal is to serve other people as the personification of the Supreme-soul, and enjoy the proximity of the Divine from moment to moment. The life of a *Sannyasi* becomes enjoyable, purposeful, and meaningful.

Initiation into *Sannyasa* is not simply a matter of changing into orange robes. It is the change in attitude both at physical and psychological levels of consciousness. Genuine *Sannyasa* is that which guides the person into the acceptance of higher moral values with sincere responsibilities. It is an attitude of selfless action that prepares the person for *Sannyasa*. A *Vanaprasthi* (a person in third *Ashrama*) naturally steps into 'Sannyasa Ashrama' in due course of time, there is no doubt about it.

For the initiation ceremony a propitious day and time is fixed at sunrise, and prior to the performance of the ritual the individual is expected to fast for three days, i.e. living only on milk and fruit, and meditate devotedly on the holy syllable

Aum in solitude. Also some men like to go for total head shaving, except for the long tuft, left at the crown *chakra*, which symbolizes their perpetual alignment in yogic unity with the cosmic-soul. It also indicates that the *Sannyasi* has snapped off all the other personal attachments, except for the one with the Supreme-soul. The procedure of head shaving for entering into *Sannyasa* is optional for men and definitely not required for females.

The learned priest starts the performance of the ritual with prayer hymns from the Vedas and after giving the initial offerings of *ghee* (clarified butter) into the holy fire of *yajna* he instructs the *Sannyasi* to recite the following hymns for the purification of mind, body, and individualized-soul.

1. "*Aum prana apana vyana udana samana mei shudhyantam*"—meaning, "May I have the purity of *Panch Prana* (five types of breath) for a healthy mind and body."

2. "*Aum annamaya, pranamaya, manomaya, vijnan-maya, anandmaya, mei shudhyantam*"—meaning, "May I have the purification of *Panch Kosha* (the five levels of awareness) for yogic alliance in Bliss."

After the *Sannyasi* completes the performance of *yajna* and gives the last oblation, he joins his hands with deep humility and recites the following hymns from Yajurveda for total surrender in God. He recites the hymn: "*Aum Ayuryajnena Kalpatam, Prano yajnena Kalpatam, Chakshur yajnena Kalpatam, Prashtam yajnena Kalpatam, Yajno yajnena Kalpatam, Prajapateh preja abhuma. Svardeva aganmamrtaabhuma.*" (Yajur.9.21)—meaning, "May my life move in a spirit of *yajna* (sacrifice) dedicated to the service of God. May my breath be tuned to the spirit of *yajna*. May my vision be aligned to the source and observe everything with equanimity. May my hearing be tuned to the selfless service of humanity. May my healthy backbone (entire body) perform the charity work in perfect alliance with the Supreme-soul. O' Lord of the universe, I offer myself from the totality of my being at your service and with Thy grace, I may experience the eternal Bliss."

After the *Purna ahutee* (last oblation) the *Sannyasi* stands up and circumambulates around the sacred fire of *yajna* three times and returns back to his seat for blessings from the learned priest and steps into '*Sannyasa Ashrama*' with an attitude of undivided devotion to the Supreme Lord and sincere service to entire mankind for his peace and liberation here and hereafter.

(16) Antyeshti Samskara (Funeral rites)

The last ritual associated with the body of the person is performed at cremation by the family members of the deceased. The performance of *Antyeshti Samskara* liberates *jivatma* (soul) from the bonds of physical body and guides towards the ever-renewing journey onto the path of eternity. The funeral rites are performed with deep respect and meticulous care because for a Hindu death is not an end itself, it only marks the time for change and a new beginning into a life hereafter. Hindu sages believed in cremation of the deceased because with the burning of the dead body the five basic elements, fire, earth, ether, air, and water, which constitute the bodies of all beings, merge into the five essential components and the soul is free to enter another body based on the individual karma. The earliest description about *Antyeshti Samskar* (funeral rites) has been mentioned in Rigveda (10.16.3-5,7,13) and Atharvaveda (12.2.40-42).

Right after death the body is placed on the ground, the head towards North and the feet towards South. The head is slightly lifted with the support of a cushion, so that the tenth gate of the body at the crown *chakra* remains aligned with the luminosity of *Jyotirlingam* for upward, peaceful journey of the soul. *Tulsi* (celestial herb) leaves are placed in the mouth with a spoonful of Holy water from Ganga. The relatives and friends of the deceased sit close to the dead body and read prayers and hymns from the holy books for the peaceful departure of the soul. The family members also start the necessary preparations for the funeral, because as long as the dead body remains in the house neither the family members nor even the neighbors can cook or eat at home. Before cremation the dead body is given a proper bath and anointed with scented paste of sandalwood. Next, the corpse is wrapped with a new white silk or cotton sheet and decorated with flowers and garlands. After preparing the body of the deceased for cremation the family members and friends carry it in a procession to the cremation ground. Generally the funeral procession is headed by the eldest son of the dead, with the chanting of hymns from Vedas and the holy syllable *Aum*. At the cremation site the dead body is laid on the funeral pyre arranged in the *Kunda* (the fire pit) and is totally covered with fuel wood. The head of the corpse is placed in the North direction. Afterwards, a close relative, or, preferably, the eldest son, lights a lamp of *ghee* (clarified butter) and circumambulates the pyre with special prayers for the liberation of the deceased. Then he lights the funeral pyre, beginning from the mouth, and slowly moves towards the legs and feet. Later the oblations are offered in the blazing fire at the *kunda* with the uninterrupted chantings of Vedic hymns. Towards the end, special oblations are made with hymns from Yajurveda for liberation of the soul from mortal body. All these hymns are followed by an address to the different organs of the body such as, "May the organs of vision proceed to the Sun—the source of origin, may the vital air merge in the atmosphere, and so on."

After the cremation, the family members and relatives go to the river or pond nearby to purify themselves with ritual bath and then return to their homes. On the fourth day after cremation, the family members and relatives of the deceased go back to the cremation ground to collect the bones and ashes from the pyre *kunda* and then leave the pot of ashes at a separate safe place at the cremation site. The mourning period is observed for 13 days that requires certain modesty, respect, and gravity. The food cooked during this time is simple and also the immediate family members and the close relatives spend maximum time in the study of Bhagawad Geeta, Katha Upanishad, and prayers. *Shanti-Karma* or purificatory worship is performed on the 13th day and charities are made in the name of the deceased. Later, after two or three weeks, the ashes of the dead are retrieved from the crematorium and taken to a holy river like Ganga, Yamuna, Narmada, or to the ocean and immersed into the ever-renewing flow of the sacred water with profound respect and special prayers. This marks the end of the performance of the 16th *Samskara* as described in Manusmriti.

Aum, Shanti, Shanti, Shanti...

"Probably no work of world literature, secular in its origin has ever produced so profound an influence on the life and thought of a people as the Ramayana."

-Prof. Arthur A. Macdonell

"In fact the Ramayana and the Mahabharata are the encyclopedias of ancient Aryan life and wisdom, portraying an ideal civilization which humanity has to aspire after."

-Swami Vivekananda

"The Ramayana is the most beautiful composition that has ever appeared at any period or any country."

-Prof. Monier Williams

"What, however, left a deep impression on me was the reading of the Ramayana… "

-Mahatma Gandhi

4

The Ramayana

The Ramayana is one of the most famous epics in the religious classics of the world's literature. It comprises 24,000 verses divided into seven sections, known as Kandas; namely Balakanda, Ayodhyakanda, Aranyakanda, Kishkindhakanda, Sundarakanda, Lankakanda, and Uttarakanda. The Ramayana as the word explains itself is a combination of two words "Ram and Ayana" i.e. the life story of Sri Rama. Apart from its poetic excellence and literary grandeur, it is also considered to be a Holy scripture by Hindus around the world.

For centuries, millions of people have been reading the great epic with utmost respect and devotion, and will certainly continue the same for years to come. In words of Makhan Lal Sen, "The appeal and freshness of the epic poems transcend all limitations imposed by time, space, age, caste, creed, society and language. All, irrespective of their age, succumb to the charms and fascinating personalities of its heroes, who have inspired countless men of different generations and spurred them on to perform almost superhuman task."

Ever since the first composition of the Ramayana in Sanskrit by Maharishi Valmiki, it has been considered to be one of the most cherished religious texts as well as an important part of Indian culture and ethos. People read it, re-read it with profound respect for authentic spiritual growth and also for the attainment of peace and harmony in daily life. For generations it has been the most favorite bedtime story for little children. Every year in the month of October/November during Navaratra worship, special dramas are organized at night that narrate the story of the great epic Ramayana. These dramas are called *Ramleelas* in which the life story of God-incarnate Rama is shared in a spiritual setting and the general public is educated and enlightened about the religious history and also the important characters and events of the great epic.

In reference to the timeless appeal of the Holy Ramayana says Swami Tapasyananda, "Here Rama is not only a great personage, an examplar of the highest ideals of *Dharma*, but the very God, the Divine incarnate, revealing and fully remembering his spiritual glory and bestowing salvation on all who came into intimate contact with him. Thrilling and evocative hymns, discourses on high spiritual themes, philosophical dissertations and directions for spiritual practice appear in every part of it. Besides the instructions they convey, these sections contribute immensely towards the devotional edification of those who adore Rama as their favorite Deity." Mahatma Gandhi, a great devotee of Rama, always upheld the Ramayana to be the glorious work on devotion. He often mentioned in his lectures about the loftiness of its ideals, the simplicity and elegance of its diction, the freshness of its enduring beauty, and unflinching devotion that exhilarates the human soul into the purity of love for God and live a life in perfect harmony with *Swadharma*. "Second only to the Bhagawad Geeta in its influence," says Professor R.C. Prasad, "popularity of the Ramayana is by no means limited to India, nor are the Hindus its only readers; the unique universal message of the great epic has fascinated the learned devoted Indians as well as the Western erudite scholars."

The glorious epic Ramayana begins with the story of King Dasharatha, the descendent of King Ikshwaku from Solar dynasty, who ruled the ancient kingdom, Kosala with its capital at Ayodhya; a beautiful city of magnificent palaces, gardens, and fabulous shopping squares. The kingdom was blessed with wise and learned Brahmins, devoted to the study of sacred text and proper guidance to society. King Dasharatha, who ruled the empire with utmost care and courage was sincerely loved and respected by his people. The King was blessed in a number of ways; but sometimes he still felt lonely and unhappy because he was childless.

One day the King called upon his royal priest, sage Vasishtha, and confided in him saying, "Oh great sage, I feel the Solar dynasty is likely to fade away because I have no successor who will carry on after me." The learned sage Vasishtha listened carefully to the king and suggested him to perform the *"Putra Kameshti yajna"* under the guidance of the wise sage Rishyashringa to be blessed with a child. Accordingly the austere sage Rishyashringa was invited to the palace to perform the *yajna* with celestial chanting of hymns from Atharvaveda. At the completion of the devoted offerings in the sacrificial fire, a resplendent *purusha* emerged from the *yajna*, holding a golden vessel of *Payasa* (milk and rice pudding). He handed over the bowl of *Payasa* to the King Dasharatha and told him to distribute it among his three wives. The Queens accepted the celestial *Payasa* and joyfully shared with each other. In due course of time they were all blessed with sons. First, the eldest Queen Kaushalya gave birth to Rama. Then Queen Kaikeyi was blessed with Bharata and later Sumitra, the third Queen, gave birth to twins named Lakshmana and Shatrughna. At the birth of the four princes great festivities were held at the palace and by the people of Ayodhya. The king enjoyed spending the blessed moments with his four glorious sons, and felt that his life had become fuller and more meaningful.

After the princes were given the sacred thread by the family preceptor Rishi Vasishtha, they went to his *Gurukul* (school) for formal education. The royal princes were educated to attain proficiency in arts and sciences, especially in archery and bowmanship. King Dasharatha felt extremely happy as he watched the princes excelling in the study of Vedas and the military sciences. The four brothers displayed quite unique characteristics during their training at the *Gurukul* (school). Rama's respect to *Dharma* and truth became quite pronounced even as a young boy. Lakshmana showed strict discipline at every step and Bharata's devotion to Rama and nobility was apparent to everyone. Shatrughna's attitude was always kind, compassionate, and dutiful.

One day when the King was in consultation with his

ministers about some important matters of the state, a royal guard entered the assembly hall and informed the majesty about the arrival of Muni Vishwamitra. King Dasharatha felt honored and received the Rishi with deep reverence. When the latter explained the purpose of his visit, the King agreed to send Rama and Lakshmana to the Ashram (monastery) of Muni Vishwamitra in order to guard his *yajna* from ferocious demons in the forest. After taking blessings from their parents and sage Vasishtha, the princes left Ayodhya in the company of Muni Vishwamitra. They passed the gates of Ayodhya in few hours and reached at the banks of river Sarayu where they camped for the night. After the prayers at sunset Muni Vishwamitra blessed the princes with special mantras, *"Bala and Atibala"* which would protect them from fatigue and other afflictions such as hunger and thirst.

The next morning both the brothers woke up with renewed enthusiasm and after their prayers at sunrise proceeded on their journey with the revered Guru. They crossed the confluence of the Sarayu and the holy river Ganga. Towards the evening, when they reached Dandaka forest, the Rishi told them about the fearsome creature Thadaka, who lived in that dark forest and constantly harassed the hermits at their Ashrams, and also killed the travelers who crossed the jungle. He further added, since it is the duty of a Kshatriya King to protect his people from wicked Rakshas (demons), the prince Rama should move forward and kill the fearsome creature Thadaka so that there can be peace and prosperity around the forest.

After the death of the dreadful Thadaka, Muni Vishwamitra was deeply impressed by the valor of the princes and initiated them into the special use of divine weapons that he had received from Brahma and Devraja Indra through his tough penances over the years. The great sage shared with Rama all the esoteric techniques of the most sophisticated weaponry, along with the special mantras associated for the proper use.

They resumed their journey the next day and soon arrived at the sage's hermitage. The Rishis at Sidhashrama welcomed the princes and soon after the morning ablutions, they started the *yajna* with the guidance of Muni Vishwamitra. Both Rama and Lakshmana guarded the sacrificial site remaining vigilant throughout the day and night till Muni Vishwamitra completed the *yajna* with other hermits. During the performance of sacred *yajna* for six days, many ferocious demons attacked the Ashram and tried to interrupt the sacred *Agnihotra*, they were either vanquished by Rama and Lakshmana or ran away in fear. After staying at the hermitage for another few days, the princes left for Mithila with their Guru Vishwamitra and other sages to visit King Janaka and attend the royal celebration for which the Kings and Princes were invited from all over the country.

In course of their journey to the capital Mithila, when they reached the outskirts of the magnificent city, Rama noticed a deserted Ashram. He inquired from his Guru about the details of the abandoned place. sage Vishwamitra told the princes that the forsaken dwelling in the dense forest used to be the Ashram of sage Gautama, who lived there with his most beautiful wife Ahilya. Once, when Rishi Gautama was quite far away from his cottage for the morning prayers, Indra approached Ahilya in the guise of the Rishi Gautama and persuaded her for sexual favors, and she yielded to his unholy desire. Although she realized her mistake at some point, but could not do anything about it. After gratifying his passion, Indra was about to sneak out of the cottage, precisely at that moment the Rishi returned and saw him leaving disguised as the sage. Rishi Gautama was terribly angry and cursed both of them—Indra to lead the life of a eunuch for some time, and Ahilya to lead a hidden life of penance and regret. He also told her that after the practice of severe austerities for many decades, she would be released from the curse by the purifying touch of Sri Rama's feet. So when the young princes and sage Vishwamitra entered the cottage of sage Gautama and the moment Sri Rama's feet touched the rock on which Ahilya was meditating for years, she was instantly liberated from the evil effects of the curse and stood aside in her exquisite beauty with her palms joined in salutation. When Maharishi Gautama came to know about this through his yogic powers; he immediately returned to his hermitage and began to live with his beautiful wife Ahilya with a cheerful heart.

On their way to the capital Mithila, sage Vishwamitra mentioned to the princes about the royal celebration, at the palace of King Janaka, in relation to the first-time display of Shiva's magnificent bow, which had been in his possession for the last several generations. After they reached the palace at Mithila, the revered sage introduced the princes to King Janaka and expressed their desire to join the celebration at the court the next day. When Rama and Lakshmana entered the royal assembly hall with their Guru, they looked at the valiant princes gathered there, each desirous to string the Shiva's mighty bow and win the hand of King Janaka's beautiful daughter Seeta. As Rama approached Shiva's bow and lifted it with utmost ease the other Kings and Princes watched quite anxiously. The moment he tried to string the enormous bow it cracked into two pieces and fell on the ground with a thundering sound that flashed across the cosmos. A wave of joy, wonder, and amazement went across the assembly hall. Princess Seeta, who watched Rama with deep reverence and love, was escorted to the ceremonial stage. She offered the wedding garland to Sri Rama and they became betrothed. Later at the special request of King Janaka, Prince Lakshmana accepted the hand of Seeta's younger sister Urmila and her cousins Mandavi and Shrutakirti were given in marriage to Bharata and Shatrughna. The royal marriage ceremonies of all the four brothers were graciously solemnized at the palace of King Janaka. Several gods and goddesses joined the celestial wedding and showered their blessings with saffron colored rice mixed with pearls.

After the wedding celebrations were over, King Dasharatha with his four sons and their beautiful brides started his journey back to his capital. The citizens of Ayodhya gave a warm welcome to the princes and their adorable brides. According to the advice of King Dasharatha, elaborate preparations were made to ensure all kinds of comforts for the newlyweds. Everyone in Ayodhya was very happy and loved to watch their princes mature into young men of service and nobility. Rama and his brothers helped their father in the management of state. People loved Rama for his clarity of vision, steadfastness in truth, and the remarkable sense of justice. Rama and Seeta continued to serve their parents and constantly guided their younger brothers and their spouses into the cherished values of ideal family life.

Thus 12 wonderful years passed by. King Dasharatha noticed the noble qualities of his son Rama and his growing popularity. Rama was very patient with others and enjoyed the company of learned and wise men. People loved him because of his unswerving honesty, hard work, dexterity, fortitude, excellence in weaponry, kindness and generosity. Everybody in Ayodhya idolized him because he was intelligent, courageous, and made himself accessible to everybody's request. King Dasharatha also felt very proud of the great accomplishments of his adorable son Rama and one day, in consultation with his royal priest sage Vasishtha and other ministers at the royal court, he decided to crown Rama as *Yuvraja* (heir apparent) and hand over the kingdom to him. The moment he made the announcement a joyous applause went across the assembly hall as if everybody had been waiting anxiously to hear the good news of Rama's coronation ceremony. The wise sage Vasishtha immediately suggested to the King that the following day when the *Pushya Nakshatra* happened to be in conjunction with Moon was the most auspicious time for Rama to be crowned as *Yuvraja*.

Later during the day Prince Rama was summoned to the court and the King told him about the proposal. Rama humbly accepted his father's decision with a natural ease and assured the King for peace and prosperity of the kingdom while upholding the cherished traditions of Sun dynasty. He touched his father's feet for blessings and then instantly went to the inner chamber of his mother Kaushalya to share the good news.

For the coronation ceremony King Dasharatha invited all the other chiefs and Kings of the neighboring Kingdoms, but because of the shortage of time he could not invite King Kaikaya and Janaka thinking that the good news would be known to them later. He also missed the princes Bharata and Shatrughna as both of them were gone to spend some time with their maternal grandfather King Ashwapathi. Right after the announcement to the public the King gave consent for all preparations for the coronation ceremony. The citizens of Ayodhya began to decorate the city. People appreciated King Dasharatha for his noble decision of assigning Rama the throne of Ayodhya.

Queen Kaikeyi had a personal maid named Manthara. The day when the crowning of Rama was announced she happened to ascend the terrace of the palace and heard about the coronation the following day. She instantly rushed to Queen Kaikeyi's inner chamber and after a vicious, elaborate persuasion she succeeded to convince her mistress to make a demand for the two boons from the King, which he had promised many years ago. King Dasharatha, after checking into the details of all arrangements at the court, decided to spend the evening with Queen Kaikeyi and also personally share the good news with her, but the King was shocked when he entered the bedroom and saw her lying on the ground very sad and angry. He stooped down and inquired softly about the cause of her sadness. After the king comforted her for a few minutes, she got up and spoke in a firm and determined voice. She reminded the king about the two boons of her choice which the latter had conferred on her a few decades ago. The King listened to every single word and promised sincerely for the fulfillment of her wishes. The Queen took a deep breath and spoke in a precise manner, demanding Prince Bharata to be crowned as *Yuvraja* (heir apparent) of the capital and Rama to be exiled to the forest as an ascetic for a period of 14 years. When the King heard the cruel words of the Queen he was overwhelmed with grief and sank down into the couch totally bewildered and confused.

In the morning when Sumantara, the chief minister entered the King's inner chamber to inform him about the arrival of sage Vasishtha and other distinguished guests in the assembly hall, he was shocked to see the king lying on the couch totally exhausted and moaning with a grief stricken heart. When the Queen Kaikeyi saw Sumantara at the door, she told him to leave and send Rama instantly. When Rama got the message he rushed to the palace of his parents and was naturally startled to see the distressed condition of his father. The King Dasharatha was in a state of deep mental agony; he opened his eyes and looked around in utter helplessness. The King whispered the word 'Rama' and then became speechless. At that point the Queen Kaikeyi stood up and spoke on the King's behalf. When Rama heard about the coronation plans for Bharata and 14 years in exile for himself, a serene smile flashed across his face. He saluted the mother Kaikeyi with complete calmness and assured to obey the commands of his father with profound respect. Rama also promised her that he would leave the palace as soon as possible without any delay.

When Rama was going towards his mother Kaushalya's palace to seek her blessing and also inform Seeta about the sudden change in plans, Lakshmana followed him in quick steps and expressed his views with roused anger about the entire situation. Rama listened to the outburst of Lakshmana quite peacefully and told him about the nobility of his father and how important it was for the King to live by the pledge he had taken. He emphasized the importance of following the path of *Dharma* for everybody.

Later, at the sincere persuasion and request of Seeta and Lakshmana, Rama gave them the permission to accompany him in exile for 14 years. When Rama, Lakshmana, and Seeta dressed like ascetics came out of the palace and stepped into the chariot with Sumantra a large crowd of grief-stricken people followed them to the borders of the Kingdom. Proceeding southwards, they crossed the rivers Tamasa, Gomati, and then Ganga with the help of Guha, the chief of the tribe in that area, who held deep respect for the kings of

Solar dynasty. On their journey through the dense forest they met sage Bharadwaja and with his advice they found a secluded comfortable place on the hills of Chitrakuta where they built a cottage by the river Mandakini and started living in peace.

When Sumantra returned back to Ayodhya, he went straight to the King's palace and conveyed Rama's loving message in a sorrow-stricken voice and then lapsed into speechlessness. He watched the King lying with his eyes closed and faintly repeating "Rama, Rama." Thus lamenting, the King breathed his last in the presence of Sumantra, the Queen Kaushalya, and Sumitra. When King Dasharatha's death was reported to the public the entire kingdom was plunged into deep sorrow. The citizens of Ayodhya lamented at the death of their adorable King, as a personal loss. The kingdom was without a ruler for the time being.

The wise sage Vasishtha immediately dispatched two swift messengers to Ashwapathi's palace at Kekaya, in order to bring Bharata and Shatrughna, from the capital of their grandfather. On their return to Ayodhya, the princes performed the cremation ceremony under the guidance of the royal priest. After 13 days of mourning, the wise sage Vasishtha and other ministers at the court requested the Prince Bharata to accept the crown and take charge of governing the state. Bharata declined all the suggestions instantly. He requested the great sage and other ministers to be ready to accompany him to Chitrakuta to see Sri Rama and make a genuine appeal to accept the crown of Ayodhya. A large number of citizens, the royal ladies and ministers, decided to join Bharata in his journey to the forest. They all stayed in Chitrakuta with Sri Rama, Seeta, and Lakshmana for a few days and Bharata continued persisting Sri Rama to return home to be the King of Ayodhya. He made many proposals from various points of views on the issue, for Sri Rama to return back to Ayodhya and accept the charge of the Kingdom, but each one of his suggestions was turned down instantly. Sri Rama explained the importance of his steadfastness in vows, inner integrity, reverence for truthfulness, obedience to the commands of his father, and above all living by the laws of *Dharma* set by the holy sages.

At some point the discussion between Sri Rama and Bharata became highly intellectual and philosophical; both of them kept convincing each other and emphasizing, "It is all yours, not mine." The Rishis, Munis, and other people from Ayodhya, who watched and heard the most exalted conversation between the brothers, were overwhelmed by their dedication and spirit of renunciation. The great sage Vasishtha was deeply touched by the devotional love of Bharata and suggested the latter to act as Sri Rama's representative till the end of 14 years. Bharata agreed to the proposal and requested Sri Rama to give him his sandals to be reverently installed on the throne as a symbol of Sri Rama's presence until the end of the stipulated period of his exile. Afterwards, holding Sri Rama's holy sandals in his hands with deep veneration, Bharata returned back to Ayodhya with his ministers and family members. He, himself lived like an ascetic on the outskirts of the capital in Nandigrama and ruled the kingdom as a devoted representative of Sri Rama.

After, the noble-minded Bharata with Shatrughna and others left Chitrakuta, Sri Rama with Seeta and Lakshmana also decided to move to some other dwelling. So within a few days they proceeded towards Dandakaranya. On their way to the dense forest they stayed at the Ashram of Maharishi Atri where Seeta received the celestial jewelry and other special gifts from Rishi's wife Anusuya, who had been quite well-known for her tough austerities and divine blessings. In course of their journey to Dandaka forest, they visited many Ashrams and met several Rishis absorbed in tough penances for their own spiritual growth and also for the welfare of humanity. They stayed at the Ashram of the great sage Agastya, who was a master in military tactics and strategies and also a well-known authority on the Holy scriptures and Vedas. He initiated Sri Rama and Lakshmana into the operation of celestial weapons. The illustrious princes received the tremendously powerful bows and inexhaustible quivers of Indra with great enthusiasm. They also promised for the appropriate use of weapons as enjoined by the laws of Kshatriya *Dharma*.

At the advice of sage Agastya they proceeded towards Panchavati situated on the banks of river Godavari. On their way they saw a giant aged eagle perched on the branches of a huge tree who introduced himself to be the sincere friend of King Dasharatha at one time. Jatayu, the wise aged eagle, accompanied them to Panchavati and assured to stay around with them in case they needed any help. At Panchavati they found a comfortable, peaceful spot in beautiful surroundings to build a cottage and decided to spend the remaining period of their exile in that enchanted forest, which was quite safe and loaded with a variety of fruit trees.

One evening after their daily prayers when Sri Rama, Lakshmana, and Seeta were sitting in a relaxed mood and talking about Ayodhya, at that time, a Rakshasi (demoness) named Shoorpnakha happened to pass by their cottage. The moment she looked closely towards the cottage, her eyes seemed to rest on Sri Rama. Shoorpnakha was overwhelmed by the passionate desire to marry the illustrious young man. She immediately assumed the form of a beautiful woman, went straight to Sri Rama and introduced herself with a mischievous smile and also spoke at length about the great powers of her elder brother Ravana. After a short conversation Shoorpnakha started making amorous advances and expressed her inner passion requesting Sri Rama to accept her in marriage. When Sri Rama repeatedly declined her proposal, she became very angry and pounced upon Seeta with a menacing gesture. Sri Rama rushed to protect his wife and Lakshmana instantly pulled out his sword from the scabbard and cut off her nose and ears. Shoorpnakha howled with pain and quickly resumed her real form of a demoness and ran away. She went straight to her wicked brothers, Khar and Dushan, who lived on the edge of the forest and constantly harassed the travelers and the sages.

It was within a few hours Shoorpnakha returned to

Panchavati with Khar and Dushan accompanied by 14,000 ferocious demons. When Sri Rama saw the army of Rakshas approaching near the cottage he told Lakshmana to hurry up and take away Seeta to a safe shelter in the mountain cave and guard her carefully. In the meantime Khar attacked Sri Rama and a fierce battle raged between them. Sri Rama shot his celestial arrows with great precision and smashed Khar, Dushan, and their 14,000 warriors in a few hours. Shoorpnakha watched everything in horror and instantly hurried to Lanka to inform her brother, Ravana, about the entire disaster.

She entered Ravana's court screaming and crying at the pitch of her throat and explained everything that had happened at Panchavati, without telling her amorous advances and demonic tricks. She described in detail the valor and unmatched strength of Sri Rama and his younger brother Lakshmana. Shoorpnakha emphasized the celestial grace and beauty of Seeta in order to infuse a passionate desire in Ravana's heart. After listening to the story of his sister, Ravana became obsessed with the thoughts of Seeta and came up with a heinous plan to abduct her secretly.

The next morning, he summoned his magic chariot and flew off alone towards the cottage of his Uncle Mareecha who was a magician and could assume the form of any human or beast. King Ravana told Mareecha about his vicious proposal and demanded help in abducting Seeta. At first, Mareecha did not approve Ravana's unholy plans, but after repeated threats from the latter he concluded woefully to move along the commands of the mighty Rakshasa. Thereafter, Mareecha and Ravana stepped into the air chariot and flew towards the cottage of Sri Rama at Panchavati in Dandaka forest. They got down at a place that was half-hidden behind the cluster of trees. There, Mareecha quickly assumed the form of a golden deer and began to stroll at the front gate of Sri Rama's dwelling. Right at that moment, Seeta came out to pick some flowers for prayers and she noticed the golden deer strolling in their front yard. She was totally captivated by the beauty of the dazzling creature and instantly requested Sri Rama and Lakshmana to catch the deer. At that point, Lakshmana had some doubts about the true identity of the golden deer. He looked at the unique creature and remarked that the golden deer was too perfect to be real. He requested Sri Rama to approach the deceptive deer with caution. Sri Rama looked at Lakshmana with a smile and requested him to stay with Seeta in the cottage as he walked swiftly towards the deer. Sri Rama chased the elusive deer for miles in the dense forest and finally when he shot his arrow at the animal the golden deer resumed the true form and screamed in the piteous voice of Sri Rama, "Oh Lakshmana, help!" At the cottage in Panchavati, when Seeta heard the helpless screams, she was seized with panic and burst into a rage insisting Lakshmana to leave immediately to help Sri Rama.

The moment Lakshmana left the cottage, Ravana quickly came out of his hiding place. He assumed the form of a mendicant ascetic dressed in Saffron clothes and moved towards the front gate of the cottage with a begging bowl in his hands. The minute Seeta stepped out of the cottage to give alms, Ravana instantly grabbed her hand and pushed her into his air chariot and flew off. As the chariot rose in the air, Jatayu the old faithful bird heard the helpless, piteous cries of Seeta, he quickly flew up in the air and tried to save her from the cruel hands of the demon, but Ravana cut off the bird's gigantic wings and talons and Jatayu fell on the ground helplessly. In the meantime Sri Rama and Lakshmana returned to the vicinity of Panchavati and noticed Jatayu brutally wounded and gasping for breath. The gallant bird spoke haltingly with his dying breath and informed them about Seeta's abduction by a demon flying southward in an air chariot. After listening to the story of the brave bird Jatayu, Sri Rama was overwhelmed with anger, grief, and unbearable anxiety and wept bitterly. He immediately resolved to finish the evildoer and the brothers began their search for Seeta.

In their journey southward a horrible creature, Kabandha, attacked them. In a battle between the three of them, the princes chopped off the monster's tremendously long arms and he fell on the ground. Before dying, Kabandha advised them to go towards the banks of Lake Pampa and seek help of Sugreeva, who lived on the Rishyamuka hills. After performing the cremation rites of Kabandha as desired by the latter Sri Rama and Lakshmana proceeded towards Lake Pampa. On their way they visited the Ashram of an aged, saintly woman named Shabri. She had been anxiously waiting for Sri Rama's arrival for many decades. The brothers rested in her lovely cottage and ate the fruits she had collected and saved for Sri Rama with utmost love and devotion. Soon after Shabri listened to the melodious sermon on nine-fold devotional love from Sri Rama, she abandoned her mortal body and ascended to the world of celestials.

The princes resumed their search for Seeta and within a few days they reached the foothill of the Rishyamuka Mountain, where they met Hanuman. He introduced himself in the guise of a young scholar and inquired about their purpose of coming into that forest. After listening to a short introduction from the princes of Ayodhya, Hanuman resumed his natural stature of a giant monkey and prostrated at the feet of Sri Rama in utter humility and requested them to visit his King Sugreeva's remote residence on the top of Rishyamuka Mountain. He instantly lifted both the princes with profound reverence, placed them on either shoulder and carried them up the hill.

Sri Rama and Lakshmana met Sugreeva and after narrating their story, expressed a sincere desire for mutual friendship. Sugreeva felt honored at the proposal and quite comfortable in confiding his personal problems with Sri Rama. He told Sri Rama about the reason of his exile and how his brother Bali had seized his kingdom and his Queen. After a short conversation both Sri Rama and Sugreeva became united in sincere friendship and promised to help each other. Later, Sugreeva told Sri Rama and Lakshmana about a woman being carried by a ruthless demon in an air chariot towards south. The lady was crying in a piteous voice, "O Rama! O Lakshmana!" and when she saw people near our cottage, she dropped a packet of personal jewelry that had been saved carefully. When Sri Rama looked at the jewelry he was overwhelmed with grief and tears rolled down his eyes as he thought about the sufferings of Seeta.

Over the following few weeks, Sri Rama and Lakshmana helped Sugreeva to restore back his lost kingdom and also his Queen, who had been enslaved by his brother Bali. After the coronation ceremony of Sugreeva as the king of Kishkindha and his nephew, Angada, as *Yuvraja* (heir apparent), both Sri Rama and Lakshmana returned to their dwelling in the forest nearby and decided to begin their search for Seeta after the rainy season.

At the arrival of calm and peaceful autumn, when the blessed sunlight swept across the green meadows, Hanuman the chief minister at the court of Kishkindha, reminded his King Sugreeva about the promise, the latter had given to Sri Rama and the search for Seeta began. King Sugreeva in consultation with Sri Rama decided to send Vanara troops into four units, led by their commanders. Each division would go in search for one month. Hanuman, Angada, and Jambavan were given the most difficult assignment of proceeding southward along the high mountain tracks through the dense forest. Since Sri Rama had been deeply impressed by the unique physical strength and wisdom of Hanuman; he gave his signet ring to the latter and said, "Take this ring, this will assure Seeta that you are my messenger. May your mission be successful." Hanuman accepted the ring with his head bowed in reverence and deep humility. He journeyed southward with his comrades and searched quite carefully but could not see any trace of Mother Seeta. It was almost the end of the stipulated period of time given for search, when the entire team reached the southernmost tip of the country by the seashore.

There, while sitting under a tree, they started discussing among themselves the sad story of Sri Rama's exile and the subsequent incidents that followed, like Seeta's abduction by Ravana in the forest, the gallant bird Jatayu's death and so on the search for Seeta. The vulture King Sampaati, the elder brother of Jatayu happened to be sitting on a neighboring hill. When Sampaati heard the name of his brother and the sad news of his death he slowly started moving towards the group of Vanaras. As he approached closer and introduced himself as Jatayu's brother, Hanuman came forward and comforted the grief-stricken bird. Sampaati told Hanuman and his associates that one evening he saw Ravana carrying a beautiful young woman in his air chariot across the ocean to his island kingdom, Lanka. He also added that the pious lady was crying for help and loudly repeating the names of Sri Rama and Lakshmana. After listening to the story of Sampaati they felt quite assured and confident that Mother Seeta was definitely imprisoned somewhere in Lanka, but when it came to the issue as who would cross the big ocean, they felt helpless and very depressed.

At that juncture Jambavan the wise, aged bear approached Hanuman and reminded the latter about his inherent, divine powers and also emphasized that Hanuman being the son of the wind god was the only one who could cross the ocean and carry the message of hope and comfort to Mother Seeta. When Hanuman listened to the encouraging words of Jambavan, he immediately woke up from a reverie, as if he remembered something that was forgotten for some reason. He stood up instantly repeating out-loud, "Jai Sri Ram" (victory to Rama) and assuming a gigantic stature leaped into the open sky over the vast ocean. Hanuman flew at a miraculous speed and with his skill and resolution he survived all the trials on his way to the kingdom of Ravana. The moment he landed on the outskirts of Lanka he resumed back his normal size and leapt over the city gate to enter the kingdom.

He walked across the golden city and peeped into all private chambers of Ravana till at last he saw a woman of exquisite beauty lolling in her bed quite peacefully. For a moment he thought it might be Seeta but the next minute he corrected himself, knowing that Seeta would not rest in a luxurious bed in separation from Sri Rama. He quickly left the palace and wandered sadly in the groves around the city until he reached Ashoka Vatika (garden) which was Ravana's favorite retreat. He spent the night sitting on a tree. In the early hours of sunrise, when Hanuman looked around, he saw a woman of celestial beauty, who was deeply absorbed in her own thoughts and constantly repeated, "Sri Rama, Sri Rama" with utmost love and devotion. He also noticed that many Rakshasa women tormented Seeta with their teasing words. The moment when Hanuman was about to approach her, he saw Ravana coming towards Ashoka Vatika and he decided to hide himself more effectively behind the thick leaves of the tree. Ravana approached Seeta with endearing words, "Seeta, please come with me and live in my palace like a Queen. My wealth, my kingdom all shall be yours to enjoy." Seeta placed a blade of grass between Ravana and herself and spurned all his proposals. She insisted to be restored back to her dear husband Lord Rama.

Ravana's frightening eyes rolled in anger and he turned back from the Vatika, hissing like a snake. Eventually when everybody left, Hanuman quickly gathered himself up and started singing the glories of Rama in the most melodious voice. Seeta looked around in total amazement and when she heard the name of Sri Rama a wave of joy went across her face. Hanuman jumped down from the tree, knelt at her feet in sincere veneration and said, "I am Hanuman." The moment he noticed fear and suspicion in her eyes he immediately gave her Sri Rama's signet ring and assured her with humility that he was indeed Rama's messenger and devotee. He also added since Sri Rama did not know about her whereabouts he could not come to rescue her. After listening to the stories of Hanuman, Seeta felt very comforted and gave him a personal piece of jewelry and requested to hand it over to Sri Rama as her memorabilia.

When Hanuman was about to leave he planned to destroy some parts of Lanka to make his visit noticeable to Ravana and also to explore the strength of the enemy. He destroyed many buildings and killed hundreds of Rakshasa warriors. Finally when Ravana's son Indrajeet attacked, he allowed himself to be captured because he wanted to meet Ravana personally at his court along with his associates. Hanuman enlightened the King about the path of *Dharma* and also warned him of his upcoming destruction at the hands of Sri Rama. Ravana became furious and ordered his soldiers to kill Hanuman, but wise Vibhishana intervened, reminding his brother that it was not proper to kill a messenger. Then in great fury he suggested to set his tail on fire and let him return to his master Sri Rama. When the soldiers got hold of his tail and started wrapping it with some pieces of silk soaked in oil, it became longer and longer. Finally when the tail was set on fire, Hanuman resumed his enormous stature, leapt into the sky and started setting fire to splendid palaces, mansions, military cantonments, and business centers.

After creating panic all over the capital, Hanuman took a quick dip in the ocean and flew back to the other side of the shore where the other Vanaras were waiting for his return. Later, they all hurried back to Sri Rama's dwelling in the forest to share the good news. Hanuman bowed in deep humility and gave a detailed account of all that had happened in Lanka and also handed over to Sri Rama the *Sikha-mani* (crest jewel) of Seeta. Sri Rama pressed the jewel close to his heart and became silent for a moment. He expressed his sincere gratitude to Hanuman and held him in his arms with tears of joy. Hanuman also informed about the safety of Seeta and emphasized upon the difficult circumstances at Ashoka Vatika in Lanka. After listening to the detailed information from Hanuman about Lanka, Sri Rama instantly turned towards King Sugreeva and requested him to make the move for battle as soon as possible. King Sugreeva immediately ordered the Vanara forces to organize themselves for a quick move. Sri Rama, Lakshmana, Sugreeva, and Hanuman with a big army of Vanaras started marching southward under the blessings of auspicious star *Uttara Phalguni*—the star of victory. They jumped and shouted—"Victory to Rama!" and at last they reached the southern seashore. They camped by the ocean beach and started looking into the serious problem of crossing the vast expanse of sea, stretching hundreds of miles.

After the departure of Hanuman from Lanka, the city was rebuilt very quickly, but Ravana was somewhat ashamed and really disturbed at the thought of panic created by Hanuman. He summoned his ministers, in order to consult and seek their opinion. His commander-in-chief, his son Indrajeet and others got up one by one in the royal court and spoke brave words to please Ravana and encourage him to go forth and finish those people who instigated the monkey warrior. Although, there were some ministers in his assembly who condemned his act of abducting an innocent woman and suggested him to restore her back to Sri Rama and seek peace with the latter for his own welfare and of the country. His younger brother Vibhishana insisted upon the right code of ethics and begged him to liberate Seeta and restore her honorably to Sri Rama. He warned Ravana of the danger and the upcoming calamities. Ravana shouted in anger and contemptuously asked Vibhishana to leave the court. Later when it became difficult for Vibhishana to tolerate Ravana's repeated insults, he gathered himself up quietly, renounced all his possessions in Lanka and flew straight towards Sri Rama's encampment with four other faithful associates. After reaching at the Vanara's camp, he declared, "O Rama, I am Vibhishana the younger brother of Ravana. I tried to convince my brother to return your wife back to you with respect but he declined all my proposals. I could not tolerate his abusive behavior anymore and so I have renounced everything and left Lanka. Now I seek your asylum, grace, and protection." Sri Rama replied, "O Vibhishana, you have relinquished the evil and decided to support the righteousness, you are welcomed here" he also added, "if a man comes as a friend and takes refuge in me how can I reject him?" He comforted Vibhishana and appreciated his honesty and also instantly requested Sugreeva and Hanuman to make arrangement for his coronation and honor him as the King of Lanka. Thereafter, Sri Rama and his comrades consulted Vibhishana at every step, while drawing their plans of attack on Lanka.

After camping on the seashore for a couple of days, Sri Rama and his associates seriously started thinking about the immediate hurdle of crossing the vast ocean. Sri Rama stood on the shoreline of the ocean and prayed to the sea god saying, "O' Sagara, please make a path for my army to cross over to Lanka." The sea god emerged from the great ocean and suggested a course of action saying, "O' Rama, you have in your army the mighty Nala, son of Vishwakarma. He is an excellent engineer. Let him construct a bridge across the waters and I shall support to hold it up." Sri Rama graciously accepted the proposal and called upon Nala to take charge of the project. Soon at the command of Sri Rama and Nala, thousands of Vanaras started working with sincere enthusiasm. They brought huge boulders, uprooted massive trees, uplifted big hills, dragged everything to the shore and used it in the construction of the bridge over the vast ocean. At every step they cheered, "Jai Sri Rama"(victory to Sri Rama). It was the magic of Sri Rama's name, which cemented the construction material together. The bridge was built within five days and Sri Rama's army marched across the bridge with renewed enthusiasm. After they landed on the outskirts of Lanka, Sri Rama's army surrounded the city. At the advice of Vibhishana the forces were carefully stationed at each gate of the capital.

When Ravana found out about the upcoming attack on Lanka, he became a bit frustrated and started playing some devious games in desperation. First, he sent a few spies disguised as Vanaras into the camp of Sri Rama to explore their strength, and also to corrupt Sugreeva's mind but the demons failed in their mission. He then ordered the skilled sorcerer Vidyutjihva to create a replica of Sri Rama's head and secretly leave it in front of Seeta's cottage as an evidence of Rama's defeat and death. The moment Seeta saw the replica, she collapsed, but within a few seconds she quickly recomposed herself and smiled at Ravana's treacherous mentality.

After the distribution of army at the assigned stations, when Sri Rama looked at the beauty and wealth of golden Lanka, he was moved with pity for the innocent citizens of the kingdom. He instantly consulted his commanders and ordered Angada, the son of gallant King Bali, to go as a peace messenger to the court of Ravana and convince the latter for peaceful negotiation; but Angada's mission failed. Immediately after Angada's return from Lanka, Sri Rama ordered his troops to march forward onto the city gates and a fierce battle raged between the two armies.

There were many duals between the individual warriors like Hanuman with Jaambumaali and Angada encountered Indrajeet. The battle raged throughout the day and at some point—Indrajeet shot serpent darts at Sri Rama and Lakshmana and both the brothers fell on the ground unconscious. When Hanuman noticed the Vanaras standing in total bewilderment, he immediately leaped to the sky in order to seek Garuda's help. The divine eagle, Garuda, the perennial enemy of Serpents, arrived in the battlefield instantly and neutralized the effect of the venomous darts. The princes woke up with renewed strength and the Vanaras' army resumed the fight with shouts of triumph, "Victory to Rama." The Vanara forces suffered greatly in the beginning, but Hanuman always kept up their spirits with the encouraging words of assured victory.

Sri Rama's forces felt quite weak and bewildered the day when a grim battle ensued between Indrajeet and Lakshmana. The brave and dashing son of Ravana, Indrajeet swooped down with his powerful weapons and killed and wounded thousands of Vanaras. Thereafter he hurled his magic arrow towards Lakshmana that pierced through his chest and the latter fell down on the ground and became unconscious. It was late in the evening and Sri Rama became extremely concerned and worried about Lakshmana and the other wounded soldiers. At that juncture, the valiant Hanuman had to fly towards the Himalayas and bring the healing herbs to the battlefield overnight, which gave a new life to Lakshmana and also helped many other wounded soldiers.

The battle went on for nine days and Rakshas' forces also suffered greatly, wailing and lamenting rose from all corners of the city. Ravana lost his commanders one by one, and also his brother Kumbhakarna, other relatives and his very dear son Indrajeet. On the last day of the war Ravana entered the battlefield with thunder and lightning. He pushed his way through the Vanaras, and made his first attack on Sri Rama with blazing arrows. His magnificent chariot was fully equipped with powerful, mysterious weapons. Sri Rama instantly countered Ravana's attack with a shower of celestial arrows that pierced through the giant Raksha's armor and made him frustrated and confused momentarily. Ravana quickly recomposed himself and invoked his Supernatural powers and a grim battle began again. Later at the suggestion of Vibhishana, Sri Rama invoked the *Brahmastra* (weapon) given by sage Agastya and aimed it straight into Ravana's belly, at the mysterious point of his invincibility. It shattered Ravana's body and he fell head long from his chariot and died instantly. Vibhishana performed the death rites for his brother with royal grandeur and then entered the kingdom with Lakshmana and Hanuman.

After the coronation ceremony of Vibhishana, Hanuman went to Ashoka Vatika to convey the good news of Sri Rama's victory to Seeta, and bring her over to the Vanaras camp. He also informed Mother Seeta that Sri Rama wanted her to be dressed with clean clothes and jewelry before coming to his presence. Later when Seeta reached the camp and came closer to Sri Rama, she sobbed in joy and happiness but also sensed Sri Rama's coldness and felt a strange barrier between her husband and herself. Sri Rama looked at Seeta and said "I waged this war not just to liberate you from the cruelty of Ravana, but also to vindicate my honor and restore respect for entire womanhood. This is the victory of goodness over evil." He further added, "I cannot take you back in my life now, because you have lived in a stranger's house for a year." Seeta was shocked to hear Sri Rama's words, and she immediately signaled Lakshmana to prepare a pyre, and declared to seek refuge in Agni (fire). Lakshmana was totally bewildered and burned with indignation; he turned around to look at Sri Rama's reaction. But Sri Rama seemed passive and remained quiet. He gathered a bundle of twigs and kindled a big fire. Thereafter, Seeta circumambulated Sri Rama with profound respect and then jumped into the fire with her hands folded in prayer for protection saying, "Let this be the test of my purity and virtuosity." She was calm and very sure of her chastity. Instantly a celestial figure emerged from the fire who protected Seeta, extinguished the flames and requested her husband to come forward saying, "O Rama accept Seeta with respect and dignity, she is pure and virtuous." Sri Rama moved towards Seeta, held her hand with a smile and apologized sincerely.

They understood each other and felt united again in the purity of love. The people who were present there and the celestials from heaven witnessed the tough ordeal Seeta had to go through.

Since the stipulated time of 14 years of their exile was going to be over the next day, Sri Rama immediately realized the urgency of keeping his promise to Bharata and requested King Vibhishana to make arrangement for their quick departure. The king summoned for the *Pushpaka Viman* and placed it at their service. Sri Rama, Seeta, Lakshmana, Hanuman, and Vibhishana all ascended the air chariot and started their journey back home to Ayodhya. At the special request of Seeta they made a brief descent at the Capital of Sugreeva to pick up the royal ladies to accompany Seeta to Ayodhya; and also at that time Sri Rama requested resplendent Hanuman to fly separately to Ayodhya in order to inform Bharata in advance about the good news of their safe arrival.

When Bharata made the public announcement of Sri Rama's homecoming, a wave of ecstatic joy went across the Capital; people started making festive preparations and decorated the entire city with festal lamps in golden vases. When *Pushpak Viman* landed at Nandigram, where Bharata had been waiting anxiously with other members of royal families and sages; there were thousands of citizens assembled from all over to greet Sri Rama with Seeta and Lakshmana and also other celebrities. In the meanwhile Sumantra brought the royal chariot yoked with white horses. Sri Rama and Seeta joyfully ascended the chariot with other honorable guests and they all proceeded towards the palace with thousands of other people who walked with them through the streets of Ayodhya. Soon after they reached the palace, the great sage Vasishtha fixed the auspicious day and time for Sri Rama's coronation. The enthronement ceremony took place in a very traditional style. Sri Rama sat on the jeweled throne with Seeta beside him under the royal white umbrella held by Bharata. The great devotee Hanuman sat at his feet in modesty with hands joined in humility and selfless service. The great sage Vasishtha placed the magnificent crown of the Sun dynasty on Sri Rama's head while other priests chanted the Vedic hymns in ecstasy of celestial blessings.

The great emperor Sri Rama ruled his kingdom with care and compassion while strictly following the path of *Dharma*. Sri Rama and Seeta the most adorable, divine couple were sincerely devoted to each other and also enjoyed serving the elders in family and the sages who visited the palace from time to time.

It was shortly after their arrival at Ayodhya that Seeta became pregnant. During her pregnancy, several Munis, Maharishis, the learned scholars in Vedas and Vedangas came to visit and congratulate Sri Rama for his victory over the ferocious demons in the forest and also in Lanka. One day when it was late in the evening and Sri Rama was about to leave the assembly hall, a spy from the secret services walked in and wanted to share a little bit of the current topics of gossip among the citizens of Ayodhya. He stood with his palms joined in deep veneration and spoke quite hesitantly. He told

Sri Rama that in general, the people of Ayodhya were content, happy, and prosperous, but some people still disapproved of Queen Seeta's acceptance by him since she had been forcibly abducted by Ravana and lived in Lanka for a year. Sri Rama was extremely hurt by the false accusation and quietly left the court. He proceeded towards the inner chamber of the palace. Although he did not tell anything to Seeta, she could sense his agony and repeatedly requested to share the silent pain. Sri Rama turned his face down, sighed deeply, and shared with Seeta the ugly rumors and lies about her chastity. Seeta was shocked to hear the false accusations and felt very sorry and concerned for Sri Rama; but she quickly recomposed herself and declared modestly that she must leave Ayodhya and spend the rest of her life in a hermitage in the forest. She further added, "O Lord of my heart, both you and I know deep in ourselves that I am chaste, pure, and virtuous but it is important that a King's wife should be above all suspicions and respected by the citizens. It is my duty to purge you from all stains of ignominy. You should still rule your people with care and justice, that's why I must leave."

Sri Rama, although deeply grieved at heart, called his brothers and explained the entire situation to them. They were stunned and bewildered because it was beyond their comprehension to understand the complexity of *Raj Dharma*—the tough, sacred duties of a king. Sri Rama told Lakshmana that tomorrow early morning take Seeta in a chariot to the forest and leave her at a safe secluded place near the hermitage of sage Valmiki. Accordingly, early in the morning before the daybreak, Lakshmana took out a chariot and escorted Seeta to the forest. After dropping her off near the hermitage of sage Valmiki, Lakshmana broke down and sobbed bitterly. His grief was unabated. He went on lamenting as he got upon the chariot and drove back to Ayodhya.

Seeta was also plunged into deep pain and cried aloud while she watched Lakshmana's chariot leaving the forest. She panted heavily with a sorrow-stricken heart for a while, and then suddenly, she heard a soft voice from behind the bushes and saw an old sage coming towards her. As he came closer he said, "My daughter, I am Valmiki a poet and a hermit. Please accept my hospitality and live in our hermitage with other hermit-women. I will make sure that they take good care of you." He further added, "I know, you are the daughter of King Janaka and the dear consort of Sri Rama and also you are pure and chaste. Don't be sorry, be patient and keep your faith alive in yourself and Sri Rama." Seeta bowed at Valmaki's feet and requested him not to disclose her identity at the hermitage and both proceeded to the Ashram.

After Seeta left the palace at Ayodhya, Sri Rama suffered the agony of separation from his most devoted wife and also abandoned all the royal comforts. He adopted the ascetic way of life, while living at the palace and performing all the duties of a king. He became more devoted to the work of administration and welfare of the citizens. Sri Rama as an ideal King, ruled his empire by the laws of *Dharma*. He sacrificed his personal comforts as well as happiness in order to honor the voice of his citizens. In Ramayana Sri Rama's character has been presented as the embodiment of *Dharma* that encompasses almost every aspect of life. An ideal King, an ideal man, an ideal son, an ideal brother, an ideal friend, a devoted husband, a valiant soldier, and above all the lover of humanity and truth.

At Valmiki's hermitage Seeta accommodated herself gladly to the circumstances and gave birth to Sri Rama's twin sons, Lava and Kush. Time passed by and the boys were well trained and educated by Maharishi Valmiki and their mother Seeta; so much so, that by the age of 12 they excelled in the studies of Vedas, music, sciences, art, archery, bowmanship, and the use of celestial weapons. During that time Muni Valmiki had completed the work of comprising his great epic Holy Ramayana and he taught the poem to Lava and Kush line by line. The illustrious boys memorized the entire story of Ramayana and could sing melodiously with flute and other musical instruments.

In the meanwhile at Ayodhya the great King Sri Rama decided to perform the *Ashwamedha yajna*—the destroyer of all sins. It was a public festival and everyone in Ayodhya and from the neighboring kingdoms was invited to participate and enjoy the performance of *Yajna*, music, storytelling, and singing. Since after the exile of Seeta, Sri Rama had strongly refused to get married again, so, for the auspicious completion of *yajna*, a golden statue of Queen Seeta was installed next to the seat of the king Sri Rama, at the sacred site of *yajna*. Public announcements were made for the beginning of the festivity and Sri Rama's *Ashwamedha yajna* began with great pomp and splendor.

Also according to the royal traditions of the Sun dynasty, at some point during the performance of the ceremony, a white horse with special gold insignia of the Ikshvaku dynasty was escorted to the site of the royal celebrations. The great royal priest Vasishtha chanted a few hymns from scriptures and the royal horse started moving out of the palace followed by a large army under the leadership of Shatrughna. When the horse reached the premises of Maharishi Valmiki's Ashram, Lava and Kush stopped the horse and as they read the proclamation placed on its forehead; they decided to tie the horse to a tree. A little after that, a few of Sri Rama's soldiers quickly entered the Ashram and ordered the boys to release the ceremonial horse. When Lava and Kush refused to do that, a terrible battle ensued between the twin princes and Sri Rama's army. The two valorous sons of Seeta used the arrows blessed with potent spells by their Guru Valmiki and defeated all the mighty warriors including Shatrughna, Lakshmana, Bharata, Sugreeva, and Hanuman. When Sri Rama heard about the terrible defeat of his army at the hands of two illustrious young warriors, he decided to visit the site of the battlefield. In the meantime sage Valmiki who was with Seeta at the banks of Tamasa river performing some rituals, visualized the entire situation with his yogic power and immediately rushed to the Ashram leaving Seeta behind. When Sri Rama approached closer to Lava and Kush the wise sage moved forward and stood between them. He introduced his disciples to the king and asked them to apologize for holding the royal horse at the

Ashram. He also added that he would bring Lava and Kush to the palace tomorrow to attend *yajna* and the singing program.

The next day the twin boys went to Ayodhya with the sage and at the request of Sri Rama, they began singing the Ramayana in presence of the Kings, Rishis, and other citizens assembled at the palace. Sri Rama was deeply touched by the story and the art of presentation by the sage's most intelligent pupils. In the course of listening to Ramayana, Sri Rama came to know that Lava and Kush were his own sons born of Seeta. His heart ached with emotions of love. The following day, he sent a messenger to sage Valmiki to convey that if Seeta was pure and virtuous she might come back to Ayodhya and absolve him from all guilt and shame. The sage agreed to Sri Rama's proposal and the next morning the Muni Valmiki entered the assembly hall with Seeta, Lava, and Kush. Everyone was moved with sorrow by that sight. Rishi Valmiki looked at Sri Rama and said, "O King, here comes your devoted wife Seeta whom you had abandoned in fear of public criticism. Allow her to prove herself pure. These twin boys, Lava and Kush, are your own sons born of your most virtuous wife Queen Seeta. Seeta approached Sri Rama in utter humility and said, "Let me prove my innocence before you and your people once and for all." Sri Rama got up from his throne, moved forward with modesty and said, "I give you my permission."

Seeta immediately took a step back and with her hands joined in sincere prayer said, "If I am pure and virtuous and have been always faithful to my husband, let mother Earth open now, and allow me to enter in its womb." Right at that moment when Seeta was taking this solemn vow, the ground rumbled with fearsome noise and from the bowels of earth emerged the goddess Earth, sitting on a magnificent throne. The goddess stretched out her arms, quickly took Seeta in her embrace with respect and then disappeared below. Flowers were showered from above and the fragrant breeze whispered blessings for the divine Queen Seeta. The earth shook again and then closed. For a moment, holy calmness swept across the universe. Sri Rama sobbed heavily with a grief-stricken heart, and cried aloud saying, "Seeta, Seeta." His Queen Seeta always remained alive in his thoughts and he never got married again.

Sri Rama ruled Ayodhya with his brothers for a long time and later assigned the different territories of the Kosala empire to Lava and Kush and the sons of Lakshmana, Bharata, and Shatrughna. He crowned his son Kush as the King of Ayodhya and Lava was assigned a prosperous kingdom in farthest north of Kosala. After some time, at the silent call of divinities from *Vaikuntha* (Heaven), Sri Rama wished to depart from the world of mortals. Sri Rama had performed and achieved what he had to as an incarnation of Lord Vishnu. Among the brothers, Lakshmana was the first one to discard his mortal body and ascend the realm of celestials. Upon the news that Sri Rama was going to depart from the world soon, King Sugreeva, Vibhishana, Jambavan, and many other celebrities came to Ayodhya to witness the last moments of the manifestation of God-incarnate on earth. Lord Rama blessed his great devotee Hanuman and said that he would continue to live in the hearts of people as long as mankind would live.

It was at a very early hour of the morning when Lord Rama left the palace to discard his mortal body by yogic transcendence on the banks of River Sarayu. When he stepped into the river a voice was heard from heaven above, "O Vishnu! Come to *Vaikuntha* (celestial abode)." The moment Lord Rama shuffled off his mortal being: Bharata, Shatrughna, and many other followers also entered the holy river in yogic alignment with Lord Rama and ascended upward filling the horizon with their radiance.

Lava and Kush ruled the empire for a long time. They traveled to far-off lands and shared the message of sage Valmiki's glorious poem, 'The Holy Ramayana' with thousands of people.

For centuries the Divine couple Lord Rama and Seeta have been worshipped as embodiments of *Dharma*, always inspiring people into the nobler values of life and their worship will continue for many more generations to come.

"The Mahabharata is not only the largest, but also the grandest of all epics, as it contains throughout a lively teaching of morals under a glorious garment of poetry."

-Sylvain Lévi

"The Mahabharata has molded the character and civilization of one of the most numerous of the world's people. How? By its gospel of *dharma,* which like a golden thread runs through all the complex movements in the epic; by its lesson that hatred breed hatred, that covetousness and violence lead inevitably to ruin, that the only real conquest is in the battle against one's lower nature."

-C. Rajagopalachari

"It will scarcely be possible to deny the Mahabharata to be one of the richest compositions in Epic poetry that was ever produced."

-Arnold Hermann Ludwig Heeren

5

The Mahabharata

The great epic Mahabharata is one of the noblest heritages of Hindu families and holds the honor of being the longest epic in the world's classical literature. It is a unique composition of more than 90,000 verses, long prose passages, and about 1.8 million words in total. It has been rightly claimed, "Whatever is there in the Mahabharata may be found elsewhere; but whatever is not here is nowhere else." This great epic of varied interests with its extraordinary length, its varied contents, its everlasting appeal and enduring freshness has been read, recited, enacted, and told in stories throughout the length and breadth of India and other countries through the ages. In the words of Dr. K.M. Munshi, "Mahabharata is not a mere epic, telling the tale of heroic men and women and of some who were divine; it is a whole literature in itself, containing a code of life; a philosophy of social and ethical relations, and speculative thought on human problems that is hard to rival; but above all, it has for its core the Bhagawad Geeta, which is, as the world is beginning to find out, the noblest of scriptures and the grandest of sagas in which the climax is reached in the wondrous Apocalypse in the Eleventh Canto." The glory of the noble epic Mahabharata has been eloquently expressed by C. Rajagopalachari. He writes, "The characters in the epic move with the vitality of real life. It is difficult to find anywhere such vivid portraiture on so ample a canvas. Bhishma the perfect knight; the venerable Drona; the vain but chivalrous Karna; Duryodhana whose perverse pride is redeemed by great courage in adversity; the high-souled Pandavas, with god like strength as well as power of suffering; Draupadi the most unfortunate of Queens; Kunti the worthy mother of heroes; Gandhari, the devoted wife and sad mother of the wicked sons of Dhritarashtra—There are some of the immortal figures on that crowded, but never confused canvas. Then there is great Sri Krishna whose divinity scintillates through a cloud of very human characteristics, His high purposefulness pervades the whole epic. One can read even a translation and feel the overwhelming power of the incomparable vastness and sublimity of the poem."

Some of the most impressive passages in the epic center round the philosophic discussions and discourses on life and conduct, attempting to explain the relationship of the individual to the society and his own inner-self. The profusion of moral and spiritual teachings in reference to the long-standing tradition of the Hindu scheme of life, which is expressed by the four-fold formula of *Dharma, Artha, Kama,* and *Moksha* has raised Mahabharata to the level of a scripture. Wrapped in the middle of the great epic Mahabharata is the holy dialogue between Arjuna and Lord Krishna, which has been upheld in profound reverence by the sages, philosophers, educators, and learned scholars all over the world. Commenting on the magnificence of the great epic

James L Fitzgerald says, "The historical importance of the Mahabharata is not the main reason to read the Mahabharata. Quite simply, the Mahabharata is a powerful and amazing text that inspires awe and wonder. It presents sweeping visions of the cosmos and humanity, intriguing and frightening glimpses of divinity in an ancient narrative that is accessible, interesting, and compelling for anyone willing to learn the basic themes of India's culture. The Mahabharata definitely is one of those creations of human language and spirit that has traveled far beyond the place of its original creation and will eventually take its rightful place on the highest shelf of world literature beside Homer's epics, the Greek tragedies, the Bible, Shakespeare, and similarly transcendent works."

The great epic is divided into 18 sections known as 18 Parvas—Adi Parva, Sabha Parva, Vana Parva, Virata Parva, Udyoga Parva, Bhishma Parva, Drona Parva, Karna Parva, Shalya Parva, Sauptika Parva, Stree Parva, Shanti Parva, Anushasana Parva, Ashvamedha Parva, Ashramavasika Parva, Mausala Parva, Mahaprasthanika Parva, and Swargarohana Parva.

The great epic Mahabharata starts with Adi Parva, in which the divine sage Vyasa gives a long description about the history of the Bharata race, also known as Kurus. The story of the Mahabharata begins with King Shantanu, the descendant of Bharatas, who ruled an ancient kingdom from his capital Hastinapur. He was the father of Devavrata commonly known by his latter name, Bhishma. After the death of the great King Shantanu, his son Chitrangada became king of Hastinapur

KURU DYNASTY

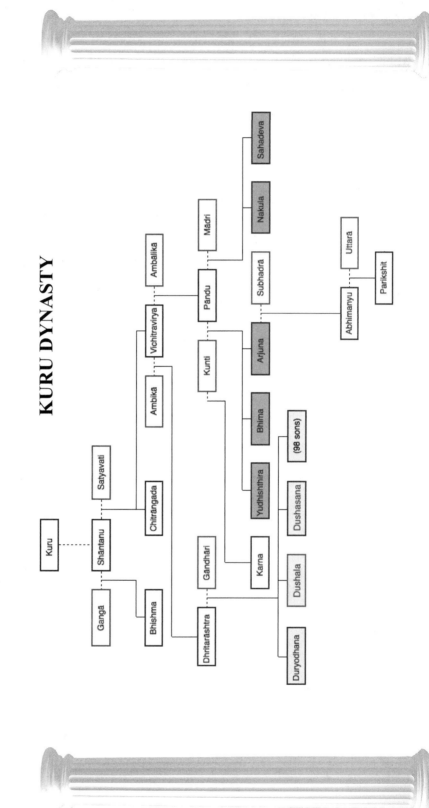

and he was succeeded by Vichitravirya. The latter had two wives Ambika and Ambalika. Ambika gave birth to a blind child who was named Dhritarashtra and Ambalika became the mother of another descendant of Bharata who was named Pandu.

Both Dhritarashtra and Pandu were brought up under the care of Bhishma. Dhritarashtra got married to Gandhari, the beautiful princess of Gandhar. Since Dhritarashtra was born blind, Pandu, the younger brother, ascended the throne of Hastinapur. He ruled the kingdom very well with the guidance of his uncle Bhishma and half-brother Vidura. Pandu got married to the beautiful Princess Kunti from Yadava dynasty who was widely famed for her celestial beauty, intelligence, and virtue. Later, with the advice of Bhishma and at the special request of the king of Madra, he got married again and took a second wife Madri, in accordance with the prevailing customs in royal families.

King Pandu was valorous and just; respected and adored by his people. He enhanced the prestige and power of Kuru dynasty in the course of his reign. One day while he was hunting in the forest, he committed a certain offence and was cursed by a celestial being that "the shadow of death will enshroud him the moment he lustfully approached his wife." King Pandu was deeply afflicted at this curse and retreated to the forest with his wives. He devoted himself to asceticism and led a life of renunciation and contentment. The thought of having no progeny and being unable to discharge his *Pitri Rihna* (debt) to his ancestors troubled him quite often and he felt very sad. His wife Kunti noticed the inner pain and turmoil of her husband and confided to him the story of divine mantra and the blessing conferred on her by the great visionary sage Dhurvasa in her young age. While relating the incident of sage Dhurvasa's visit at palace, momentarily her mind rolled back into past memories, when she was unmarried and lived at her father's palace. One day, out of total innocence and curiosity, she had invoked the Sun god with celestial mantra and was blessed with a baby boy. The boy was born encased in divine armor and wearing bright earrings. Kunti was over-whelmed with fear and in order to avoid the humiliation, she placed the baby boy in a basket and set it afloat in a river. She remembered crying in agony at the separation of her first born and prayed for his well-being. The baby boy was picked up by a childless couple, Adhiratha and his wife, who dwelt on the riverbank. They accepted the baby as a great gift of God and named him Karna.

On hearing the magical power of the divine mantra given to his wife by the visionary sage Dhurvasa, King Pandu urged Kunti to prepare herself immediately to invoke the blessings of *Dharma*, the god of justice, and pray to be blessed with a child. Queen Kunti called upon the celestial power with deep humility and genuine request. She uttered the divine mantra in meditative unity, *Dharma* responded to her invocation instantly and thus she was blessed with her son, Yudhishthira. As soon as the baby was born, a voice was heard from heaven, declaring, "the newborn to be virtuous, truthful, endued with celestial prowess and who will be a great emperor."

After some time, Pandu requested Kunti to pray for another son. Kunti invoked Vayu, the god of wind and was blessed with a son endowed with extraordinary strength. The child was named Bhima. After this the King Pandu and his most virtuous Queen Kunti observed the sacred vows for one full year and prayed to Lord Indra for progeny. On an auspicious day Kunti invoked the blessing of Indra (the king of gods) who thereupon blessed her with a son. The child was named Arjuna. At the sincere request of King Pandu, Kunti shared the sacred mantra with Madri. She invoked the Ashwins and was blessed with heavenly twins Nakula and Sahadeva. These five sons of celestials from Kunti and Madri came to be known as the Pandavas. In the meantime, Queen Gandhari and King Dhritarashtra were also blessed with their first son Duryodhana, the second Dushasana, and later on the other sons for a total of one hundred, who came to be known Kauravas. They were also blessed with one daughter named Dushala. Duryodhana, the eldest son of Gandhari and Dhritarashtra, was a year younger than Yudhishthira.

The Kuru King Pandu lived for many years in the forest and joyfully watched his five sons being brought up by the great Rishis dwelling in the forest monasteries. One day in the season of spring when Pandu was alone with his wife Madri, he approached her passionately; in spite of her repeated protest and reminder of the curse. The moment when Pandu's resolution broke down; the curse of the sage took effect instantly and he died in Madri's arms. Queen Madri felt herself responsible for the death of the King and decided to ascend the funeral pyre of her husband, entrusting her sons to the care of Kunti.

When the Rishis in forest reported the death of Pandu to the royal family in Hastinapur, the entire kingdom was plunged into sorrow. The public lamented it, as a personal loss. The sages took Queen Kunti and the five sons of Pandu to Hastinapur to live under the care of Bhishma and Dhritarashtra. The five brothers with their cousins (the sons of Dhritarashtra) grew up together. They got their early education and the initial practice of arms from the royal Guru, Kripacharya and later for the proficiency in the special use of arms they were guided by the well-known Guru Dronacharya, also known as Drona. He coached the princes with deep sincerity and in a short time taught them the science of arms, in all its branches. He also imparted the same training, into the use of arms, to his only son, Ashwatthama.

When the princes had completed their training, Guru Drona reported to Bhishma and the King Dhritarashtra about the completion of their education and requested for a performance and test, in the presence of the royal family and general public. An auspicious day was fixed for the royal tournament. People from all over the kingdom came to witness the performances of their adorable princes. The great teacher Drona entered the arena and introduced to the public the names and the accomplishments of his students. On seeing the handsome Princes the whole assembly was delighted, and after the auspicious chanting of sacred mantras the Princes started displaying their superhuman skills with their extraordinary weapons. The spectators were spellbound at the marvelous presentation of Arjuna. Everybody was lost in wonder and amazement, the way Arjuna had mastered the *astras* (weapons) and the special mantras that charged each one of them with specific power.

It was almost towards the close of Arjuna's miraculous deeds, there was a sudden uproar at the entrance of the arena. An illustrious young man dressed with divine armor and wearing celestial earrings entered the arena and challenged Arjuna in a thundering voice. This was Karna, the son of Kunti from the Sun god, whom she had left in a basket and floated down the river years ago. The young warrior looked around proudly and gave a casual salute to elders in the royal family and declared with confidence the superiority of his efficiency in use of *astras* (weapons). With the permission of Dronacharya, he almost repeated every act that Arjuna had performed earlier. Duryodhana felt extremely delighted at each performance of Karna and hugged him, extending his hand of sincere friendship. He was very happy at discovering a rival to Arjuna. When Karna challenged Arjuna to a single combat, the latter with Drona's permission came forward instantly. As they were ready to enter into combat with each other, the royal teacher, Kripacharya, who was well-versed in the rules of regulating duels stepped between them and addressed Karna, saying "This prince, the youngest son of Queen Kunti and Kuru King Pandu will engage in combat with you, only after you tell us your royal lineage because princes from royal families don't engage in single combat with unknown adventurers." When Karna heard these words, he stood quiet and helpless.

At this juncture Duryodhana leapt forward to Karna's help and immediately declared him the new king of Anga, for which he had the authority. When the coronation ceremony was being held, the old charioteer Adhiratha, the foster father of Karna entered the assembly, and supporting himself on a staff, he moved towards the stage. The moment Karna noticed the old man coming towards him, he immediately bowed his crowned head at his feet in deep reverence. Adhiratha the charioteer embraced Karna, addressing him son, and the tears of joy rolled down his wrinkled cheeks. After the coronation ceremony was over, there were confused murmurs in the crowd. It was late evening and since there could be no combat after sunset the assembly dispersed.

Observing the popularity of Pandavas and sincere affection for his nephews, Dhritarashtra appointed Yudhishthira the eldest son of Pandu as his *Yuvraja* (heir-apparent) of the kingdom. It was within a short time that Yudhishthira, on account of his benevolence, fortitude, and unswerving honesty, won the hearts of his people. He listened to public grievances, inspected the army, and expanded the territories of Kurus. He made himself accessible to everybody. The Pandu brothers became heroes because of their hard work, dexterity, excellence in weaponry, kindness, and generosity. People idolized Yudhishthira and his brothers.

Duryodhana felt threatened by the popularity of Pandavas and kept telling his father Dhritarashtra that the latter made a big mistake in declaring Yudhishthira as his heir-apparent to the throne of Hastinapur. His jealousy began to grow deeper and he constantly sought into schemes to kill the Pandavas. Duryodhana, Dushasana, their Uncle Shakuni, and the best friend Karna, in consultation with one another, formed an evil conspiracy; and with the approval of Dhritarashtra, they resolved to kill Queen Kunti and her five sons. With the help of the wicked wretch Purochana, who was a well-skilled architect, they decided to build a mansion in Varnavata with highly flammable materials like jute, wax, oil, and straw. They persuaded Dhritarashtra to convince Yudhishthira to take a short vacation with his mother Kunti and younger brothers, and visit the Varnavata during the famous festival of Shiva. In the meantime, Purochana, the wicked architect, furnished this exclusive mansion with luxurious beds, carpets and all kinds of royal comforts.

A few days before the famous festival of Pashupati in the town of Varnavata, Yudhishthira, with his brothers and mother Kunti, took leave of his uncle and other relatives in Hastinapur. A large number of citizens with grandsire Bhishma, Guru Drona, escorted the Pandavas for part of the journey and then returned to their respective abodes. Vidura, the man of heightened intuition, could clearly visualize the unholy contrivance and the hideous plot of Duryodhana. He accompanied them a little farther and before leaving he warned Yudhishthira about the upcoming danger in Varnavata, in a code language. He indicated that the luxury palace built for their stay in the city was actually a trap of death. The wise

Prince Yudhishthira grasped Vidura's message immediately and they both parted with a silent promise of help.

The citizens of Varnavata received Queen Kunti and her sons with great enthusiasm and they enjoyed the most spectacular celebration of the Shiva festival. The Pandavas were invited as resplendent celestials everywhere at public festivities, and people rejoiced at their presence in the town. They went on hunting during the day and kept armed vigil during night as instructed by Vidura. The wicked steward Purochana was instructed by Duryodhana to wait for a few months, in order to make the murderous fire appear like an accident.

One day Queen Kunti invited the citizens of Varnavata for a grand feast at their mansion. After everybody left at night Yudhishthira called his mother and brothers and told them to prepare for the escape through the secret tunnel constructed by the expert miner of Vidura. While escaping, Bhima was given the responsibility to set fire in the back of the palace and all the brothers accompanied by their mother hurried out through the subterranean passage unnoticed, groping their way out in the darkness. They marched along the difficult pathways suffering many hardships. The people of Varnavata informed the royal family about the disaster. Dhritarashtra and his sons although genuinely happy at heart, went to the river with sorrowful kinsmen and performed the propitiatory funeral rites. Vidura took the grief-stricken Bhishma aside and told him the entire truth, Bhishma felt relieved and praised Vidura for his far-sightedness.

After their escape from Varnavata, the Pandavas lived in disguise as Brahmins, at Ekachakra for a long time. One day at the quiet hours of sunset, the great sage Vyasa visited them, and they were advised to move on to a new shelter in the kingdom of King Drupada. On their way to the kingdom a traveler informed them about the *Swayamvara* of King Drupada's daughter at the royal palace. Queen Kunti, with her motherly instinct, told her sons to join the groups of other Brahmins going to witness Draupadi's *Swayamvara*.

After a long journey they reached the beautiful city of the King of Panchala and found a shelter at the house of a potter, down an old obscure street. On the day of *Swayamvara*, the Pandu brothers disguised as Brahmins left home quite early and moved towards the palace. They entered the royal assembly hall and sat with other Brahmins watching the unequalled affluence of the King of Panchala. They looked at the valiant princes gathered there, each desirous of winning the hand of the Princess. They noticed the sons of Dhritarashtra also sitting in a group at one corner of the hall. Karna the most gifted in archery, was also there. In that concourse there was also the king of Dwarka, Sri Krishna—the eighth incarnation of Lord Vishnu. He came with his brother Balarama.

The beautiful princess Draupadi escorted by her brother Dhrishtadyumna entered the assembly. She looked at the valiant princes with profound respect and ascended the dais. After the performance of auspicious rituals by the royal priests, the suitors started coming forward one by one. The beautiful princess Draupadi watched the noted kings and princes coming forward haughtily and returning to their seats abashed and ashamed with humiliation. When Karna approached the mighty bow and lifted it with ease, the princess Draupadi spoke in a clear and precise manner, that she would not accept him. Karna dropped the bow and returned to his seat. Finally Arjuna, disguised as a Brahmin, came forward. He lifted the bow in his hand strung it effortlessly; and shot five arrows in succession into the target. Draupadi who watched him anxiously, approached Arjuna with respect, offered the ceremonial garland putting it round his neck, and they became betrothed. Arjuna clasped her hand and the Pandu brothers proceeded to the house of the potter accompanied by Draupadi. When they reached home, and announced at the door saying, "Dear mother come out, look what we got in *Bhiksha* (alms) today." Kunti answered from inside the house, "Share equally" but when she came out at the door and saw the princess Draupadi, she felt very embarrassed and regretted it deeply. At that juncture, when the king Drupada and his daughter Draupadi, the Pandu brothers and their mother Kunti were confused, the great Rishi Vyasa came to their help. He told a long story about the previous lives of Draupadi and explained that her unusual marriage to five Pandu brothers was the result of her own previous karma. King Drupada was amazed and stunned on hearing the words of sage Vyasa, but finally he yielded to the advice given by the great sage.

The King Drupada was definitely happy to know that the five brothers were the sons of the great Kuru king Pandu. The marriage of the Pandu brothers with Draupadi was duly solemnized at the palace of King Drupada. Sri Krishna the king of Dwarka and his brother Balarama were the most honorable guests at the royal wedding. In the rituals of the marriage ceremony the first to accept Draupadi's hand was the eldest brother Yudhishthira and all others one after the other. The brothers agreed to follow the strict discipline. The Princess was advised to live with each brother for one full year and during that period the others swore to eradicate her image from their thoughts completely. Anybody who violated the practice of the code of conduct, exiled himself from the family for at least one year. After the wedding, the Pandu brothers with their mother were invited to stay at the palace and enjoy the royal treats.

When the news of the Pandavas' wedding to the princess of King Drupada reached Hastinapur, a wave of shock and unease flashed through the hearts of Dhritarashtra and the Kaurava Princes. They were totally bewildered. On the other hand Bhishma, Vidura and Drona were comforted to know the well-being of the sons of Pandu and also overjoyed at the news of the relationship that was established between the two royal families through the marriage of the Pandavas. Bhishma the grandsire suggested that Dhritarashtra should send a proper messenger to Panchala, and duly invite the sons of Pandu with their bride; welcome them back with respect and hand over the half of the Kuru kingdom. He emphasized that the citizens of the state also desired a kind of fair settlement. Vidura went to the city of King Drupada and requested him on behalf of Dhritarashtra to send Pandavas with their beautiful bride to Hastinapur. The Pandu brothers and their mother Kunti consulted Sri Krishna, the king of Dwarka, who happened to be at the palace at that time. Sri Krishna suggested that the Pandu brothers should go back to Hastinapur and also he promised to accompany them. At Hastinapur the Pandu brothers with their bride Draupadi and Queen Kunti with her nephew Sri Krishna the king of Dwarka, were given a warm welcome by Bhishma, Drona, Dhritarashtra, and other members of the royal family.

The next day after their arrival at the palace, Dhritarashtra made the announcement at the court about dividing the kingdom between the cousins and blessed the newly crowned king Yudhishthira. The Pandavas in their share got the Khandavaprastha, the ancient capital of their ancestors the Paurvas, which was nothing more than a desert. They accepted the offer without any complaint, in the hope of avoiding a war and living in peace with their cousins. They worked very hard, and with help of Sri Krishna transformed the barren land into a most prosperous and wealthy city. They named the new kingdom Indraprastha, because it matched the grandeur and splendor of the capital of Indra. The Pandavas ruled their new kingdom in all glory.

After being settled for few years, Arjuna decided to go on a pilgrimage. In the course of his journey he visited Dwarka with a desire to spend time with Sri Krishna. There he met Sri Krishna's younger sister the beautiful princess Subhadra and with the approval of elders in Vrishni's family they were united in marriage. After his marriage with Subhadra, Arjuna spent a few months in Dwarka and then returned to Indraprastha with his beautiful bride. In due course of time

Subhadra gave birth to an illustrious son. The child was named Abhimanyu, who became the joy of everybody in the family, especially Vasudeva. Queen Draupadi by then had been also blessed with five sons and the Pandavas were happily settled at Indraprastha. They led a peaceful and contented life.

The great King Yudhishthira devoted himself to the welfare of his people. The citizens of Indraprastha urged him to perform the *Rajasuya yajna* and assume the title of an emperor. The Pandu brothers agreed to the wonderful proposal made by the public and the preparations for the grand *Rajasuya yajna* started with great enthusiasm. Thousands of Kings from neighboring kingdoms were invited, Sri Krishna from Dwarka being the most distinguished among all of them. The Kaurava brothers with the elders of Kuru family from Hastinapur were also invited and received with profound respect at Indraprastha. They were given special attention and honor throughout the performance of grand *yajna*.

After the spectacular coronation ceremony of the great emperor Yudhishthira, all the guests left loaded with rare gifts and honors. Duryodhana was deeply tormented to see the unimaginable prosperity of the Pandavas. He felt very uncomfortable throughout his stay at Indraprastha and wished to snatch everything from his cousins. After he returned to Hastinapur, he discussed his emotional unrest with his uncle Shakuni and they made a plan to invite Yudhishthira and his brothers to the game of dice. Shakuni was quite familiar with Yudhishthira's weakness for the game and also about his ignorance of tricks, during the play. He assured Duryodhana that the game of dice was the only way to snatch Indraprastha from Pandavas and drive them out of the Kingdom. They persuaded king Dhritarashtra to invite Yudhishthira and his brothers for a game of dice at the newly erected crystal palace of games in Hastinapur. When Vidura presented the invitation at Indraprastha, he expressed his personal impressions and judgment to Yudhishthira, but in spite of the warning, the latter accepted the invitation and went to Hastinapur, accompanied by his brothers, Queen Draupadi and his mother Kunti.

After arriving at the magnificent palace, they rested for the day and next morning the Pandava brothers proceeded to the hall of games. The assembly hall at the crystal palace was packed with visitors. The royal seats were occupied by Dhritarashtra with Sanjaya at his side, Vidura, Karna, Bhishma, and some other members of family. After the exchange of customary greetings, Yudhishthira with his brothers and Duryodhana with Shakuni moved to the central portion (stage) of the hall. Yudhishthira was a bit hesitant in the beginning but at the repeated challenges of Shakuni he could not resist and the game started. At first they started modestly with a handful of pearls but later the stakes became bigger and the cunning gambler Shakuni kept winning. Yudhishthira got carried away by the intoxication of game and lost everything he possessed at the instigation of the wily Shakuni. He lost his brothers, even himself and eventually Draupadi, who was dragged to the assembly hall by wicked Dushasana. She was about to be stripped naked by force, when she cried for Divine mercy in utter helplessness and invoked the help of Lord

Krishna, who came to her rescue (not visible to the mortal eyes) and created an endless supply of cloth around her body. As one *sari* (piece of wrap) was pulled off, another appeared immediately and endlessly. Although the wicked Dushasana withdrew a huge mass of cloth from Draupadi's body but she still remained covered with her original *sari*. Everyone in the assembly hall was touched by this miracle and cursed Duryodhana and his supporters, who drugged and dragged the Pandavas into disaster. When Draupadi came out of her trance, she opened her eyes and loudly swore in the assembly that one day she will be avenged. Dhritarashtra got frightened at the angry words of portending calamities echoing from the walls of the palace. He quickly apologized to her and gave back to Pandavas everything they had lost.

The next day, early in the morning the five brothers and Draupadi started their journey back to Indraprastha, but they had not gone too far, when a messenger of Dhritasthra cordially approached them and presented the invitation for one more round of dice. Yudhishthira thought it over, paused for a second, and then decided to drive back to Hastinapur. The game started and within a few rounds, the vicious Shakuni threw the dice and screamed out-loud "I win." At the end of the game, Pandavas and Draupadi were penalized to spend 12 years in exile in the forest, and spend the 13th year in an unknown place; and if by any chance they were recognized in the 13th year, they must spend another 12 years in exile. When Yudhishthira with his brothers and Draupadi walked in silence, through the streets of Hastinapur there arose an outcry of lamentation from public. The entire city was plunged into grief. A group of citizens with the royal priest Dhaumya went along with them until they reached the banks of river Ganga. The learned priest Dhaumya advised Yudhishthira to seek the blessing of the Sun god for the supply of food during their exile. At the early hour of the Sunrise, Yudhishthira meditated by reciting the 108 names of Surya (Sun) while standing in the knee-deep water. His prayers were duly granted. He received a *Akshyapatra* (a celestial bowl) from the sun god with a promise of an inexhaustible supply of food required for daily consumption for 12 years to come. The celestial voice made it very clear, that the bowl will be filled every morning at Sunrise and will remain overflowing with food until everyone has been served at the end of the day.

After crossing the holy river Ganga and treading along the difficult roads they reached the Kamyaka forest surrounded by peaceful lakes and fruit trees. They decided to live there in the company of learned Rishis. During their stay at Kamyaka Vana (jungle) they had visitors from Hastinapur, and other neighboring kingdoms. When King Drupada and Sri Krishna visited the Pandavas, Draupadi wept bitterly and sobbed in pain at the memory of the traumatic incident, when she was grabbed by her hair and dragged before an assembly of monsters. Sri Krishna was deeply touched and consoled her with a promise that all those who tormented and insulted her would be punished severely in the due course of time. He took a solemn vow to help the Pandavas to restore their lost empire.

One day a serious argument on the concept of *Dharma*

began between Draupadi and Yudhishthira and later on Bhima also joined to support Draupadi. The great sage Vyasa arrived at the crucial moment and appeased everybody. He assured that the virtue of tough austerities is never lost and declared their victory over the wretched Kauravas at the end of their exile. He initiated Yudhishthira into a very powerful mantra called '*Pratismriti*' and asked him to impart the mantra to Arjuna, which would give him the ability to access the higher states of consciousness and become invincible. After sage Vyasa left the forest, Draupadi and the Pandavas felt relieved and quite encouraged with the blessing of the Rishi. Later, as advised by the sage Vyasa, Yudhishthira transferred the holy mantra '*Pratismriti*' to Arjuna for the purpose of entering into tough austerities and receiving celestial weapons from Indra, Varuna, and Lord Shiva.

On an auspicious day, after due preparations, Arjuna took leave and moved northward towards the foothills of sacred Himalayas and settled down to meditate on Lord Shiva. After tough ascetic austerities for years, Arjuna was blessed with the sacred vision of Lord Shiva who bestowed upon him the most powerful weapon, *Pashupati*. The other gods Varuna, Yama, and Kubera also appeared in his meditative unity and gave him the celestial weapons assuring victory against the Kauravas. The vision and the divine touch of Lord Shiva was an overwhelming experience for Arjuna. He remained absorbed in ecstatic trance for a while and when he opened his eyes, he saw Matali with the chariot of Indra, waiting to drive him to Amravati the kingdom of celestials. At the palace of

Devraja Indra, Arjuna received a warm welcome and also in due course of time he obtained all the celestial weapons. One day Indra suggested him to learn music and dance that could be of great benefit in the future. The great teacher Chitrasena was appointed for tutoring. During his stay at the capital of Indra, the celestial dancer Urvashi fell in love with Arjuna. When he disregarded the relationship, she flounced out in anger and cursed him saying, "You will lose your virility and become a eunuch." Later at the request of Indra, the duration of his curse was reduced to one year. Devraja Indra appeased Arjuna and explained to him that Urvashi's curse would be a blessing in disguise during the 13th year of their exile. After learning the secret use of all celestial *Astras* (weapons) and proficiency in dance and music, Arjuna joined his brothers after an absence of five years.

They all met at a certain spot in the Himalayas and then moved southward to Kamyaka Vana (forest). One evening after their daily prayers when they were sitting in a relaxed mood and listening to the stories of Arjuna about the *Astras*, which he acquired from the divine sources, suddenly a few soldiers entered their hermitage and begged for help and protection for Duryodhana, who was captured and severely beaten up by Gandharvas in a battle across the river from Kamyaka forest. Bhima was extremely delighted at Duryodhana's defeat and disgrace—but when Yudhishthira heard a cry of agony from Duryodhana he got worried and immediately dispatched Bhima and Arjuna to rescue Duryodhana saying, "After all they are our brothers." Bhima and Arjuna were able to liberate Duryodhana and the latter thanked the Pandavas for help, and went back to Hastinapur disgraced and humiliated.

The Pandavas' stipulated period of exile for 12 years was drawing closer. Although it was going to be the last year of their exile it appeared to be quite difficult. They began to discuss the serious issue of living in disguise for one whole year. One day, in the late afternoon when the brothers were seriously talking over the various possibilities of how they should live in disguise during the 13th year of their exile, a Brahmin arrived at their cottage, totally confused and tormented. He explained, that a deer with its long antlers entered his sacred *Agnihotra* shrine and while rubbing its horns against the churning staff and fire-sticks, got entangled in those and fled wildly into the forest. He requested the Pandava brothers to go after the deer quickly and bring back his special items for prayer. He spoke for help in his extremity. Yudhishthira became exceedingly concerned and so with his brothers, they decided to chase the deer. Tracking the foot-prints, they spotted the deer from a distance and shot their arrows. The deer sped in great leaps and bounds enticing them far into the forest and then vanished suddenly. Losing sight of the deer the noble minded sons of Pandu sat under a banyan tree to rest. They were very thirsty, disappointed and exhausted. Yudhishthira told his younger brother Nakula to climb the tree and look for any pool or river close by. Nakula noticed a beautiful crystal clear pond at a little distance. At the command of Yudhishthira he came down the tree and walked towards the pond to fetch some water for everybody. When he reached there and the moment he touched the water, a voice came echoing from the pond and said, "Stop! This pond belongs to me, you cannot drink the water from here until you answer my questions." Nakula however, who was exceedingly thirsty ignored the warning, and quickly drank the water. He immediately fell down by the pond and died.

After a while Yudhishthira sent his brother Sahadeva to find out what delayed Nakula's return. He also disregarded the voice from the pond, rushed eagerly to drink water and instantly fell dead. Puzzled and concerned that Sahadeva also did not return, Yudhishthira asked Arjuna to leave quickly in the direction of the pond. When Arjuna reached at the pond he was shocked to see the bodies of his younger brothers but driven by the desperate thirst, he also ignored the warning of the unseen voice, quickly drank the water and died. After that Bhima racked with anxiety, rushed swiftly towards the pond and saw his three brothers lying dead. He swung his mace and shouted in anger, but as he descended into the pond to drink water a voice was heard again from the pond; he also ignored the warning and fell dead among his brothers. Later, when Yudhishthira himself went to the pond and saw his brothers lying there, he was shocked and grief stricken. He lamented aloud and wondered what was behind all that. He observed the dead faces and concluded for certain, they could not have been killed by mortals. He stepped into the pond and the moment he touched the water, the invisible voice warned as before and said, "This pond belongs to me. Do not drink water until you answer my questions; your brothers died because they disregarded my warning." Yudhishthira, the man of wisdom, immediately guessed the presence of Yaksha and realized what had happened to his brothers. He saluted the unseen voice and spoke with profound respect, "I will not touch the water without your permission, I will definitely answer your questions as well as I can."

The unseen voice started putting questions very rapidly one after the other without giving Yudhishthira enough time to pause and think, and the questions moved from one topic to another very quickly.

Q—What makes the Sun rise?

Ans—Brahma the creator makes the Sun rise every day.

Q—By what does a man become wise and learned?

Ans—It is by the study of *Shastras* (Holy scriptures) a man becomes learned and it is by the ascetic austerities and the association with learned he attains wisdom.

Q—Who is a true Brahmin, by birth, study of scriptures, or conduct?

Ans—Not by birth, but by the knowledge of the Holy scriptures, purity of mind and body, and right conduct.

Q—What is most important for those who sow?

Ans—Rain.

Q—What is important for those who seek prosperity?

Ans—Offspring.

Q—What is more nobly sustaining than the earth?

Ans—Mother.

Q—What is higher than the heaven?

Ans—Father.

Q—What is faster than the wind?

Ans—Mind.

Q—What is more numerous than grass?

Ans—Thoughts.

Q—Who sleeps with eyes open?

Ans—Fish.

Q—What is that which does not move after birth?

Ans—Egg.

Q—Who is the friend of the exile?

Ans—The companion on the way.

Q—Who is the friend of the householder?

Ans—A Wife.

Q—Who accompanies a man at the time of death?

Ans—*Dharma* and charity.

Q—What is more blighted than withered straw?

Ans—A grief-stricken heart.

Q—What is the biggest vessel?

Ans—Earth.

Q—What is happiness?

Ans—Happiness is the result of good conduct.

Q—What is the highest duty or *Dharma*?

Ans—Non-Violence.

Q—Who is truly happy?

Ans—The one who feels he has enough and is free from debt is truly happy.

Q—What rescues man in danger?

Ans—Courage.

Q—By giving up what, a man becomes rich?

Ans—Desire.

Q—By abandoning what, a person becomes adorable to all?

Ans—Ego.

Q—By renouncing what, one becomes free of sorrow?

Ans—Anger.

Q—What is the greatest wonder in the world?

Ans—Everyday people die and corpses are being carried along, yet the onlookers never realize the truth that they are also going to die one day, they think they will live forever. This verily is the greatest wonder in the world.

Q—What is the Path?

Ans—The Path is what the men of wisdom and inner enlightenment have followed.

Thus, at the end of all questions and answers, Yaksha the unseen voice revealed its true identity and said, "O Yudhishthira, I am very pleased with your answers. From your dead brothers, you may choose one to revive." Yudhishthira answered "Let my brother Nakula, son of our mother Madri come back to life." Yaksha was pleased with Yudhishthira's impartiality and therefore, he revived all his brothers; and also conferred another boon that they would have the special blessing of remaining unrecognized in the last year of their exile.

After Yaksha disappeared, the Pandavas retraced their steps back to the hermitage where Draupadi was anxiously waiting for them. They gave to the Brahmin his churning staff and sticks and sat down calmly to discuss the plans for the last year of their exile. They talked over various possibilities and finally decided to spend the 13th year at the palace of Virata, the king of Matsya. The Pandu brothers with Draupadi took leave of the holy sages in the forest and moved towards the kingdom of Virata. They bundled up their armors in a sack and tied on the top of a tree in a hidden place outside the capital. With the special blessings from Yaksha to remain incognito, they entered the palace with courage and confidence. Yudhishthira took the assignment as a courtier; Bhima named himself Vallabha and offered his services at the King's kitchen in the palace. Arjuna reminding himself about the curse of *Apsara* (celestial dancer) Urvashi decided to hide himself in the guise of a eunuch Brihannala and teach dance and music to the royal ladies. Nakula and Sahadeva took the work of taking care of horses and cows at King Virata's stables. Draupadi became Sairandhri—the personal companion and attendant of the Queen and princess.

The Pandava brothers and Draupadi stayed happily at the palace of King Virata until the death of Kichaka who harassed Draupadi and was secretly killed by Bhima. General Kichaka was Queen Sudeshana's brother and also a powerful man and head of the army. His death created a commotion in the country and when Duryodhana and his allies heard the news, they immediately suspected that it was definitely Bhima, who had killed Kichaka. It did not take them long to conclude that Pandavas were in Virata's city. Since the stipulated period of Pandavas's exile was going to end in few days, Duryodhana and his supporters decided to attack the kingdom of Virata as soon as possible. He knew that if the Pandu brothers were discovered (exposed) while living in disguise before the stipulated time, that would extend their exile for another 12 years, and if by any chance their judgment happened to be incorrect still there could be no loss in their attack on Virata's kingdom. Although Bhishma and Drona did not approve the proposal, they still joined the Kauravas' army and invaded the kingdom of Matsya. Pandavas, due to their loyalties to the King, decided to support him while remaining in disguise. It was the evening of the last day of Pandavas' exile when Arjuna disguised as Brihannala entered the battle and blew his famous conch. When Duryodhana heard the sound, he screamed instantly and said, "That is Arjuna, we have discovered the Pandavas! Since the 13th year is not over yet, they should be exiled for another 12 years." The grandsire Bhishma interrupted him instantly and said, "According to the astrological calculation the period of exile is already over."

In the meantime, Karna attacked Arjuna and a fierce battle raged between the both armies. Arjuna shot his arrows with great precision. First he drove Karna from the battlefield, and later Drona, Ashwatthama, Kripacharya and Duryodhana. When a spectacular fight raged between Arjuna and Bhishma—Arjuna used a magic weapon which made all the warriors unconscious and they collapsed in the battlefield. Later on, the Kauravas' army returned to Hastinapur after the humiliating defeat. Arjuna, with the Prince of Matsya, returned back to the capital after a glorious victory. The next day, at the court the victorious Prince Uttar revealed the true identity of the Pandavas and Draupadi. King Virata was overwhelmed with amazement and joy. He thanked and apologized to the Pandavas and offered his wealth and a large number of other gifts. He also proposed the hand of his beautiful daughter Uttara in the marriage to Arjuna, but the latter immediately declined the offer. Arjuna said, "O' King, the princess learnt music and dancing from me and I have always looked upon her as a daughter. I will be honored to accept her as a daughter-in-law, married to my son Abhimanyu." The preparations for the royal wedding started instantly. The most honorable among the guests was Sri Krishna, who came with his sister Subhadra and her son Abhimanyu—the bridegroom. The marriage of princess Uttara and Abhimanyu was solemnized according to Vedic rites in presence of many kings and princes from other kingdoms.

On the next day, after the wedding celebration the Pandavas with their friends and relatives assembled in the council hall at Virata's palace. Sri Krishna addressed the assembly, "All of you know how Yudhishthira was deceitfully defeated at the game-board by son of Suvala (Shakuni); and robbed of his kingdom, and exiled for 13 years to the forest with his brothers and Queen Draupadi. Now having fulfilled their pledge, Pandavas have every right to demand their kingdom back. While keeping in mind the laws of *Dharma* and the welfare of both Pandavas and Kauravas, we should send an ambassador to Hastinapur, who can persuade Duryodhana to a peaceful settlement by giving back, half of the kingdom to Yudhishthira with respect and dignity. They are asking for only what lawfully belongs to them." After a short discussion between King Drupada, Satyaki, Balarama, Sri Krishna, and Yudhishthira the meeting was adjourned. Sri Krishna left for Dwarka with his people and Pandavas dispatched their messenger to Duryodhana for a friendly peaceful agreement.

After waiting for few months quite patiently to receive any reasonable reply from Duryodhana (Hastinapur), King Drupada and Yudhishthira started sending out messengers to other Kings, those were likely to favor their cause. Arjuna himself left for Dwarka to seek Sri Krishna's support. Duryodhana who was constantly being reported through his spies about every single move of Pandavas, he also started sending his messengers to various kingdoms and set out himself to Dwarka for help. Arjuna and Duryodhana reached Dwarka at the same moment, while Sri Krishna was fast asleep. They both entered his bedroom together, Duryodhana picked a good chair and sat comfortably near the headboard of the bed while Arjuna took his seat near Sri Krishna's feet in a respectful posture. When Sri Krishna woke up his eyes fell on Arjuna and being aware of the other visitor at the head, he greeted both of them and asked what brought them to Dwarka. Duryodhana spoke first, He said "O' King of Dwarka, it looks like a war may ensue between Kauravas and Pandavas, if it does I request for your help." Sri Krishna answered, "O' Son of Dhritarashtra when I woke up and opened my eyes I saw Arjuna first, so he gets the first choice." He further added, "that in the distribution of assistance, my fully equipped and heroic forces will be on one side and Me alone as an individual person on the other and also I will not fight. Now tell me your choice Partha?" Arjuna's answer came instantly, "O' Keshava I definitely want you to be on my side, even if you don't fight. I request you to steer my chariot through the battlefield." Duryodhana was overwhelmed with joy to get the support of a vast army. He thanked Sri Krishna wholeheartedly and returned to Hastinapur in high spirits, still wondering over Arjuna's choice.

In the meantime, Yudhishthira's peace messenger reached Dhritarashtra's court and launched into a narrative of the situation. He spoke with respect, "O' King since Pandavas have duly honored their pledge of living in exile for 13 years, now they want their share of the Kingdom which legitimately belongs to them; and if they are denied what is due to them, they will definitely take it back by force." Bhishma was the first to answer "How fortunate that they desire only peace." He advised Dhritarashtra to return Indraprastha to the Pandavas, but Duryodhana got furious and Karna supported him. Dhritarashtra silenced everyone and told the envoy that he would send the answer through Sanjaya as soon as possible. It was after a few days that Sanjaya was dispatched to Upaplavya, another place in Matsya territory, where the Pandavas were staying. There he presented a formal document of King Dhritarashtra. After sharing the elaborate message of peace from Dhritarashtra he said, "O' Yudhishthira, even if Kauravas do not give back your kingdom, you should not abandon the path of *Dharma* by waging a war against your cousins." Yudhishthira replied instantly, "As a Kshatriya king I would be failing in my *Dharma*, if I did not make enough efforts to take back my lost kingdom and share with my citizens what is lawfully theirs. Give us back at least a small part of it." He further added, "For five of us, give at least five villages and make peace with us. Even that will make us happy and content."

After the exchange of messages Sanjaya took leave of the Pandavas. He returned to Hastinapur and conveyed the message of Yudhishthira at the court next day. He praised Yudhishthira's words of wisdom and his genuine desire of peace among the cousins. Bhishma, Drona, Vidura, Kripacharya, and even Dhritarashtra honored the peace settlement from Pandavas but wicked Duryodhana could not tolerate the appreciative words of Sanjaya anymore; he stood up and shouted, "Yudhishthira is well aware of our strength; that's why now he has decided to come down from half of the kingdom, to settle for just five villages. Why a man of power will settle for less? Pandavas will not receive even a needle point of territory from us." Karna and Dushasana supported him out-loud and they left the court.

On the other hand at Upaplavya, after Sanjaya left for Hastinapur, Yudhishthira felt very sad and told his brothers that they should avoid the war at all costs; especially when they were certain of their victory. At this juncture, he turned towards Sri Krishna for help, who had already arrived at Upaplavya with the special request of Arjuna. Sri Krishna replied, "O' Yudhishthira I know your mind is always steeped in righteousness, for your sake I will visit the Kauravas at their court and try to persuade them for a peaceful treaty. We must make this one last effort to avoid war."

When Sri Krishna reached Hastinapur, he was received with profound respect and enthusiasm by Bhishma, Drona, Kripa, Vidura and others. Next morning he appeared at the court of Dhritarashtra and explained his mission quite clearly. He sincerely proposed for a peaceful settlement. Sri Krishna turned towards Duryodhana and said, "Make peace with your cousins by giving them half the Kingdom or at least give them five villages and they will live happily." The evil Duryodhana looked at Sri Krishna and said, "No I will not give them any land, not even enough to cover a needle point. That is final." He walked out of the assembly hall accompanied by his brothers.

Outside the hall he consulted his allies and plotted to seize Sri Krishna by force and confine him in the prison. When Sri Krishna heard the news, he laughed and disclosed His Divinity. It is believed, that Dhritarashtra also regained his sight for a moment to behold the *Vishvarupa* (Universal Form). After a few seconds Sri Krishna resumed his mortal form and walked out of the court with Satyaki and Vidura. He got into his chariot and set out towards Upaplavya. War became inevitable.

The next day, he met the Pandu brothers in the assembly

hall and reported the results of his visit at Hastinapur. Yudhishthira immediately looked at his brothers and said, "You have heard the final word from Duryodhana, and also, how he is already swaggering about his 11 division military force led by Bhishma and Drona. There is no hope for peace anymore, now we must prepare for war without delay. Pandavas started sending emissaries to all the friendly rulers and soon they also had a fully equipped powerful army of seven divisions, led by seven distinguished warriors, King Drupada, Virata, Dhrishtadyumna, Sikhandi, Satyaki, Chekitana, and Bhima. Dhrishtadyumna was selected to be the commander-in-chief for the army of Pandavas. At Hastinapur the troops were assembled in millions, equipped with many kinds of weapons. Duryodhana arranged his 11 divisions led by Bhishma, Drona, Kripacharya, Salya, Karna, Vikarna, Somedetti, Dushasana, Ashwatthama, and others all skilled in the strategy of warfare. The Kauravas' army was marshalled by revered grandsire Bhishma.

The Holy land of Kurukshetra was picked for the site of war, where the great sages of antiquity had performed tough austerities and *yajna*, hoping that the sacredness of the place would be conducive to the victory of truth and establishment of *Dharma* (righteousness). Kurukshetra was also the land of the ancestors of the Kurus usually called *Tapkhetra* (field of Penances and discipline). According to astrological calculations a certain date was fixed for the commencement of the war and as the time approached closer, slowly the troops began to march. Yudhishthira personally supervised the transportation of food supplies, medicines, physicians, fodder, machines and weapons. Before the troops had started moving to Kurukshetra the great sage Vyasa made a visit to Hastinapur and at the special request of King Dhritarashtra he granted an extraordinary divine vision to Sanjaya, by which the latter could visualize, the day-to-day activities at the battlefield and relay the entire scene of the war to Dhritarashtra, while sitting next to him in his palace.

It was at the dawn of Mokshada Ekadashi—Vaikuntha Ekadashi, the 11th day of the ascending phase of the Moon in *Margashirsh shukla*,when the armies of the Kauravas and the Pandavas marshalled by their respective commander-in-chiefs met face to face at the holy battlefield of Kurukshetra. It was at the critical juncture, just a few minutes before the commencement of the war, when Arjuna looked at his grandsires, teachers, cousins, grandsons, brothers, relatives, and friends stationed between both the armies, he was touched with deep sorrow, pain, and compassion. He felt unsteady, agitated, emotionally confused, and very sad at the entire situation. He requested Sri Krishna for guidance saying, "O' Keshava, my heart is overpowered by the weakness of pity and my mind is confused about my duty. I request Thee, to tell me for certain, which is decidedly good for me." Arjuna recoiled back from his assigned duty and felt totally confused and depressed. After listening to the self-contradictory state-ments of Arjuna for a few minutes, Sri Krishna opened the conversation saying, "O' Arjuna, the soul is immortal. There was never a time when I or you or these rulers of men did not exist; nor will there be any time in the future, when all of us shall cease to be. One soul enclosed within the mind has gone through many births before, and keeps entering into new wombs. The soul is eternal, all pervading, unchanging immutable, and primordial."

Throughout the dialogue Arjuna was enlightened about the mysteries of yogic unity and how a person becomes wise and integrated just by learning to live in the consciousness of the Supreme-self. The words—*Tasmatsarveshu Kaleshu yog yukto bhava Arjuna,* literally means, "O' Arjuna remain aligned in yogic unity with the soul, and do all your work with the guidance of the Supreme-soul." Arjuna was persuaded to re-evaluate the entire scenario on the basis of his guidance from the indwelling-soul and fight the battle in the spirit of service to his countrymen. Sri Krishna guided Arjuna step by step into the gospel of selfless action and also revealed His true identity as God-incarnate saying, "O' Arjuna, whenever there is decline of *Dharma* (righteousness) and moral values; I manifest myself in order to re-establish the values of righteousness and to restore orderliness on earth. For the protection of the virtuous for the destruction of the wicked, and for the establishment of *Dharma* (righteousness) I come into being from age to age." Later, during the dialogue Arjuna was blessed with *Vishvarup Darshana* (The universal form of Lord Krishna). He was overwhelmed with amazement and thrilled with joy at the most blessed sight of the Supreme Lord as 'One unified field' and realized that he was a co-worker with God in the great work of eliminating negativity and destroying the wicked and vicious people. He was awakened to the truth that behind the veil of entire activity, it is the 'Will' of God which prevails and keeps everything in motion.

After giving a long sermon about the importance of performing one's duty with detachment, in a spirit of dedication, Lord Krishna convinced Arjuna in making a complete surrender to the Lord without any trace of reservation. He said, "*Sarvadharman parityajya mamekam saranam vraja aham tva sarvapapebhyo moksayisyami ma sucah*" meaning—"O' Arjuna forget all about your mixed notions of *Dharma*, take refuge in Me. Be in eternal union with me, I will take care of you and liberate you from all fears". When Arjuna surrendered to the call of the Divine, from the very core of his being and from the totality of his heart; Lord Krishna's grace descended unconditionally. He immediately became aligned with the source and said, "O' Krishna my delusion is destroyed and I have regained my memory (knowledge of the self) through your grace. Now I am totally integrated, and free from all doubts. I shall act according to thy word." Arjuna felt light-hearted, relaxed, stabilized, confident, integrated and motivated in carrying the command of Sri Krishna, sincerely and devotedly. When Arjuna picked up his Gandiva, a wave of joy swept across the ranks of the Pandavas and the angels showered their blessings from heaven.

At the spur of the moment when all the chiefs in Pandavas' army were ready to blow their conches, suddenly Yudhishthira was seen descending from his chariot and walking towards the commander of the Kauravas' forces. Yudhishthira went directly to his grandsire Bhishma and touched his feet for blessings and asked for permission to begin the battle. After formally seeking the approval from Bhishma; he also went to Dronacharya for blessings. The moment Yudhishthira bowed down and touched his feet; Dronacharya spoke in very assertive words, "*yato dharmastato Krishna, yato krishnastato jaya*" meaning, "where there is *Dharma* (righteousness), Sri Krishna is there, and where there is Sri Krishna, victory is assured." He further added "although, I am bound to the Kauravas and must fight on their side; "O' Dharmaputra, my blessings are going to be with you, rest assured." Yudhishthira also approached Kripacharya, and his uncle Salya, obtained their blessings and then returned to his military station and gave the signal for attack. The battle began with single combats between the leading chiefs equipped with equal weapons. The initial move was made by Bhima and later when all became engaged in heroic combats the noise of battle rolled and rent the air. A fierce battle went on for 18 days, on the field of Kurukshetra, sometime in favor of Kauravas and sometime in favor of Pandavas. Each morning the troop formations were changed. On Kauravas' side, after Bhishma's command for ten days, Drona took the lead and after the latter's death, Karna succeeded to command, till the 17th day of the war. The Pandavas' forces suffered greatly in the beginning but Sri Krishna always kept up their spirits with his encouraging words and assured victory to Yudhishthira. The Great War came to an end with a duel between Duryodhana and Bhima in which the latter pounced on wicked

Duryodhana and smashed him down to die helplessly. The same night Ashwatthama, Kripacharya, and Kritvarma, the sole remnant of Kauravas' army killed Dhrishtadyumna and all the sons of Draupadi while they were plunged in deep sleep at their tents. After the tragic incident, the Pandavas returned to Hastinapur. They spent one month period of mourning outside the city at the banks of a sacred river and performed the special rites for the peace and salvation of the departed souls. Yudhishthira lamented loudly and shed tears in pain while paying oblations. He remained grief-stricken and depressed for a long time.

The coronation of Yudhishthira was duly solemnized with the blessing of Sri Krishna, sage Vyasa, and elders in the royal family, but before taking up the duties of the state; he went to visit the great grandsire Bhishma, who patiently awaited his death while lying on his bed of arrows. At the advice of Sri Krishna, Yudhishthira sat at the feet of his grandsire Bhishma and sincerely requested him for guidance in the management of state, especially the duties of a King. The venerable Bhishma shared his profound wisdom with Yudhishthira, blessed everyone in the family and discarded his mortal body in peace.

Yudhishthira, after his enthronement, ruled the country with the cooperation of his brothers and great guidance of Vidura and the chief royal priest Dhaumya. The old king Dhritarashtra and Queen Gandhari were served with deep respect at the palace. It was after 15 years of pleasant stay with the royal family; one morning Dhritarashtra expressed his desire to retire and live in the forest with Gandhari and spend rest of his life in contemplation. The great Queen Kunti a veritable embodiment of *Dharma*, also decided to accompany them. Yudhishthira made all the comfortable arrangements for their stay at the Ashram in the forest and visited them quite often—until one day, a fierce forest fire raged around the Ashram and three of them died in the conflagration while deeply absorbed in *Samadhi* (meditation).

After the great war of Kurukshetra was over, Sri Krishna stayed in Hastinapur for few months in order to protect Abhimanyu and Uttara's unborn child Parikshit, and then later returned to Dwarka with Balarama, Satyaki and other Yadava heroes. He ruled the kingdom for about 35 years and in the 36th year of his regime the Vrishnis and Yadavas destroyed each other in a mutual feud, leaving no trace of themselves. Sri Krishna and Balarama witnessed the entire massacre. Balarama was overwhelmed with shame and decided to renounce his mortal being in meditation. Sri Krishna, Himself, had performed and achieved what He had to as incarnation of Lord Vishnu. So, reflecting over the completion of His mission as God-incarnate, He concluded that the time of his own departure from the world of mortals had come. The Supreme deity Sri Krishna, although perpetually aligned with *Parabrahman*, wished to depart from the world like other human beings.

One day while he was lying on the sand at the wooded beach and absorbed in yogic meditation, a fierce hunter mistook the sole of his foot for a bird and shot an arrow. Thus the illustrious deity, the cosmic energy, the creator as well as the destroyer of all, ascended upwards, filling the entire welkin with splendor and reached His own inconceivable region.

When the Pandavas received the news of Sri Krishna's departure from the world they were grief-stricken and very depressed. They lost their interest in life on earth and decided to renounce the world. They crowned their grandson Parikshit as a King of the empire and the five brothers with Draupadi left Hastinapur. They went out on a pilgrimage proceeding to the North and visited several holy shrines. As they moved towards the high-peaked mountain path in the Himalayas; the four Pandu brothers and Draupadi died one after the other. Dharmaputra Yudhishthira alone was blessed to ride into the celestial chariot of Indra and after going through his final trial successfully, he renounced his physical body and entered the realm of celestials, where he was greeted warmly by the gods and also his brothers and Draupadi.

The great King Parikshit, the son of Abhimanyu, ruled Hastinapur for many years and thus continued the Pandava dynasty.

"I owed a magnificent day to the Bhagawad Geeta. It was the first of books; it was as if an empire spoke to us, nothing small or unworthy, but large, serene, consistent, the voice of an old intelligence which in another age and climate had pondered and thus disposed of the same questions which exercise us."

- Ralph Waldo Emerson

"In the morning I bathe my intellect in the stupendous and cosmogonal philosophy of the Bhagawad Geeta, in comparison with which our modern world and its literature seem puny and trivial."

- Henry David Thoreau

"When doubts haunt me, when disappointments stare me in the face, and I see not one ray of hope on the horizon, I turn to the Bhagawad Geeta."

- Mahatma Gandhi

"When I read the Bhagawad Geeta and reflect about how God created this universe everything else seems so superfluous."

-Albert Einstein

6

The Bhagawad Geeta

The Bhagawad Geeta is the most luminous dialogue in the legacy of Vedic literature. There are hundreds of commentaries on the Bhagawad Geeta—both in Indian and in many foreign languages. This is perhaps the most widely translated scriptural text of the world. In the words of Dr. S. Radhakrishnan, "For centuries people have found comfort in this great book which sets forth in precise and penetrating words the essential principles of a spiritual religion which are not contingent on ill-founded facts, unscientific dogmas, or arbitrary fancies. With a long history of spiritual power, it serves even today as a light to all who will receive illumination from the profundity of its wisdom, which insists on a world wider and deeper than wars and revolutions, can touch. It is a powerful shaping factor in the renewal of spiritual life and has secured an assured place among the world's greatest scriptures."

The message of Geeta synthesizes almost all the well-known teachings of ancient scriptures of the world and it is addressed to the entire mankind. In the words of Dr. Annie Besant, "Among the priceless teachings that may be found in the great Hindu poem of the Mahabharata, there is none so rare and precious as this, 'The Lord's Song.'"

The Bhagawad Geeta presents a profound insight into the working of human nature and provides the appropriate guidance that is needed in almost every field of life. Ever since the teachings of Geeta have become known to the people in Europe and America, it has quickly won the interest and admiration of millions. Many philosophical and religious groups in foreign countries hold the same respect for Geeta as the people in India. Dr. Paul Brunton, a great British scholar, has written: "This ancient book can satisfy the modern needs. Nearly every literate yogi in India carries with him a small edition of this inspired and profound classic, the Bhagawad Geeta... The Geeta summarizes various approaches to the Overself and also describes the latter. Sri Krishna not only represents the embodied spiritual teacher, He is ultimately the Overself within man, the God within who can illuminate all dark corners and answer all questions."

The great educator and philosopher of India, Mr. Madan Mohan Malaviya, has said about Geeta, "I believe that in all the living languages of the world, there is no book so full of true knowledge, and yet so handy as the Bhagawad Geeta." The well-known professor of religion at Oxford University, Mr. Zaehner, has written about the glory of the sacred song in these words, "Geeta is a first-hand guide to the ancient roots of Vedic religion. Although in Shvetashvatara Upanishad the transcendence of the personal God has been affirmed to some extent—with Geeta has come the devotional religion." The great respect and appreciation for Geeta has been voiced by

Warren Hastings, the first British Governor General of India, in year 1773. He has said, "When the British Empire is lost in the oblivion, when its sources of wealth and prosperity are not remembered, this scripture and the lessons it contains will continue to inspire millions of people in this world." Sir Edwin Arnold has called Geeta the incomparable religious classic of India.

The perennial philosophy of the Bhagawad Geeta has been a rich source of guidance and inspiration to the entire mankind for centuries. In the words of Barbara Stoler Miller, "The dramatic moral crisis that is central to the Bhagawad Geeta has inspired centuries of Indian philosophers and practical men of wisdom, as well as Western thinkers such as Thoreau, Emerson, and Eliot." In her translation of the Bhagawad Geeta she mentions Thoreau and Emerson's fascination for the holy dialogue, and ponders why Thoreau took the Bhagawad Geeta to Walden Pond. She writes, "Among the many works of Asian literature that were studied in Concord, Massachusetts, in the mid-nineteenth century, none was more influential than the Bhagawad Geeta." She quotes the profound response of Thoreau to the study of the Holy sermon in these words: "In the morning I bathe my intellect in the stupendous and cosmogonal philosophy of the Bhagawad Geeta, since whose composition years of the gods have elapsed, and in comparison with which our modern world and its literature seem puny and trivial." She has also quoted some beautiful lines from one of the journals of Ralph Waldo Emerson, "It was the first of books; it was as if an empire spoke to us, nothing small or unworthy but large, serene, consistent, the voice of an old intelligence which in another age and climate had pondered and thus disposed of the same questions which exercise us."

The Bhagawad Geeta, has been called a *Yogashastra* because it explains the theoretical knowledge of the soul and also the techniques to experience the unity with the soul. The colophon *Srimad Bhagawadgeeta supanishatsu brahmavidyayam yogasastre*—towards the end of each chapter clearly indicates that Bhagawad Geeta is the science of the Absolute—Supreme *Parabrahman* and the great scripture of yoga.It is both the knowledge of the Supreme reality and the art of union with reality. The entire yogic philosophy written by any sage has been summarized in the holy sermon.

Vishadyoga (Chapter 1)
(The Yoga of the Despondency of Arjuna)

The most luminous dialogue in the Bhagawad Geeta opens with *Vishadyoga*—Arjuna's grief. *Vishad* is a depressed state of mind when everything in life appears to be unsettled and confused. In moments of loneliness, when we feel helpless and depressed; we are persuaded to seek help from God and take refuge in the Supreme-soul. Communion with the indwelling Lord in moments of depression is called *Vishad yoga*. An honest surrender to the Supreme Lord in pain and innocence is *Vishadyoga*. It is a fact, when a person cries out for help from the purity of his heart, the guidance comes from the indwelling-Lord, which helps to release the aching past and move on in life with a new concept of truth. Every person has to pass through the self-created egocentric boundaries of 'I and Mine' in order to comprehend the inner-Bliss and alliance with the source. Arjuna grieves at the painful memories of the past and the dreaded images of the future. The moment he finishes one statement, he brings another in support of the previous one. Weighed down by emotional conflict, confused and depressed Arjuna seeks an escape from the performance of his assigned duties. Sri Krishna remains silent; he knows that Arjuna is depressed.

Samkhyayoga (Chapter 2)
(The Yoga of Transcendental Knowledge)

Arjuna detracts from his assigned duty and feels helpless. He says, "O' Krishna, my heart is overpowered by the weakness of pity and my mind is confused about my duty; I request Thee, to tell me for certain, which is decidedly good for me."

Sri Krishna opens the conversation saying, "O' Arjuna, the soul is immortal." He explains that the entire manifestation of Supreme *Parabrahman* represents the real and unreal, the immortal and the mortal, the Supreme-Self and the conditioned-self. The real is eternal, and the unreal is ever changing and perishable. The body goes through all kinds of changes in life but the one who perceives the entire change, the soul ever remains the same. Even at the time of death the soul goes from one body to another forced by the thoughts and memories. The soul at one time becomes someone's father, at another time, the son, the elder brother and yet another time the younger brother. One soul enclosed within the mind has gone through many births before, and keeps entering into new wombs. The process of understanding the nature of the soul is really very subtle and difficult; it cannot be described in words.

Sri Krishna gives some examples, which are within the comprehension of the human mind, i.e. the fire cannot burn it nor can water make it wet and also weapons cannot cut it. The soul is eternal, all pervading, unchanging, immovable and primordial. The saints and philosophers who live in the awareness of the soul, for them death is only a change; in which the soul leaves one body and enters into another which is new.They know very clearly that the physical body was meant to live only for a limited time, between the two events the birth and death.The journey of the soul is ever renewing on the path of eternity.

Sri Krishna enlightens Arjuna about the subtle meaning of *Karmayoga*.The word yoga has been derived from the Sanskrit word '*Yuj*'—which means to bind, and join together the various levels of consciousness, in order to experience a union and communion with God. It is the conscious communion of the individual-soul with the Supreme-soul. The discipline of yoga makes the individual receptive to the voice of the indwelling-soul and initiates him into the performance of action in a co-partnership with God, and thus transforms his action into the yoga of action. Living a life in the awareness of the Divine, and performing all work in the consciousness of the Divine is *Karmayoga*.

After listening to the glories of inner wisdom and *Karmayoga*, Arjuna makes a request to know more about the man of wisdom who has been blessed with yogic unity and becomes firmly grounded in the transcendental nature of the Supreme-soul. Sri Krishna tells Arjuna that the person who has the experiential knowledge of the transcendental-self, he definitely shows the grace of his inner unity, even in his day-to-day life. There is a beauty in his countenance, satisfaction in his manners and harmony in his words. A man of integral wisdom, who is ever united in the yoga of transcendental knowledge, makes quick, firm, impartial and very determined decisions. He is highly intuitive and his discerning ability is remarkable. His decisions come from the purity of his heart. The eloquence of his speech and the careful analysis of his words manifest the serenity of his mind. He performs his duties very regularly, efficiently, and relapses back into the stream of inner Bliss whenever he wants to. Sri Krishna glorifies the practice of transcendental yogic unity, which forms the foundation for all types of progress in material life as well as in spiritual.

Karmayoga (Chapter 3)
(The Yoga of Action)

The dialogue opens with a question from Arjuna. He says, "O' Krishna if the knowledge of the Supreme-self and unity in yoga is the only means to the realization of the Self, then how can the gospel of selfless action be helpful in it?" He makes a request for proper explanation.

Sri Krishna declares that in this world there are two types of spiritual disciplines, the yoga of knowledge and the yoga of action. The yoga of knowledge means, the type of knowledge that helps the individual to be in unity with the Higher Self; while the yoga of action—means the type of work which helps to experience union and communion with God. Both the yoga of action and the yoga of knowledge do complement each other. A man of integral wisdom who is perpetually settled in the transcendental knowledge of the Self, definitely performs all his work in a co-partnership with God. In his practice of devotion-cum-action, a spontaneous flow of inner awareness is perceived, that ultimately, prepares him for the direct experience of unity in yoga. He tells Arjuna that a person has to blend both the yoga of knowledge and the yoga of action in order to achieve the highest fulfillment in any activity. Both the methods of yoga are inter-dependent. A person needs the proper knowledge of both in order to attain perfection in either one of them. Both *Samkhyayoga* (the yoga of knowledge) and *Karmayoga* (yoga of action) revolve around the performance of action selflessly and skillfully.

Sri Krishna tells Arjuna that a person does not have to renounce the world in order to make the spiritual advancement; because the performance of duties with love, devotion, and detachment itself purifies the individual. It is the practice of devotion-cum-action which educates the individual in all dimensions. When a person performs his work with proper knowledge and undivided devotion, the procedure itself modifies the behavior and actually the process itself becomes both the training and the teacher.

Jnana-Karmayoga (Chapter 4)
(The Yoga of Action and Knowledge)

In continuation of the philosophy of *Jnana-Karmayoga*, Sri Krishna tells Arjuna that the yoga of selfless action is not a new concept, it has been handed down in regular succession. The ancient kings and sages always respected the sacred doctrine and performed all their duties in the spirit of sacrifice. It is the perennial wisdom that has assisted the sustenance of life on earth through ages.

He also enlightens Arjuna about the concept of *Dharma*. The word *Dharma*, which comes from the root word *Dhar*— means to uphold and maintain. It's a unique system of values determined and supported by the voice of the inner-self, which guides us to perform our duties by keeping in mind the global welfare. It is the direct guidance from the source of life that prevails at the heart of the entire creation.

In a society where people become very materialistic, and when every person moves single-mindedly, in the pursuit of wealth, the spirituality is usually pushed to the very far end. With the negligence of spiritual values, usually people become selfish, and ignore *swadharma*. Any type of material progress and happiness, which is preferred over ethics, becomes another form of misery. It is the consciousness of the Divine, which guides the person to live by the code of conduct upheld by *Dharma*.

The decline of *Dharma* (righteousness) starts at the individual level and gradually spreads throughout the community and nation causing a downfall of the entire society. This is what Sri Krishna declares, "Whenever there is the decline of *Dharma* (righteousness), and the rise of unrighteousness, O' Arjuna, then I manifest Myself, in order to maintain the code of ethics so that the society can function peacefully and harmoniously."

Here Sri Krishna is speaking to Arjuna as the Higher-Self of each and every one of us. The Lord incarnates Himself, to enlighten people so that they can recognize their own divinity by their own efforts. He guides people by the example of His personal life. The God-incarnate comes down to the level of human beings, in order to educate them into graciousness of the human life. He strengthens their faith in God and also their respect for the laws of *Dharma*.

Karma-Sannyasayoga (Chapter 5)
(The Yoga of Action and Renunciation)

In context to the doctrine of *Karma-Sannyasayoga*, Sri Krishna starts with the meaning of *Sannyasa* (renunciation). He tells Arjuna that the renunciation and the performance of actions in Yoga, both lead to the highest good; but of the two, *Karmayoga* (the yoga of action) is indeed superior. In general, the word *Sannyasa* is related to complete renunciation of the world. Sri Krishna calls that person a perpetual *sannyasi*, who has risen above the dualities of life; who is peaceful and works with the serenity of yogic alliance.

He makes it very clear that renunciation of the world, without proper knowledge of *Karmayoga* can be really difficult. It is the performance of action in yoga that prepares the person for total renouncement of worldly life. The gospel of selfless action makes the path of relinquishment enjoyable and interesting. *Karmayoga* is a means for attaining the state of renunciation.

Sri Krishna glorifies the importance of devotion, dedication and unity with the Supreme-soul, which is the basis of genuine renunciation. He explains that by living in constant awareness of the soul, one develops an intimate relationship with the Divine. As the bond of love for God becomes stronger, the detachment and renunciation come spontaneously. The inner purification, renunciation and liberation—all this is an ongoing process towards self-realization and the attainment of *Nirvana* or *Moksha*.

Dhyanayoga (Chapter 6)
(The Yoga of Meditation)

The dialogue opens with the words of Sri Krishna. He repeats once again that renunciation and the yoga of action are essentially the same. He makes it very clear that the attitude of selfless action is a means for the person, who wants to make progress in yoga; and when perfected in *Karmayoga*, peace within becomes the guidance. A quiet mind enjoys reposing in God. Sri Krishna makes it very clear that detachment from the fruit of action comes from inner peace, and the inner peace comes from yogic unity with the Supreme spirit. Learning to work with the guidance of the Supreme-soul is *Karmayoga* and renunciation in essence.

In reference to the philosophy of karma and the rise and fall of the human soul, Sri Krishna says, "Let a man lift himself by his own self, let him not degrade himself; for he himself is his own friend and he himself is his own enemy" (6.5-6). Anybody can rise to the height of a genius and can become the glory of the world, but if he ignores the voice of the inner-self, then he drifts away from *swadharma*, and he falls. A human being can be the splendor and majesty of the world but also its ridicule. For example, if a person remains aware of the voice of God and the activities of the mind he definitely acts like a friend of his own self. On the other hand, when a person acts carelessly under the slavery of his conditioned behavior, ruled by the lower-self, he becomes his own enemy.

Sri Krishna tells Arjuna, it is through regular practice of meditation that we can purify our thoughts and thus, can improve the quality of life. Meditation means to attend to the thoughts with attention and intention. In meditation we learn to attend ourselves by watching, observing and beholding the movements of our thoughts, ideas, and aspirations. It is the method of exploring the inner dimensions of our personality and ultimately being introduced to the essentiality of our nature. Real meditation is the liberation from the clutches of our conditioned behavior and living in Bliss, where the different aspects of our personalities blend into one harmonious whole.

After listening to the glories of meditative unity in transcendence, Arjuna makes a request to know more about the destiny of a person, who makes some efforts but falls in yoga and fails to achieve perfection. Sri Krishna assures Arjuna that the virtue of good work is never lost. Any one who falls in yoga and fails to achieve perfection in present life, definitely remains eligible for perfection in the life hereafter. The pursuit goes on to his next life. He is reborn in a family that gives him an opportunity for suitable completion of the task, which remained incomplete in the previous life. He is intuitively persuaded towards the path of self-realization and God-realization. He regains all the knowledge of his previous births and makes use of that for the yogic unity. The progressive realization of the Supreme-soul is a very difficult task to accomplish in the short span of a single lifetime. According to the law of karma the soul keeps evolving around the *samskaras* (latencies) until it finally becomes settled in the Supreme-soul.

Once again Sri Krishna glorifies the greatness of Yoga and tells Arjuna to become a devoted yogi. He tells that living a life in yogic unity with the indwelling-soul is far better than all the austerities and scriptural knowledge. A yogi's life is gracious, glorious and becomes an example for others. He tells Arjuna, to be a Yogi in order to achieve the very best in human life here and hereafter.

Jnana-Vijnanayoga (Chapter 7)
(The Yoga of Wisdom and Knowledge)

After giving a long description of yogic unity in meditation, Sri Krishna draws Arjuna's attention towards the similarities in the macrocosm and the microcosm. He declares that the Divine and the manifestation of the Divine are not separate from one another. Both are very intimately connected. It is the knowledge of the Supreme-soul which reveals the mysteries of the universe. It is the yogic unity in transcendence, which helps us to know everything in the universe. In general, people start their study from the gross to the subtle, and from matter to the spirit, means the analytical study of the relative and Absolute. In that process of scientific inquiry, it is very hard to comprehend the truth, because after some analysis, our answers itself become the questions. On the other hand when we move intuitively from the subtle to the gross, the inner intuition guides us, helps us and the understanding of the unmanifest and manifest Divinity becomes easy. He tells Arjuna that it is necessary to experience the silent flow of divine energy in macrocosm as well as in microcosm in order to realize the unity that prevails in the universe.

In reference to the glories of devotion and worship, Sri Krishna tells Arjuna, "There are four kinds of virtuous people who worship Me: the person in physical agony, the seeker of knowledge, the seeker of wealth, and the man of wisdom." Sri Krishna declares all of them to be noble and virtuous, but the man of wisdom to be very special, because he loves Him for His sake only. Loving the Self for the sake of the Self is very rare.

Sri Krishna concludes the conversation declaring that after going through many births, the man of wisdom and true devotion is intuitively led to the subjective apprehension of Supreme Divinity and comes to the realization—"*Vasudeva Sarvam Iti*"—that *Vasudeva* is everything. Here *Vasudeva* stands for the Supreme consciousness, which presides over the cause, space and time; and is also above all. He takes refuge in *Vasudeva* being the highest goal and also the means to attain his goal. His mind works in unity with the universal mind. Sri Krishna calls this enlightened person a Mahatma which literally means a noble and virtuous soul; who stands above the rest of the crowd, and who becomes an embodiment of the Divine.

Akshara-Brahmayoga (Chapter 8)
(The Yoga of the Imperishable Brahman)

The dialogue opens with a bundle of questions from Arjuna. He says, "O' Krishna what is *Brahman*? What is *Adhyatma*? What is Karma? What is *Adhibuta*? What is *Adhidaiva*? What is *Adhiyajna*? And how a person concentrates on you at the time of death?" He makes a special request to know more about the realization of God at the time of death.

Sri Krishna starts with the words, *"Aksharam Brahma Paramam,"* which means, "The Supreme imperishable is *Brahman*." The entire world is rooted in *Brahman*. The nature of *Brahman* is inexplicable, but during the process of learning and austerities as we move from one perceptual experience to another, we are ushered to the realization that 'Bliss is *Brahman*'. All the beings are born from Bliss, sustained by the Bliss and into the Bliss they merge again.

In reference to the answer of second question what is *Adhyatma*? Sri Krishna tells that the nature of the Self is addressed as *Adhyatma*, the path of spirituality is also *Adhyatma*, so is the science of the soul and the study of the self. He also adds that the creative force, which gives momentum to the wheel of creation is called Karma. In answer to the fourth question, what is *Adhibhuta*? Sri Krishna explains, that the elements that contribute towards the composition of everything in the world are *Adhibhuta*—the perishable aspect of the divine potency.

Answering Arjuna's next question, what is *Adhidaiva* and *Adhiyajna*? Sri Krishna says, "O' Arjuna in the macrocosm as well as in the microcosm all the gods and goddesses are controlled by the Supreme-Lord. The controller of these *Daivas* is *Adhidaiva*." There is one vital force that presides over the inner cosmos and guides the entire functioning of the body. This work order of perfect co-operation for the sustenance of the body is called *Yajna*. All the voluntary and involuntary activities of the body are only the various manifestations of the transcendental consciousness. God is not only remote from us in some supreme status beyond but he is here too, in the body of every being; in the heart of every man and in nature. Although perennially established in peaceful transcendence, the Lord is *Adhibhuta*, *Adhidaiva*, and *Adhiyajna* dwelling in the bodies of all beings.

After giving answers to six questions, Sri Krishna proceeds to Arjuna's last question, in reference to the realization of the God at the time of death. He tells very clearly, that the individual-soul goes into the thought where the mind is settled at the time of death. It is the ruling thought at the moment of departure from the body, which is the culminating point of all our memories and *samskaras*.

Sri Krishna tells Arjuna that living a life in perpetual awareness of the Divine should become a state of mind—a way of life. At the time of death it is the yogic practice of living in the consciousness of the soul, which helps the person to experience the inner vision, and guides him to a single-minded concentration on the Supreme *Purusha*.

Sri Krishna also mentions about closing of the doors of the senses and firmly confining awareness to the primordial sound of *Aum*; which guides the soul in the realms of Divine consciousness. He makes it very clear to Arjuna that the person who lives his life in harmony with the primordial *nada* (sound), definitely departs in perfect peace with the primordial-Self. When the yogic unity with the Supreme-self becomes the joy of life and the richness of every moment, the life becomes a celebration. The yogi knows how to celebrate life and death as well. That is why, Sri Krishna repeats several times, during the dialogue, "*Tasmat sarveshu kaleshu yogayukto bhavarjuna*," which means, "O'Arjuna stay aligned in yogic unity from moment to moment."

Rajavidya-Rajaguhyayoga (Chapter 9)
(The Yoga of the Sovereign Science and Sovereign Secret)

In reference to the experiential knowledge of the Self, the dialogue opens with the words of Sri Krishna. He tells Arjuna that the royal science, the royal secret and the experiential knowledge of the Supreme-soul gets revealed with pure unconditional love, and sincere undivided devotion. He makes it very clear that for understanding the mysteries of the soul, one really doesn't need to have much pre-requisite in philosophy and religion. The knowledge of the

Supreme Divinity is inherently present in all of us, and it is revealed, by itself; when the individual remains aligned with the source of life and follows the guidance of the Higher-Self with love, innocence, and honest devotion. He upholds the path of devotion to be the noblest and highly rewarding in the spiritual journey. It has been called the Supreme purifier because it is the fulfillment in itself and also a means for increased fulfillment at the same time.

He tells Arjuna that each and every person can find a personal relationship with God. It does require sincere love, willingness, devotion, discipline, commitment, and complete surrender with an honest desire to be accepted in service. Here the yoga of action, the yoga of knowledge and the yoga of devotion are graciously blended into the holy formula— Learn to live in the consciousness of God and make yourself available to the selfless service of the Divine.

Sri Krishna knows that Arjuna will cooperate enthusiastically and peacefully only when he is blessed with the experiential knowledge of the soul. It is only after self-actualization, he will feel more like an instrument in the hands of the Divine power.

Vibhutiyoga (Chapter 10)
(The Yoga of The Divine Manifestations)

In the description of the omniscience of the Supreme-soul, Sri Krishna has used the word '*Vibhuti*' which means magnificence. *Vi* signifies *vishesha* (special) and '*bhu*' implies being. *Vi* + *bhu* means appear, expand, and manifest. The entire universe is an expression of the power and the majesty of the creator. He draws Arjuna's attention towards the unity in diversity as experienced in the universe. Everything is the manifestation of divine potency.

The dialogue becomes interesting when Arjuna expresses his desire to know more about the attributes of the Divine and understand the mystery of that Supreme power which prevails at the substratum of the universe. He makes an appeal for a clear, detailed explanation of the various significant manifestations that can spontaneously help him to maintain his perpetual unity with the Lord.

Sri Krishna opens the conversation with words, *"Aham atma gudakesa sarvabhutasayasthitah ahamadisca madhyam ca bhutanam ante eva ca"* (BG 10.20), meaning, "O'Arjuna, I am the indwelling soul, seated in the hearts of all beings; I am the beginning, the middle as well as the end of all beings." He further adds, "Among the Adityas, I am Vishnu and of the Vedas I am Samaveda. I am the Shankara among the Rudras," and so on.

After giving a short description of the attributes, Sri Krishna concludes the description saying, *"Vistavhyahamidam krtsnam ekansena sthito jagat—O'* Arjuna I exist supporting the whole universe with the single fragment of Myself."

These words convey the ultimate declaration, that the entire universe is being held together by a small fraction of the Lord's yogic power. The divine potency is holding everything together and also reflecting through everything. In words of Swami Chidbhavananda, "Lord is expressing Himself.

Whatever catches our imagination, draws our attention, sends us into raptures and infuses bliss into us that is none but the glory of the God." It is very difficult to comprehend the infinitude of the Supreme; the human understanding can catch only a small fraction of it, so it is just enough to remember that the Lord is everything. This attitude of seeing the Lord's opulence and majesty in everything keeps us perpetually connected with the Supreme-Self and strengthens our closeness with the Divine.

Vishvarupa-Darsanayoga (Chapter 11)
(The Yoga of The Vision of the Universal Form)

After listening in detail about the attributes of the Divine, Arjuna makes another request, he says, "*Manyase yadi tac chakyam maya drastumiti prabho yogesvara tato me tvam darsayatmanamavyayam*" (11.4), meaning, "O' Lord of yoga, if you consider me worthy of beholding your universal form please show me your eternal majestic Self." In *Vishwarup Darshan*, Arjuna is awakened into a specific field of super-consciousness. He looks at the universal body as 'One' unified field in which everything settles eventually. He beholds the cosmic body, enclosing the entire creation in one unit. The cosmic vision gives Arjuna an opportunity to understand the relativity of time and that, which is beyond the concept of cause, space, and time. He feels exhilarated and starts singing the glories of the Lord with love and devotion. He says, "O' Lord you are *Anantah* (Infinite). You are the God of gods, the abode of the entire universe."

Arjuna comes to the realization that he is a co-worker with God in the great work of eliminating ignorance and tearing down the vicious cycle. Establishment of morality and *Dharma* is a co-operative enterprise of God and man. He is awakened to the truth that behind the veil of entire activity, it is the 'Will' of God that prevails and keeps everything in motion.

Sri Krishna tells Arjuna that the experience of Divine vision is indeed a special blessing of the Lord. He says, *"Jnatum drastum ca tattvena pravestum ca parantapa—* O' Arjuna only by sincere undivided devotion a person understands Me, perceives Me in essence and enters into My essentiality." This is what Vedas have declared—Being, Becoming, and Bliss.

Bhaktiyoga (Chapter 12)
(The Yoga of Devotion)

The dialogue opens with a question from Arjuna. He says, "O' Krishna, some worship You with sincere undivided devotion and some others meditate on the unmanifest—which one of these two is the better knower of yoga?" Arjuna wants to know the comparative relevance of devotional services offered to the personal God and contemplation upon the unmanifest, Divinity. As a student of Vedic tradition, Arjuna has been taught that the Supreme-soul is attributeless, formless, omniscient, and omnipresent; but after visualizing the God's cosmic form, his old concept has taken a new meaning. Although, throughout the conversation, Sri Krishna has mentioned the worship of the personal form of God, apparently Arjuna missed the inner meaning of His statement. He is convinced that devotion to a personal God is the best approach in spiritual journey but he still requests Sri Krishna to confirm it.

Sri Krishna tells Arjuna, "Those who concentrate their mind on Me, live in unity with Me; those are steadfast in their faith; worship Me with undivided devotion are the knowers of yoga." He also enlightens Arjuna about the devotion to the unmanifest and says, "Those who worship the imperishable, the indefinable, the unthinkable, the immovable, omniscient, and eternal with complete self-control, they also reach Me." It is really difficult to draw a line between the worship of *saguna* (God with form) and the meditation on *nirguna* (formless); at which point one ends and the other starts. In the process of worshipping *saguna*, we actually meditate on *nirguna*, the formless, that hides behind the *saguna*. So by being devoted to either, one is indeed worshipping both at the same time. The worship of God with form and shape spontaneously leads us to contemplation upon the unmanifest Supreme Divinity.

In reference to the modes of concentration on the Self, Sri Krishna explains some methods, generally applied in training of yogic communion. He starts with *Abhyasayoga*, which means constant practice with repeated effort of living in the consciousness of the Divine. Repeat the name of the Divine consciously and witness the process. Constant remembrance of the Lord purifies the mind and creates the most intimate relationship with the Divine that eventually leads to yogic unity with the soul.

In explanation of the various methods for unity in yoga, in verses 10-12, Sri Krishna concludes, that knowledge is indeed better than that practice, which is followed without proper insight. Meditation is of course, superior to knowledge but renouncing attachment to the fruits of actions is even better, "*Tyaga chantir rantiram*," which means, "With renunciation peace follows quickly."

He declares that renouncing the attachment to the fruits of actions is the key for perfection in yogic unity with the Self; because it eliminates the sources of unrest and brings about dynamic quietude, which is the foundation of meditative life. The gospel of selfless action definitely leads to the subordination of all the other methods used by the aspirant in the spiritual journey. It is the touchstone of success in religious life.

After giving a short description of the concept and the modes of devotion, Sri Krishna describes in detail the hallmarks of a genuine devotee. These are the characteristic features of a man of sincere devotion and the guidelines for spiritual progress. He starts from the word *adveshta*, which means no jealousy. A true devotee of the Lord who is perpetually aligned with the essential nature of the Higher-Self, is very peaceful, secure and contented. He is also very generous, kind, caring and compassionate. He looks upon the entire creation as a living organism united within the essentiality of the Supreme Lord. He enjoys cosmic unity and touches the heart of entire creation with love and kindness.

The next hallmark of an enlightened devotee is inner integrity and determination. A man of steadfastness becomes very familiar with the power of providence and knows how to express yogic alliance through his words and deeds. His life is tuned to the Divine symphony and his words are always very clear and influential. He is constantly aware of his goals and moves ahead with full confidence. Sri Krishna concludes, that these hallmarks of a true devotee are the codes of primordial *Dharma*.

Kshetra-Kshetrajna-Vibhaga-Yoga (Chapter 13)
(The Yoga of the Knowledge of the Field and the Knower of the Field)

The dialogue opens with words of Sri Krishna, "*Idam sariram Kaunteyakshetram ity abhidhiyate,*" which means, "O' Arjuna, this body is a field." The word "field", which is used by a physicist to describe the forces of nature, has also been used by Sri Krishna in relation to the forces that express through the bodies of all beings.

The physical body is a field—a manifestation of thoughts, memories, and latencies enclosed in the subtle body (mind, intellect, and ego).

The subtle body is a field of information. Every single thought that goes through the mind is duly recorded and saved in the field of information and later expressed in action. The recorded data in mind gives shape to all the activities of daily life. Every expression in the physical body has its roots in the data of the subtle body, which is a field of memories, and *samskaras*. If we closely observe the entire span of life till the present date, we can realize that the entire life is only a bundle of memories, which have been duly recorded and saved in the field of the subtle body—the memory bank.

Sri Krishna tells Arjuna that the entire life is a vast field of actions and also revolves around the wheel of thoughts, memories and *samskaras*. Just as a seed yields the corresponding type of crop, the memories saved in the field of information take shape into actions and yield their fruits in due course of time. No one can escape the law of karma. People reward and punish themselves because of their own karma. It is the principle of cause and effect, which gives momentum to the wheel of creation.

Earlier in the dialogue Sri Krishna has explained to Arjuna about the immortality of the soul, here He repeats the same truth in a different way. He says, "Those who know the reality of this body as a field and the one who controls this body, as the knower of the field, he is called a man of wisdom." He further explains, about the inter-connection of these fields and how each one is sustained by the knower of the field. He wants Arjuna to be awakened from the systematic, self-deceptive explanations of the conditioned-self and pursue the validity of the knower of the field beyond the masks of eternity.

Sri Krishna declares that the field and the knower of the field both exist in a very mystical union. When we are introduced to our essential nature as the knower of the field we live as a spectator, as a witness and give ourselves a chance for self-analysis and self-improvement. We also experience the essential truth that 'I am separate from the body and I am the knower of the body' and that is when our real education begins. Self-realization is to be able to realize the Self as the witness of all activities. So it is essential to have a clear understanding of the distinction between the thought and the one who is aware of that thought.

Sri Krishna assures that anyone who goes in unity with the soul and understands the distinction between the body and the Master of the body; becomes liberated in due course of time.

Guna-Triya-Vibhaga-Yoga (Chapter 14)
(The Yoga of the Division of the three Gunas)

In reference to the yogic alignment with the supreme-soul through the knowledge of transcending the three *Gunas* (*Sattva, Rajas, Tamas*), Sri Krishna says, "*Param bhuyah pravaksyami jnananam jnanamuttamam.* O'Arjuna I must tell you more in detail about the highly revered supreme knowledge and ancient wisdom." The transcendental knowledge of the Supreme-soul is within the access of every human being. It is not something to be acquired from somewhere else; it actually needs to be revealed to us from our own indwelling-self. This knowledge of the Supreme-self becomes alien to us because of our negligence and ignorance. It is only when a person transcends the limitations of his physical body and the masks of the conditioned-self he can comprehend the essentiality of his luminous, pure, unconditioned nature and the Bliss of the Supreme Divinity.

Sri Krishna enlightens Arjuna about the mystical union of spirit and matter. He declares the *Prakriti* (primordial nature) to be the '*Mahat Brahma,*' the cosmic womb of all beings, in which the Divine consciousness becomes seated as the seed-giving Father. It is the potency of the Divine, which energizes the inert nature and makes it grow and manifest itself as the most spectacular creation. One Supreme power is expressed through innumerable forms and shapes within various grades of potentialities bound by their own latencies. Matter is indeed the cosmic mother of the entire spectacular universe and Supreme Lord is the cosmic father.

Sri Krishna tells Arjuna about the masks of the conditioned-self. He talks about the instinctive nature of man, its analysis and the melodies. The thinking faculty of every person does express the three *Gunas* (qualities of nature), such as, *Sattvic* (purity), *Rajasic* (passion) and *Tamasic* (nescience). He tells Arjuna that it is very important to understand these qualities of matter, and the way we become conditioned by them. *Sattva* is pure light, illumination and enlightenment. It is generally represented by the color white. A *Sattvic* person is always in unity with the purity of the Divine. He thinks clearly and can differentiate between the right and wrong.

Rajasic attitude, which is generally recognized with the color red, is marked by excessive activity. A *Rajasic* person is always very anxious, restless, and stressed. His life becomes primarily devoted to the pursuit of money and power. *Tamas* (nescience) is symbolized by the color black and the navy blue. A *Tamasic* person lives in a deluded world of total ignorance, which is far beyond the realities of life. He is always confused and thinks that he is being destined to live by chance and not by choice.

The realization of the presence of Supreme-soul beyond the slavery of the *Gunas* is realized only when we are able to develop our conscious relationship with the Supreme-soul and realize the essentiality of our pure divine nature. It is only in human life that we get an opportunity for self-analysis, self-realization, and liberation. It should be our endeavor to learn to live a life, which is consciously connected with the soul. Human life should become a means of God-realization and salvation.

Purushottamayoga (Chapter 15)
(The Yoga of the Supreme Person)

Realization of the Supreme-Self is the *Purushottama-Yoga*, means going into yogic communion with the Supreme *Purusha* who is beyond all the fields; and the knower of the fields. It is the experiential knowledge of the unified field. Sri Krishna opens the dialogue with the words *"Urdhvamulamadhahsakham asvattham prahuravyayam,"* which means, "Having its roots above and branches below, the tree of life is primordial." Earlier during the dialogue Sri Krishna has given an elaborate description of the *kshetra* (field of experiences) and also the *kshetrajna* (knower of the field) separately. Here He describes the field of experiences with the unique allegory of an *Aswattha* tree. *Aswattha* means, "that which will not remain the same till tomorrow." It is perpetually changing, constantly growing and expanding in all directions. The roots of this tree are strongly entangled deep down in the world of mortals; nourished by actions and experiences.

Sri Krishna tells Arjuna that understanding the tree of *samsara* is very difficult. It is the manifestation of various inter-connected events. It is too difficult to trace back its origin because every single root comes from the preceding one. The history of the entire universe is the evolutionary chain of alterations, which is being worked out by a specific law of karma (cause and effect). The entire process is constant and orderly flow of birth, death, and rebirth. Everybody and everything has its heritage in the One, which existed before. Understanding the law of karma is very difficult as long as we are involved in the pursuit of material comforts. Sri Krishna tells Arjuna to wake up from the circular patterns of conditioned thinking and comprehend the truth, behind the perceptual boundaries of the senses. He declares very clearly that the human beings are not just the passive victims of some unknown destiny. Every person has the ability and strength to improve the quality of life and be liberated from the bonds of karma.

After presenting a detailed description of *samsara* Sri Krishna tells Arjuna about the essential nature of *jivatma*. The word *jiva* comes from a Sanskrit word *jiv* means 'to breathe'. *Jivatma* (embodied-soul) means a fragment of *atma* (pure-soul) who identifies with *jiva*. *Jivatma* is essentially one with *atma* but also distinct because of its separate self-assumed identity, which is enclosed in personal thoughts and *samskaras*. *Paramatman* (cosmic-soul) is the eternal reality behind the mask of *jivatma*. Individual life is a wave, which emerges from the wholeness of pure consciousness without disturbing its peace and serenity.

As a wave in ocean is essentially a part of the ocean the individualized-soul is eternally a part of the cosmic-soul. The experience of alienation occurs because of duality; but when the individual-soul goes in unity with the Supreme consciousness, from the gross to the subtlest realms of awareness; the embodied-soul resumes its true identity and feels a part of the Supreme-soul again. It is the experience of being restored to the wholeness of Divine and freedom from false identifications.

The *Purushottamayoga* is the ultimate identification of the individual-soul with the Supreme-soul. It is the realization of the *uttamapurusha* (Higher-Self) within, which goes beyond the mutable and immutable. Realization of transcendent-Self, the *uttamapurusha*, is being awakened into heightened awareness where the individual-soul enters into the unified field of super consciousness and actually becomes a witness, of both the field and the knower of the field.

Sri Krishna tells Arjuna to look behind the veil of his localized, individualized consciousness and experience the presence of silently witnessing Supreme-soul who upholds the infinite dynamism of the entire universe.

Devasursampatti Vibhaga-Yoga (Chapter 16)
(The Yoga of the Distinction between the Divine and Demoniac Endowments)

Sri Krishna opens the dialogue and enlightens Arjuna about the field of positive and negative forces. He explains the marked distinction between the *Devas* (divine) and the *Asuras* (demonic). *Deva* means the one who knows how to give and share. The other word, which is used for *Deva*, is *Sura*, which signifies the one who is consciously in tune with the Divine symphony. The *Asura* (demonic) means the one who is not consciously in tune with the soul. Sri Krishna tells Arjuna that the divine nature is marked by an acme of fearlessness, purity of heart, performance of *yajna*, respectful study of scriptures, charity, austerity, modesty, straightforwardness, renunciation, humility, forgiveness, generosity, self-study, non-violence, truthfulness, self-discipline, persistence, fortitude, and universal love.

In description of the demonic nature, Sri Krishna explains that the deluded people cannot see the difference between the right and wrong. The concept of purity, good conduct, truthfulness and cleanliness does not exist for them. These people are consciously or unconsciously disconnected from the voice of the indwelling-self and do heinous crimes in order to satisfy their passionate desires.

Although every *Jivatma* (individual-soul) is potentially divine and a fragment of the Supreme-soul; but when the soul takes upon the human body, he becomes possessed with two strong desires. The individual-soul likes to enjoy everything in the material world; but being a fragment of the Divine, the soul feels comforted in the closeness of the Supreme-soul. In the human body *Jivatma* (individual soul) becomes confused about the mixed identities. The spiritual impulses give peace and harmony, while the primitive impulses create restlessness and confusion. Every person has the potential to rise in spirituality and work in a co-partnership with God but if he becomes a slave of his conditioned behavior, he falls. Although every person is essentially spiritual, the degree of spiritual awareness differs from one person to another. In general, people divide themselves into two categories; the men of divine qualities and the men of demoniac qualities.

After giving a long description of the divine and demonic qualities of human beings, Sri Krishna declares desire, anger, and greed to be the triple gate of hell; that brings about the downfall of the individual-soul. These Hi-three in human behavior act in a close co-partnership with each other and do appear as uninvited friends. Victory over these three gates of hell brings enlightenment and liberation.

Sri Krishna concludes that in order to live a peaceful life at the individual level and also as a the member of family and society, it is indeed the *swadharma* of mankind to remain conscious of the divine qualities by staying in touch with the voice of the indwelling-soul.

Sraddhatriya Vibhaga-Yoga (Chapter 17)
(The Yoga of the Threefold Division of the Faith)

The dialogue opens with a question from Arjuna. He requests Sri Krishna to explain the mysterious power of *Shraddha* or faith. Sri Krishna starts the answer saying, "The faith of the embodied beings is threefold, born of their innate disposition—the *sattvic* (pure), the *rajasic* (passionate) and the *tamasic* means rooted in ignorance." All the personal concepts, ideas, thoughts, and activities of a person revolve around the type of faith he holds. The quality of faith reflects the inborn nature or *swabhava* of the person.

The *sattvic* people are spiritually awake and enlightened. A *sattvic* person performs the worship as a duty and makes all offerings to the gods and goddesses without any desire for reward. His attitude is enlightened and supportive of universal life. On the other hand, a *rajasic* person worships God in order to seek all kinds of boons and bounties. His act of charity shows his hidden desire for name, and fame. About the *tamasic* worship, Sri Krishna tells that it is generally performed out of fear and superstition. A *tamasic* worship is hardly in conformity with the ordinances of the sacred books.

He also enlightens Arjuna that people, who practice violent austerities and torture their bodies; they also hurt Me, who lives in the body. Sri Krishna makes it very clear to Arjuna that self-discipline and self-control should not be confused with the physical torture of the body. The practice of self-mortification is painful and unworthy; it should not be followed at all.

After giving a short description of the various types

of austerities and services performed for self-realization and God-realization, Sri Krishna tells Arjuna that all kinds of services should be dedicated to God with the holy words "*Aum-Tat-Sat.*" *Aum* is pure cosmic energy, which connects us to everything in microcosm and macrocosm. *Aum* is the primordial sound that prevails at the heart of entire creation. The word '*Tat*' stands for the supreme reality in essence. '*Sat*' signifies the Truth behind everything and also for the work, which is auspicious. Sri Krishna declares that all types of worship, *yajna*, and austerity should start with the holy syllable *Aum* and completed with the dedicated words of "*Aum-Tat-Sat*" which indicates, that the worship has been initiated by the grace of the Lord, and is dedicated in His service. In this way the worship becomes purified and the means for liberation.

While concluding the mysterious power of faith and *Aum-Tat-Sat*, Sri Krishna repeats once again the genuine role of *shraddha* or faith in the progressive realization of the Supreme Divinity. *Shraddha* signifies the honest faith, which proceeds from the yogic unity with the Supreme-soul. As a matter of fact, the person's relationship with the Divine is primordial and perennial, but the individual perceives the grace only in proportion to the degree of his faith, reverence and devotion. *Shraddha* is the dynamic force that nourishes the mutual intimacy with the Divine. *Vishwasa* or faith should be our *Swasa* means the breath of life. It is *shraddha*, the sincere faith and honest devotion, which gives peace, happiness, liberation and *Nirvana* eventually.

Moksha-Sannyasayoga (Chapter 18)
(The Yoga of Liberation through Renunciation)

The dialogue opens with a specific question from Arjuna in reference to the concept of *sannyasa* (non-attachment) and that of *tyaga* (renunciation). Although Arjuna has heard about the words *tyaga* and *sannyasa*—many times during the dialogue but he could not understand the subtle meaning of these terms clearly and precisely. Sri Krishna tells Arjuna that renunciation of all actions promoted by personal desires is *sannyasa*; while giving up the desire for fruit of actions is called *tyaga*. The literal meaning of both words *sannyasa* and *tyaga* is to renounce; and both the words are used in the sense of relinquishment, but *tyaga* is slightly different from *sannyasa*. It is the giving up of all anxieties, related to the enjoyment of the fruits of actions.

Sri Krishna declares that renunciation of obligatory actions is not proper. The obligatory actions include, both the daily duties at the individual level and also the special duties, which we are expected to perform as a member of family and society. If we ignore these duties, our renunciation is immature and ignorant. Anybody who neglects his obligatory duties disturbs the continuity of action in nature and brings about a chaos in society. His renunciation is marked as escapism from the realities of life. He degrades himself and becomes a burden for himself and for others in the family and community.

Genuine *sannyasa* is that, which guides the person to the acceptance of higher moral values with greater responsibilities. A man of clear vision knows exactly the expectations of the family and the society in which he lives. He performs all his duties skillfully, intelligently, and diligently. He is quite clear about the appropriate age and time in life, when he should prepare himself for partial renunciation and for total renunciation.

In reference to the philosophy of God-realization through the devoted performance of assigned duties, Sri Krishna tells Arjuna, "That the type of work selected by the Brahmins, Kshatriyas, Vaishyas as well as Shudras, is generally in accordance with their own inborn qualities of nature." A Brahmin is an embodiment of *sattvika* (purity). Serenity, self-control, asceticism, simplicity, honesty, knowledge of the Holy scriptures, sincere faith in God, are the characteristics of a Brahmin born of his innate nature. He is expected to be learned and guide others into a pure and enlightened lifestyle from the example of his own purity of mind, body, and speech. The other class is the Kshatriya. The duty of a Kshatriya is to enforce the law and order for the well-being of the society. The protection of the country, society, and community is the first and foremost duty of a Kshatriya. The next on the four-fold division is the Vaishya, endowed with more *rajasic* nature. They are instinctively interested in business and trade. The fourth is that of the Shudras naturally inclined to manual work and maintenance.

Each station of duty is very significant and important for the development of society. Every person is guided by his own *swabhava* and finds inner satisfaction in the special field of action as initiated by his inborn nature. This classification in society is psychological and universal. It is created by the people, of the people, for the people. Sri Krishna declares that by being devoted to one's own duty, a person can attain perfection and liberation. The Supreme-Lord of the universe should be worshipped through the dedicated performance of one's own duty.

After explaining all the profound mysteries of yogic unity and how by adhering to *Karmayoga* a person becomes eligible for attaining the Supreme Bliss in human life, Sri Krishna answers the appeal made by Arjuna in the beginning of the dialogue, He says, "O'Arjuna disregard your mixed notions of *Dharma*. Take refuge in Me. Be in eternal union with Me, I will take care of you—I will liberate you from all your fears. Grieve not." The concept of *Dharma* becomes mixed, confused and complex when a person is consciously disconnected from the Supreme-soul and screens reality through some fixed individualized, localized, egocentric ideas. It is the personal attachment to that notion or idea which creates disturbance in the spontaneous flow of guidance from the indwelling Supreme-Self and creates confusion.

Sri Krishna persuades Arjuna to make a complete surrender with guileless heart without any traces of reservations. It means shedding of all pretenses and striping of all the masks of conditioned-self. The idea is that as long as *Jivatma* (individual-soul) clings to its separate self-created, limited egoist individuality, the person becomes bound to move along with the instructions of his conditioned nature; but when he surrenders to the Lord, he becomes a co-worker and co-creator of his circumstances. It is only through the grace of the Divine that he is introduced to the secret codes of his programmed life and the programmer. He becomes intuitively awakened and receptive to the call of the indwelling-self and his different concepts of *Dharma*, start blending into one essential *Dharma*, 'accept to live in the consciousness of the soul and follow your Bliss.'

Sri Krishna is very well aware of the process of inner awakening and that is why after introducing Arjuna to the call of the Divine with total surrender, His immediate next question is: "O'Arjuna, have you heard attentively whatsoever we have discussed so far. Did you understand the meaning of My message?"

Arjuna's answer, *smritir labdha*, is very significant. *Smritir* literally means memory and *labdha* means regained. *Smritir* is to remember something, which has been forgotten for some reason. It is the realization of the primordial relationship with the pure, luminous soul. It is the experience of going back to the wholeness in which the individual-soul finds unity with the Supreme-soul.

Arjuna who has descended earlier into the limitations of mind and body, now wakes up once again to the majesty of being the controller of the situation. His mind, which was plunged earlier in *Vishad* (depression)—now wakes up into a blessed state of receiving *Prasad* (grace). The *Vishad* is changed into *Prasad* of the Divine. Arjuna feels totally oriented to a new concept of life, relaxed and peaceful.

Sanjaya glorifies the phenomenal dialogue between Sri Krishna and the enlightened soul Arjuna. He says, "Wherever there is the contemplative wisdom and the yogic power of Sri Krishna; the devoted yogic unity and the practical efficiency of Arjuna in performing the work; there is morality, welfare, unfailing righteousness, success, victory, glory, and everything else."

May the teachings of the Bhagawad Geeta bless everyone with the power of enlightened love, devotion, and true knowledge—restoring peace, happiness, and harmony on earth.

"Tileshu tailam dadhiniva sarpir apas srotassuaranishu cagnih. Evam atmatmani grhyate'sau satyenainam tapasa yo'nupasyati."

Shvetashvatara Upanishad (1.15)

"Just as the oil in the sesame seeds, butter hidden in the curd, water in the sediments of the spring, fire in the wood, so is the Supreme-Self veiled within one's own self and can be perceived by true austerity and knowledge of the soul."

7

The Concept of God in Hinduism

The hymns of Vedas and the other Holy scriptures of Hinduism describe clearly that *Parabrahman* is the omnipotent substratum from where the plurality of the world is projected. The Supreme power exists diffusing its abundance in everything within the boundaries of perception and everything beyond that. The entire universe is rooted in *Parabrahman*—the non-local spiritual domain, from where the information and energy emerge, creating millions of forms and names in space and time. Hindu cosmology explains this as Supreme-soul, individual-soul, and matter.

The Hindu trinity—Brahma, Vishnu, and Maheshwara (Shiva)—are the three expressive aspects of *Parabrahman*. Lord Brahma as distinct from Supreme *Brahman* is the creator, Lord Vishnu is the sustainer, and Maheshwara (Shiva) is the annihilator as well as the regenerator. If we look closely at the ancient Hindu trinity we see three identical faces of the Divine; the power projection of eternity. All the deities may appear to be independent; in fact they are the different facets of the pure consciousness. The omniscience of *Parabrahman* is the only truth that prevails at the heart of the entire creation. The Vedic Rishis have declared jubilantly, *"Ekam sad vipra bahudha vadanti"* (Rig.1.164.46)—meaning, "One alone exists; sages and mystics call it by various names."

Hindu gods and goddesses are the personification of the ultimate Supreme Reality, guiding and satisfying the devotees who seek help with prayers and meditation. For instance, the worship of Lord Vishnu initiates people to live a life with the spirit of *yajna* (sacrifice), which means, helping each other selflessly. The word *yajna* conveys the ideal of inter-dependence, continuity, and the survival of creation. Similarly the worship of Shiva in which the water is offered on the top most part of *Shivalingam* creates a remarkable harmony at physical, psychological and spiritual levels of awareness; while hands pour the water, the chanting of hymns guides the mind to remain absorbed in the joy of divine love with intention and attention. Gradually as the mind becomes involved in the offering, the devotee enters into the ecstatic trance and the inner alignment is perceived in meditative unity with the source. It is the flawless apprehension of the pure consciousness, which creates, sustains and nurtures the entire universe. It is a subjective experience of visualizing the divine light, when the devotee enters into the higher states of consciousness and perceives, "I am created by the light of the Self, sustained by the light of the Self, I am indeed that light of the Self."

In the worship of Sri Ganesha, which forms an important part of almost all the Hindu rituals, the devotee seeks blessing for enlightenment, clarity of vision, purity of mind and intellect. The symbolism in prayers indicates the efforts of the individual-soul seeking liberation from the seven deadly sins such as, lust, anger, greed, envy, sloth, egoism, and gluttony. The icon of Sri Ganesha is a geometrical figure created to produce a profound and lasting spiritual experience of inner peace and tranquility.

In Hinduism, there are some goddesses who are worshipped independently as well as with their Divine spouses. Goddess Saraswati, the consort of Brahma, is worshipped as the embodiment of knowledge, wisdom, purity, and serenity. Sri Lakshmi, the Divine consort of Lord Vishnu, is worshipped for wealth, prosperity, peace, and happiness on almost all important occasions, especially Deepavali. Mother Durga, the personification of the totality of the powers of Brahma, Vishnu, and Maheshwara, is worshipped for annihilation of negative tendencies. The consort of Kala the all devouring time is Kali—another aspect of divine potency of *Parabrahman*. Mother Kali is worshipped to seek victory over time and the ability to live in the tissue of the present moment. The goddess Parvati, the Divine consort of Shiva, is worshipped for alignment with *Para Shakti*. In the worship of Mother Parvati the individual is introduced to his inherent potentials and blessed with deep physiological rest, inner peace and yogic unity in transcendence.

In some Hindu temples there is also a shrine of Bhoodevi—the goddess Mother Earth, where the devotee seeks blessing to be respectful to the reservoirs of earth and use everything with a sense of responsibility. He calls upon the divine energy that aids the earth's evolution and helps to balance the impact of human life.

In ritualistic worship of gods and goddesses the devotee offers flowers, leaves, water and food while chanting mantras from the Holy scriptures. The offerings are made in several steps, each having its special significance. The food that is offered to God with love and devotion becomes sacred because of the positive energy released during the worship. It is called *Prasad*—the blessed food, and our partaking of it gives inner peace and fulfillment. According to Hindu tradition, *Prasad* is always shared with others so that everyone is blessed with purity of thoughts, words, and deeds.

Although, it is very difficult to trace back when the deity worship was added to the ritualistic performance of Vedic *yajna* in Hindu families, it became very popular and enjoyable in due course of time. The human mind, in general, needs some kind of expression of the omniscient, inexplicable as an *ishta deva,* or chosen deity, in order to concentrate and develop the intimate personal bond with God. There have always been two types of devotees worshiping God with form and shape or without form and attributes; but they all know they are pursuing the same goal i.e. alignment or anchorage with the source.

It is a fact that in course of spiritual progress from *saguna* (God with form) to *nirguna* (God without form), an inspired devotee is blessed with subjective experience of the eternal truth. In reference to this there is a very interesting story in our Puranas. Once Lord Rama, the God-incarnate, asked his great devotee Hanuman, "O' son, tell me what is your relationship with Me and how you meditate on Me?"

Sri Hanuman replied, "O' Rama sometime I look upon You as '*Purna*' –the undivided 'One' –at other moment I see your presence reflecting through everything and everybody and I look upon myself as a fragment of You. Yet another time, I meditate on You as my Divine master and think of myself as your humble servant. When, however, I am blessed with inner unity and the experiential knowledge of the Self then I feel '*Tat tvam asi*'—Thou art That." As a matter of fact, monotheism itself becomes a spiritual monism for eventually the individual-soul discovers that its own essentiality is the same as that of the God worshipped.

Tat tvam asi is one of the four key statements described in the Vedas about the concept of God:

1. "*Aham brahmasmi*" from the Yajurveda meaning, "I am *Brahman*—I am the totality."

2. "*Tat tvam asi*" from the Samaveda meaning, "Thou art That," —*Brahman*.

3. "*Ayam atma Brahma*" from the Atharvaveda meaning, "This *atman* (Self) is *Brahman*."

4. "*Prajnanam Brahma*" from the Rigveda meaning, "*Brahman* is pure-consciousness." (Bliss)

These are *mahavakyas*, meaning the great sentences or the combination of highly sacred words that are shared by the spiritual teachers (Gurus) with their disciples during mantra initiation. In these key mantras, the sound flows quite spontaneously, and can set up powerful vibrations in the body which assert union with the pure consciousness.

Although each individual-soul is potentially divine and eligible for Divine status, the realization of the presence of the Supreme Lord beyond the veils of eternity is experienced by the degree of self-awareness and inner alignment to the source of life. When an aspirant remains consciously united with the purity of the Supreme-soul, gradually the individual-soul starts resuming its true identity and moves step-by-step, from *Jivatma* (individualized-soul) to *Mahatma* (the great enlightened soul), and eventually *Paramatma* (The Cosmic soul)—the 'One' perennially aligned with *Parabrahman*. It is the experience of being restored to the wholeness of the Supreme-soul and freedom from the masks of the egoistic conditioned-self. Free at last! It is being awakened to one's own completeness—'*Aham Brahmasmi*', I am *Brahman*—I am the totality.

This exalted experience of yogic unity in transcendence has been eloquently expressed in Brihdarayanka upanishad, "*Aum Purnamadah purnamidam purnata purnamudachyate, Purnasya purnamadaya purnamevavasisyate*" (5.1.1), meaning, "That is the whole, this is the whole, the whole comes out of the whole, even when the whole comes out of the whole, what is left behind is also the whole." Everything in the macrocosm as well as in the microcosm declares the wholeness of *Parabrahman*. The universe emerges out of infinitude, it is sustained by the infinitude and into infinitude it goes back again.

Hinduism believes that the Supreme power that prevails at the substratum of the universe also manifests as God-incarnate—*Paramatma* or *Bhagwan*. God-incarnate, although appearing to be an ordinary human being, remains rooted in transcendental-Self. His body is the cosmic body and his mind is the cosmic mind. He is beyond the limitations of cause, space and time. The Supreme-soul incarnates to enlighten that each and every human being is an eligible candidate for Divine status. He shows his personal compassion for people and initiates them into the realization of their innate potential. As observed in Bhagawad Geeta, the God-incarnate, Lord Krishna tells Arjuna about his inherent divinity and educates him about the secret of living in the consciousness of the soul. He repeats several times during the dialogue, "O'Arjuna, wake up! and achieve which is yours."

In reference to the immanence of the Divine, Sri Krishna explains to Arjuna, although the Supreme consciousness dwells in each and every molecule of the body, the presence of the soul can be intimated and experienced easily at the shrine of heart. Contemplation at the heart center has been highly emphasized in almost all the religious scriptures of Hinduism. It is at the heart center where love for God is awakened and the grace of the Divine is personally experienced. In affinity to the love of God at the cave of our heart, the great poet, Rabindranath Tagore writes, "The most distant course comes nearest to thyself, and that training is the most intricate which leads to the utter simplicity of a tune. The traveler has to knock at every alien door to come to his own, and one has to wander through all the outer worlds to reach the innermost shrine at the end. My eyes strayed far and wide before I shut them and said 'Here art thou!' The question and the cry 'Oh, where?' melt into tears of a thousand streams and deluge the world with the flood of the assurance 'I am!'"

In the Bhagawad Geeta Sri Krishna also tells Arjuna, "*Upadrastanumanta ca bharta bhokta mahesvarah paramatmeti capyukto dehe smin purusah parah*" (BG.13.23), which means, "The presence of the Lord in the body can be experienced as playing various roles at the different levels of consciousness, such as an observer, experiencer, sustainer, controller, spectator and the silent witness of all our activities." The indwelling-soul observes every single wisp of thought that flashes through our mind and acts as a guide to the individual in counseling what is right and what is wrong. The inner voice suggests, and then steps back for us to decide. Human beings are free to choose their actions but definitely bound by the good or bad results.

With regular practice of meditation and daily prayers, when we are introduced to our essential nature as the knower of our mind and body; we live as a spectator, as a witness and give ourselves a chance for self-analysis and self-improvement and that is when the real education begins. Self-realization is to be able to realize the Self as the witness of all activities. It is the blessed experience of understanding the distinction between the thought and the one who is aware of that thought. This is the meaning of the famous aphorism—

"Know Thyself"

For a Hindu, God is a living reality and there is a constant effort to stay aligned with the pure luminous soul. People have shrines at homes, at work places, schools and hospitals. There are rituals to bless a new car, new house and business etc. People greet each other with words—'*Namaste*' meaning, "The one in me salutes and bows to the one in you." It is honoring divinity in others, which promotes cosmic intimacy and brings people closer to each other in a relaxed spiritual bond.

In an effort to maintain inner unity with the soul, the performance of certain rituals starts from the day when the mother conceives the baby. There is a special worship during the pregnancy and within a couple of days after the birth of the baby, the infant is blessed with some sacred words. The father whispers in baby's ear, "*Tvam vedo-asi*" meaning, "You are the knowledge of the Vedas." He also writes *Aum* on the lips of the newborn with a gold or silver spoon while repeating the Holy syllable *Aum* accompanied by the celestial sound of conches. Every child is spiritually initiated at the age of six or seven and given a personal mantra, which helps the child to stay aligned with the indwelling-soul and become receptive to the guidance of the soul. Later in life the youngster learns several mantras and prayers from his parents and spiritual teachers and is constantly reminded to stay connected with the indwelling-soul from moment to moment. Also the rituals performed on almost all the Hindu festivals are intended to purify the individual and prepare him step by step to experience the exalted state of '*Sat Chit Anand*,' which means, 'Truth, Awareness, and Total Bliss.'

The famous key statement of Vedic literature, '*Sat Chit Anand*,' has been explained beautifully by Mahatama Gandhi. He always said that staying firm on '*Sat*' (Truth) leads to '*Chit*' (Pure-Consciousness), which leads to '*Anand*' (Infinite Bliss). Since God Almighty combines all the three, that's why God is addressed as '*Sat Chit Anand*'. Be truthful and let the Absolute Truth be revealed to you.

In Hinduism there are some powerful religious symbols used in rituals and meditation. These symbols present the totality of the Supreme-soul and also the path leading to alignment with the indwelling-soul, gods and goddesses and the cosmic bodies. The Holy syllable *Aum* is the most well known symbol of Hinduism. This primordial religious symbol has been highly glorified in the Vedas. The sound of *Aum* is the whisper from the unified field of pure consciousness to itself and the entire universe is the orchestration of that whisper. This sound from *Brahmanada* wraps the entire creation. Everything in the macrocosm as well as in the microcosm is the sequential unfoldment of this mysterious sound, which is whispering and manifesting through every little molecule and every little atom.

According to the Mandukya Upanishad, (1.3-4-5) *Aum* symbolizes the triads in time and space and also the four states of consciousness. 'A' stands for the waking state (conscious level), 'U' describes the dream state, and 'M' stands for the dreamless, deep sleep. (*Sushupti*). When written in Sanskrit, there is a curved line on the top, which indicates the fourth state of consciousness that is beyond dreamless—deep sleep. It is called *Turiya* in meditation when the individual-soul goes through the gap into unity with the universal-soul. This half syllable leads the meditator into deep silence and inner peace. The dot on the curved line represents the Supreme Divinity in us. Meditating on the dot is going into the silence of the Self. Three syllables also describe the three stages of evolution in the universe. A stands for *adimata* (beginning), U stands for *utkarsha* (sustenance) and M stands for *mitti* (annhilation). It also describes *Akara, Ukara,* and *Makara*— combined together *Omkara. Akara* stands for *Ishwara, Ukara* for *Moolaprakriti* and *Makara* for *Maya Shakti.* This means that everything we see in the universe is going through an evolution. It comes into existence, it is sustained for a while and then it is gone. Everything is enclosed within the grasp of the swift moving time. The mystic syllable also stands for Brahma, Vishnu, and Shiva. The cosmic cycle of creation, sustenance and destruction. The primordial sound of *Aum* is called the *Brahma nada*, which holds within itself the totality of everything in the universe. The philologists believe that all the vowels have originated from *Aum*, and have asserted that if one concentrates and repeats the vowels for a few minutes, like A E I O U, the sound of *Aum* can be heard resonating very clearly. *Aum* is considered to be the source of all the alphabets in Sanskrit and the source of all the languages. It is also assumed that the basic seven sounds of music have originated from the primordial nada *Aum*

Other popular symbols used in meditation and ritualistic worship are the '*Swastika*', '*Dharma chakra*', '*Sri chakra*' and '*Saligrama.*' '*Swastika*' comes from the word *Swasti*, which means 'auspiciousness.' It represents the omniscience of the all-pervasive intelligence that prevails at the substratum of the entire creation. The symbol of '*Swastika*' represents the symbol of *Aum* written in *Brahmi lipi*, one of the old scripts of ancient India.

'*Dharma chakra*' represents the wholeness of the Divine. It is symbolic of the eternal cosmic law of birth, death and rebirth which gives momentum to the wheel of creation. It also represents the universal field of energy and information always in motion.

Similarly the symbol of '*Nataraja*', the dramatic dancing posture of Shiva with a ring of flames all around the figure, indicates the pulsating rhythm of comic energy, which has no beginning and no end.

The '*Sri Chakra*' is one of the most popular religious symbols used in worship and meditation. It is a geometrical diagram with a star at the center, which leads the aspirant to the shrine of heart, under the wish granting mythological tree—*kalpataru*, where the individual goes into unity with the Divine mother.

'*Saligrama*' is a black rounded stone with a natural hole showing visible spirals inside which indicates that the true nature of the soul is veiled in many layers of conditioned consciousness and is indeed very difficult to comprehend. '*Saligrama*' is supposed to be endowed with mysterious powers which guide the individual to unity in transcendence and desire for selfless service to humanity.

Hindu philosophical treatises assert clearly, our perennial relationship with the Supreme-soul and also suggest the appropriate means and methods to experience it. The grace of God is inherent in every individual, it just needs to be perceived and called forth at the conscious levels of awareness and then it starts manifesting through us by itself. The joy of this inner-anchorage with the soul has been gloriously expressed by the great Hindu poet Rabindranath Tagore in *Gitanjali*: "Through birth and death, in this world or in others, wherever Thou leadest me it is Thou, the same, the one companion of my endless life who ever linkest my heart with bonds of joy to the unfamiliar. When one knows Thee, then alien there is none, then no door is shut. Oh, grant me my prayer that I may never lose the bliss of Thy touch of the one in the play of the many."

"Ekam sad vipra bahudha vadanti"

Rigveda (1.164.46)

"One alone exists;
sages and mystics call it by various names."

8

Hindu Gods & Goddesses

Worship of gods and goddesses in Hinduism emerged from the ancient religious traditions of *Sanatan Vedic Dharma* as an endeavor to seek harmony with the forces of nature, which support the sustenance of life; such as fire, air, ether, earth, water, Sun, Moon, and constellations. These forces of nature were worshipped separately and also together as eight *vasus*—meaning, "In which the entire creation exists." Later people started addressing these cosmic bodies as gods and goddesses, and started worshiping in rituals of daily life.

The Sanskrit word for god and goddess is *Deva* and *Devi*—the word *Deva* comes from the root word *Div* meaning, "to shine" or "who radiates the potential dynamism, the splendor, the glory and charisma of the Supreme Lord and showers blessings." Since time immemorial all the early morning prayers are addressed to the eight *vasus* with special offerings to the Sun god—the giver of life on earth.

There are so many hymns in the Vedas that describe the festival of sunrise when the golden light is scattered through the rift of clouds. In Sun worship, water is offered facing east with special hymns; the water reflects the seven colors of sunlight, stimulates the seven *chakras* in body, and creates balance of the five basic elements that constitute everything in the physical world. The early morning sunlight rejuvenates each little cell in our body, helps in absorption of calcium, eliminates harmful toxins, strengthens the immune system, and brings significant improvement in general health. There are 12 yogic postures for *surya namaskara*—or worship of Sun god, each flowing into another very gracefully, graciously and energizing the whole body. The rich experience of early morning unity in yoga remains with the person for the rest of the day and the heavenly after-glow of morning sunlight is carried on in the activities of daily life. The great Gayatri mantra has been dedicated to the worship of the Sun god in which the aspirant calls upon the Divine Mother Savitur for inner enlightenment, purity of mind and intellect, inner integrity, and right guidance in the activities of daily life.

The midday offerings are made to the Rudras—the vital airs, *pran, apan, vyan, saman, udan, naga, kurma, karkalla, devdatta, dhananjaya,* and the consciousness. The wind god is also worshipped as Anila. The offerings in the evening at sunset are made to Agni—the fire god. In prayers the fire god is addressed as Agni, Pavakka and also Anala. Worship of Agni has been highly glorified in the Vedas. The first hymn of the Rigveda starts with the adoration of Agni as an embodiment of Supreme *Parabrahman*: "*Aum Agni Meede purohitam yagasya deva ritvajam hotaram ratna dataram,*" which means, "I salute to Agni the fire god, the most bounteous, the giver of wealth on the planet." In the Vedas there are hundreds of hymns dedicated in appreciation of Agni that manifests as fire on earth, as lightning in the sky (Indraloka), as the Sun in heaven, and as a mediator carrying the offerings of men to gods. All the traditional Vedic rituals are performed around the ceremonial fire, the personification of Supreme Lord Himself.

The worship of cosmic powers initiates the individual to be respectful to the reservoirs of earth and use everything with a sense of responsibility. The earth has been always addressed as mother, symbolic of fertility. There are so many hymns in ancient scriptures describing the glory of Mother Earth with other cosmic powers, such as, "Let the earth full of fragrance, the water having different tastes, the wind whose touch is very pleasing, the lustrous light of Sun, the sky full of words make my life pleasant and enjoyable." There are hundreds of hymns in the Vedas addressed to Mother Earth in which the devotee calls upon the divine energy that aids the earth's evolution and helps balance the impact of human life. The *Prithvi Sukta* of the Atharvaveda gives a beautiful description written to the glory of Mother Earth (12.1.11-13), "O' Earth let thy hills, snowy mountains, and valuable forest be pleasant, enjoyable and useful. Upon the brown and black multi-colored earth, which is guarded by Indra, may I stand unharassed, unhurt and unwounded."

"I call upon thee O' Mother Earth who has nurtured us since the beginning of creation. Thou are bounteous, beautiful, pure, and patient, maintained by the ordinance of *yajna*. May thou help us to have quick growth and enjoy our share of food."

Varuna the Lord of water has always held a very revered place among the Vedic gods and goddess. There are many hymns in the Vedas dedicated to the worship of Varuna that encompasses the whole world. In some of the hymns the Varuna is also addressed as Mitra Varuna. Besides these deities the others generally worshipped in rituals are Adityas and Indra. According to the ancient Hindu scriptures there are 12 Adityas—the special aspects of sunlight over the 12 months of the year. In the worship of Adityas the aspirant seeks blessings for making the appropriate use of time throughout the year. Indra is usually addressed as Devaraja Indra the Lord of gods and goddesses. There are hundreds of hymns, especially in the Rigveda describing the glory of Indra.

Moon the most important star in the Vedic astrology is worshipped as the source of *Ojas*—the elixir of life. In the worship of the Moon especially on the fourth, eighth and 11th day, and also on the full Moon day of the lunar calendar, the individual seeks blessings for happy, healthy and prosperous life on earth. There are many hymns in the Vedas and other ancient scriptures that describe the glory of Moon and the nectarean *soma*, which nourishes the food, herbs, and healing plants on earth.

The Vedic sages have described God as omnipresent,

omniscient, the Supreme *Parabrahman* and all the gods and goddesses in nature as the expressive aspect of that Supreme power. They made it very clear that Supreme Divinity and His manifestations cannot be separated and declared jubilantly, "*Ekam sad viprah bahudha vadanti*"— (Rig. 1.164.46), meaning, "One alone exists; sages and mystics call it by various names." Worship the Supreme Divinity in any revered form you like and address Him by any name, it all goes to the one ultimate infinite, Supreme Reality—*Parabrahman*, the pure consciousness. In reference to this the holy sage of Shvetashvatara Upanishad has also written beautifully, "The all-pervading Supreme Power is Agni—the fire god, Aditya—the Sun god, Vayu—the wind god, Chandera—the Moon god, Shukra—shining and pure, Brahma—the womb of creation, Apah—the water, Prajapati—Lord of progeny, creator of all" (4.2).

Although it is very difficult to trace back when the deity worship was introduced to the ritualistic worship of Hindu families, it is definitely clear that the sages like Vasishtha, Vyasa, Kashyap, Atri, Bharadwaj, Angira, Bhrigu, and Vishwamitra, believed in God as *Nirakara* (unmanifest) and *Sakara* (manifest). There is also a description of a personal God addressed as *Ishwara, Paramatma, Bhagwan, Narayana, and Jagdishwara.*

Worship of God with form and shape became very popular in due course of time because the human mind in general needs some kind of expression of the omniscient, inexplicable as an *Ishta Deva* (chosen deity) to concentrate and develop the intimate personal bond with the Supreme Divinity. In order to experience the Absolute which is beyond the reach of sensory perceptions, either the person has to transcend above the finite to experience the infinite or to bring the infinite to the level of finite perception in some form and shape. Hindu gods and goddesses are the personification of the ultimate, infinite, Supreme Reality, answering and satisfying the devotees those who seek help with prayers and meditation. Each deity is addressed with specific mantras imbued with a specific kind of energy. Shrines become powerful because of the constant repetition of deity mantra recited millions of times in daily prayers. The moment we enter the shrine, we feel engulfed with collective spiritual energy at the holy sanctuary. In prayers and meditative unity with the deity, the aspirant is introduced to his own inherent potential and guided to make the best use of it. This revelation comes as a grace of the Divine and opens the new vistas of self-understanding and ushers the individual into the accomplishment of his desired goals in life. All the deities may appear to be independent, but in fact they are the different facets of the pure consciousness. The omniscience of the *Parabrahman* is the only truth that prevails at the heart of the creation.

The entire universe is rooted in Supreme *Parabrahman*. The Hindu trinity of Brahma, Vishnu, and Maheshwara (Shiva) are three expressive aspects of the Supreme *Parabrahman*. Lord Brahma is the creator, Lord Vishnu the sustainer, and Maheshwara (Shiva) the annihilator as well as the regenerator. Brahma the creator must not be confused with the Supreme cosmic spirit *Parabrahman*; Brahma is only one aspect of the *Trimurty*—Brahma, Vishnu, and Maheshwara.

Lord Brahma

Brahma is the source, the seed of all that is in the universe. The word Brahma has been derived from root word '*brh*', meaning to grow and expand, boundless immensity, from which space, time, and causation originate; names and forms emerge. Everything in the macrocosm as well as the microcosm is the orchestration of this mysterious power, which is whispering and manifesting through every little molecule and every little atom. Brahma is the cosmic subtle body, *Hiranyagarbha* (the womb of creation), the sum total of all the thoughts and memories of the living beings. Subtle body is the software of the individual-soul created by mind, intellect, and ego, which projects the physical body and the world. Each individual body is the subtlest spark of Brahma, the creator of the universe. Brahma is also addressed as the Vedic deity Prajapati—meaning the Lord of progeny, *Hiranyagarbha*—the golden embryo, and also the *Vishwakarma*—meaning the architect of the world.

The Lord of creation, Brahma, is generally depicted, as standing on a lotus, with four faces and four hands; holding a water pot, the four Vedas, the sacred ladle or spoon and the *kusa* grass. Brahma standing on the lotus with stem rooted in the fathomless water indicates the conditioned consciousness perennially aligned with the source—the Supreme *Parabrahman*. The four faces of Brahma indicate the omniscience of the creator in four directions; consciousness moving within itself and creating millions of forms and shapes in space and time. Holding the Vedas, the holy manuscript in one of his hands suggests the importance of Vedic knowledge, which is sacred and secular. Hymns of the Vedas describe the glories of the Supreme power and the perennial inter-dependence, which exists between God, nature and the other created beings. The Vedas are the source of all knowledge—arts, literature, music and sciences. The *kusa* grass, the ladle, and spoon in the other two hands signify the importance of *yajna*, living with the spirit of sacrifice means give and share. The water pot in his hand indicates the importance of respect for Varuna—associated with water bodies, clouds, and rain. Since life comes out of water, sustained by water and goes back into water, worship of Varuna has been highly emphasized in ancient Vedic rituals.

Lord Brahma's vehicle is a swan, the symbol of enlightened discrimination, heightened intuition, purified intellect, and also indicates that justice should be dispensed to all creatures. Divine Mother Saraswati the goddess of knowledge is the Divine spouse of Brahma. Although Brahma, the Vedic deity Prajapati's presence is invoked in almost all Hindu religious rites, there are only two temples exclusively dedicated to Brahma in India; one is at Pushkaraj in Rajasthan and the other in Tamil Nadu.

Lord Vishnu

Worship of Lord Vishnu has been highly glorified in the ancient scriptures of India. There are innumerable temples and shrines of Lord Vishnu where people seek blessings for good health, wealth, love, peace and success in life. The devotees of Lord Vishnu are called *Vaishnavas* and they generally wear a U-shaped sandalwood mark on their forehead. The word "Vishnu" literally means, "The one who has entered into everything, pervades at the heart of the entire creation, supports and sustains." The word "Vishnu" also means "*yajna* (sacrifice)."

The worship of Lord Vishnu initiates people to live a life with the spirit of *yajna*, which means, helping each other selflessly. The word *yajna* conveys the ideal of inter-dependence, continuity, and the survival of creation. The whole universe functions through the spirit of mutual interdependence. It is the network of services performed selflessly by gods, human beings, other species, plants, trees, water bodies, stars, and planets. Lord Vishnu is the transcendent Supreme Lord as well as the immanent reality of the whole universe. The entire world is held together by the power of the Lord himself.

Lord Vishnu is addressed by many different names

such as Parmeshwara, which means, the most intimate friend of human beings who can be reached and intimated as the indwelling-Self at the shrine of heart in yogic unity. The Realization of Lord at the temple of heart is easy and the most rewarding experience of life. Lord Vishnu is also addressed as Sri Venkateshwara, Balaji, and Satyanarayana. *Vishnu Sahasranama*, written by Adi Shankaracharya explains the meaning of the thousand names of Lord Vishnu, generally used by the devotees in their prayers.

Traditionally Lord Vishnu is worshipped as standing upon a lotus with four hands, wearing a yellow silk wrap, a garland of gems or fragrant flowers and the magnificent crown, which signifies His sovereignty over creation. Holding the celestial conch in one hand and blessing with the other known as '*Varda hasta*' indicates the call of the Divine to the higher and nobler values of life. If the individual can learn to live in alignment with the voice of God, his life becomes a blessing. The mace and discus in the other two hands signify the corrective and punishing power of the Lord. The individual who does not live by the guidance of the Supreme God and disrespects the laws of *swadharma,* he is knocked down occasionally with the mace of the Divine. Also, if the entire society becomes corrupt and people start losing their moral and ethical values, the Lord uses the annihilating discus to punish the wicked people in order to bring peace and harmony in society. Lord Vishnu is the protector of *Dharma* and initiates people to live with mutual respect while keeping in mind the global welfare. The discus also stands for the wheel of time in creation. Lord Vishnu standing on the lotus flower indicates that the pure consciousness, although involved in the sustenance of the world still remains detached and rooted in the essentiality of Supreme *Parabrahman*. It also indicates the *Swadhishthana chakra* the seat of Lord Vishnu in human body. *Swadhishthana chakra* is located in the region of pubic bone a little below the navel. The elemental quality of this chakra is water in which floats the *padma*, the seat of Lord Vishnu.

There are some temples where Lord Vishnu is enshrined in *Anantashayana* posture—the *yoganidra*, which means the yogic sleep—the Lord reclining peacefully on the body

of a multi-headed coiled serpent floating in the ocean. The coiled serpent, '*Adi Sesha*', represents the *Kundalini shakti*, which unfolds magnificently at *Sahasrara* (crown *chakra*) in '*yoganidra*'.This is a highly allegorical picture of the Supreme *Purusha* resting in the body on the soft bed of '*Vasuki*' (celestial serpent) the *kundalini shakti*. Lord Vishnu is indeed the Supreme *Purusha* who dwells in the city of the physical body. '*Puri*' means the city, the dwelling place of the soul and the '*purishayat*' means who is resting in the body. This is the vision of the indwelling *Purusha* (Supreme-soul), who is experienced as the silent witness by yogis in deep meditation. This reclining posture of Lord Vishnu is installed only in a few temples where people make offerings and seek blessings for peaceful meditative unity in transcendence. The Divine consort of Lord Vishnu is Sri Lakshmi the goddess of wealth and prosperity.

Lord Shiva

The Worship of Lord Shiva has been one of the most cherished rituals in the religious tradition of ancient India. Across the country there are innumerable temples and shrines with the images of Shiva in the form of *Yogi Raja*—as well as the symbolic *Lingam* form, rounded both at the top and bottom to indicate that it doesn't stand or arise from anywhere in space or time. It has neither beginning nor end. At some temples it is in the shape of an egg symbolic of the cosmic womb, *Hiranyagarbha*—the source as well as the support and resort of the entire creation. *Shivalingam* symbolically represents the complete eternal cosmic principle of creation, sustenance and annihilation. The three horizontal lines on *Shivalingam* indicate the three qualities of the polarized creative force of nature— the three *Gunas: Sattvic, Rajasic,* and *Tamasic.* In worship, all the offerings are made on the topmost part of *Lingam*. *Shivalingam* is also worshipped as *Jyotirlingam*, the ball of radiance, the bright flame. Everything in the universe is the transformation and configuration of cosmic energy—the flame of fire is the manifestation of God. *Jyotirlingam* is the embodiment of divine light.

The glorious form of *Jyotirlingam* stands out in all majesty—the Supreme Divinity out of formlessness emerges in the form of bright flame, declaring that there is nothing beside the Omniscience of the Lord. Worship of *Jyotirlingam* is symbolic of both, the unmanifest and manifest Divinity. The literal meaning of *Lingam* is 'symbol', 'mark', or 'sign' that ushers to the hidden principle of the absolute truth. There are many hymns in ancient scriptures where Shiva has been identified with 'Agni' (fire) the cosmic energy conceived as an element of life force, as well as destruction. *Jyotirlingam* is the distinctive symbol that represents the divine light, which forms the substratum of the universe.

The most important ritual associated with the worship of Shiva is *abhishekam*. The holy sage of Shivapurana describes *"abhishekapriyoshiva"* which means, "Lord Shiva is pleased with *abhishekam*." Shiva *abhishekam* is the offering of water on the topmost part of *Shivalingam* in an unbroken stream with uninterrupted chanting of sacred hymns and one pointed concentration. In the process of *abhishekam* the devotee prays for unity with the source of life in an unbroken stream of devoted thoughts; even though only momentary this phenomenal experience of connectedness brings inner awakening which is closer to any other spiritual experience of life. The ancient rishis have described it as, *'sajatiya vritti pravah'*, which means, "continuous single pointed contemplation on God." Shiva *abhishekam* creates a remarkable harmony at physical, psychological and spiritual levels of awareness; while hands pour the water, the chanting of hymns guide the mind to remain absorbed in the ecstasy of Divine love with attention and intention. Slowly and gradually as the mind becomes involved in the process, the devotee enters into the ecstatic trance and the grace of the Lord is revealed in the meditative unity. It is the subjective experience of visualizing *Jyotirlingam* (the ball of radiance) at a specific level of yogic unity in transcendence.

There are hundreds of shrines across the country where Lord Shiva is worshipped as *Jyotirlingam* but the most well known are the *Dwadasha Jyotirlingam*. Shivapurana declares although all the shrines of Shiva are auspicious but these 12 are of special importance and significance for meditative unity with the indwelling Supreme-Self. These shrines are described in Jyotirlinga Stotra:

1 Somnath in Saurashtra (Kathiawad), Gujarat

2 Mallikarjun or Mallikeshwar in Sri Sailam AP (also listed as a Shakti Pitha site).

3 Mahakal in Ujjain or Mahakaleshwar at Ujjain, MP state.

4 Omkar in Mamaleshwar (at Omkareshwar on the river Narmada, MP)

5 Vaijnath in Parli (Vaidyanath at Deogarh, Bihar)

6 Bhima Shankar in Dakini northwest of Poona, in Dhakini, Maharashtra

7 Rameshwar in Setubandha, Tamilnadu

8 Nagesh, Naganath/Nageshwar, in Darukavana, Maharashtra

9 Vishweshwar/ Vishawanath in Banaras/Varanasi, UP

10 Trimbakeshwar near Nasik on the banks of river Gautami/Godavari, Maharashtra

11 Kedarnath/Kedareshwar in Uttarakhand Himalayas, UP

12 Ghurmeshwar in Shivalaya or Grineshwar in Visala-kam, near Ellora caves, Maharashtra.

According to the ancient holy books of Hinduism, it is believed that anybody who goes to these shrines with sincere devotion is definitely blessed with yogic communion to the source of life and attains liberation in due course of time.

Lord Shiva is addressed by many different names, such as Rudra (the life force). The holy sage in Shvetashvatara Upanishad declares, *"Eko hi Rudro na dwitiyaastu,"* meaning, "Rudra is 'One' without a second." The great saint calls upon Rudra in profound reverence with heart-felt devotional love. The hymns known as *Kritanjali* from Shvetashvatara Upanishad are highly melodious, poetic, and also deeply philosophical.

There is a detailed description of 11 expressive aspects of Rudra in other Hindu scriptures; such as Hara, Bahurupa, Triyambaka, Aparajita, Vriskapi, Sambhu, Kapardi, Raivata, Mrigavyadha, Sara, and Kapali. These Rudras are the bestower of blessings, exalted joy and Bliss; or can be described as bestower of personal desires. Since Rudra is also addressed as the *Prana Shakti* (life force), the 11 aspects of *Prana* are also addressed as Rudra i.e. *Prana, Apana, Vyana, Samana, Udana, Naga, Kurma, Krikala, Devadatta, Dhananjaya,* and *Chita.*

Lord Shiva is known as Shankara (auspicious) and also Shambho—meaning, the world of joy and the one who helps us to live in yoga and work through the uninterrupted consciousness of the Divine. It also means who helps in self-control at all levels of consciousness. There is another beautiful hymn in Vedas—*"Aum namah shambhavaya cha mayobhavaya cha, namah shankaraya cha, mayasakaraya cha namah shivaya cha shivataraya cha"* (Rigveda 16.41), meaning, "I salute and bow to Lord Shiva who leads us into austerities, who is the giver of joy, peace, and happiness. I salute and bow to the bestower of everything in the physical, mundane, as well as the spiritual world." Shiva is also addressed as Mahadeva—which means the controller of all the gods and goddesses in the macrocosm as well as in the microcosm. It is the indwelling light of the Self, the vital force that presides over the inner cosmos and guides the entire functioning of the body. It is the light of the Self, which sustains and maintains order in body. When the divine light leaves the body, the individual light goes into cosmic light; a spark merging into the wholeness of the Divine radiance.

There are many hymns in ancient scriptures where Shiva is worshipped as *Omkara*—the holy syllable *Aum*. *Omkara* represents the cosmic cycle of creation, sustenance, and destruction. *Omkara* is a combination of three words *Akara, Ukara,* and *Makara,* combined together *Omkara. Akara* for *adimata* (creation), *Ukara* for *utkrishta* (sustenance), and *Makara* for *miti* (annihilation). The manifestation of Divine power *Aum* is Uma—the creative force—which is holding everything together and is reflected through everything. Shiva is addressed as Triyambaka, which means "having three eyes." Beside the two eyes, the third eye is the eye of higher perception, wisdom, and increased intuition where the presence of indwelling-Self is perceived in the form of light in meditation. It is also known the eye of contemplation and concentration, the focal point between the two eyebrows from where the breath control starts and the meditator goes into unity with the indwelling-Self. This is the most powerful psychic station in human body known as *Ajna chakra*—the command center, where the individual becomes receptive to the guidance of the Higher-Self. Spontaneous concentration at the command center makes us very contemplative, concentrated, intuitive and we are blessed with the clear understanding of the past, present and future. This specific level of awareness is *Trikala Darsana.* It is to be awakened to exalted awareness from where one can perceive and visualize the present, the past, as well as the mysteries of the future. It is a three-fold experience all at once. *Trikala Darsana* is to enter into unity with the universal mind that encompasses everything in the microcosm as well the macrocosm. When the mind is purified in yoga the light of the Self is perceived in mediation at the command center. This is the personal experience of visualizing the spark of energy at *Triveni—Ajna chakra*; where the two psychic currents *Pingala* from the right and *Ida* from the left merge into *Sushumna nadi*. It is that specific level of purified consciousness where the individual is blessed with special powers such as clairvoyance, telepathy and clairaudience.

Lord Shiva is also addressed as Mahakala and Kaleshwara—which means the master and controller of all devouring time. The great *Mahamrityunjaya mantra* is also addressed to the indwelling Shiva for liberation from the fear of death. With constant repetition of this mantra the person remains connected with the source of life and he is blessed with the experiential knowledge of his own immortality, which brings liberation from the fear of death and also the rich experience of being ageless, timeless, and immortal.

Another sacred, famous name for Shiva is Nataraja, which literally means, "the master of everything and everyone involved in the play of life." The symbol of Nataraja shows a marvelous unity of the various levels of consciousness, from gross to the subtle and to the unified field when the individual-self goes into unity with the cosmic-self. This dramatic figure indicates that Shiva, although involved in the dance of life remains perpetually absorbed in the serenity of the Supreme-soul. The face is calm and peaceful as a spectator in the play of his own creative impulse. The peaceful face indicates the yogic unity in transcendence. The ring of flames all around Nataraja is the cosmic energy, the divine potency which has no beginning and no end.

Lord Shiva

There are some holy shrines, especially in North India where images of Lord Shiva are enshrined in the form of a '*yogi Raja*' sitting in peaceful meditation, totally absorbed in the ecstasy of inner Bliss. Shiva the god of austerity is always shown wearing the tiger skin with holy ashes smeared all over, and hair rolled upward at the top of the head on the crown *chakra*. The snakes around the neck indicate the awakening of *Kundalini shakti*, the crescent moon on the forehead signifies the enjoyment of the mystical divine nectar *Soma*, which originates in the *Sahasrara*—crown *chakra*, cascades through *Binduvisarga* and drips through *Lalana chakra* located on the left side of the forehead. This elixir of life gives blissful intoxication in deep meditation and radiates the exhilarating joy of yogi in ecstatic trance. The sacred Ganga flowing from the top of the head, the crown *chakra*, indicates the release of spiritualized consciousness from the bottom of the spine, the *Muladhara chakra*. "Ganga" literally means "the flow of knowledge." In yoga meditation with the proper alignment of neck, head, and lower back the *Sushumna Nadi* is awakened and the pure spiritualized energy is released like a fountain from crown chakra at the top of the head. The Trishul, or trident, of Shiva is the symbol of His sovereignty as creator, the sustainer and the annihilator. The small drum hanging around the trident signifies the rhythm of time in the universe.

Although Shiva *abhishekam* forms an important part of daily rituals at the shrines of Shiva; the special worship performed on Shivaratri holds great significance. Shivaratri— literally, the night dedicated to the worship of Shiva is observed on the 14th night of the descending phase of moon in the month of January-February. It is the auspicious night when the presence of Lord Shiva is perceived from the depth of our own inner-Self. The night of Shivaratri has been given special importance for meditative unity in transcendence, which brings liberation in this life, and life here after. Some people who aspire for authentic spiritual growth in life they hold fast on this special day and also meditate at home from sunset to midnight. It is believed that the cosmic combination on this special night is conducive to meditation and the mind becomes very receptive to the call of the Divine and unity in meditation is experienced very naturally and spontaneously. The quietness of the night makes the meditative experience very rich and rewarding.

Sri Ganesha

Sri Ganesha worship forms an important part of almost all the Hindu rituals in which the devotee seeks the blessings of Ganapati for inner enlightenment, clarity of vision, purity of mind and intellect, precision of thoughts, inner integrity, peace, prosperity, and right guidance into the activities of daily life. The Rigveda declares *"Gana nam tva ganapatim hava mahe,"* (2.23.1), which means, "I invoke the blessings of Ganapati, the master of *ganas*—the chief elements that constitute the body of the universe." Ganesha or Gananayaka also means the Lord of the groups of deities in the human body as well as in the cosmos; which are working in perfect co-operation with each other for the sustenance of life on earth. Gananayaka controls the combined movement of every little atom and every little molecule that keeps the wheel of creation in motion.

In some ancient scriptures there is a description of a geometrical figure of Sri Ganesha, known as *Pancha bootatmaka ganesha*—which means that Sri Ganesha is the embodiment of the five chief elements that constitute the body of the entire universe. It is for this reason, that the blessings of Lord Ganesha are invoked with words *"Aum Sri Ganapataye Namah"* at the beginning of all auspicious worships. The icon of Sri Ganesha is a geometrical figure created to produce a profound and lasting spiritual experience, which liberates the individual from the lingering shadows of conditioned behavior and gradually aligns with the source. Beside the names such as Sri Ganapati, Sri Ganesha, Sri Vinayaka, and Gananayaka there is a long description of names in the *Ganapatiatharvashirsha*, each explaining the specific attribute; such as *"Aum ek dantaya vid mahe vakratundaya dheemahi, tahno danti prachodayat, "* which means, "May we meditate on Lord Ganesha, who is identified as *'ek dantaya'* and *'Vakratundaya'*. O' Lord, May thou purify our intellect and motivate our thoughts in the right direction."

There is also a drawing in *Mudgulapurana,* which describes the particular significance of all those prayers recited by the devotees during the worship.

'Aum Vakratundaya Namah'–praying for liberation from *matsura* (carelessness) born of *pramada* (negligence).

'Aum ek dantaye Namah'—pursuing freedom from the clutches of *madsura* (conceit).

'Aum lambodharaya Namah'—seeking strength for cosmic unity and liberation, from anger, jealousy and violence.

'Aum Dhoomravarnaya Namah'—aspiring for liberation from inner darkness and ignorance.

'Aum Gajnaya Namah'—seeking victory over *lobhsura* (greed).

'Aum Vikataya Namah'—praying for liberation from lust.

'Aum Vighna hartaya Namah' and *'Vinayakaya Namah'*, which means the Supreme leader who removes all the possible obstacles both at physical as well as psychological levels of consciousness. The symbolism in prayers indicates the efforts of the individual soul seeking liberation from the seven deadly sins—such as lust, anger, greed, envy, sloth, egoism, and gluttony.

The ancient religious literature of Hinduism describes the worship of Gananayaka not only in images but also in *lingas, saligramas, yantras* (geometrical diagrams), *swastikas,* and *kalashas.* There are thousands of temples and shrines of

Ganapati all over India and in many south-east Asian countries like China, Japan and Indonesia.

The image of Lord Ganapati with elephant head, large ears, four hands, big belly, dressed in yellow silk, with a lovely carved crown, and a little mouse sitting near his feet was introduced by the sages of Puranic literature. In this form Sri Ganapati is worshipped as '*Sudh, Budh, Swarupa*', which means the embodiment of purified intellect who is perennially absorbed in the transcendental wisdom and silence of the Supreme-soul. 'Ga' means *buddhi* (intellect), 'na' means the *vijnana* (wisdom), 'pati' means the master. So, another meaning for Ganapati is the master of the intellect and wisdom. Lord Ganesha is also addressed as *Pranava Swarupa*, which means the embodiment of the Holy syllable *Aum*

The large ears of Sri Ganapati indicate the importance of silent intelligent listening to the teacher, which leads to increased learning ability, creativity, attention span, and comprehension. The trunk coming down the forehead of the elephant face and turned to the left indicates the alignment of the mind and intellect to the psychic current '*Ida*' arising from the left side of the spine which ushers the aspirant into exalted awareness, systematic orderly thinking, and contemplation. It also represents the holy syllable *Aum* or '*Pranava*' and appropriate introspection and acceptance while reflecting carefully upon the teachings of a Guru. It is the ability to make independent choices on the basis of one's own inner confirmation. In a few rare cases the trunk will curve to the right to touch the *modaka* on the right hand. Also the trunk of the elephant has the peculiar efficiency to uproot a tree or pick up a pin from the ground, which suggests that anybody who remains aligned with the eye of intuition, located between the two eyebrows, he is blessed with special intuitive ability to solve all kinds of problems in life. The four arms of Ganapati indicate the sovereignty of the master of *ganas* in four directions. In one hand he holds '*pasha*' (axe) and in the other a 'rope' which symbolizes that with one hand he helps his devotees to cut off the attachments to the fruit of their actions and be free from the bondage of karma; and with the other hand he pulls them closer to the realization of truth which ties them to the enjoyment of inner Bliss. In his third hand he holds *Modaka* a rice ball or *ladoo*, which signifies the *Prasad* (grace) that one receives by being close to the Divine. With the fourth hand the '*abhaya hasta*' he assures love, peace, prosperity, security and protection under all circumstances. Lord Ganesha's big belly with a snake wrapped around it declares, that the entire creation exists in *Panchabootatmac Ganesha*; invoked at *Muladhara chakra*, where the Lord of *Ganas* gives boons in the form of *Riddhi* (prosperity) and *Siddhi* (inner-alignment). *Ganapatiatharvashirsha* of Atharvaveda explains this beautifully. "*Tvam Muladhara sthitosi nityam, tvam shakti trayatmaka, tvam yogino dhyayanti nityam,*" which means, "O' Lord Ganapati you are the embodiment of tri-fold power—the *Kundalini shakti*, enshrined in *Muladhara chakra* at the bottom of the spine; where the great yogis concentrate in meditation for unity in transcendence."

In some of the old *Tantric* geometrical drawings, which

provide a detailed explanation of seven *chakras* in the human body, there is generally a picture of *Airavata* (the celestial elephant) at the *Muladhara chakra* the seat of Lord Ganesha. It is the hiss of the elephant at the *Muladhara chakra* that moves the *Kundalini shakti* (spiritual energy) upward and leads the individual towards the achievement of higher goals. *Airavata* represents determination, steadfastness, loyalty, stability, power, and prosperity. This is one reason, why the elephant is traditionally considered auspicious and symbol of prosperity in Hinduism; and it also explains the symbolism in connection with the icon of Lord Ganesha.

At the shrine of Sri Ganesha close to the seat of the Lord, we always see a mouse of ridiculously small size sitting in the midst of offerings and looking up at the master for permission to touch the food offered in prayer. The Sanskrit word *Musaka* (mouse) has been derived from the root word '*mus*' which literally means to steal. A mouse stealthily enters a house and starts destroying things quietly. The mouse connotes the worldly desire that quietly sneaks in our mind and stealthily starts creating bondage and slavery, but if it is checked; it works at the command of the '*sudh budh swarupa*' (purified intellect) and is definitely harnessed into the useful channels. The mouse stands for the desire in this world. The man of steadfast wisdom who is spontaneously settled in the serenity of the Supreme *Parabrahman* is definitely above and beyond the slavery of desire. He acts as a master or Lord of his desire and makes it a vehicle to serve the humanity.

Although Sri Ganesha worship forms an important part

of the Hindu rituals in daily life and every month on the fourth day of lunar calendar, special prayers are held at the temples for Sri Vinayaka, the Ganesha festival in the lunar month of *Bhadrapada* holds special significance. Ganesha Chaturthi, which is celebrated on the fourth day of the ascending phase of Moon in *Bhadrapada* is one of the most popular festivals of Hindu families especially in Maharashtra and some parts of south India. The festival starts on the fourth day with worship of clay-molded images of Sri Vinayaka and the celebration culminates on the day of *Ananta Chaturdashi*, the 14th day of the lunar calendar. On this day the images are taken in a procession to the river or seacoast nearby and immersed in the water with prayers and special offerings of rice balls, the most favorite *naivedyam* of Sri Ganesha. This immersion of the clay images in the ocean is called the *Visarjana* ceremony, which forms the culmination of the worship. *Visarjana* means giving away the concept of fo rms and names and entering into the essentiality of the ideal behind the image of Sri Ganesha. On Ganesha Chaturthi some people fast and seek blessings for good health, wealth, and spiritual growth in life.

Goddess Saraswati

Mother Saraswati the Divine consort of Lord Brahma is worshipped as the embodiment of true knowledge, wisdom, purity, and serenity. There are innumerable shrines of the goddess Saraswati at temples, educational institutes, schools, *Gurukuls*, Ashrams and the homes of artists, musicians and devotees who are inclined to experience inner enlightenment and spiritual maturity.

The word Saraswati explains itself—'*sara*' means the essence and '*swa*' means the indwelling light. Mother Saraswati is the personification of divine light who intimates us with the essentiality of everything in the world. The goddess is also addressed as *Jnana Shakti* means the pure luminous divine knowledge, which awakens the inherent abilities of the individual to experience and comprehend higher realities, both in physical and the spiritual world.

The image of the goddess Saraswati represents the Divine Mother; not only the embodiment of all knowledge—arts, sciences, crafts and skills but also the ideal Guru, the greatest spiritual teacher perennially absorbed in the subjective experience of transcendental reality. The great goddess is always shown wearing a beautiful white silk *sari*, holding the four Vedas in one hand, a rosary in the other and playing *Veena* with the other two. The white color of her *sari* indicates *sattvika* (purity) and serenity. The Vedas indicate the sovereignty of Vedic knowledge, which forms the basis of learning in the multiple branches of education and the rosary in the other hand reminds us about continuous *manan* (contemplation and reflection). It indicates that the study of the Vedas and contemplation should always move hand in hand. It is not only the knowledge gathered and absorbed from books which brings awakening but also the continuous introspection and reflection. Book knowledge remains merely information until it is fully contemplated and personally experienced. '*Manan*' or contemplation opens the doorway to the deepest mysteries of the world and the actualization of our inherent potential.

The other two hands of the goddess are engaged in holding the celestial music instrument *Veena*—which indicates the call of the Divine for our constant alignment with the primordial sound of *Brahmanada—Aum*. The sound of *Brahmanada* wraps the entire creation. It is a connecting link to the entire universe as well as to the deepest mysteries of the Supreme-Self. The celestial melody of *Veena* initiates the individual to stay tuned to the sound of *Aum* in order to live in peace and harmony with the indwelling-self with society and nature. It tunes up the mind and intellect into the natural rhythm of '*nada*' (sound) and prepares the individual to experience and comprehend higher realities. It creates alignment with the Supreme power from where the flow of life receives guidance.

At the shrine of the goddess Saraswati there is always a peaceful looking swan sitting next to the holy feet of the Divine Mother proudly waiting to serve with humility. Swan, the vehicle of the goddess, is the symbol of purity, heightened intuition, and discriminative intelligence. The bird swan, called *Hansa* in Hindi is believed to have the special ability to separate milk from water, thus representing the power of adopting only that which is desirable and rejecting the undesirable. The symbolism indicates that anybody who seeks the blessings of Saraswati develops the remarkable discriminative ability to differentiate between right and wrong choices, what should be adopted and what should be avoided. He becomes highly intuitive very organized and his goals are always very clear to him. This is one reason why the enlightened sages who are perennially aligned with the source and live with the guidance of the Divine Mother are designated as *Paramahansa* such as Swami Ramakrishna *Paramahansa*, which means highly enlightened sage. The other title used for the highly learned sage, and the man of wisdom is 'Saraswati', such as Swami Dayananda Saraswati.

The Divine Mother Saraswati is also addressed as Vageshwari (goddess of '*vac*' or speech), Brahmi (the Divine consort of Brahma), Maha Vidya (the supreme knowledge) and Sharada. Saraswati also means the flow of pure celestial energy from which the organized creation proceeds.

Although the worship of the goddess Saraswati forms an important part of prayers in Hindu families, there are some Vedic rituals especially performed for children in which Saraswati worship is highly emphasized such as the *Vidya arambha* ceremony when the child starts pre-school. The worship is performed at the holy shrine of the goddess Saraswati. The youngster is advised to seek blessings of the Divine Mother while the learned priest recites hymns invoking the presence of the goddess. Towards the completion of the worship the child repeats the prayer "*Mata saraswati namastubhyam varde kamarupini, vidyarambha karisyami sidher bhavatu mei sada,*" which means, "O' Divine Mother

Saraswati I salute and bow to you.You are the giver of boons and bounties; today as I start my education please be with me, guide me and bless me with success in the field of education I choose."

Saraswati worship also forms a very important part of *Upanayana Samskara*, the sacred thread ceremony generally conducted at the age of nine and above; when the youngster is enlightened about the importance of good education and his responsibilities as a respectable member of family and community. The other auspicious occasion for Saraswati worship is the *Vedaarambha Samskara* when the high school graduate starts higher education at college. In worship of the Divine Mother, he recites special hymns from the Holy scriptures and seeks blessings for a good academic career, clarity of vision, purity of intellect, and right guidance into the activities of daily life.

Besides these special ceremonies, Saraswati worship also forms an important part of the festival Vasant Panchami celebrated in the month of February, on the fifth day of the lunar month *Magh* in the ascending phase of Moon. The goddesss is decorated with fresh flower garlands, and special prayers are held in schools, Ashrams and at homes. People seek blessings for the enlightened love of God, peace and happiness in the family. It is the most important day of the year for musicians, artists, poets, and educators when they worship their musical instruments, sacred books and other equipments at the altar of the holy mother seeking her blessings for increased awareness, sacred knowledge, spiritual maturity, and success in life.

Sri Lakshmi

The Goddess Sri Lakshmi the Divine consort of Lord Vishnu is worshipped for wealth, prosperity, peace, and happiness on important occasions, especially the festival of Diwali. In the worship of Sri Lakshmi, the royal form of *Adi Shakti* the individual seeks guidance for making money by appropriate means and making the appropriate use of wealth while keeping in mind the global welfare. The sacred hymns that are recited during the worship literally mean, "May we become respectful to the bounties and reservoirs of earth and honor the mutual inter-dependence which exists between human beings, other species and mother nature; may the money float in the hands of wise and virtuous, helpful in providing good education, well-equipped labs, libraries, proper medical care, hospitalization, and the businesses conducive to the proper growth of society."

Sri Lakshmi, the royal *Adi Shakti*, is worshipped wearing a beautiful red *sari* with garlands of fragrant flowers; magnificently sitting or standing on a fully blossomed lotus flower. The four hands of the goddess signify the four-fold purpose of life: *Dharma* (duty), *Artha* (wealth), *Kama* (desire), and *Moksha* (liberation). The goddess of wealth is holding the lotus flowers in each of her two upper hands and the other two are always engaged in pouring out wealth and bestowing prosperity. The lotus flower, the highest concept of all that is sacred and pure, also indicates detachment. The symbolism of lotus flowers in two hands and pouring gold coins from the other two gives the profound message of being blessed with wealth and riches from the Divine Mother and at the same time remaining detached from it—which speaks gloriously of the Hindu way of life *Dharma, Artha, Kama* and *Moksha*.

The great goddess is generally seen with two celestial elephants one on each side carrying garlands and pouring water from pitchers held in their trunks, that also signifies power and prosperity. Although the worship of the goddess of fortune, Sri Lakshmi forms an important part of the rituals performed on all auspicious occasions, the worship on Deepavali holds special importance. Deepavali, the festival of lights, is celebrated on the last day of the descending phase of Moon in the lunar month of *Ashwin*, generally in October or November. On this special festival, Sri Lakshmi is worshipped along with Sri Ganesha. It is a three-day long festival, which starts with *Dhantehras* on the 13th day of the lunar calendar and the celebration culminates into the worship of the goddess Lakshmi on Deepavali. The worship of the Divine Mother Sri Lakshmi with a special variety of sweets, candies, gold and silver coins and gifts is really spectacular. Deepavali or Diwali is one of the most popular Hindu festivals celebrated throughout the country.

Goddess Durga

Mother Durga—the personification of the totality of the powers of Brahma, Vishnu, Maheshwara, and other gods, is worshipped for the annihilation of negative tendencies. Durga is addressed as *'Dur gati harani'*—which means, "Who helps us to remain awake and transcend the darkness, which exists in the form of lust, greed, gluttony, anger, arrogance, jealousy, envy and illusion." The sincere worship of *Adi Shakti* purifies the mind and accelerates our day-to-day emotions towards the journey of self-purification. Mother Durga is generally worshipped dressed in a gorgeous red *sari*, wearing several ornaments and the royal crown. She is magnificently seated on a lion with ten hands each signifying the combined powers of Brahma, Vishnu, Maheshwara and other gods. For example the great goddess is holding the *brahmastra* and water pot of Brahma, the mace, the discus, conch and the lotus flower of Sri Vishnu, the trident and drum of Maheshwara, the rope and *'pasha'* (axe) of Sri Ganesha.

The goddess Durga is addressed by various names; each having an importance and significance of its own, in connection with one or the other episode. The goddess is addressed as Mahishasuramardini (the conqueror of Mahisha—the buffalo demon), Vindhyavasani, (the one who lives in the Vindhyas), and Vaishnavi Shakti (the mysterious power of Lord Vishnu). The Divine Mother Durga is also addressed as Bhavani, Kanakadurga and Kousaki Durga. Devi Bhagavatam and Markandeya Purana, the highly venerated ancient scriptures, describe the most enchanting poetical hymns in adoration of the great goddess, in which the Divine Mother is invoked by hundreds of different names simple and melodious.

The great goddess is worshipped with sincere love and devotion on several important occasions, especially during Navaratra. Durga Puja in Bengal during the *Ashwin* Navaratra is really extravagant. It is a special nine days worship starting with the first day of the lunar month *Ashwin Shukla* generally in September or October. The gorgeous clay images of the goddess are beautifully decorated, sincerely worshipped for nine days and then taken in triumphant procession from all over the town to the nearby river or ocean where the images are ceremonially immersed in the water with special prayers. In south India this special nine days worship starts as Mahalaya and is concluded with the celebration of Mahishasuramardini and Vijayadashmi which indicates, step by step self-purification and victory over the demonic selfish behavior ruled by lower-self. The Devi temple in Chittorgarh (Rajasthan) is also famous for the unique celebration of Durga puja during the Navaratra festival.

Goddess Kali

The consort of Kala the all devouring time is Kali— another aspect of the divine potency of Supreme

Parabrahman. Mother Kali is worshipped for victory over time and blessings for living in the tissue of the present moment.

The concept of time has existed ever since the beginning of creation. It is deeply grounded in the psychological make up of man. Time is a measure in the world of relativity. The entire creation functions under the concept of time. Kala, or time, is the expression of divine potency that works behind everything. It modifies, transforms, deteriorates, and slowly brings everything to final destruction. Everything we see is caught within the grasp of swift moving time.

The image of the goddess Kali, the awe-inspiring ferocious aspect of divine power, always shows her standing in a challenging posture, wearing a garland of 50 human skulls, and her red tongue protruding from her mouth. Being the personification of all devouring time, the ultimate end of everything striking awe and fear, her complexion is extremely dark black, bordering on deep blue. The goddess is generally shown with four hands, holding a dagger, and the head of a demon in two of her hands, and the other two are in *Abhaya* and *Varada Mudras*; which clearly indicates that although time is swallowing and gobbling up everything that comes into existence, if we learn to live in the awareness of the present moment, we are blessed with mastery over swift moving time and can make the very best use of it. We learn to live by choice and not by chance.

There are many shrines of the goddess Kali all over India,

especially in Bengal, where people go to seek her blessings on special occasion. Kali worship forms an important part of the Navaratra and Deepavali festival in Bengal, which helps the aspirant to move beyond the conditions created in time momentarily; enjoy the blessed state of inner unity with the indwelling-soul and maintain the awareness of Bliss for the rest of the year.

Divine Mother Parvati

Goddess Parvati, the Divine consort of Shiva is worshipped for alignment with *Para Shakti* (pure-consciousness). Mother Parvati is also addressed as Uma—the personification of the divine power of the holy syllable *Aum*. Uma is the creative force, which is holding everything together and is reflected through everything. Parvati being the mother of the universe is worshipped by many different names such as Bhavani, Rudhrani, Ishwari, Gauri, Sarvamangala, Girija, Rajeshwari, Bhuvaneshwari, Katyayani, Hemavati, Lalita, Tripurasundari, Shambhavi, Maheshwari and Mahadevi.

The image of the Supreme goddess Parvati is shown wearing a beautiful *sari*, the traditional *mangal sutra*, garlands of fragrant flowers, and always blessing her devotees with love, peace, happiness, and experiential knowledge of the Supreme-soul. The worship of Parvati forms an important part of many rituals, but before the wedding ceremony Gauri worship is considered to be very auspicious. In some parts of South India and especially in Maharashtra the wedding ceremony does not start until the bride has sincerely completed the worship of Gauri (Parvati) and received blessings for love, peace and harmony in married life.

Although the worship of goddess Parvati is conducted every Friday at the shrine with '*Lalita Sahasranama*' (the thousand names of the goddess), the special worship performed on *tritiya* in the lunar month of *Bhadrapada*— which is the third day of the bright phase of the Moon in August/September, is really unique. The image of the great goddess is decorated with a beautiful silk *sari*, expensive ornaments and fresh flowers. Delicious sweets are offered with special prayers and devotees seek blessings of the *Para Shakti* for good health, wealth and perennial unity with the source of life. Some devotees who aspire for increased spiritual enlightenment observe fast on this special day and meditate on '*Kundalini Shakti*' at *Muladhara chakra*, located at the bottom of the spine. The Divine Mother makes their meditative experience extremely rewarding and they generally witness the *Kundalini Shakti* gradually moving upward through the *chakras* (the psychic stations) and merging into its source at '*sahasrara*' the *Jyotirlingam* located at the top of the head. In the subjective experience of the journey to infinite Bliss, the individual is introduced to his inherent potential and blessed with deep physiological rest, inner peace and tranquility.

Navagraha Mandala

The Worship of the nine celestial bodies, known as *Navagraha* forms an important part of the rituals performed on special occasions in Hindu families. In most of the temples, especially in South India, besides the important shrines of Lord Shiva, Lord Vishnu, Sri Hanuman, Lord Rama, Lord Krishna, and other gods and goddesses there is generally a shrine of nine celestial bodies known as *Navagraha Mandala*, where the devotees seek alignment with the cosmic bodies for peace, good health, and prosperity.

According to Vedic astrology there is indeed a strong relationship between human mind and body and the stars and planets. The shrine of nine celestial bodies represents the Sun, the Moon, and the five planets i.e. Mars, Mercury, Jupiter, Venus, and Saturn along with the ascending and descending nodes of Moon known as Rahu and Ketu—the *chhayagrahas* (shadow planets). The image of the Sun is always placed in the center of the shrine facing east and the others are installed around the Sun god each facing in a specified direction.

Surya, the Sun god, the personification of the Lord himself, the source of *tejas*, the giver of life on the planet, is always shown wrapped in a red silk scarf, facing east, radiating the charisma of celestial light and blessing the devotees with a positive attitude towards life and good health. 'Chandera' or the Moon, the source of *ojas*, the elixir of life, is shown wearing a white silk scarf facing west and showering blessings for peace of mind and inner integrity. 'Mangal' or Mars is presented, wrapped in a vermillion silk scarf, facing south and proudly blessing his devotees with physical strength, self-confidence, success, and prosperity in life. 'Budh' or Mercury the Lord of wisdom, pure intellect, and creativity is always shown wrapped in a green silk scarf standing in deep modesty, facing east and blessing his devotees with peace and harmony. 'Bruhaspati' or Jupiter also known as Guru, which means the great spiritual teacher, is always shown wearing saffron scarf, symbolic of light and enlightenment, facing north, and blessing his devotees with, authentic spiritual growth and peaceful happy family life. 'Shukra' or Venus the god of love, peace and prosperity in married life is presented wearing a white silk scarf, facing east and blessing the devotees with efficiency in work, success in academic performances, and happiness in worldly life. 'Shani' or Saturn the slow moving planet is always shown wearing a black or dark navy blue silk scarf facing west and helping people to eliminate darkness from their lives. Rahu the *chhayagraha* (shadow planet) is usually shown as the head of a serpent, wrapped in a light brown silk scarf, facing south; and Ketu its counterpart, another *chhayagraha*, is generally depicted as the tail of a serpent wrapped in a multi colored silk scarf also facing south and blessing people with the pleasures of life.

These nine heavenly bodies in the sky called *Navagraha* radiate a specific type of celestial energy, which is closely connected with the physical as well as the psychological make up of the human beings and forms a significant part of the Vedic astrology. According to the latest studies in relation to the direct influence of these cosmic bodies on human mind and body, the great Vedic scholar Maharishi says that the nine parts of DNA have their counter parts in nine heavenly bodies—the *Navagraha*. DNA revolves around hydrogen bonds which correspond to the Sun god, the giver of life on planet, phosphate corresponds to Moon, cytosine to Mars, sugar to Mercury, guanine to Jupiter, thymine to Venus, adenine to Saturn, and the enzymes that act within the DNA and yet are not a part of it to Rahu and Ketu, the shadow planets. This clearly indicates the bond that exists between the man and the cosmos, between the human intelligence and the cosmic intelligence. As is the macrocosm so is the microcosm.

It is because of the direct influence of the activity of these cosmic bodies on human beings, '*Navagraha Shanti Puja*'—the worship of the nine celestial bodies is performed for peace and prosperity. *Navagraha* worship is performed with flowers and the nine types of grains, symbolic colors of the nine kinds of gems people wear in order to be in alignment with the specific type of energy of each planet and luminary body. For example, for Leo, the master of the birth sign is the Sun god and the gemstone is *Manik* (Ruby), generally found in a variety of deep, crimson, and scarlet red colors. The recommended weight of the stone is at least two to four carats, or more. The gem stone ruby should be always mounted in gold and worn in the ring finger of the right hand. *Moti* (Pearl) is the gemstone for Cancer and Taurus related to the Moon, the master of their birth sign. The weight of the pearl should be anywhere from one to three carats or more. Mounted in silver, the pearl ring should be worn in the ring finger or the little finger of the left hand. For Aries and Scorpio the presiding planet is Mars and the recommended stone by astrologers is the deep red *Moonga* (Coral) mounted in gold or silver. The ideal weight of coral as suggested by the gem specialists should be two to four carats or more depending upon the age of the person. The coral ring should be worn on the ring finger of the right hand in such a way that the gemstone touches the skin.

Mercury is the ruler of two birth signs, Gemini and Virgo. The suggested gemstone for these birth signs is *Panna* (Emerald). The preferred weight of an emerald should be three to five carats or more. This gemstone is generally mounted in gold and worn on the little finger or the ring finger of the right hand. For Sagittarius and Pisces the master of their birth sign is Jupiter and the auspicious gemstone is *Pukhraj* (Yellow Sapphire) which is often found in light, yellow, or golden color quite transparent and self-luminous. The weight of this auspicious gem should be anywhere from three to five carats or more. The yellow sapphire ring is always mounted in gold and worn on the first finger of the right hand, which corresponds to the energy of Jupiter.

The gemstone for Libra is *Heera* (Diamond) and the ruling planet is Venus. This luminous gem radiates a white gleam of light all around. A diamond ring should be set in silver, white gold, or platinum and worn on the ring finger of either the right or left hand. For full benefit from the diamond the weight of the gem should not be less than one carat. Saturn rules over two birth signs, Capricorn and Aquarius, and its gemstone is *Neelam* (Blue Sapphire). The weight of this precious gem should be anywhere from two to four carats or more. The setting of blue sapphire is preferably in gold or silver and the ring is worn on the middle finger of the right hand, which corresponds to the special energy of Saturn in the body.

For Rahu, which is a shadow planet, the recommended stone is *Gomed* (Hesonite). The weight of this gemstone should be at least three to six carats or more. It is generally mounted in silver and worn on the middle finger or little finger of the left hand, which activates its energy in the human body. Ketu, which is considered to be the counterpart of Rahu, also holds an important role in ancient astrological treatises. The gemstone for Ketu is *Lahsunia* (Cat's Eye). It is generally mounted in a mixture of special metals like silver, copper, or gold or any one of these. The weight of this gemstone should be always two to six carats and the ring is worn on the little finger of the left hand.

The treatises written on astrology and Ayurveda highly recommend the use of gems in order to create favorable effects in mind and body. Since the gems absorb energy from the seven rays of sunlight and other cosmic bodies, their interplay with the human body is natural. The color of these gems radiate energy at certain frequencies of light and therefore can set-up some powerful vibrations at the various levels of consciousness. The gemstones absorb, reflect and radiate the specific type of energy of each cosmic body and definitely create distinctive effects on the human organism, which facilitates good health and progress in life. In *Navagraha* worship the devotee seeks blessings with special hymns that describe the connection of energies between the human body and the celestial body.

Sri Hanuman

Worship of Sri Hanuman, a great devotee of Sri Rama, is one of the most popular rituals performed every Tuesday and Saturday in Hindu temples. Across the country, almost in every village and town there are shrines and temples with the image of Sri Hanuman standing in modesty with hands joined in humility; or sitting with his head slightly bent forward in a devotional posture before the image of Sri Rama and Seeta. At some other shrines, he is portrayed as Veer Hanuman (noble hero) holding a mace in his right hand, with a promise to uphold *Dharma* with courage, bravery and humility. Also there are shrines where Sri Hanuman appears either seated with deep humility at the feet of Sri Rama and carefully listening to the mysteries of *Parabrahman* or singing the glories of the Lord with bells and cymbals in his hands totally absorbed in the ecstasy of divine love.

In the highly revered great Hindu epic the Ramayana, Maharishi Valmiki presents Hanuman as the embodiment of undivided devotion to Sri Rama. Although a very learned scholar well-versed in the study of *shastras*, a man of super human strength, and valor, the master of eight *siddhis* and nine *niddhis*, Hanuman has been portrayed as a humble servant of the Lord. For Hanuman, Sri Rama is everything. Entrusted with the most intricate task by his master, he crosses the ocean and enters the kingdom of Ravana very tactfully. He consoles the Mother Seeta. He creates a panic in Lanka and breaks the morale of the Rakshas. He also gives a sermon to Ravana and preaches him the lessons of the ethical code. Hanuman returns safely, back to his master and reports about the well being of Seeta with reassurance. He saves the life of Lakshmana by fetching the life giving herb '*sanjeevani*' from the Himalayas. Sri Rama entitles Hanuman as *Sankat Mochan*, which means, "the one who appears at the time of difficulty."

Besides the great epic Ramayana which gorgeously illustrates the valorous achievements of Sri Hanuman there is another small scripture Hanuman Chaleesa that describes many facets of his illustrious personality and the devotional love for Sri Rama and Seeta. Reciting Hanuman Chaleesa with sincere devotion forms an important part of the worship, which is conducted for Sri Hanuman on every Tuesday and Saturday.

The festival of Hanuman Jayanti, honoring the birth of Sri Hanuman is celebrated with deep respect and enthusiasm every year on the full Moon day of *Chaitra Purnima* in the month of March or April. Generally people hold fast for the day and visit the temples where the statue of Sri Hanuman is decorated with a new coating of vermillion mixed with butter. At some temples the worship starts in the evening at sunset with *abhishekam* and recital of selected *shlokas* from the Ramayana. *Vada* garlands, bananas, mangoes, and other sweets are offered in prayers and later shared with the devotees. People seek blessings for increased awareness, good health, physical and emotional strength, courage, determination, power of eloquence, steadfastness in the vows of celibacy, true devotion, unconditional love and selfless service to the Supreme Divinity.

Lord Rama

Lord Rama, the God-incarnate, is worshipped with profound respect, sincere love, and ardent devotion by the devotees seeking good health, peace, and prosperity in life. There are innumerable old and new temples of Lord Rama all over India and in other countries of the world. The God-incarnate, Lord Rama is traditionally shown standing with His Divine consort Seeta by His left side, the younger brother Lakshmana by the right hand, and His great devotee Hanuman kneeling a little in front with deep humility.

The Ramayana, the great Hindu epic, which describes the life story of Lord Rama, ranks among the greatest religious classics of the world. In the Ramayana, Sri Rama's character has been presented as the embodiment of *Dharma* that encompasses almost every aspect of life; an ideal king, an ideal man, an ideal brother, an ideal friend, a devoted husband, a valiant soldier and above all a lover of humanity and truth. Throughout the life story of Sri Rama, the great sage Valmiki has tried to illustrate the truth that the virtues and ideals of a perfect man upheld by Sri Rama are indeed quite possible to practice for every human being. Rishi Valmiki has presented Sri Rama as *Purushottama*, which means, "the One most honorable among the human beings," a man of highest perfection. Throughout the long story of the Ramayana, one observes Sri Rama at ease within himself. He is always calm, peaceful, forgiving, pure minded, self-disciplined, humble, polite, very determined, and adorable. His life sets an example of purity and nobility as great as human mind can imagine.

Ramnavami, the auspicious day that honors the birth of Sri Rama, is held on the ninth day of *Chaitra Shukla* in the month of March or April. The temples are beautifully decorated with flowers and lights. The floors are covered with artistic drawings from Ramayana and walls are decorated with golden leaves. The images of Sri Rama along with Seeta, Lakshmana, and Hanuman are decorated with beautiful silk shawls, rich ornaments, flowers, and garlands and worshipped with *Sahakeertana* (group chanting). Verses from the great epic Ramayana are recited with sincere devotion highlighting the chief events of Sri Rama's life. In Ayodhya, the birthplace of Sri Rama, the celebration is incredible.

The great sage Valmiki presents Lord Rama and Seeta as embodiments of *Dharma* always inspiring people into higher and nobler values of life. For centuries the Divine couple has been worshipped by millions of people with sincere respect, love and devotion and their worship will certainly continue for many more years to come.

Lord Krishna

Lord Krishna, the God-incarnate holds a very adorable place in the spiritual and religious life of people in India and in many other parts of the world. There are temples and shrines of Lord Krishna almost in every village and in every town of India where people seek his blessings for devotional love, peace, harmony, and yogic unity in transcendence. The incarnation of Lord Krishna represents the descent of the Supreme-Self in the material world. The Divine manifestation of Sri Krishna has touched almost every aspect of life, religion, poetry, philosophy, mysticism, music, dancing, art, literature, sculpture, painting, yoga, and meditation. For thousands of years, His glorious life, profound wisdom, and divinity have influenced deeply the philosophical, spiritual and cultural life of people.

In the dynamic incarnation of Sri Krishna, we see an ideal figure imbued with a subtle gleam of divinity, the sweet melody of flute, an elusive fleeting smile, and inspiring words of profound wisdom that have fascinated poets, writers, great saints, sages, mystics, educators, and warriors for centuries through the length and breadth of the planet. His lifestyle sets an ideal example of love, compassion, purity of heart, fearlessness, steadfastness, self-sacrifice, renunciation, endurance, nobility, and purity, as great as the human imagination can comprehend. We see in Lord Krishna the universal-Self revealing Himself to the individual-self as the most sincere caring compassionate friend and guide.

The Bhagawad Geeta, the holy dialogue between Lord Krishna and Arjuna is one of the most well-known and revered texts among the other scriptures of the world. The teachings of the Holy Geeta are universal, broad and meant for the welfare of humanity. The general theme of the dialogue is the importance of yogic unity with the source of life while being engaged into the activities of daily life. Sri Krishna makes it very clear that unity in yoga is not merely a practice in isolation; it is the discipline of living in the awareness of the self and performing all the duties of life with the guidance of the Supreme Divinity. The great message of Sri Krishna in the Bhagawad Geeta has been held in deep reverence by sages, philosophers, and learned scholars all over the world. There are hundreds of commentaries on Geeta, both in Indian and foreign languages.

Sri Krishna Janmashtami, the auspicious day dedicated to the birth celebration of Lord Krishna is one of the most popular Hindu festivals. It is celebrated on the eighth day of the dark fortnight of the lunar month *Bhadrapada* generally in August or September. In Mathura, the birthplace of Sri Krishna and also in Vrindavan, the celebration is really spectacular. Cradles with the image of baby Krishna are decorated with flowers, beads and bells with sincere love and deep devotion. At sunset special cultural programs are organized in the temples. There are dance performances and skits staged by children, based on the stories from the boyhood of Sri Krishna. Towards the early hours of night starts the special music program of devotional songs. Everybody joins the singing with the fervor of divine love and waits for the midnight celebration when the devotees rock the cradle with the chanting of hymns, blaring of the conches, and the ringing of bells. The *janmakal puja* is performed with offerings of sweets made with milk and butter and everybody goes to the shrine to receive blessings. The sweet melody of the flute and the ringing of bells at midnight makes the spiritual experience very rich and rewarding.

Geeta Jayanti is the other festival that commemorates the auspicious day when Lord Krishna enlightened Arjuna with the holy teachings of Bhagawad Geeta. Geeta Jayanti is also celebrated all over India and in other parts of the world with deep religious fervor and enthusiasm. Thousands of pocket-sized copies of the Geeta are distributed at conferences and temples. The great sages recommend that everybody should always keep a small edition of Geeta in his pocket for the study of selected verses whenever there is an opportunity. This helps the person to be in harmony with the voice of God and receive sufficient guidance in the activities of daily life.

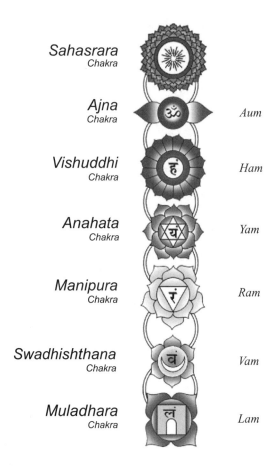

Sahasrara Chakra

Ajna Chakra — *Aum*

Vishuddhi Chakra — *Ham*

Anahata Chakra — *Yam*

Manipura Chakra — *Ram*

Swadhishthana Chakra — *Vam*

Muladhara Chakra — *Lam*

"Concentration (*dharana*) is holding the mind at a specific place within the centers (seven lotuses) of pure consciousness in the body." *(3.1)*

"Meditation (*dhyana*) is the uninterrupted flow of awareness towards the object of concentration." *(3.2)*

"When the mind is liberated from all kinds of distractions and becomes settled in the purity of the Self, it enters the state called *samadhi*." *(3.11)*

-Patanjali Yogasutra

9

Patanjali Ashtanga Yoga
&
Chakra Meditation

The Practice of yoga and meditation originated from the ancient religious traditions of Vedic *Dharma* as an effort to seek alignment with the source of life in order to live a healthy, happy, spiritual, peaceful, and prosperous life, which is in peace and harmony with our own inner-self, with others in society and with nature. A yogi is one who seeks union with the indwelling Supreme-soul for self-realization, God-realization, and attainment of eternal Bliss. The word yoga has been derived from the Sanskrit root word *yuj* meaning to combine or join together the mind, body and spirit in order to experience union and communion with the indwelling-soul. It is the unity of the conditioned-self with the pure luminous Higher-self. Yoga is an art, which helps the person to bring his scattered thoughts together into a reflective and meditative state of mind to comprehend the presence of divinity within. It is an effort to learn to live in the awareness of the self and develop the special ability of maintaining the presence of mind under all circumstances. It integrates almost every aspect of our personality and sets up a spiritual force, which is effective, radiant and shines through our activities. Ordinary work is performed with extraordinary efficiency and enthusiasm.

Yogic discipline is a systematic practice of exploring the inner dimensions of our personality and being introduced to our ownselves and others. It reorients the entire personality so that thoughts, words and deeds blend into a homogeneous whole. It really improves the quality of life because of the perpetual alignment with the source. In general, people who practice yoga and meditation are alert, active, creative, diligent, intuitive, relaxed, spiritually awake, and live a healthy life. A yogi's life is gracious, glorious, and becomes an example for others.

According to the ancient scriptures of Hindu religion, the yogic discipline as we know today was collated and written down by the great sage Patanjali in his *Patanjali Yogasutra*, which describes 196 *sutras* divided into four sections. The first part deals with the theory of yoga, the second with the art of initiation into practice. The third describes the method of comprehending the inherent powers and the fourth describes inner unity with the soul in meditation.

This expanded form of *Yogasutra* was further simplified as *Patanjali Ashtanga Yoga*—the eight-limbed framework intended to initiate the individual into physical fitness and a disciplined lifestyle, which gradually leads to exalted awareness, spiritual enlightenment and liberation. It is a systematic approach to the apprehension of human potential and the hidden mysteries of divine powers accessible to each one of us. *Ashtanga yoga* ushers the individual step by step into the practice of a sophisticated cleansing process of body and mind which creates favorable conditions at the sacred shrine within the body for yogic communion with the supreme-soul in meditation. It is the most specialized holistic eight-fold approach that provides profound insight into the understanding of our body, mind, the codes of moral ethics and social obligations those serve as the prerequisites for spiritual enlightenment and direct perception of truth.

The eight limbs of yogic discipline that encompass the entire field of our existence; physical, psychological and spiritual are: *Yama, Niyama, Asana, Pranayama, Pratyahara, Dharana, Dhyana,* and *Samadhi.* Each one of these holds its proper role for the spontaneous advancement into the next stage leading the aspirant step by step from known to unknown, from body consciousness to the eternal Bliss, peace and liberation.

Yama is a collective name for universal moral commandments such as *Satya* (truthfulness,) *Ahimsa* (non-violence), *Brahmacharya* (continence), *Asteya* (non-stealing), and *Aparigraha* (non-covetousness or non-accumulating). These are called *Mahavratas*—which means the vows taken for self-purification, right interaction with others and advanced yogic practice. The practice of these *Mahavratas* in daily life purifies the individual, and accelerates the day-to-day emotions towards the pursuit of higher goals in life.

Niyamas are the rules, the spiritual practices for inner growth and for the purification of mind and body such as *shoucha*, (internal and external cleanliness), *santosha* (contentment), *tapas* (austerities), *swadhyaya* (self-study and the regular study of Holy scriptures), and *Ishwarapranidhana* (surrender to the will of God). *Niyamas* are the principles necessary for progress in personal yogic practice. Anybody who is disciplined about eating, daily exercise, recreation and work, his day-to-day life becomes synchronized and for him yogic unity becomes a way of life. *Niyamas* constitute the foundation for a disciplined lifestyle that gives self respect, improves the quality of work, and promotes good health, peace, and spiritual growth.

The next limb of *Ashtanga yoga* is the *Asana* (physical exercises) an important part of the sacred science that encompasses the physical, psychological, as well as the spiritual levels of consciousness. Some people think that yoga practice is only a bunch of physical exercises, while it is only a small fraction of the Patanjali's yogic framework, which is meant to achieve alignment of mind and body. Physical exercises are a part of *Hatha yoga* which improves flexibility, the flow of energy and prepares the mind and body for yogic unity in meditation. Yogic exercises are helpful in the concentration of mind and proper functioning of the nervous system. *Hatha yoga* integrates our thought pattern and helps the body, mind and spirit to function in unison. It is a systematic cleansing of the body, which creates free flow of energy in the body. There are 48 *mukhya asanas* (well known yoga postures) each flowing into another very gracefully, and energizing each cell in the body. Also there are *Mudras*—the fixed positions, and *Bandhas,* which means, to hold and lock energy at a certain part of the body and then release as needed. There are three basic *Bandhas* i.e. *Jalandhara* (chin-lock), *Uddiyana* (abdominal lock), and *Mulabandha* (anal lock) which refers to *Muladhara chakra* and also to the muscles of the region between the anus and genitals.

The next step is *Pranayama*, a combination of two words *prana* and *ayama*. *Prana* is the life force and *ayama*, which means stretch, extension, expansion, regulation, prolongation, restraint, or control. Thus *pranayama* means the conscious control of breath. It is an art of rhythmic *Puraka* (inhalation), *Kumbhaka* (retention), and *Rechaka* (exhalation). In the practice of meditation, *Pranayama* plays a significant role because there is a very subtle and powerful relationship between breath, mind, and body. When the breathing is relaxed and peaceful, senses and mind spontaneously surrender to the quietness of the self. *Pranayama* improves our breathing capacity and gradually tunes the mind into the habit of deep breathing which helps to eliminate build-up toxins from body, makes the lungs flexible and strong, brings significant changes in body structure and promotes efficiency in our day-to-day activities. It is an evolutionary rejuvenating process.

There are many types of *Pranayama*—the breathing techniques quite simple to practice; such as *Nadi Shodhana* means the alternate nostril breathing, which leads to deep relaxation and yogic unity in meditation. The other important ones are *Surya Bhedana pranayama, Chandra Bhedana pranayama, Ujjayi, Anuloma-Viloma, Sheetali, Sithkari, Bhastrika, Kapalabhati,* and *Bhramari.* These breathing techniques are designed to nourish the physical, psychic and spiritual pathways and to balance heat and cold in the body, which creates a relaxed flow of awareness. These are some of the special yogic *Pranayama* taught by most of the yoga teachers for the general well-being of mind and body.

The other important aspect of *Ashtanga yogasadhna* is *Pratyahara*—meaning conscious withdrawal from the enjoyment of the senses. It also means developing control over external influences or being aware of the activities of mind and body. The organs of perception such as hearing, sight, touch, taste, and smell serve as windows to the world outside. The messages are conveyed through the senses of perception; mind interprets the data, stores it and feeds it back to the physical body with new and old information. So in order to achieve inner peace, stability of mind, yogic unity in meditation and overall progress in spiritual life; the practice of *pratyahara* forms a very important limb of the yogic framework. Following the footsteps of this sacred yogic discipline the individual lives in total vigilance of the self and cultivates within himself a new and awakened lifestyle which operates under the direct guidance of the Supreme-soul. His life becomes very integrated and disciplined with intelligent moderation in everything. He performs his worldly duties very regularly, efficiently and relapses back into inner calmness whenever he wants to. For him moving into the advanced steps of *Ashtanga yoga* i.e. *Dharana—Dhyana* and *Samadhi* becomes quite spontaneous and effortless.

Dharana is one pointed concentration with faith and

determination. It integrates the thinking faculty and gradually ushers the mind into the serenity of *Dhyana* and later into *Samadhi*, the meditative unity with the source. Concentrated attention is a prerequisite for success in meditation. It prepares the mind and body for the journey to the infinite Bliss. There are many *Dharana* techniques on the path of yogic unity, such as concentration on sound which helps to get tuned to the sound of the primordial *nada* at the heart center— *Anahata chakra. Tratak* or fixing the eyes on some external or internal object, is also a powerful method of concentration. The practice encloses the thoughts into a small circle and scattered attention into collectiveness, which is slowly followed by a state of peaceful meditation. The great mystics also recommend the use of a sacred mantra for concentration and contemplation. Persistent repetition of mantra awakens the dormant energy and tunes the mind to enter the point of singularity, which connects different levels of consciousness. *Dharana* evokes the inner awareness, integrates the flow of thoughts, and initiates the mind to be receptive to the silent call of the divine.

The next step is *Dhyana* or meditation which leads to *Samadhi*, means unity with the pure luminous Self in transcendence. It is being, becoming, and Bliss.

Meditation, the most familiar word associated with yoga and quite familiar to the modern generation is still a mystery. Sometime people wonder what meditation is; and how this strange practice of being silent within ourselves can be so valuable. Meditation literally means to attend to the thoughts with attention and intention, which gradually leads to the silence of the soul from where the whole universe unfolds, from where we are nourished and sustained. Meditation practice has been highly glorified in all the ancient scriptures as the final means for inner awakening and the subjective experience of higher states of consciousness i.e. unity consciousness, cosmic consciousness, and transcendental consciousness. Each level of consciousness has its own style and capacity of comprehending the inherent knowledge of the soul; and as the aspirant moves from fields of conditioned consciousness into the mysteries of super-consciousness, each step provides a basis for the spontaneous awakening at the next. It is to be introduced to the masks of the conditioned-self as well as to the pure luminous peaceful nature of the Higher-self. The quiet and restful mind learns to restore positive energy in meditation and remains in perpetual communion with the transcendental-self even while engaged in the activities of daily life.

Anybody who meditates regularly is blessed with increased creativity, improved academic performance, efficiency in work, increased job satisfaction, and an enthusiastic attitude towards life. Regular practice of meditation provides deep psychological and physiological relaxation, heightened awareness, and systematic orderly thinking. It improves our intellectual abilities, memory, comprehension, emotional and physical coordination, and our relationship with others. Daily practice of moving into the restful state of consciousness strengthens the stability of the conscious mind and gradually helps to break the cycle of erroneous stressful thinking. It improves the sleep pattern, dream pattern, and definitely cures insomnia because of a shift in awareness, cultivated during the peaceful moments of meditative unity with the soul.

With regular meditation we can access the software of our conditioned-self. Inner alignment with the source helps to download the information and be aware of the dormant memories and *Samskaras* those initiate new actions. In silence we are introduced to the secret codes of our programmed life and the programmer. It allows us to become a witness of our life. We learn to live in the awareness of the self, become alert about the activities of the mind and body, and the way we evolve in everything. Self-observation in meditation helps to renounce the addictive habits and compulsive behavior; many stubborn age-old conditioned habits simply disappear due to the psychological transformation that occurs in daily meditation.

The disciplined practice of daily yoga and meditation strengthens the immune system, promotes healing ability and definite decrease in the use of prescription and non-prescription drugs because of the total body synchronicity achieved in regular meditation. Perfect health is indeed an expression of our body's ability to function in total alignment with the inner wisdom. Modern medical science agrees to the fact that most of the physical ailments originate primarily from emotional stress caused by anxieties, worries, and resentment from memories of the past. The cure for these psychosomatic sufferings is within the reach of every individual only if he or she learns to follow the Bliss. We live under the false impression that healing is only in the hands of therapists and doctors; we often forget our own healing ability which comes from the intelligence of our own body. It is indeed a fact that sustained healing takes place with the proper guidance of a doctor and our own inner healer. Mood elevation, an enthusiastic attitude towards life, improved health, enhanced awareness, self-confidence, self-reliance, increased learning abilities are the expression of total body coherence maintained in daily meditation.

According to modern medical studies, on average in waking consciousness, the brain waves of a person when measured in EEG are most commonly in beta frequency. The pattern is random and incoherent; all parts of the brain showing different wavelengths. But in meditation as the person moves into deeper layers of consciousness the pattern starts changing; the brain waves are more coherent, orderly and normally in the alpha frequency, quite characteristic of deep relaxation, peace and harmony. In some cases theta waves have been also noticed in meditation indicating a deeper state than alpha, and the pattern is more synchronous. It has been also noticed that usually, advanced meditators are able to maintain the resonance of inner unity even while engaged in the activities of daily life. It is really interesting to know that the experience of deep rest, relaxation and inner silence perceived during meditation is far deeper than what one receives during sleep. In general, meditators are able to lock the resonant field of the brain with the resonant field of the heart to create total body coherence, total alignment of mind, body, and spirit; when every cell in body becomes tuned to the sound of primordial nada and the guidance of the Higher-Self. It is also true that with the sustained practice of meditation the aging process can also be controlled to some extent because of daily connection with the source of life. People who meditate are very relaxed, peaceful, creative, precise, and live a long healthy life.

Now coming to the meditation techniques, as explained earlier, yoga and meditation are not separate. Regular practice of yoga gradually leads into yogic unity with the source; where mind, body and spirit are totally aligned and the yogi enters into exalted wakefulness, unity consciousness, and silence. First of all, it is important to select a quiet place and try to meditate every day at the same spot. It works wonders because the particular spot of meditation becomes energized with positive vibrations. The moment we take the seat quietness begins to flow towards the goal in meditation. It is also important to sit facing east or north in meditation. East for enlightenment and north for stability; besides it brings the special advantage of alignment with the magnetic field of the earth. The most beneficial time for meditation is early sunrise and sunset. The glories of dawn and dusk when the day and night meet have been beautifully described in the Vedas. This is the time when the air is charged with spiritual energy; the mind is refreshed and free from the activities of daily life, ready and receptive to the guidance of the soul.

According to *Patanjali Ashtanga Yoga*, the recommended posture for meditation requires proper alliance of lower back, neck, shoulder, and head. This is the vertical alignment, which creates balance and allows a spontaneous flow of energy in the body. It is important to start with a simple posture, the crossed-legs position with a cushion supporting the seat called *sukhasana,* which helps to move into *siddhasana* and later into full lotus posture the *padmasana.* The techniques used by the yogis, saints, seers, mystics, and the householders do vary to some extent but in general everyone follows the similar guidelines—such as tuning the mind to the rhythm of the breath as it moves in and out and simply witnessing the thoughts as they go by; gradually as the breathing becomes relaxed a specific silence is perceived between the thoughts and the meditator enters into unity with the breath and later with the Supreme-Self.

Some yoga teachers highly recommend the use of a mantra for concentration in meditation. The word 'mantra' is a combination of two words *man* (mind) and *tra* (liberate). The aphorism '*manatrayate iti mantra*' means, the word that liberates the mind is mantra. Mantra has the power to awaken within the mind the corresponding God consciousness and thus prepares the mind for unity in silence. When we start meditation with internally repeating the mantra, slowly we observe our thoughts passing by and leaving some trails behind but gradually disappearing. At the beginning of meditation we watch our thoughts and then we begin to watch ourselves repeating the mantra. Slowly our mind settles and our breathing also becomes slow, we feel that instead of repeating the mantra we are only listening to the mantra. As we move into the deeper realms of consciousness, the syllables of our mantra start disappearing, leaving behind a mesmeric experience, which leads the mind into total silence.

Meditation with the primordial sound of *Aum* has been also highly glorified by the Vedic sages. This mystic syllable is known as *Brahmanada*, heard by the Vedic sages in deep meditation at a specific level of yogic unity in transcendence. At the beginning of meditation with the primordial sound of *Aum*, it is merely the repetition of the mystic syllable at the conscious levels of awareness. We simply float with the sound as it moves in and out with breath while our attention deeply focused on its vibration.

As the melody moves into the deepest layers within consciousness, the beat of our heart and the sound of *Aum* start merging into one another. Gradually when the mind joins the sound and exhilarates in spiritual ecstasy, a specific silence is perceived between two successive syllables. Slowly we become unaware of the sound and breath, and gently enter into the unified field of consciousness. Although, in the beginning we are in unity with the source only for few seconds but with gradual practice as the silence extends longer and longer the meditation period becomes long, effortless and very enjoyable.

Journey to the infinite Bliss through the seven psychic stations in body is *chakra* meditation, upheld in profound reverence since time immemorial. In *chakra* meditation the consciousness is guided from the bottom of the spine to the top of the head while monitoring the breath, visualizing the changing colors of heavenly light at each *chakra* and remaining tuned to the sound of mantra at each psychic station till the yogi enters into infinite Bliss. This is the awakening of the *Kundalini shakti*, the life force coiled up at the base of the spine. The *Chakras* are psychic centers along the route of *Sushumna nadi* in the spinal cord. The first one is *Muladhara chakra* located in the region of perineum at the base of the spine. This is the seat of *Kundalini shakti* the reservoir of energy physical, emotional, psychic and spiritual. The elemental quality of *Muladhara* is earth; the symbol is a lotus of four petals with a square in the middle. Within the square is the *Svyambhulingam*, surrounded by the 'deep red' glow of celestial light. The mantra is '*Lam*'.

The second psychic station is *Swadhishthana chakra* located in the region of the pubic bone in front of the body a little below the navel. The elemental quality or *tattva* is water; the symbol is the lotus of six petals with a crescent moon shining in the middle. The mantra is '*Vam*' and 'vermillion' divine light is visualized in meditation. This psychic station is the reservoir of present and remote memories and the instinctive behavior which relates to the survival of the species.

The third is *Manipura chakra* means the city of jewel; the reservoir of solar energy located a little above the navel in the region of solar plexus. The symbol is a lotus with ten petals, within which is a triangle pointing downward. The elemental quality or *tattva* is fire and the heavenly glow is 'yellow'. The mantra for meditation is '*Ram*'. At *Manipura chakra*, the yogi perceives the energy of the Sun radiating and permeating the whole body. Meditation at *Manipura chakra* strengthens the immune system and helps to enhance the elemental qualities of Agni such as purity, vitality, self-assertion, dynamism and dominance.

The next psychic center is *Anahata chakra* located between the two breasts. It is also known as heart *chakra* and shrine of pure consciousness. The symbol of heart *chakra* is a lotus of 12 petals, with two intersecting triangles in the middle, in the form of a six pointed star. Air is the elemental quality, the mantra is '*Yam*' and 'green' divine light is visualized in deep meditation. It is the focal point of emotional and psychological maturity, spiritual intimacy, love, compassion and cosmic unity. Yogis and mystics in India generally guide their disciples to concentrate on this light at the heart center appearing in the form of *Bana Lingam*; in order to enter the higher states of consciousness. Just below this psychic station is the *Anand Khanda*—the cave of Bliss where the meditator is blessed with the glimpses of *Kalpataru*, the wish granting celestial tree.

The fifth psychic station is the *Vishuddhi Chakra*, located in the back of our throat where the mystical divine nectar drips from *Binduvisarga* and gives a feeling of blissful intoxication in meditation. Ether is the elemental quality and the symbol is the lotus of 16 petals. The mantra is '*Ham*' and the divine light is visualized as bright 'cerulean blue'. It is the junction point in the body which purifies and synchronizes the opposites. In meditation on *Vishuddhi chakra* the individual is blessed with serenity, purity, melodious voice, command of speech and the special ability to communicate influentially.

The sixth psychic station located between the two eyebrows is *Ajna chakra* means command center. It is also called the eye of intuition, meditation and contemplation, where the two psychic currents *Pingala* from the right of the spine and *Ida* from the left merge into *sushumna nadi* and the individual is guided into the subtle realms of the preliminary super-conscious state. The corresponding element of this *chakra* is mind and the symbol is a circle with two petals, representing the third eye surrounded by the two physical eyes, indicating the power of this chakra to transcend space and time. The divine light that surrounds the *Ajna chakra* is cool 'indigo blue' and the celestial mantra is the holy syllable *Aum*. Meditation at *Ajna chakra* ushers the individual into the realms of pure consciousness where he is blessed with mystical powers called *ashta siddhi* and also at the same time the desire for liberation, salvation, and *moksha*.

Meditation on the sound of *Aum* at *Ajna chakra* gradually leads the yogi towards the crown *chakra* located at the top of the head—the *Sahasrara*—means thousand petaled lotus. It is the seat of the self-luminous soul that holds all the other *chakras* within itself. It is like a radiant dome of celestial spectrum with a heavenly glow of violet light. To enter into *sahasrara* is the culmination of yoga meditation where *prana* and the consciousness merge into one another, the ego-centric conditioned-self disappears and the mind settles in the pure void of *shunyamandala* (infinite). The illusion of individual-Self disappears and yogi enters into the unified field of pure-consciousness—*nirvikalpa samadhi*. After the experience of unity at crown *chakra* the yogi lives in an expanded state of illumined consciousness. He has the special ability to stay in union with super-consciousness as long as he likes and then descend to other *chakras* whenever he wants to. He becomes the controller of his mind and body. The crown *chakra* is both the entry and the exit point in the human body. It is the doorway through which the divine light enters the body and this is the exit that leads the yogi to liberation and *moksha*. Journey to the infinite Bliss along the route of these psychic stations is a unique experience which enlightens the individual about the mysteries of *Kundalini shakti* and the inherent powers of mind and body at each station. The mode of inner awakening and gaining knowledge is different at each *chakra* and meditation on each one of these provides a basis for the spontaneous alignment at the next.

Chakra meditation is the flawless apprehension of the pure consciousness and the spontaneous experience of inner unity, which promotes perfect health, longevity, systematic orderly thinking, love, peace, harmony, and desire for liberation. *Chakra* meditation practiced systematically and devotedly brings about a sustained single-pointedness more efficiently than many other hasty methods of meditation.

"The Mantra is a link between you and the cosmos, between you and the deeper mysteries of the universe. Its meaning is purely metaphysical and relates directly with the very core of your existence"

-Swami Satyasangananda

"When a spiritually advanced soul repeats the Mantra, it becomes charged with its power and it becomes 'living'. When he gives the Mantra to a disciple, the power is transmitted also."

-Swami Yateshwarananda

"Mantras are Sanskrit invocations of the Supreme Being. Reinforced and propelled by *Japam* meditation, they pass from the verbal level through the mental and telepathic states, and on to pure thought energy."

-Swami Vishnudeva Nanda

10

Mantra

Mantra, the word of power, is like an atom pulsating with enormous latent energy, which is released with devoted constant repetition. Each mantra is a *Shakti-Kendra* (Energy center) that is activated as the initiate curves back to the source and attunes himself to its dynamic potential.

A mantra can be a syllable, a single word, a hymn or a verse. It is a concise prayer imbued with powerful vibrations. It is only by contemplating and meditating on mantra with faith, humility, and sincere devotion, the person is able to comprehend its inherent powers in the appropriate spirit; and if he is able to be in unity with the words of mantra the results are bound to be highly beneficial, rewarding and absolutely astonishing. The word mantra is a combination of two words—*man* and *tra* —*man* means mind, our thinking faculty and — *tra* means to liberate. The ancient scriptures describe it as *"manatrayate iti mantra"*—means, the word which liberates the mind is mantra. According to Swami Tapasyananda, "Mantra is something more than a prayer. It is in itself a word of power. It is a thought-movement vehicled in sound and words."

Regarding the source of mantras, it is said that at the beginning of creation, some privileged souls were blessed with inner vision. In their deep contemplation and yogic unity in transcendence they heard a celestial sound, that later came to be known as *Brahmanada* or the Holy syllable *Aum*. In Vedic literature, *Aum* has been identified as the root mantra and all the other mantras are the mystic revelation of this sacred sound—the *Brahmanada*. These mantras are universal and have been written for the welfare of entire mankind.

Any particular mantra which is given by a teacher to his disciple is known as Guru mantra. In general, a Guru mantra is a combination of one or more holy names of the Supreme Lord. *Aum* is usually included in the beginning of the sentence. This special mantra becomes charged with a specific type of energy and brings blessings from the teacher. The Guru gives a new life to the disciple and also helps the aspirant to awaken his own inherent potential.

Since Vedic times the holy sages in India have emphasized upon the necessity of a spiritual teacher. They believed that a deep psychological change occurs in the mind of a disciple at the time of mantra initiation. Swami Sivananda used to say, "Although an aspirant may feel nothing miraculous at the time of his initiation, the effect of the mantra given by an enlightened Guru is unfailing."

There is nothing secretive about mantras, and the use of a self-selected mantra does help the individual, but when a mantra is given by a self-realized teacher, it becomes a living seed. The Guru, by his spiritual power, gives life to the word, and thus awakens the specific dormant energy of the disciple. That is the secret of the teacher's initiation. Besides, the mantra given by a revered Guru is a *Jagrat* (awakened) mantra. It has been recited by the Guru himself for many years, over a million times; and also it comes from a lineage. It is a link in a spiritual chain; as the disciple is being initiated by his Guru so the Guru himself was once initiated in the past, by some holy man whose power is thus being passed on to the disciple. Once the disciple makes the sincere promise, the light of the Guru's guidance always remains with the aspirant and helps him on the path of self-realization and God-realization. Another important fact is that the quick awakening impulse that comes from the words of a Guru cannot be received from a self-chosen mantra. In general, the individual-soul receives awakening from the words of another pure and contemplative soul. In the words of Swami Yateshwarananda, "when a spiritually enlightened soul repeats the mantra, it becomes charged with its power and it becomes 'living.' When he gives the mantra to a disciple, the power is transmitted also."

The practice of reciting a mantra is called mantra *Japam*. There are some important steps in learning the practice of *Japam*, in order to achieve the full benefit of mantra. Right after initiation from a spiritual teacher, the disciple is advised to whisper the mantra few times, and then repeat it silently with sealed lips. Silent *Japam* is a kind of internal dialogue and the most powerful method of creating unity with the indwelling-soul. It strengthens our mutual bond with the Divine, and the true grace of the Supreme Lord begins to pour into our lives. As the silent communication becomes stronger the spiritual energy begins to flow into the conscious states of mind. It awakens all the latent energies of the aspirant and connects the individual to the source of life. At this point, the mind remembers the mantra and lets it go on as naturally as possible. It becomes a tool for relaxation, and instead of reciting the mantra, the individual listens to its words and sound. It is believed that a beginner makes efforts to practice mantra with concentration, while an advanced aspirant simply remains aware of it. *Japam* (recitation) goes on without much effort.

In some schools of 'Mantra Yoga', the aspirant is advised to practice mantra *Japam* by writing the words on a piece of paper. This is called *Likhet Japam*. This is a very tough austerity but it prepares the individual for quick success in mantra *Siddhi*. In this process of writing and reciting simultaneously, the words of mantra are etched in the memory and are recorded in the deepest layers of our consciousness. *Likhet Japam* is a very devoted and interesting way of achieving concentration and the full benefit of mantra recitation. The person can write the mantra in any script he likes but more advisable is in his own language. Like any other austerity, for *Likhet Japam* the aspirant should select a specific spot and time for daily practice.

Some yoga teachers recommend the use of a rosary or *mala* with quiet mantra recitation. In *Japam* with a rosary the aspirant moves one bead with each mantra. The movement of fingers along the rhythm of quiet recitation creates yogic alignment of mind, body and spirit, which amplifies devotion and concentration.

The great sage Patanjali has emphasized upon the significance of understanding the meaning of mantra. It should be recited with full meaning in thoughts. When we repeat the mantra dwelling upon its meaning, our thoughts move along the meaning of the words and slowly but definitely our thoughts start taking the shape of the words. Both the mantra *Japam* and its personal experience are important for spiritual growth.

Mantra and Meditation

Meditation with mantra has been highly glorified in almost all the ancient scriptures as a powerful means for inner awakening and subjective experience of the higher states of consciousness.

According to the ancient spiritual masters, mantra *Japam* is a very important pre-requisite for meditation. Constant recitation of a mantra has the power to awaken within the mind the corresponding God consciousness and thus prepares the mind for concentration in meditation. Mantra *Japam* encloses the thoughts into a small circle and the scattered attention into collectiveness, which is slowly followed by a state of inner peace and silence. It creates an aura of divine love at the sacred shrine within the body, for Holy communion and union with the indwelling soul. As a matter of fact, relaxed meditation is a continuation of quiet mantra recitation. It is a preliminary training, which is necessary for yogic unity in transcendence.

Describing the power of mantra *Japam* as an important tool in meditation, Swami Yatishwarananda writes, "In the beginning of spiritual life you need not bother about real meditation. Do mantra *Japam* and dwell on your *Ishta Devata.*

In due course, *Japam* will develop into *dhyana*, which means unbroken thought on the theme for meditation like the unbroken current or flow of oil from one cup to another. Through mantra *Japam* the Divine spirit will become more real than the world. And only then will real *dhyana* become possible. Do the first thing first, and then the next thing will come by itself."

Meditation with a mantra is a universal idea, but in Hinduism and Buddhism it is more predominant. The Nichiren sect in Japan makes use of a *sutra* for meditation and the belief is that the recitation and repetition of the holy name can lead to the achievement of the desired goal in meditation. For a Tibetan yogi mantra *Japam* plays a very significant role in meditative austerities. Both in Judaism and Christianity the repetition of a prayer or holy formula from the Bible is used to guide the mind into a contemplative mood for meditation. In Sufism also there is a description of *Dhikr* means repeating the name of God and recollecting the thought of God with intense concentration. The most popular practice of transcendental meditation as taught by Maharishi Mahesh Yogi also involves the simple practice of internally reciting the holy mantra, given to the meditator by the spiritual teacher. Quiet recitation leads the aspirant into yogic unity with the source, where mind, body and spirit are totally aligned and the meditator enters into peaceful transcendence.

When we start the meditation session by repeating a mantra, we observe our thoughts passing by and leaving many trails behind. At the first stage, we watch our thoughts and then we begin to watch ourselves repeating the mantra. Slowly our mind settles and our breathing also becomes slow, we feel that instead of repeating the mantra, we are only listening to the mantra. As we move into the deeper realms of consciousness, the syllables of our mantra start disappearing, leaving behind the mesmeric experience, that leads the mind into total silence. Although in the beginning the experience of transcendence lasts only for few seconds but with gradual practice as the silence extends longer and longer the meditation period becomes long effortless and extremely enjoyable.

Mantra – The Gateway to Freedom

Freedom is one of the most cherished dreams of human beings. Our desire to be free from restrictions and limitations, expresses itself everywhere. The individual soul longs for freedom. "Go home" is the cry of a heart that feels suffocated in bondage. Although, the joy of living in freedom is a human prerogative, only few know how to achieve it.

Absolute freedom, liberation—*Mukti, Moksha,* or *Nirvana* is right here in the middle of *samsara.* It is simply being aware of our true nature, which is pure, luminous and unconditional. It is to be in touch with the center of our being the *sahaja avastha* (at ease) where we are not compelled by any desire, where we have no regrets, no expectations, no fear and we can hold on to our essential nature, which is peaceful, pure and absolute Bliss. Freedom is living in the tissue of the present moment, which is free from the lingering shadow of the past and the worries of the distant future. Time bound awareness is the cause of bondage, while the timeless awareness is freedom.

In general, the mind is conditioned to remain involved in those ideas and objects to which it has been attached for some reason. It forms the habit of thinking about the same thing. If we watch our thoughts in silence, we will realize that the thoughts of today are the repetition from yesterday or somewhere in past. So at some point, we have to learn to become aware of our thoughts and actually come out of the self-created web. It is through the constant repetition of mantra that we are introduced to the secret codes of our programmed life and the programmer. Quiet mantra *Japam* works at our sub-conscious level and gradually brings some dramatic changes in our day-to-day life.

In reference to this, I like these words of Swami Sri Yukteswar; he writes, "Forget the past. The vanished lives of all men are dark with many shames. Human conduct is ever unreliable until anchored in the Divine. Everything in the future will improve if you are making a spiritual effort now." Hence the secret of freedom lies in the experiential knowledge of the indwelling-soul—mantra *Japam* is the means, the highly recommended austerity for the accomplishment of the desired goal. Mantra *Japam* is the gateway to liberation and freedom in life here and hereafter.

Mantra – A Mystical Experience of the Pure-Self

Purity of heart has been highly emphasized in all the religious traditions of the world, because it reflects the pure luminous nature of the soul.

The pure, divine nature unites people, brings them

closer and makes them caring, sharing and loving; while the conditioned nature separates and disintegrates people and makes them mean, selfish, jealous, and ruthless. This is what it means, *"Blessed are the pure in heart for they shall see God"* (Matthew 5:8). Although, every individual-soul is essentially spiritual and very pure at heart, but since the degree of spiritual awareness differs from one person to another that's why, generally, some people are very pure while others are not. So in order to be blessed with purity of heart, it is really important to remain grounded in the awareness of the soul with the devoted recitation of mantra.

When the holy name of the Lord starts touching the subconscious levels of the soul, gradually the thought pattern becomes tuned to the purity of the Supreme-soul, and slowly the mind learns to settle in there. It is a fact that devoted repetition of the holy mantra purifies the entire thinking faculty and helps the person to regroup his thoughts into a new and pure image.

Mantra—Phenominal Help in Yogic Communion

'Mantra and Yoga,' the two closely related spiritual practices, are rooted in the ancient religious traditions of Hinduism. 'Mantra Yoga', means to develop a union and communion with God by constant repetition of mantra. Mantra *Japam* can be very useful and beneficial in the accomplishment of all the preliminary and preparatory steps for yogic communion. Mantra initiation awakens the dormant energy and the *Japam* channelizes it harmoniously and systematically. When the energy of mind and body is in harmony: the observance of ethical codes, the practice of *Asanas* and the inner alliance in meditation comes spontaneously.

In 'Mantra Yoga', a person is initiated to live his entire life in the awareness of the soul and perform all his work through guidance of unity in yoga. It is a discipline of living in the consciousness of the Self. It is the manifestation of inner unity into the activities of day-to-day life.

'Mantra Yoga' evolves around a remarkable way of living, which blends: devotion, meditation, creativity, inner peace and perfect health. It is indeed a fact that the highest goal of life can be actualized and realized when a person is consciously grounded in 'Mantra Yoga' and becomes aware of the truth that he is in perpetual alignment with the soul. Silent recitation of a mantra is the seed, the beginning, the nucleus around which a person constructs his entire yogic discipline.

Mantra—The Discovery of Life-In-Itself

Self-realization is the most valuable and rewarding gift of life. It is a shift in awareness—it is coming out of a certain type of life frame and stepping into another, in which we feel enlightened and blessed. In the realization of the Self, a person moves step by step into new dimensions of self-awareness and subjective apprehension of his behavior. He observes himself as he really is—exposing himself to the Self.

Quiet recitation of a mantra strengthens our relationship with the indwelling-self and works as a tool to know more about our ownselves. Mantra *Japam* is a unique way of exploring our personality at the conscious and sub-conscious levels of the soul. It enlightens the person about the complexities of mind and helps him to screen the reality through guidance from the Higher Self.

Mantra—The Silent Call of the Divine

The phenomenal power of the secret melody created by the rhythmical repetition of Holy syllable at the sub-conscious level of our awareness always remains with us, no matter where we are and whatever we are doing. It keeps collecting the scattered energy and maintains the awareness of the indwelling Lord, conscious and alive. It helps us to become more and more receptive to the silent call of the Divine and live in harmony with the rhythm of the universe.

At the beginning, we may not develop any personal, intellectual, or spiritual association with mantra, but gradually as the *Japam* becomes a part of our internal rhythm, its presence becomes very intimate and familiar. It is difficult to put into words its subtle companionship, we cannot touch it with our hands, we cannot see it with our eyes, yet something that vibrates from it mysteriously takes hold of us and can be perceived from moment to moment. The blessed experience of its mesmeric touch is totally inexplicable.

In reference to the joy of spiritual intimacy with mantra, says Rabindranth Tagore, "I will utter your name, sitting alone among the shadows of my silent thoughts. I will utter it without words; I will utter it without purpose. For I am like a child that calls its mother a hundred times, glad that it can say 'Mother.'"

"Enjoy the celestial fragrance in spring,
Silently overflowing across the green meadows
and flowering groves.
The summer with its own beauty of sighs and murmurs,
Calls upon the blessed showers from heaven with thunder
and dazzling flashes, to nurture the life on earth.
The serene whisper of leaves in autumn,
And cool breeze in winter with new hopes and promises,
All are the expressions of divine magnificence in space and
time."

The Samaveda (616)

11

Hindu Festivals

In the Hindu religion there are colorful festivals celebrated throughout the year associated with India's rich cultural and religious heritage. Although each festival is associated with several legends and marks the commencement of a new season and a fresh crop; the purpose of celebrating these festivals is self-purification, inner enlightenment, and living in peace and harmony with others. It is an effort to be respectful to the bounties of nature, celebrate the changes in nature in order to get full support of nature. The rituals performed on these festivals are intended to purify the individual at physical as well as at psychological levels of consciousness and prepare him step by step towards self-realization and God-realization.

Performance of the religious ceremonies attached to these festivals dates back to the ancient civilization of the Indus Valley. These traditions along with the wisdom of the elders in family, learned sages and spiritual teachers have been passed from one generation to another so that prosperity in society may evolve both intellectually and spiritually making the life peaceful, creative, enjoyable and prosperous.

Celebration of festivals promotes peace and harmony among the families and brings them closer in a relaxed spiritual bond. On these occasions when family and friends cook and eat together sharing their common experiences, a special relationship of mutual understanding is developed which encourages spiritual intimacy and increased desire to help each other. These joyous festivities not only give us the opportunity for merrymaking, but it also reminds us about our duties towards family and the community in which we live. Celebration of these festivals has been created and supported by some spiritual concepts and loyalty to perseverance of these rich traditions have been emphasized over centuries.

Lohri, Pongal, and Makara Sankranti

In January, people celebrate Lohri, Pongal, and Makara Sankranti when the Sun shines closer to 90° on the Tropic of Capricorn. This marks the beginning of an enlightened and prosperous time for mankind. Although the winter solstice occurs on 22nd of December, the *puniya kala*, means the auspicious time when the Sun is in the zodiac birth sign Capricorn is on January 14th marking the Makara Sankranti celebration. It is the beginning of *Uttarayana*—meaning the journey of sunlight towards the northern hemisphere for six months. *Uttarayana kala*—the enlightened time, is considered auspicious and generally people schedule important events during this period.

The celebration for Makara Sankranti starts early in the morning after a bath in sacred water. Generally people go in groups for a ceremonial dip in the nearby open reservoir of water. The worship starts by offering water to the Sun god with the recital of hymns from the Holy scriptures. There are many hymns in the Vedas that describe the glory of sunrise, when the golden light touches the horizon with blessings.

The Sun god, the personification of celestial light, is the source of *tejas* and the giver of life on the planet. The light of the Sun changes many colors, activates each *chakra* along the spine and rejuvenates each cell in the body. It strengthens the immune system and brings significant improvement in general health. After the worship of Sun god people generally concentrate on the celestial light and meditate for a while. The quietness of the crimson dawn charged with spirituality helps in alignment with inner light of the Supreme-soul. The peace and purity of the auspicious hours of Sankranti lingers in the memory long after the moment itself is gone.

Makara Sankranti is the time when special emphasis is made on giving to charities. On this auspicious day people pledge to donate a certain amount of money. The great merit received by pledging charities on Makara Sankranti is a thousand times more than any other day during the year.

A day before the Makara Sankranti, on January 13th, Lohri is celebrated in North India, especially Punjab. People light the camp fire and sing folk songs with great enthusiasm. A few days prior to this evening celebration, the young boys and girls go around the neighborhood and collect the contribution for the celebration. People visit their friends and relatives and share the sweets made with sesame seeds and jaggery. Fresh harvested corn is also cooked and shared.

In South India the Makara Sankranti is a harvest festival called Pongal. It is a four day long festival celebrating the arrival of the new crop and the prosperous time of the year. January 13th, the first day of the festival is called Bogi when people light the camp fire in the neighborhood and discard old clothes and some of the old household articles symbolic of making a new start for the year.

The second day, the 14th, is the Makara Sankranti, or Surya Pongal, when the special food called pongal is prepared from the newly harvested crop, first offered to the Sun god and later shared with friends and relatives. Mattu Pongal is the third day of celebration, dedicated to the worship of cows, and on fourth day, the Kanum Pongal, people visit their friends and share special sweets cooked with rice, sugarcane and coconut. In Kerala, Makara Deepa Puja is celebrated on Makara Sankranti, the first day of the Malayalam month of Makaram. The Makara Deepa Puja commemorates the day on which the statue of Lord Ayyappa or Dharma Sastha was enshrined in the famous Sabarimala Temple. On this day, Lord Ayyappa is decorated with the royal ornaments of Pandalam (where he was raised as a prince in his human incarnation). At twilight, a celestial light appears on Ponnambala Medu in an adjoining hill called Kantha Malai. This light, known as the *Makara Jyothi*, is believed to be Lord Ayyappa blessing his devotees.

Makra Sankranti is celebrated in Assam as Magha Bihu. The kite flying season starts in India from this day and kite flying competitions are held in some places. Makara Sankranti is a *Puniya Kala* (auspicious time) celebrated by Hindu families all over India with great enthusiasm.

Vasant Panchami

The festival of Vasant Panchami is celebrated on the fifth day of the lunar month *Magh* in the ascending phase of the Moon in February, as a welcome to the spring season, when the trees are in full blossom and the sky is filled with the choirs of birds. This is the time when the cold weather starts fading, replaced by balmy soft lingering breeze and the meadows are covered with lush green grass and thousands of flowers.

On Vasant Panchami the great goddess Saraswati is worshipped for good education, increased creativity, clarity of vision and success in art and music. Everyone in the family wears a yellow scarf, which signifies warmth, auspiciousness, inner enlightenment, and harmony with nature. The Divine mother Saraswati is decorated with flower garlands and worshipped with melodious hymns from the Vedas. Special sweets and rice cooked with saffron are offered in worship and later shared with friends and relatives.

Towards the evening special entertainment programs are held in parks and fairgrounds where music concerts and art exhibitions are organized. The great musicians and artists are honored. It is the most important day of the year for musicians, educators, and artists when they worship their musical instruments at the shrine of the great goddess and seek blessings for success.

In Bengal, it is celebrated as Sri Panchami. People

worship the images of the goddess in the morning, and towards the evening the images are taken in a procession to the nearby river for the *visarjana* ceremony. People go in procession singing the glories of the goddess and praying for enlightenment, peace, and happiness. After the ceremonial worship the images of the goddess are immersed in the river with respect and devotion.

Shivaratri

Towards the end of February and beginning of March the festival of Shivaratri is celebrated on the 14th night of the descending phase of the Moon in the month of *Magh* all over India with deep religious fervor. Shivaratri—literally the night dedicated to the worship of Shiva—is observed with the most sacred ritual of *abhishekam*, in which the devotee seeks alignment with the source of life. Shiva *abhishekam* is the offering of water on the top most part of the *Shivalingam* in an unbroken stream with uninterrupted chanting of sacred hymns and one pointed concentration. The worship creates a remarkable unity of mind, body, and spirit; while the hands pour the water, the chanting of hymns guides the mind to remain absorbed in the ecstasy of divine love with attention and intention. Gradually, as the mind becomes involved in the process, the devotee enters into an ecstatic trance and the grace of the Lord is revealed in the meditative unity. It is difficult to pinpoint when the mind becomes settled in worship but the concentration definitely leads to higher fields of yogic communion with the Supreme-soul. This is direct, instant realization of the presence of Divine and sudden, spontaneous experience of inner unity; when the limited individuality of the embodied-soul finally gets absorbed into the totality of the cosmic-soul and the devotee enters into blissful transcendence.

Shivaratri is the night of enlightenment when a person goes into the perceptual experience of divine light and feels, "I am created by the light of the Self, sustained by the light of the Self, surrounded by the light of the Self and I am indeed that light of the Self," — "*Tat tvam asi.*"

Some people who aspire for authentic spiritual growth in life hold fast on this special day and also meditate at home from sunset to midnight. It is believed that the cosmic combination on this special night is conducive to meditation and the mind becomes very receptive to the call of the Divine and unity in meditation is experienced very naturally and spontaneously. The subtle joy of unity is really exhilarating and it opens the new vistas of self-realization and God-realization.

Holi

The festival of Holi is celebrated on full Moon day of the lunar month *Falgun* in March. It is one of the most popular festivals celebrated by Hindu families. It is a two-day long celebration. The night before the full Moon day a special worship with campfire is organized in each neighborhood. Every family contributes for the offerings of sweets, coconuts, and the special *samagri* (the mixture of herbs). The learned priest starts the fire with hymns from the scriptures and then everybody makes offerings. After worship people go around the fire singing the glories of Lord Vishnu. This special celebration in the evening symbolizes the victory of positive forces over negative. The auspicious night of Holi which is dedicated to the worship of Lord Vishnu is also conducive for yogic unity in meditation.

On the next morning of the full Moon day, people collect the auspicious ashes, and take them home for good fortune and happiness. Collecting the ashes from the holy fire is called *dhooli vandan*. The ashes are used as a remedy for many common ailments. People rub ashes all over their body which protects it from mosquito bites and other insects.

It is hard to trace back when people started mixing colors with the ashes and made the festival so colorful. At present the Holi celebration is unique, especially in North India. In Mathura and Vrindavan where Lord Krishna spent his childhood, Holi *Purnima* is celebrated with increased enthusiasm. The joy of playing with colored water takes momentum when everybody starts singing songs which describe the childhood games, fun, and frolic of baby Krishna. There is dancing and singing in every neighborhood. Some people walk in groups around the town with colored powder in their hands, singing and inviting everybody to join the celebration. This is one of the most enjoyable times in villages near Mathura, Gokul, and Vrindavan. People prepare special sweets with milk and butter and share with their friends and relatives.

In Bengal, Holi is celebrated as *Dhool Purnima* and the festival is also dedicated to Lord Krishna. The images of Lord Krishna are decorated with all kinds of colored powder and then taken out in a procession. The other reason why *Dhool Purnima* is significant for people in Bengal is because of the birthday of Chaitanya Mahaprabhu who was born in 1485. He was a great devotee of Lord Krishna who believed that the essence of true devotion to God is the constant loving remembrance of Lord. He started *sahakeertana* (group chanting) and people worshipped him as the embodiment of Lord Krishna. This is the most colorful festival in India which also marks the beginning of spring season.

New Shaka Samvat and Ugadi Parva

Towards the end of March and beginning of April starts the New Shaka Samvat celebrated as New Year's Day of the Hindu lunar calendar. In South India it is celebrated as Ugadi Parva. The celebration starts early in the morning at sunrise with special prayers for the upcoming year and continues till late night. People decorate their homes with *rangolis* and special prayers are held at home as well as at the temples where the learned priest reads predictions from the *panchang* made on the basis of astrological calculation. It also marks the beginning of Spring Navaratra, the nine days worship of the Divine Mother. This is the time to meditate, to reflect and purify our life style. Navaratra literally means "the nine nights," the nine days worship which helps us to eliminate the darkness and ignorance from our lives and makes us more receptive to the guidance of the Supreme-soul. Generally people make a small shrine in the house for this special nine days worship where the whole family joins for the evening prayer. Food cooked during the Navaratra time is strictly vegetarian with a variety of sweets. The devoted worship culminates in the celebration of Ramnavami the birth of Sri Rama the God-incarnate.

There is a beautiful description of Rama's birth in the Ramayana, "*Navami titi madhu mas punita, shukla paksha abhijit hariprita*—the beautiful time of spring, the ninth day of holy *Chaitra Shukla*, when divine mother Koushalya was blessed with Rama." In Ayodhya, the birth place of Sri Rama, the celebration is really unique. The temple premises are decorated with flowers and lights. The floors are covered with artistic drawings and the walls are decorated with golden leaves. The images of Sri Rama, along with Seeta, Lakshmana, and Hanuman, are decorated beautifully with rich ornaments, flowers, and worshipped with *sahakeertana* (chanting of hymns).

In the temples of South India Ramnavami is celebrated as Seeta Rama *kalyanam*. The festivities start very early in the morning with *yajna*, celebrating the birth of Rama with special rituals such as *Naamkarana, Annaprashana*, and *Upanayana Samskara*; later, before noon, starts Sri Seeta Rama *kalyanam*, the auspicious wedding ceremony of the divine mother Seeta with Sri Rama the God-incarnate. Special arrangements are made for the divine wedding with artistic drawings around the ceremonial *mandap*. It is indeed a unique experience to be a part of the blessed moments when the celestial music is in the air and the divine couple is being blessed with yellow rice, mixed with translucent pearls. Towards the evening Sri Rama *Pattabhisheka* (the royal crown ceremony) is celebrated with great enthusiasm, and afterwards Sri Rama and Seeta are worshipped, representing the highest ideals of man and woman. The celebration ends with *Hanumad Vahana utsavam* and *Maha mangala Aarti* with the auspicious sound of conches.

In Maharashtra this festival is celebrated as Gudi Padava when all kinds of decorative silk banners are placed in front of the house and worshipped with deep respect and enthusiasm. Special sweet dishes are prepared for lunch; people visit each other and exchange greetings and gifts.

Hanuman Jayanti

Hanuman Jayanti, the birth of Sri Hanuman is celebrated on the full Moon day of *Chaitra* in the month of April. Hindu families worship Sri Hanuman the divine devotee of Lord Rama with deep respect. The birth celebration starts in the afternoon and continues till early hours of the night. The learned priest starts the worship with *abhishekam* and later he decorates the statue of Sri Hanuman with fresh flowers and vermillion mixed with fresh clarified butter. Fresh fruit, especially bananas and mangoes, are offered in worship with constant readings of Hanuman Chaleesa and verses from the Ramayana.

Vaishakhi

The Festival of Vaishakhi is celebrated on 13th of April with great enthusiasm all over North India, especially Punjab. It is around the time of Vaishakhi festival when the first crop of the year is harvested and sold. The farmers feel relaxed and celebrate the blessed time by sharing food, giving charities to the poor and donating money to temples and Gurudwaras. Special charitable feasts are organized for the poor and homeless. People visit their friends and relatives for lunch parties and exchange gifts and greetings. Community celebrations are organized in fair grounds where people perform *Bhangra* dances with folk songs to the beat of the rolling drums. Vaishakhi is a special celebration for the new born baby in the family. A special worship is conducted either at home or at the temple or Gurudwara in which the first drink of holy water is given to the baby with rose petals. Both the mother and the baby receive special gifts from elders in the family.

The festival of Vaishakhi also commemorates the birth of Sikhism—the auspicious day when Guru Gobind Sahib, in the year 1699, initiated five men of purity and dedication with holy water and started *khalsapanth*, which means the brotherhood of the pure and dedicated to the service of humanity.

Vaishakhi is a very sacred festival for Sikhs and is celebrated in all the Gurudwaras with sincere respect and devotion. The celebration is really spectacular at the Golden Temple Amritsar, Anandpur Sahib, and Keshghar where thousands of people are initiated with holy water for unity, integrity and service to mankind. In an initiation ceremony the individual pledges to uphold the principles of Sikhism as ordained by the great Gurus. The celebration of Vaishakhi brings contentment, joy, happiness, and hopes for the future.

This festival also marks the beginning of a long pilgrimage to the holy shrines of Badrinath and Hemkund Sahib in the Himalayas. The temple of Badrinath is located at the bank of the sacred river Alaknanda at the height of 3,660 meters above the sea level. Sri Hemkund Sahib, located at the height of 4,329 meters, approximately 15,210 feet above the sea level in the lap of Himalayas, is the pilgrimage center for Sikhs and Hindus. Badrinath and Sri Hemkund Sahib are located in the *tapo bhoomi*, where the great sages performed *yajnas* and tough austerities in the past. This has been the home of the great hermits and yogis for centuries. Every year thousands of pilgrims from all over the world visit Badrinath and Sri Hemkund Sahib with respect and devotion.

Buddha Jayanti

Buddha Jayanti, the birth of Lord Buddha, is celebrated on *Budhpurnima*—the full Moon day of the lunar month *Vaishakha*, in May. Special prayers are held at temples in Lumbini, the birthplace of Buddha and also at Saranath, Sanchi, and Bodh Gaya. At some places the images of Buddha with the sacred remains are enshrined under a magnificent *stupa* and later taken out in a procession all over the town. Meditation workshops are organized at temples and Ashrams where thousands of monks join to recite Tripitaka the most sacred teachings of Buddha.

Nirjala Ekadashi

In the month of June, close to the time when summer solstice occurs on June 21—Nirjala Ekadashi is observed on the 11th day of the ascending phase of the Moon in the lunar month *Jyestha*. The celebration starts early in the morning with worship of Lord Vishnu, which includes special offerings to the ancestors for peace and blessings. People donate in the name of their ancestors to the family priests, temples, educational institutes and orphanages generally in the form of cash and gift items which are needed during the hot summer months. Free food stalls with iced water and soft healthy drinks are organized for the public. After the morning worship and a special lunch the entire afternoon is utilized in the study of Holy scriptures especially the Bhagawad Geeta and Bhagavatam. Some people observe a strict fast for the entire day and spend time in group chanting and meditation. The faithful sincere observance of the fast and charities given on Nirjala Ekadashi ensure inner peace, longevity, prosperity, spiritual growth and liberation both in life here and hereafter.

Teej

Next is Hariyali Teej, the joyous festival celebrated in July on the third day of the ascending phase of the Moon in the lunar month of *Shravana* in welcome of the monsoon—the rainy season. This is the time of year when there are swings on trees and beautiful girls are seen everywhere swaying merrily in the embalming cool breeze, singing love songs filled with ecstasy.

The celebration starts in the afternoon with ceremonial worship of the goddess Parvati, the consort of Lord Shiva. Young maidens seek the blessings of the goddess for a handsome, good, educated husband and married women pray for peace and prosperity in family life. The worship of the Divine mother Parvati is performed by groups of women in the neighborhood. Towards the evening special dinner parties and *dandiya* dances are organized where beautiful ladies dressed in glamorous *saris*, *lehngas*, jewelry, and especially colorful bangles, dance with the rhythmic beats gently moving the *dandiyas* back and forth. People exchange greetings and celebrate the arrival of the monsoon. It is a very colorful festival.

Rakhi or Rakshabandhan

The festival of Rakhi or Rakshabandhan is celebrated in the month of July or August on the full Moon day of the lunar month *Shravana*. The word *Raksha*, means protection, and *Bandhan* means sacred bond. It is the celebration of the sacred bond of the pure unconditional love between brother and sister. This auspicious day brings back the warmth of special moments shared by the brother and sister since childhood. The bond between brothers and sisters is very special and remains unchanged by time or distance. It is the understanding of any situation and forgiving of any mistake.

The festivity begins early morning with prayers. The lady of the house prepares the special tray with *kumkum*, rice, flowers, sweets, and colorful *rakhis*. The sacred thread of loving bond is called *rakhi* which is generally made with colorful silk threads. The celebration starts with chanting of the Gayatri mantra. Next, the sister puts the *teeka* on the forehead of her brother and ties the sacred thread on his right wrist, wishing him good health and happiness. The brother graciously accepts the *rakhi*, shares some gifts with her and also makes the promise to give her due respect and protection. The sister shares sweets and other delicacies especially cooked for the festival. Rakshabandhan is indeed a sacred festival of cherished love and affection between brothers and sisters.

In temples of South India and also in some parts of the North the full Moon day of *Shravana* is also celebrated as Avani Avittam, the auspicious day when the sacred thread *Upanayana* or *yajnoupaveet* is changed with special offerings to the Gurus and spiritual teachers. The new sacred thread is washed with turmeric water and then given to the individual by the learned priest with blessings.

Sri Krishna Janmashtami

After the observance of Rakshabandhan, the next festival is Sri Krishna Janmashtami, the birth celebration of Lord Krishna—the God-incarnate. This is one of the most popular Hindu festival celebrated in the month of August or September on the eighth day of the dark fortnight of the lunar month *Bhadrapada*. The incarnation of Lord Krishna represents the descent of the Supreme-soul.

According to the basic belief of Hinduism, although the Supreme-Lord is beyond cause, space and time, yet, resorting to His essential transcendental nature, the Lord manifests through His divine potency. Whenever there is a decline of *Dharma* and rise of *Adharma* (the loss of moral values) the Supreme power incarnates to uphold the ethical values and to restore orderliness in society.

The Supreme Lord incarnates to enlighten people so that they can recognize their own divinity by their own efforts. He guides people by the example of his own personal life. God-incarnate comes down to the level of human beings in order to educate them about the graciousness of human life. He shows his personal compassion for people and inspires them into godliness. Although the God-incarnate can accomplish His work without manifesting Himself, He likes His work to be accomplished through a human being in order to teach about the greatness of human life.

The Divine manifestation of Sri Krishna has touched almost every aspect of life, religion, poetry, philosophy, mysticism, music, dancing, art, literature, sculpture, painting, yoga, and meditation. For thousands of years, His glorious life, profound wisdom and divinity has influenced deeply the philosophical, spiritual, and cultural life of people. In the dynamic incarnation of Lord Krishna, we see an ideal figure imbued with a subtle gleam of divinity, the sweet melody of flute, an elusive fleeting smile, and inspiring words of profound wisdom that have fascinated poets, writers, great saints, mystics, educators and warriors for centuries through the length and breadth of the planet. His lifestyle sets an ideal example of love, compassion, steadfastness, fearlessness, nobility, and purity, great as the human imagination can comprehend. We see in Sri Krishna the universal-Self revealing Himself to the individual-self as the most sincere, caring, compassionate friend and guide.

Krishna Janmashtami is celebrated all over India and

in other parts of the world with deep religious fervor and enthusiasm. In Mathura, the birthplace of Sri Krishna and Vrindavan, the celebration is really spectacular. People from all over the world congregate to participate in the festival. Everything in temples and around the banks of river Yamuna speaks about the spiritual mystery of Lord Krishna's birth, childhood pranks, and penances. The presence of the Lord is perceived everywhere in the movements of people, in the choirs of devotees, in the bells of temples, and in the whisper of the breeze coming from the groves of Gokul.

The celebration starts early morning after a bath in the holy river Yamuna and prayers. Special *Prasad* is prepared for midnight offering at the birth of the Lord. Temples and homes are decorated with pictures of Sri Krishna illustrating his birth in Mathura, childhood pranks in Gokul, education at Sandeepani with Sudama and the message of Bhagawad Geeta, he shared with Arjuna in Kurukshetra. Cradles with image of baby Krishna are decorated with flowers, beads, and bells with sincere love and deep devotion.

At sunset special cultural programs are organized in the temples. There are dance performances and skits staged by children, based on stories from the boyhood of Sri Krishna. Towards the early hours of night starts the special music program of devotional songs. Everybody joins the singing with the fervor of divine love and waits for the midnight celebration that announces the birth of Sri Krishna the God-incarnate. The birth celebration starts with the chanting of hymns, blaring of the conches, ringing of bells while everybody rocks the cradle with lullaby, "*Jhulina Jhulai bhrij Bala, Jhulay Nandalala—Resham ki dori chandan ka palana Jhulina Jhulai bhrij Bala, Jhulay Nandalala*". The *Janmakal Puja* is performed with offerings of sweets made with milk and butter and everybody goes to the shrine for *prasad*. The sweet melody of flute and the ringing of bells at midnight make the spritual experience very rich and rewarding. Sri Krishna Janmashtami is celebrated every year in order to be blessed with the vision of the Lord, once again at the Holy shrine of our own heart and remain aware of our mutual communion in the middle of everything that goes on in life.

Onam

Another famous festival celebrated in the month of August or September is Onam. It is the most vibrant and colorful festival of Kerala. Onam is a harvest festival characterized by ten days of feasting, merry making and reuniting the families and friends. The festivity starts with Atham, the first day and culminates into Thiruonam—the most auspicious feature of the unique festival.

People make elaborate preparations to celebrate Onam. This is the time of the year in Kerala when the rice and fruits are available in abundance; the trees are in full blossom and the rivers are calm and navigable. People decorate their courtyard with fresh flowers prior to the worship of Mahavishnu as Vaman. Children in the neighborhood compete with each other in designs created with various kinds of flowers.

The worship starts early morning with special offerings to Lord Vishnu and everybody receives gifts from the head of the family. A grand feast is prepared and lavishly shared with neighbors and friends. Towards the evening people go to the riverside to participate in the boat races conducted all over Kerala. The dance performances such as *Kathakali* are organized by the families that adds to the zest of celebration.

Ganesha Chaturthi

Another important festival, Ganesha Chaturthi, honoring Lord Ganesha, is also celebrated in September on the fourth day of the lunar month *Bhadrapada Shukla.*This is one of the most popular festivals of Hindu families especially in Mumbai, and South India.

The festival starts on *Chaturthi* (fourth day) with worship of clay molded images of Sri Ganesha and culminates on the day of *Ananta Chaturdashi*, means the 14th day of the lunar calendar. On this day, the images are taken in a procession to the river or seacoast nearby and immersed in the water with prayers and special offerings of rice balls, the most favorite *naivedyam* of Sri Ganesha. This immersion of the clay images in the ocean is called the *Visarjana* ceremony, which forms the culmination of the worship. *Visarjana* means giving away the concept of forms and names and entering into the essentiality of the worship of Sri Ganesha. It is really exciting to be a part of the procession as it moves slowly with hundreds of people holding the images of Sri Ganesha and repeating the holy hymns such as *Aum Sri Ganeshaya namah* with the sound of celestial conches. On Ganesha Chaturthi some people fast and seek blessings for good health, wealth and spiritual growth in life.

Navaratra, Dussehra, or Vijayadashmi

Towards the end of September and the beginning of October again comes the nine days Navaratra worship of Durga, Lakshmi, and Saraswati, which culminates into the celebration of Vijayadashmi, the victory of goodness over evil. Navaratra worship is held twice a year, exactly 180 days apart. The celebration in the month of April is *Chaitra* Navaratra when the nine days worship culminates into celebrating the birth of Sri Rama and the *Ashwin* Navaratra in the month of October, the nine days worship concludes in celebrating the victory of Sri Rama.

The Navaratra worship starts on the first day of the ascending phase of Moon in *Ashwin Shukla*. The nine days worship at home and also in temples gives us the opportunity to reflect upon our lives and how we can improve the quality of life. On the first three days, the goddess Durga is invoked. Durga literally means *Durgati Harani*, or the power that helps us to be aware of the activities of our mind and body, and gradually by fasting and prayers transcend the darkness, which exists in the form of negative forces such as greed, gluttony, anger, arrogance, jealousy, envy, and illusion.

In the next three days goddess Lakshmi is worshipped for wealth and prosperity and the last three days in Navaratra are dedicated to the worship of goddess Saraswati for inner enlightenment, peace and harmony. Nine days worship helps the individual to be in touch with his inherent potential and make the very best use of his abilities while keeping in mind the global welfare.

In some parts of South India Navaratra is celebrated as Mahalaya (great dissolution) in which the nine days austerity gradually leads the individual step-by-step into self-purification and self-realization. During the nine days worship special *Sattvic* vegetarian food is cooked which promotes longevity, purity, peace, good health, and happiness. Some people fast for the entire Navaratra worship, eating only one meal a day or eating only fruits and milk products, while others fast only for one or two days. For these nine auspicious days music, dance and dramas are organized at night narrating the story of the great epic Ramayana. These dramas are called *Ramleelas*, in which the religious history is repeated and people are enlightened about the important events of the distant past.

In Bengal and Nepal, Navaratra Puja is celebrated with great enthusiasm and devotion. The whole festival is devoted to the worship of the Divine Mother Durga. The images of the goddess are beautifully decorated and sincerely worshipped for nine days and then taken in triumphal processions from all over the town to the nearby river or ocean where the clay images are ceremonially immersed in the water with special hymns and prayers. The *Visarjana* ceremony marks the enlightened steps in worship helping the aspirant to move from less awareness to increased awareness from the finite to the infinite.

After the Navaratra worship and nine days drama presentation of Ramayana to the enthusiastic religious audience who shared every event of the life story of Sri Rama, comes the festival of Vijayadashmi—honoring the victory of Sri Rama against the demonic forces of Ravana—the victory of *Dharma* over *Adharma*. Vijayadashmi celebration is held at many fair grounds in the city. Huge effigies of Ravana stuffed with large quantities of fireworks are raised at various open grounds. The celebration starts in the afternoon and at sunset the man acting as Rama from the play of Ramayana shoots an arrow straight into the body of Ravana declaring the victory of the divine being over the devil. People browse around in the fair ground, enjoying the fireworks, food and shopping, and exchanging greetings with their friends and relatives. Vijayadashmi, also known as Dussehra, is a very popular festival celebrated with great enthusiasm all over India, Burma, Nepal and some islands of far-east Indonesia.

Dussehra festival held in Mysore is one of the most colorful celebrations in India. The dance and drama performances presented by the professional troops are really incredible. On this auspicious day Lord Rama along with Seeta and his younger brother Lakshmana are worshipped for peace and prosperity.

Deepavali (Diwali)

The festival of Deepavali is celebrated exactly 20 days after Vijayadashmi, on the last day of the descending phase of the Moon in *Ashwin*, generally in October/November. Deepavali, also known as Diwali, the festival of lights, is associated with several legends and also marks the advent of the new crop and winter season.

Few days before the celebration, houses are thoroughly cleaned and decorated. The courtyards, the front doors and the shrines inside the house are decorated with silk flowers, leaves and colorful lights. Special sweets are prepared for worship and to share with friends and relatives. The preparations for Deepavali start right after the celebration of Vijayadashmi and everybody in the family joins very enthusiastically. Shops all over the town are beautifully decorated and there is brisk buying of sweets, kitchen utensils, clothes, jewelry and especially the gold and silver coins.

Deepavali is a three-day long festival which starts with *Dhantehras* on the 13th day of the lunar calendar and the celebration culminates into the worship of the goddess Lakshmi on the night of Deepavali. On *Dhantehras* Lord Dhanwantri, the celestial physician, who blessed humanity with the science of Ayurveda, is worshipped. People seek his blessings for good health and a wholesome homogenous life style. After the worship at the shrine, a few lighted candles are placed at the front door and also near the sidewalk. The day prior to Deepavali is dedicated to the worship of Sri Hanuman the great devotee of Lord Rama who came flying to Ayodhya to inform the royal family and kingdom about the arrival of Sri Rama, Seeta, and Lakshmana on the following day of Deepavali.

After a short worship in the evening and lighting of candles in the courtyard people visit their friends and exchange greetings. Special gifts and sweets are also shared with co-workers, maids, and assistants at office and at home. Deepavali is the time for the family and friends' reunion and also celebrating the commencement of the fresh crop of the year. It is the continuation of the enlightened time which started with Navaratra. It is sharing of inner light, peace and happiness.

On Deepavali the goddess Lakshmi is worshipped along with Sri Ganesha. The worship starts at sunset. A special *puja thali* is prepared with decorated candles, red powder, rice, red thread, and the silver and gold coins. After everybody in the family has taken a seat at the shrine, the head of the family ties the red thread around the wrist of everyone, also puts *teeka* on their forehead and starts the Sri Lakshmi *puja* with hymns such as '*Aum Sri Mahalakshamyai namah.*' In the worship of Sri Lakshmi along with Sri Ganesha people seek the blessings of the goddess for making money by appropriate means and making the appropriate use of the money; also being respectful and appreciative to the blessings of God. After worship and *Aarti* everyone eats the *Prasad* and starts lighting the candles in the front yard, around the house and along the sidewalk. The fireworks start after dinner and everybody joins in fun and frolic. The celebration continues till midnight with feasting, rejoicing and sharing the blessed moments.

In Bengal, people worship the Divine Mother Kali on Deepavali. The goddess Kali is the expressive aspect of Lord

Kala—the controller of time. Worship of Kali initiates the individual to learn to live in the tissue of the present moment and be appreciative of the blessings of the Divine Mother. Worship of Kali Bhadra helps the aspirant to move beyond the conditions created in time momentarily; enjoy the blessed state of alignment with the source and maintain the awareness of the Bliss for the rest of the year. As mentioned earlier the festival of Deepavali is associated with several legends such as it commemorates the return of Lord Rama to Ayodhya, the victory of Lord Krishna over the ferocious demon Narakasura and the return of Guru Hargobind Sahib to his kingdom. Deepavali is celebrated as a day of liberation and *Moksha* for Lord Mahavira, Swami Dayanand Saraswati and the great sage Swami Ramateertha. It is one of the most important festivals celebrated throughout the country.

Gurpurab

In the month of October/November on *Kartiki Poornima*—the full Moon day of the lunar month *Kartik*, the birth of Sri Guru Nanak Sahib is celebrated, who was the founder of Sikhism. The celebration is known as Gurpurab— means the festival celebrated in the memory of the great Guru. Sri Guru Nanak Sahib was born in 1469 C.E. in the village Talwandi now known as Nankana Sahib. The festival is celebrated with profound respect and great religious fervor all over India especially at Nankana Sahib where thousands of people congregate from all over the world to take a bath in the sacred water at the holy tank of Gurudwara and enjoy the blessed teachings from Guru Granth Sahib. The celebration starts early morning at the shrine inside Gurudwara with the devotional hymns from Sri Japji Sahib and kirtan goes on very enthusiastically for the whole day with the distribution of *Prasad*. Healthy nutritious food is prepared with sincere devotion at the kitchen in Gurudwara and lavishly served throughout the day.

Geeta Jayanti
(Mokshada Ekadashi)

Geeta Jayanti is celebrated on the 11th day of the lunar calendar *Margashirsh shukla* in the month of November or December. This is the auspicious day when Lord Krishna enlightened Arjuna with the holy teachings of the Bhagawad Geeta.

The message of the Bhagawad Geeta has been held in deep reverence by the sages, philosophers, and learned scholars all over the world. The teachings of the this holy dialogue are universal, meant for the welfare of mankind. There are hundreds of commentaries on the Bhagawad Geeta, both in Indian and in many foreign languages. This is perhaps the most widely translated scriptural text of the world. Ever since the teachings of Geeta have become known to the people in Europe and America, it has quickly won the interest and admiration of millions. Sir Edwin Arnold has designated the Holy Geeta to be the incomparable religious classic of the world. Similarly, Dr. Annie Besant, Dr. Paul Brunton, Mr. Von Humboldt, F. Max Muller, Ralph Emerson, Henry David Thoreau, Franklin Edgerton, Aldous Huxley, and many other scholars and educatators of the world have taken Geeta as a text for the exposition of their thoughts.

Geeta Jayanti is celebrated all over India with great respect and enthusiasm especially at Jyotisar in Kurukshetra (a small place in north-west India), where Lord Krishna enlightened Arjuna with the sacred teachings of the Bhagawad Geeta. In Jyotisar, everything speaks about the subtle gleam of divinity and the spiritual mystery of Lord Krishna—as a God-incarnate, a great warrior and a guide of nations, the protector of *Dharma* (righteousness) a compassionate and a caring friend of Arjuna, the speaker of the Bhagawad Geeta, and the greatest teacher of the world.

On Geeta Jayanti, the temples are decorated with paintings that describe the story of the Mahabharata and the long dialogue between Lord Krishna and Arjuna. Geeta recitals are organized in large groups of people for collective illumined consciousness. Talks and discourses on Bhagawad Geeta are arranged to enlighten the public. The great celebration is marked by philosophical discussions, Geeta recitations and the recognition of scholars through awards and cultural programs.

Thousands of pocket-sized copies of Geeta are distributed at various conferences and temples. The sages recommend that everybody should always keep a small edition of Geeta in his pocket for the study of selected verses whenever there is an opportunity. This helps the person to be in harmony with the voice of God and receive sufficient guidance for the activities of day-to-day life.

Geeta Jayanti is also celebrated as Mokshada Ekadashi and Vaikuntha Ekadashi—the auspicious day especially recommended for meditative unity with the indwelling Supreme-soul which brings liberation in this life and the life hereafter.

Vaikuntha Ekadashi

Although, Vaikuntha Ekadashi may not fall on the same day as per the Hindu Lunar Calendar, it is indeed a very important festival for Hindu families. On this special Ekadashi (11th day of the lunar calendar) the entire worship is dedicated to Lord Vishnu for peace and liberation. In all Hindu temples, a sacred Vaikuntha Dwara (the door to heaven) is constructed for auspicious entry into the abode of Lord Vishnu. A special worship is conducted in the morning with the recital of *Vishnu Sahasrara Nama* (one thousand holy names of Lord Vishnu) and the magnificent door of Vaikuntha is opened for blessings. People who aspire for the blessed vision of Lord Vishnu, fast on the Vaikuntha Ekadashi and pray the entire time, sitting at the lotus feet of Lord Vishnu with sincere unswerving devotion.

"The woman should be respected and honored for blessing the family with children, and conducting the household chores with love, peace and humility. She illumines everything and brings good fortune and prosperity."

Manusmriti (9.26)

"A woman is the embodiment of Lakshmi (goddess of wealth)."

Shatapatha Brahmana (13.2.6.7)

"The son and the daughter both have equal rights to the inheritance of their parent's property."

Manusmriti (9.130)

"Let your mother be the embodiment of God to you."

Taittiriya Upanishad (1.11.2)

12

Status of Women In Hindu Society

The ancient Hindu scriptures declare graciously, *"Yatra naryastu pujyante, ramante tatra devata, yatretastu na pujyante sarvastra aphla kriya"* (Manusmriti.3.56), meaning, "To the family where women are given due respect and protection, the celestials (gods) shower their blessings perennially— but where they are not respected, all other efforts to seek happiness become ineffectual and the downfall of that family is inevitable." There is another famous saying in the sacred books of Hindu *Dharma*, "Next to God we are indebted to woman, first for the life itself and then for making it worthwhile." A woman is indeed the nucleus around which everything in family and society revolves.

Since Vedic times (which is anywhere beyond 5000 B.C.E) Hindu women have enjoyed an honorable status in society. Enter any Hindu temple of any era, all the deities have their female companion standing next to them and both are worshipped with equal respect and devotion. For example the Divine consort of Shiva is Parvati, Lord Vishnu's consort is

Sri Lakshmi and goddess Saraswati is the consort of Brahma, the creator. The *Devi* (Divine Mother) worship has been a unique feature of Hindu culture since time immemorial. The ancient sages have composed many hymns in adoration of *Devi*—such as *Lalita Sahasranama* and *Durga Stotras* that describe the thousands of holy names of the Divine Mother. The devotional lyrics of Adi Shankaracharya known as *Soundarya Lahri, Kanakdhara Stotra*, and *Annapoorneshwari Stotra*, are also really melodious and deeply saturated with pure love for the Divine Mother. Kena Upanishad glorifies Uma and Markandeya Purana the goddess Durga. A famous prayer from the Holy Vedas, "*Tvameva mata ca pita tvameva*"—O' Lord you are my mother and father—indicates clearly the honor and respect of women in the ritualistic Vedic worship. According to the Taittiriya Upanishad the first lesson a child learns from the teacher is, "*Matridevo bhava*", (1.11.2), meaning, "Let your mother be the embodiment of God to you." A mother's influence is the most powerful factor in molding the character of an individual. In a Hindu family, the mother is the epitome of purity, chastity, and unselfish love for her children. The special bond of unconditional, pure love that exists between the mother and the child remains unchanged by time or distance. It is the understanding of any situation and forgiving of any mistake.

In the Vedic Era women held a respectable status in society. Good education was regarded as an important accomplishment to be well placed in life. At homes as well as at the Gurukuls (schools) of ancient India, both boys and girls were educated together. Fine arts, music, dancing, needlework, cooking, and painting were especially included in the academic curriculum for girls. In some ancient scriptures there are descriptions of women being great archers, skillful chariot riders in the army, and great teachers par-excellence. A mantra from the Rigveda asserts this, *"aham keturaham moordhaa aha–urgraa vivaachanee"* (10.159.2), meaning, "I am the flag that leads the society and I am the lawyer who can argue well."

Seclusion of women was unknown in Hindu society. Young girls led free lives and had a decisive voice in the choice of their academic career. On festive occasions and at tournaments like horse riding, archery, debates, and literary discussions, girls appeared in public with their specialized caliber, dressed in the traditional garments of Hindu culture. The young girls were also given the *Upanayana* (sacred thread) and encouraged to study the Vedas and be an active participant in the performance of rituals at home and also in society. Yajurveda (8.1) documents clearly, "A young daughter who has observed *Brahmacharya Ashrama* should be married to a man who is educated and learned like her." In general, young girls got married in their late teens or sometimes even later than that and they also had a decisive voice in the selection of their husbands. The divine sage of the Rigveda mentions that parents invited suitors at their homes and the daughter had the freedom of choosing her husband. This tradition was called '*Swayamvara*' meaning, "the self-choice of husband by the woman." In the Vedic

Era, women dominated the social scene and were the virtual head of the family, "*Samraajyedhi shwashu-reshu samraajyut devrishu nanaanduh samraajyedhi samraajyut shushravaah*" (Atharva.14.1.44), meaning, "May your father-in-law respect you as the head of the household, may your brother-in-law and sister-in-law accept your instructions and may your mother-in-law respect you as the Queen in the family." In the ritualistic worship the woman's role was very significant. Both the husband and wife offered all the prayers jointly. The ancient Hindu scriptures also indicate only one wife in marriage.

In reference to higher education of women, Harita the great educator of that time holds clearly that there were two classes of educated, married women *Brahmavadinis* and *Sadyovadhuies*. The former pursued higher education and spiritual enlightenment throughout their life and complimented and supplemented their learned husbands in the pursuit of spiritual growth while performing the other duties of family life. The latter enjoyed being a housewife and helped in raising a good family.

The *Brahmavadinis* of Vedic period were epitomes of intellectual and spiritual attainments and distinguished themselves not only as great scholars but also as eloquent speakers and debaters at the religious conferences organized by the kings and learned sages of that time.

The most enlightening dialogue between the great sage Yajnavalkya and the lady philosopher Gargi in the Brihadaranyaka Upanishad has always drawn the attention of scholars and men of letters around the world. Once the great King Janaka organized a philosophic assembly at his palace, in which the lady philosopher Gargi stood as the most outstanding personality among the philosophical interlocutors questioning the great Vedic scholar sage Yajnavalkya. She challenged the eminent sage with a volley of intelligent questions in reference to the nature of the *atman* (soul) that confounded the learned sage momentarily. The reply to Gargi's questions given by sage Yajnavalkya constitutes one of the most memorable passages of the entire debate at the King's palace. It is also mentioned in ancient literature that the great scholar Gargi served as a judge at the King's court because of her superior erudition, precision of thoughts, and clarity of vision.

When it comes to the description of the most learned Vedic female scholars there are 11 highly venerable *Brahmavadinis*, whose compositions of mantras have been recorded in the Holy scriptures. The names of these famous revered women who achieved the most honorable status in Hindu society through their own efforts and caliber are Gargi, Maitreyi, Lopamudra, Appala, Ghosha, Sulabha, Vaach, Romasha, Ambhrini, Vishwavara, and Shashwati. In the Vedic Era the women were also allowed to remain unmarried and practice tough austerities, for example Dhritvrata, Srutavati, and Sulbha decided not to get married by their own free choice and pursued a spiritual life.

Atharvaveda refers to highly educated women as head of the educational institutes, and government offices. In the

Vedic Era women neither covered their heads nor veiled their faces, they enjoyed sufficient freedom at home and also in their involvement of public affairs. But due to the repeated attacks on India by Arab invaders and other foreigners over the past centuries, the entire setup in Hindu families was disturbed. During such hostile aggressions and also when invaders became the rulers, the chastity and dignity of women was often threatened. In many cases Hindu women sacrificed their life instead of yielding to the humiliations and insults enforced by the assailants.

Gradually Hindu society became very concerned and quite protective about the honor of women. Their freedom was curtailed and in order to protect their personal respect and chastity they started veiling their faces in public. The formal education of woman also became a serious issue of genuine concern for parents. The Hindu girls stayed at home and received the little tutoring that could be provided by parents and private teachers or none at all. They lost their privilege of active participation in social gatherings and also their presence in community celebrations became limited. Hindu girls who had been highly educated in the Vedic Era and led a free life for centuries were confined to the four walls of the house with several restrictions. The child marriages also became a necessity because unmarried girls were kidnapped by the assailants. Many other evils like the abnormal rite of *Sati* (self-immolation) means the woman jumping in the funeral pyre of her husband, also sneaked into a small section of Hindu society. The *Sati* custom was prevalent mostly among the Rajputs who were constantly attacked by the Muslim invaders. This custom started because when a Rajput king was defeated or killed by a Muslim invader, he snatched not only the state but also the Queen and the wives of the generals. So in order to save their honor, the proud Rajput women preferred to burn themselves alive with their husband rather than to be enslaved, abused, and insulted by the cruel invaders. As the chastity of women was at peril, Hindu community created a fortress of social norms around itself to protect women.

In the early 19th century when India was being ruled by the British Empire, some great Hindu leaders raised a strong voice against the prevailing custom of *Sati* (self-immolation), the child marriage, the seclusion of women and many other issues related to the suppression and education of woman in Hindu society. They started several reform movements in cooperation with the government. Raja Ram Mohan Roy took up the lead in connection with the abolition of *Sati Pratha* (self-immolation). He strongly condemned this cruel custom by writing letters to the government and rousing strong public opinion. In connection with *Sati* custom he examined all the *Smriti* texts from the great sage Manu downward and pointed out clearly that *Sati Pratha* had absolutely no Hindu scriptural backing. It was in 1829 when *Sati Pratha* was finally declared illegal by the British government. Ram Mohan Roy also raised his voice against polygamy, which had become prevalent in some parts of India. He proved on the authority of ancient Hindu lawgivers like

Manu and Yajnavalkya that a Hindu was permitted to have only one wife in marriage except under certain circumstances like barrenness or an incurable illness of the woman. In addition to that he made several other sincere efforts towards reviving the ancient rights of females in society.

Swami Dayanand, the great Vedic scholar and the founder of Arya Samaj in 1875, emphasized the need of education for women in society. He traveled across the country, and every place he visited he pleaded for the establishment of new schools and colleges for girls. In the history of social freedom and education for women in India, Swami Dayanand's name will always be gratefully remembered. The Ramakrishna Mission under the lead of Swami Vivekananda also started many schools for the formal education of women. Pandit Vidyasagar pioneered the movement of widow re-marriage and secured the first act of its legalization in 1856. The child marriages were stopped in 1929 under the Sharda Act—and the marriageable age for a girl was fixed to be 16 years and later was increased to 18 years.

At the dawn of 1901 when Mahatma Gandhi started the movement of India's freedom from the British Empire, he wrote extensively in newspapers and also spoke fervently in a decisive voice about the importance of social freedom and education of women in Hindu society. A wave of awakening went across the country and thousands of women came out of seclusion and entered the public domain with men. Gandhiji was fully convinced that a new India could be born only with women's full participation and so he drafted new political roles for them. In one of his lectures he said, "Woman is the incarnation of *ahimsa*, meaning infinite love and compassion, which again means infinite capacity for suffering. And who but woman, the mother of man, shows this capacity in the largest measure? Let her translate her love to the whole of humanity—and she will occupy her proud position by the side of man." Thousands of women rallied to Gandhi's call for civil disobedience. They set aside their suppressed and oppressed roles of being confined to the four walls of their homes, cast off their veils and started taking part in social events.

After the independence of India in 1947 equal rights for men and women have been incorporated in the constitution. The democratic secular government of India has been genuinely struggling with its enacted laws to protect the rights of women. For example, the Hindu Marriage Act of 1955 has recognized the equal rights of man and woman in the matters of marriage and divorce. The Hindu Succession Act of 1956 explains the equality of rights for women in the inheritance of property. The Dowry Prohibition Act of 1961 has aimed to abolish the custom of giving and taking dowry at the time of a wedding. These are some of the important legislations that have helped women to achieve a higher status, recognition and respect in society. Slowly over the last 50 years the status of Hindu women has changed immensely.

In modern Indian society women have reasonable freedom and enjoy their rights of equality in almost all fields of social structure. A woman can pursue the higher education as much as she desires, special seats are reserved for them in medical and engineering colleges. In modern India there are thousands of women teachers, professors, scientists, software engineers, medical doctors, nurses, physical therapists, lawyers and members of parliament. At present, women's participation in social services and administration is becoming quite vibrant. Hundreds of Hindu women are holding high positions in civil services and also in police and military services of the Indian government. For instance Mrs. Indira Gandhi the daughter of Jawaharlal Nehru was very active in the freedom campaign of MK Gandhi and later became the prime minister of India. The number of educated women in Hindu society has increased rapidly over the last 40 years. Only three decades ago about 90 percent of married women needed financial security from their husbands but not anymore. At present in big cities as well as in rural areas, young ladies are earning well, and in some cases they are financially helping their parents before marriage and their families afterwards.

In spite of the higher education and holding high positions in society an Indian woman still lives by the laws of *Dharma* set by the Vedic sages. Arranged marriages are still in vogue, but the Hindu woman has a sufficient say in the choice of her spouse and the families are quite integrated and peaceful. Hindu marriage to this day is essentially a fellowship between husband and wife who plan to live together for fulfillment of four cherished goals of life— *Dharma* (duty), *Artha* (prosperity), *Kama* (raising children), *Moksha* (liberation). The cherished ideals that have been passed from the Vedic Era are still highly emphasized in the performance of the marriage ritual. During the ceremony the woman is addressed as Lakshmi (goddess of wealth), Isha (the goddess of prosperity) and respectable, effective partner in life. At one point the groom says, "*Sumargaleeriyan Vadhu Rimaam Sameta Pashyata*" meaning, "Look at this beautiful bride whose arrival in my family will be all auspicious. May our married life be full of love and prosperity." Both the bride and groom touch others' heart and pray, that they may enclose each other in the purity of their hearts and honor the sacred relationship of marriage. And also towards the completion of seven steps around the sacred fire, the husband addresses his wife thus, "*Sakhe Saptapadi bhava*—meaning O' dear having completed seven steps, be my life long companion and may I become your most reliable friend." In married life the woman's position is supposed to be the exalted one. She is encouraged to be the head of the household bearing various responsibilities. The Hindu scriptural teachings have strongly emphasized that all religious ceremonies should be performed together by both husband and wife side by side. In general the marriage relationship is regarded to be enjoyable and permanent. The Hindu traditions believe even to this day, that a married woman who sincerely devotes her life to the well being of her husband and family becomes the embodiment of a goddess and is blessed with numerous spiritual powers in due course of time.

Although, it is quite true that in Hindu society, there is still a small fraction of social structure where women are not treated equally and that is due to the lingering deep rooted influence of previous generations when India was ruled by foreigners. In modern India, generally, women do not cover their heads or veil their faces except in some remote villages. After independence, the democratic secular government of India has been constantly struggling to safeguard the women's interest and bring back the ancient glory of Vedic Era when women were privileged with equal rights in almost every single field of life. At present, a Hindu woman enjoys sufficient freedom at home and in society, while living by the time-honored cherished ideals of Hinduism.

Index

A

C

D

L

T

Notes

Notes

Notes

Notes

Other Books and Audio CDs
By Prabha Duneja

Audio work available in Hindi

- Mangal Dhwani
- Shiv Mahima
- The Great Gayatri Mantra
- Bhaja Govindam
- Samarpanam
- Hanuman Chaleesa
- Celestial Chants for Relaxation (Sahakeertana)
- Geeta Satsang (2 volume CD set)
- Talks on Bhagawad Geeta (10 volume CD set)
- Bhagawad Geeta Recital (5 volume CD set)

Global support of education is one of the most cherished functions of Geeta Society. All proceeds from books and CDs beyond production cost is used in support of orphanages, schools for the handicapped and blind, educational institutions in India and other countries. These proceeds are intended to provide quality education for underprivileged children so that they may become productive and responsible members of society.

Contact Information
Prabha Duneja
2822, Camino Segura Pleasanton, CA 94566, U.S.A
Tel. : 925-484-5411, Fax : 925-417-5946
email : duneja@aol.com
Website : www.holygeeta.com

Other Books and Audio CDs
By Prabha Duneja

Books

- The Legacy of Yoga in Bhagawad Geeta
- Mantra and the Modern Man
- Bhagawad Geeta: The Gospel of Timeless Wisdom
- The Holy Syllable Aum
- An Introduction to Bhagawad Geeta
- Shiva
- Holy Geeta
- Bhagawad Geeta: The Gateway to Freedom

Audio: CDs and Cassettes

- Shiva
- Hinduism
- Geeta Chaleesa
- Hindu Festivals
- Poems of Rabindranath Tagore
- Primordial Sound Meditation
- The Great Gayatri Mantra
- Journey to the Infinite Bliss/Chakra Meditation
- Patanjali Ashtang Yoga & Guided Meditation
- Mantras for Yogic Unity in Meditation & Everyday Bliss
- Concept of God in Hinduism
- Our Journey Through Panch Koshas (Guided Meditation)
- Opening the Heart Chakra (Guided Meditation)
- Meditation at the Seashore
- Mantra Meditation
- Hindu gods and goddesses (2 volume CD set)
- Lectures on Bhagawad Geeta (10 volume CD set)
- Talks on the Power of Mantra (7 volume CD set)